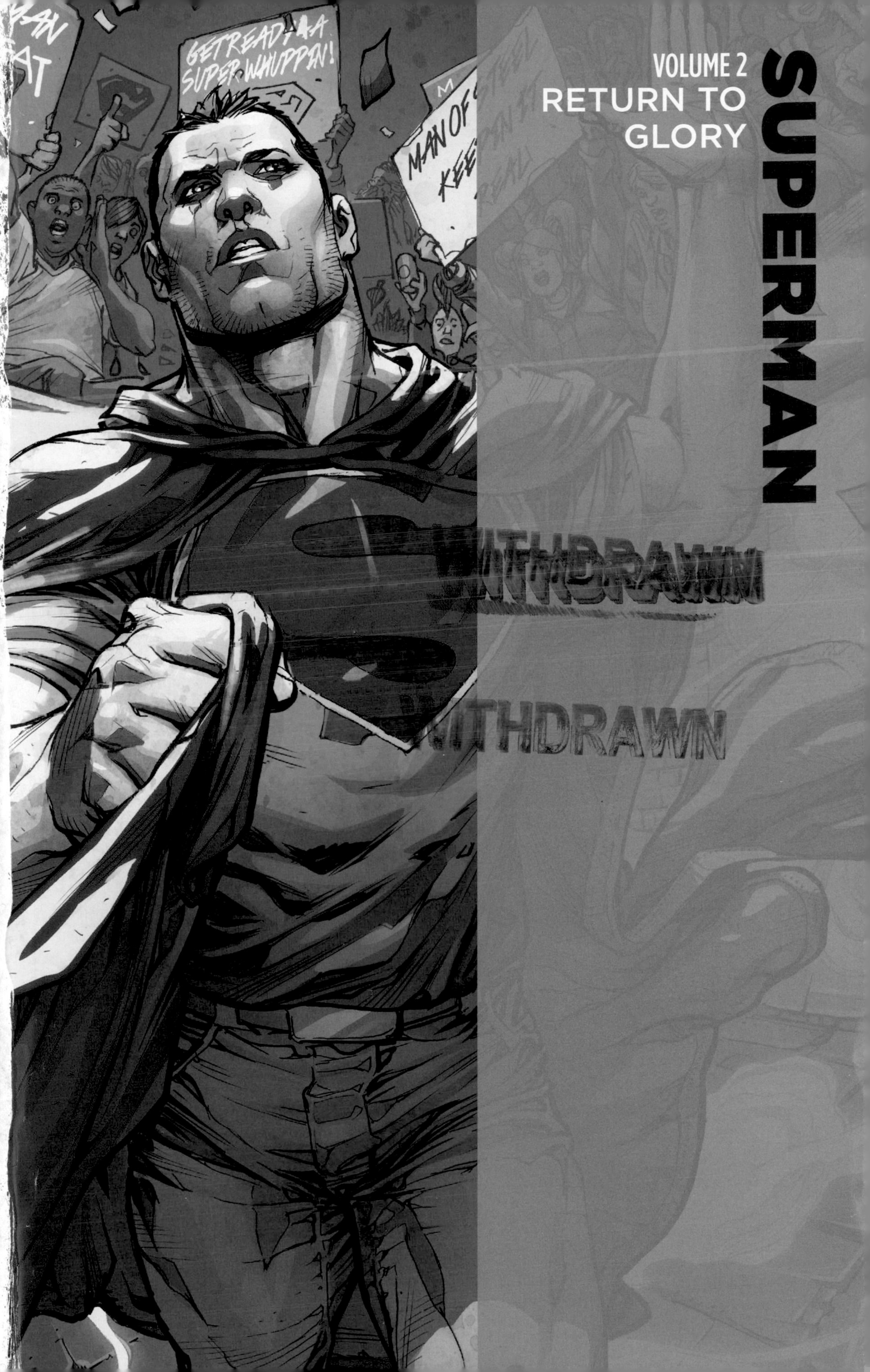
GET READY 4 A SUPER WHUPPIN'!

SUPERMAN

VOLUME 2
RETURN TO GLORY

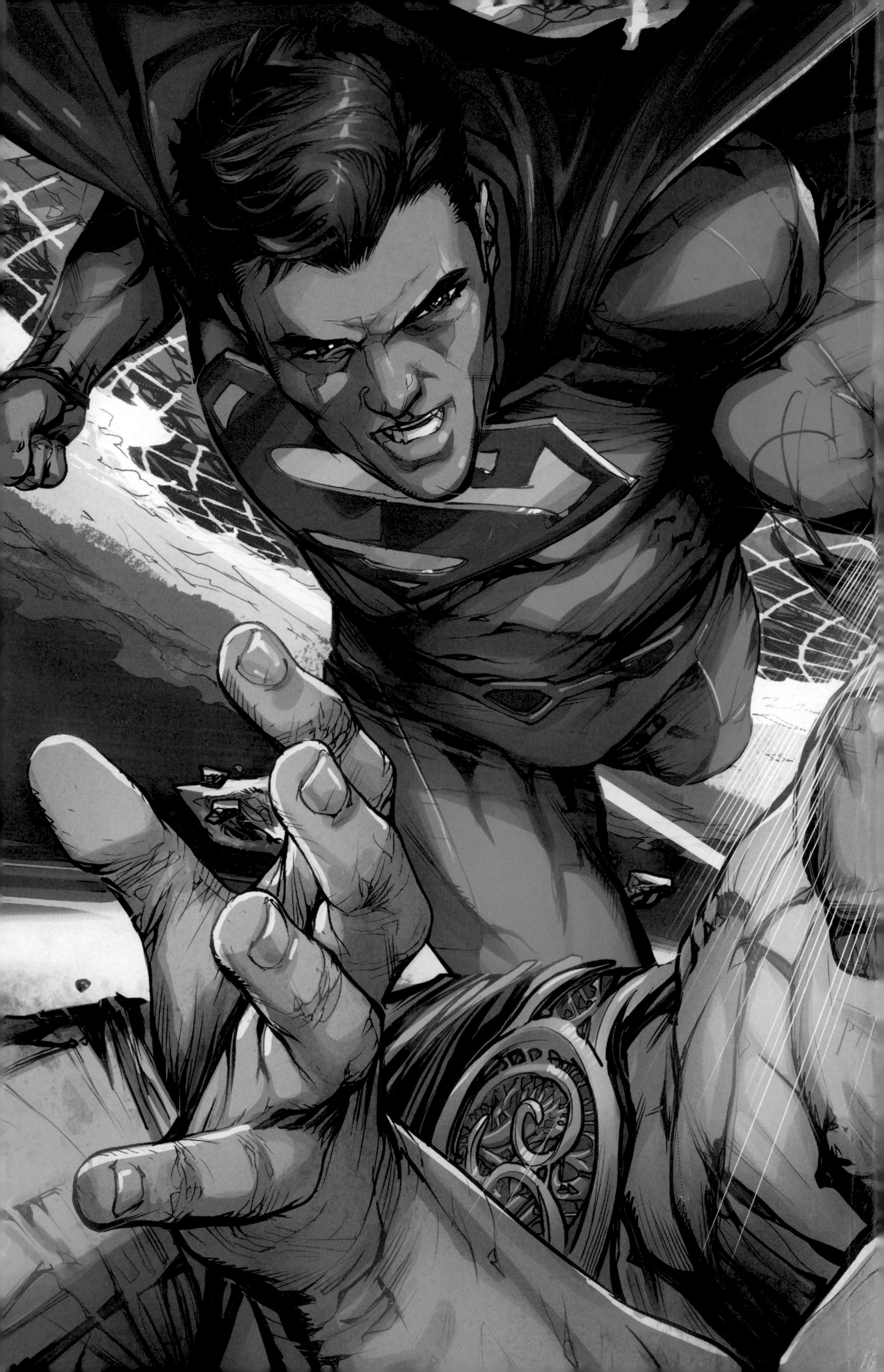

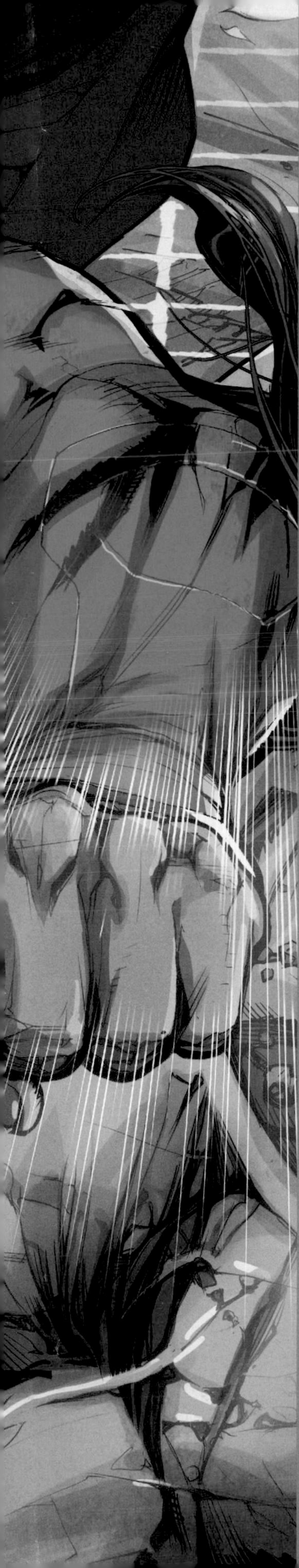

SUPERMAN

VOLUME 2

RETURN TO GLORY

WRITTEN BY
AARON HUDER GREG PAK
PETER J. TOMASI GENE LUEN YANG

PENCILS BY
RAYMUND BERMUDEZ
JON BOGDANOVE TOM DERENICK
JACK HERBERT DAN JURGENS BEN OLIVER
HOWARD PORTER MIKEL JANIN
RAFA SANDOVAL MIGUEL SEPULVEDA
ARDIAN SYAF PATRICK ZIRCHER

INKS BY
RAYMUND BERMUDEZ
JON BOGDANOVE TOM DERENICK
JACK HERBERT DON HO MIKEL JANÍN
HOWARD PORTER JEROME K. MOORE
BEN OLIVER MIGUEL SEPULVEDA
BILL SIENKIEWICZ ARDIAN SYAF
PATRICK ZIRCHER

COLORS BY
BLOND JEROMY COX HI-FI MIKEL JANÍN
TOMEU MOREY TRISH MULVIHILL
LEE LOUGHRIDGE BEN OLIVER

LETTERS BY
A LARGER WORLD STUDIOS
ROB LEIGH STEVE WANDS

COLLECTION COVER ART BY
HOWARD PORTER HI-FI

SUPERMAN CREATED BY
JERRY SIEGEL AND JOE SHUSTER

BATMAN CREATED BY
BOB KANE WITH BILL FINGER

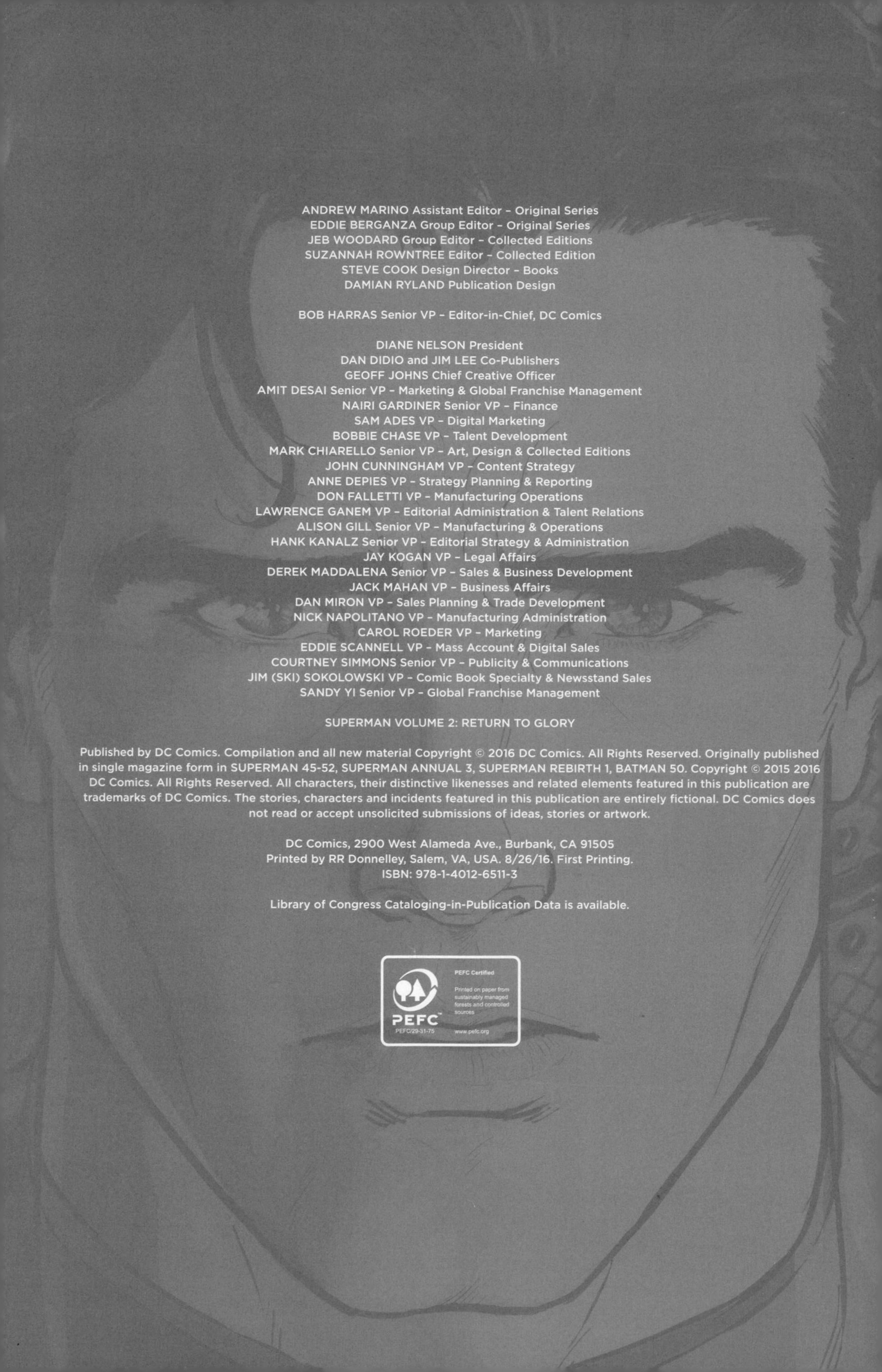

ANDREW MARINO Assistant Editor – Original Series
EDDIE BERGANZA Group Editor – Original Series
JEB WOODARD Group Editor – Collected Editions
SUZANNAH ROWNTREE Editor – Collected Edition
STEVE COOK Design Director – Books
DAMIAN RYLAND Publication Design

BOB HARRAS Senior VP – Editor-in-Chief, DC Comics

DIANE NELSON President
DAN DIDIO and JIM LEE Co-Publishers
GEOFF JOHNS Chief Creative Officer
AMIT DESAI Senior VP – Marketing & Global Franchise Management
NAIRI GARDINER Senior VP – Finance
SAM ADES VP – Digital Marketing
BOBBIE CHASE VP – Talent Development
MARK CHIARELLO Senior VP – Art, Design & Collected Editions
JOHN CUNNINGHAM VP – Content Strategy
ANNE DEPIES VP – Strategy Planning & Reporting
DON FALLETTI VP – Manufacturing Operations
LAWRENCE GANEM VP – Editorial Administration & Talent Relations
ALISON GILL Senior VP – Manufacturing & Operations
HANK KANALZ Senior VP – Editorial Strategy & Administration
JAY KOGAN VP – Legal Affairs
DEREK MADDALENA Senior VP – Sales & Business Development
JACK MAHAN VP – Business Affairs
DAN MIRON VP – Sales Planning & Trade Development
NICK NAPOLITANO VP – Manufacturing Administration
CAROL ROEDER VP – Marketing
EDDIE SCANNELL VP – Mass Account & Digital Sales
COURTNEY SIMMONS Senior VP – Publicity & Communications
JIM (SKI) SOKOLOWSKI VP – Comic Book Specialty & Newsstand Sales
SANDY YI Senior VP – Global Franchise Management

SUPERMAN VOLUME 2: RETURN TO GLORY

DC Comics, 2900 West Alameda Ave., Burbank, CA 91505
Printed by RR Donnelley, Salem, VA, USA. 8/26/16. First Printing.
ISBN: 978-1-4012-6511-3

Library of Congress Cataloging-in-Publication Data is available.

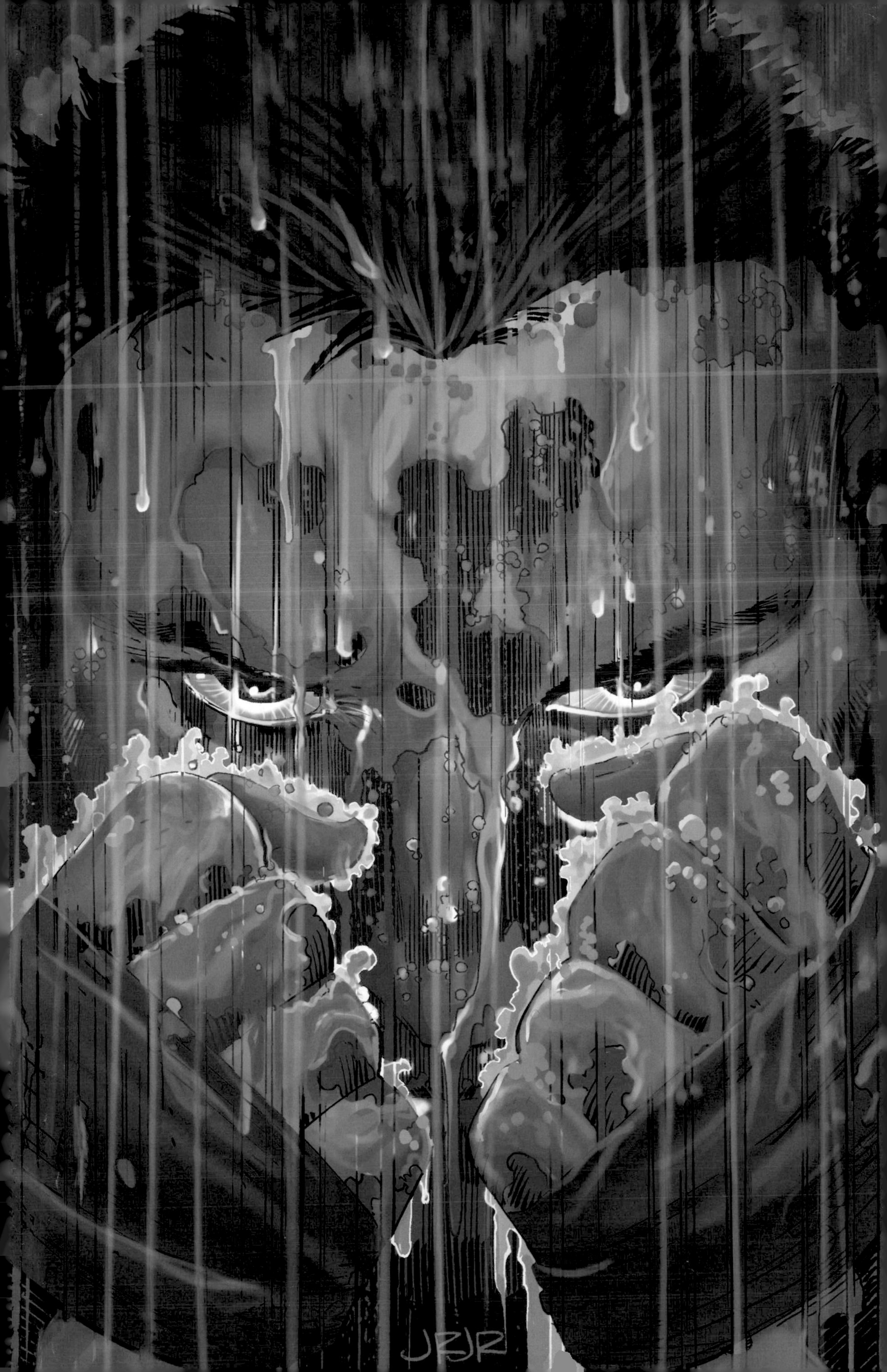
JRJR

STREET JUSTICE

GENE LUEN YANG writer HOWARD PORTER artist HI-FI colorist ROB LEIGH letterer JOHN ROMITA JR., KLAUS JANSON, DEAN WHITE cover

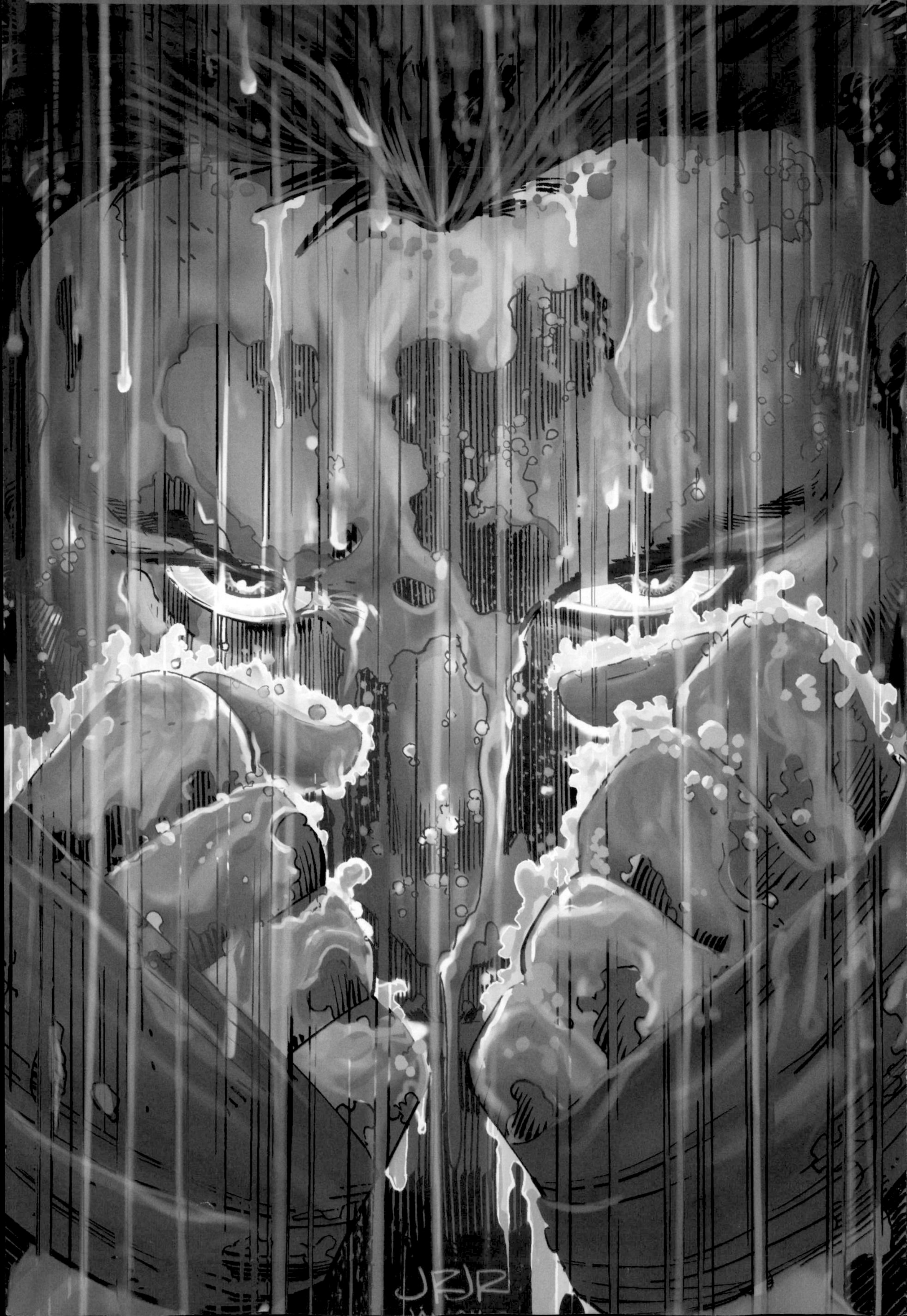
JRJR

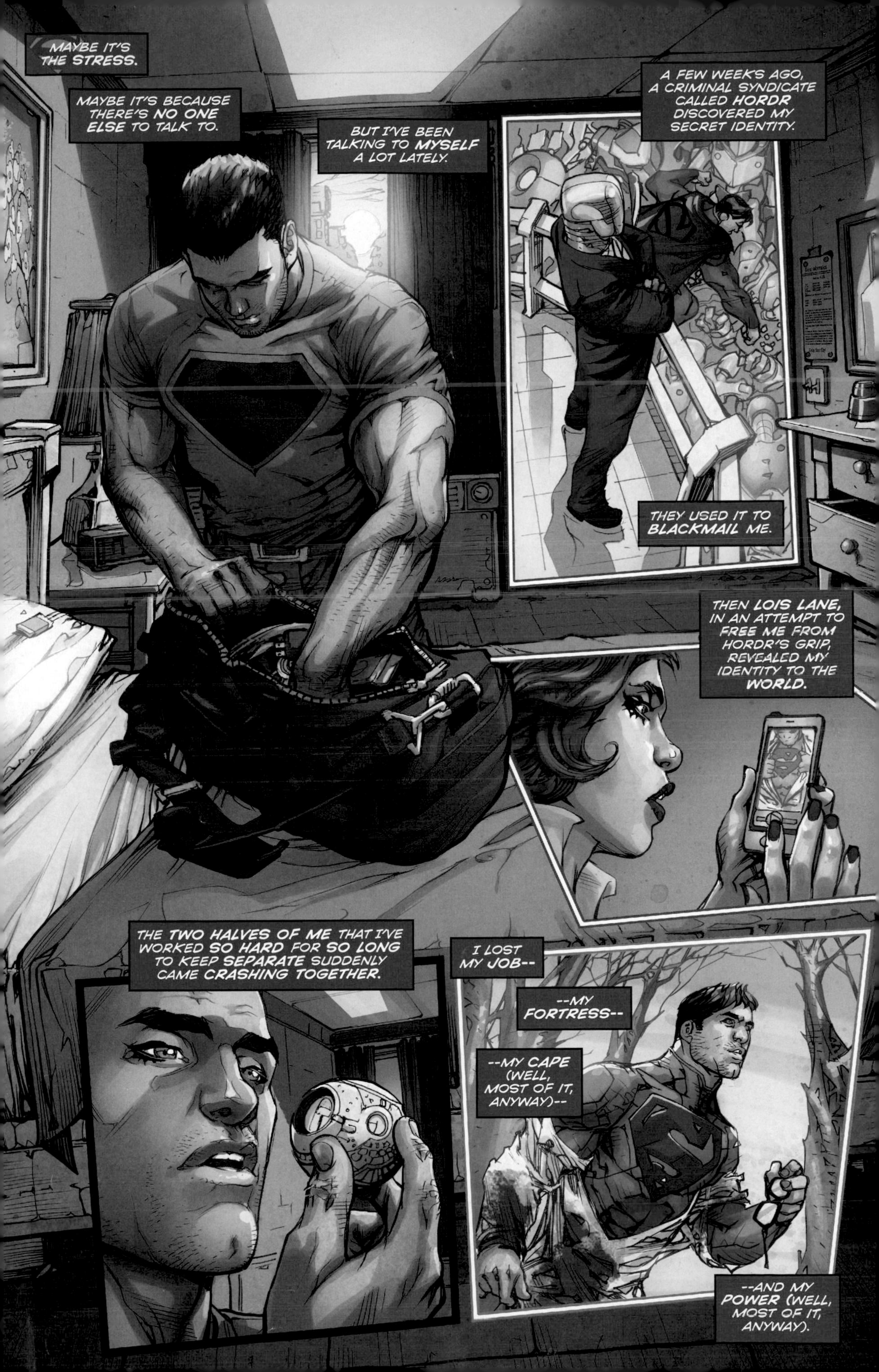
MAYBE IT'S THE STRESS.
MAYBE IT'S BECAUSE THERE'S NO ONE ELSE TO TALK TO.
BUT I'VE BEEN TALKING TO MYSELF A LOT LATELY.
A FEW WEEKS AGO, A CRIMINAL SYNDICATE CALLED HORDR DISCOVERED MY SECRET IDENTITY.
THEY USED IT TO BLACKMAIL ME.
THEN LOIS LANE, IN AN ATTEMPT TO FREE ME FROM HORDR'S GRIP, REVEALED MY IDENTITY TO THE WORLD.
THE TWO HALVES OF ME THAT I'VE WORKED SO HARD FOR SO LONG TO KEEP SEPARATE SUDDENLY CAME CRASHING TOGETHER.
I LOST MY JOB--
--MY FORTRESS--
--MY CAPE (WELL, MOST OF IT, ANYWAY)--
--AND MY POWER (WELL, MOST OF IT, ANYWAY).

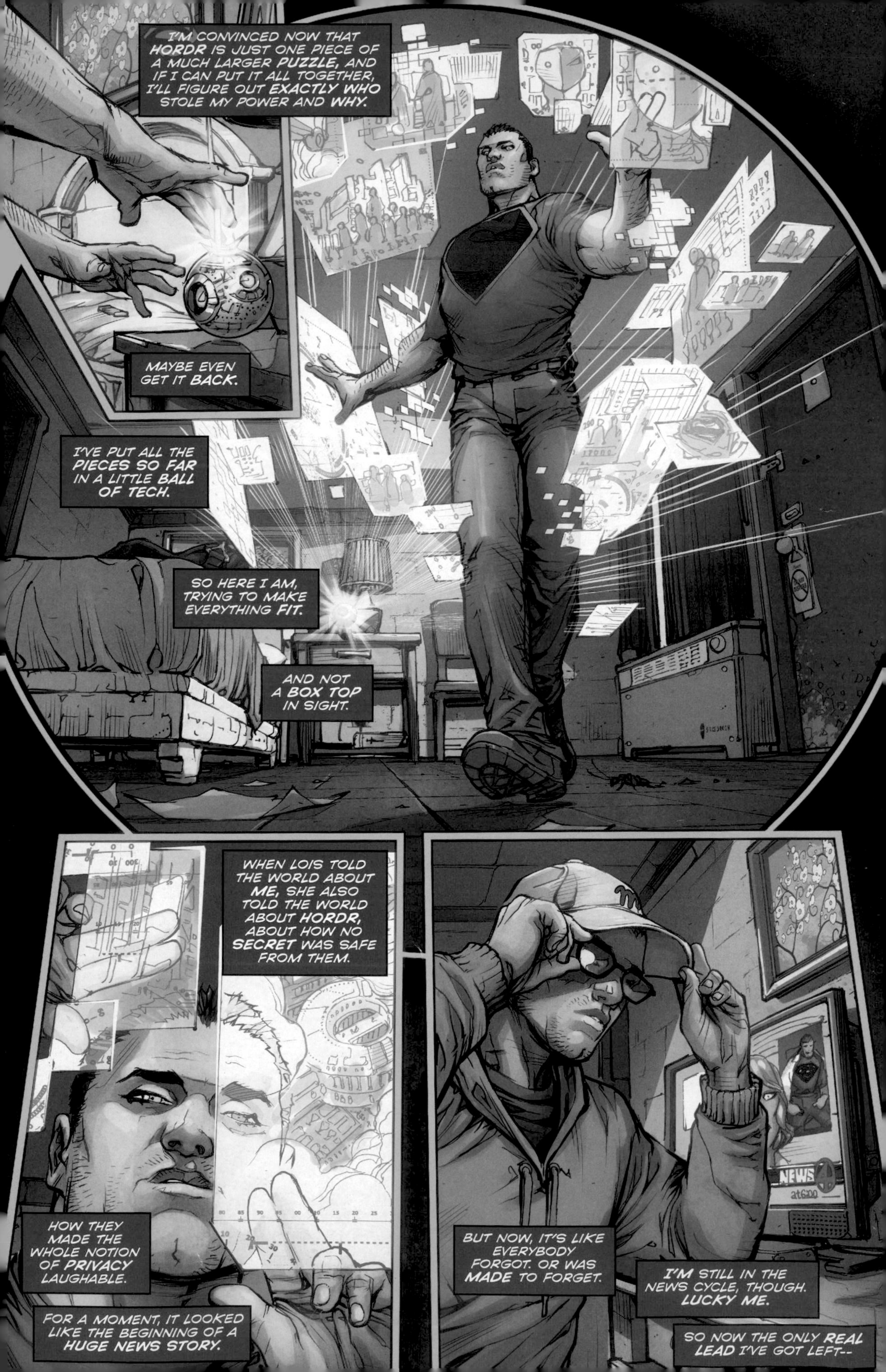

I'M CONVINCED NOW THAT HORDR IS JUST ONE PIECE OF A MUCH LARGER PUZZLE, AND IF I CAN PUT IT ALL TOGETHER, I'LL FIGURE OUT EXACTLY WHO STOLE MY POWER AND WHY.
MAYBE EVEN GET IT BACK.
I'VE PUT ALL THE PIECES SO FAR IN A LITTLE BALL OF TECH.
SO HERE I AM, TRYING TO MAKE EVERYTHING FIT.
AND NOT A BOX TOP IN SIGHT.
WHEN LOIS TOLD THE WORLD ABOUT ME, SHE ALSO TOLD THE WORLD ABOUT HORDR, ABOUT HOW NO SECRET WAS SAFE FROM THEM.
HOW THEY MADE THE WHOLE NOTION OF PRIVACY LAUGHABLE.
FOR A MOMENT, IT LOOKED LIKE THE BEGINNING OF A HUGE NEWS STORY.
BUT NOW, IT'S LIKE EVERYBODY FORGOT. OR WAS MADE TO FORGET.
I'M STILL IN THE NEWS CYCLE, THOUGH. LUCKY ME.
SO NOW THE ONLY REAL LEAD I'VE GOT LEFT--

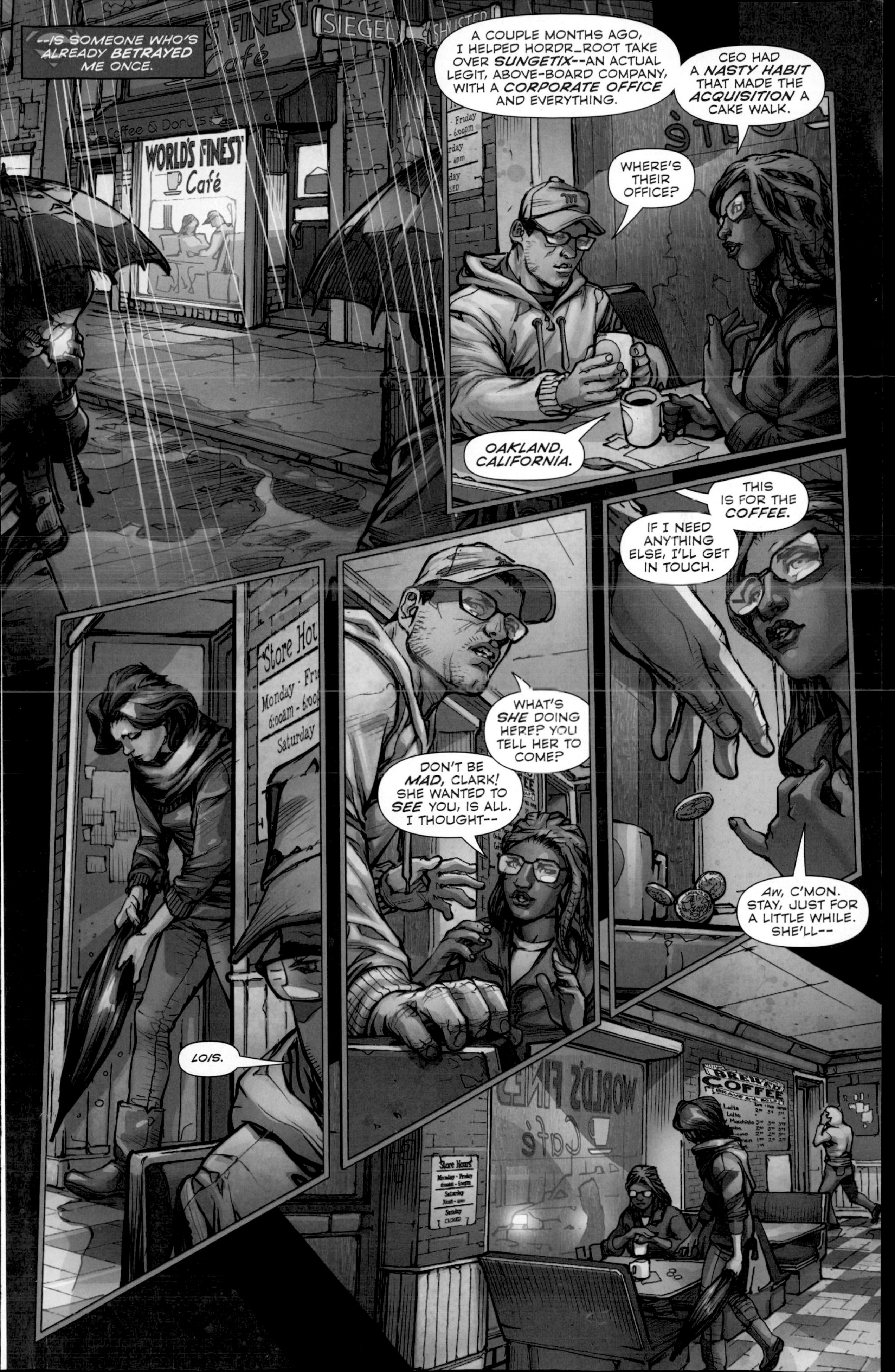
--IS SOMEONE WHO'S ALREADY BETRAYED ME ONCE.
WORLD'S FINEST
SIEGEL
SHUSTER
Café
Coffee & Donuts
WORLD'S FINEST Café
A COUPLE MONTHS AGO, I HELPED HORDR_ROOT TAKE OVER SUNGETIX--AN ACTUAL LEGIT, ABOVE-BOARD COMPANY, WITH A CORPORATE OFFICE AND EVERYTHING.
CEO HAD A NASTY HABIT THAT MADE THE ACQUISITION A CAKE WALK.
WHERE'S THEIR OFFICE?
OAKLAND, CALIFORNIA.
THIS IS FOR THE COFFEE.
IF I NEED ANYTHING ELSE, I'LL GET IN TOUCH.
WHAT'S SHE DOING HERE? YOU TELL HER TO COME?
DON'T BE MAD, CLARK! SHE WANTED TO SEE YOU, IS ALL. I THOUGHT--
Aw, C'MON. STAY, JUST FOR A LITTLE WHILE. SHE'LL--
Store Hours
Monday - Friday
6:00am - 6:00pm
Saturday
LOIS.
BREWED COFFEE

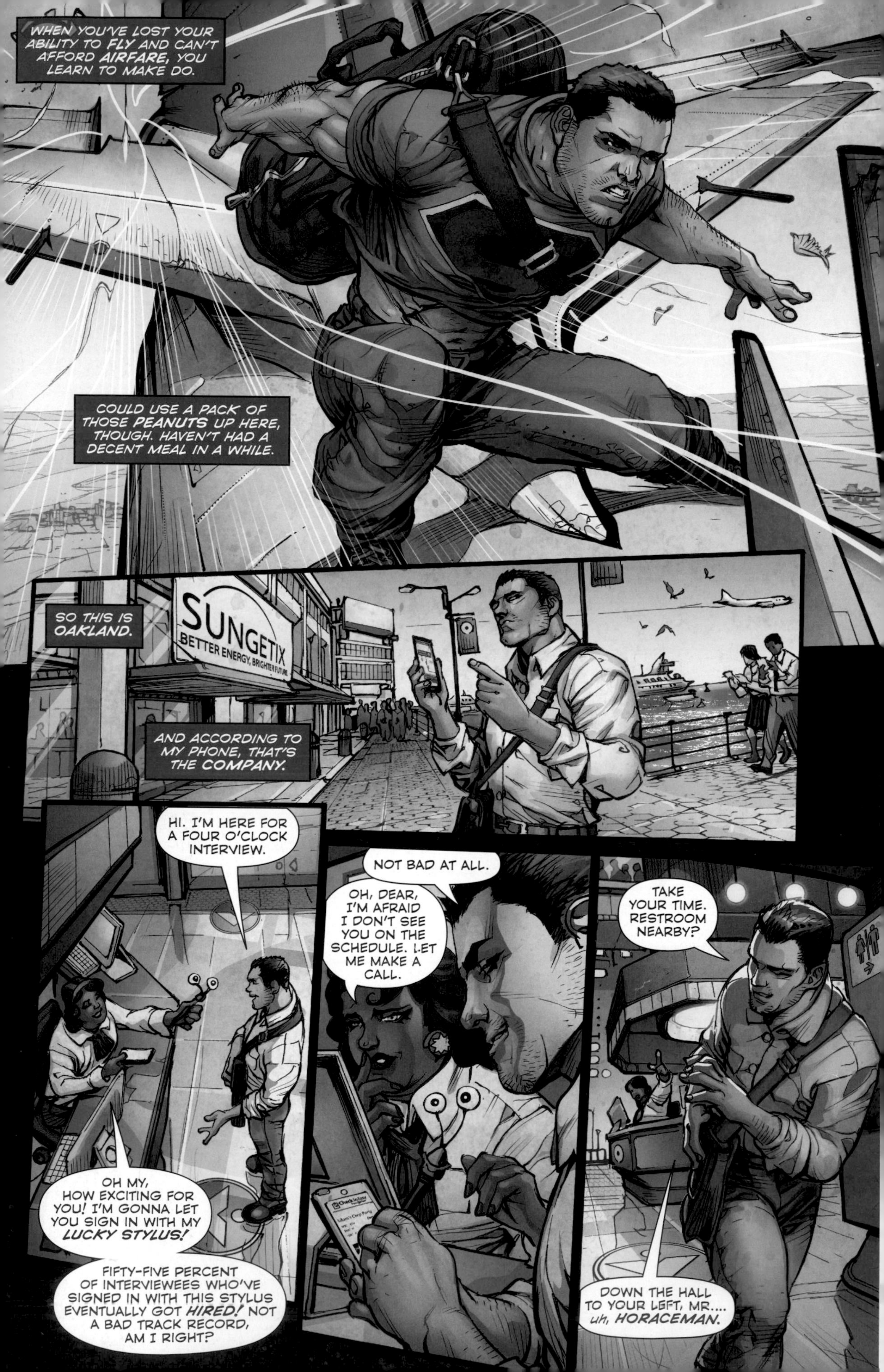
WHEN YOU'VE LOST YOUR ABILITY TO FLY AND CAN'T AFFORD AIRFARE, YOU LEARN TO MAKE DO.
COULD USE A PACK OF THOSE PEANUTS UP HERE, THOUGH. HAVEN'T HAD A DECENT MEAL IN A WHILE.
SO THIS IS OAKLAND.
SUNGETIX
BETTER ENERGY, BRIGHTER FUTURE
AND ACCORDING TO MY PHONE, THAT'S THE COMPANY.
HI. I'M HERE FOR A FOUR O'CLOCK INTERVIEW.
OH MY, HOW EXCITING FOR YOU! I'M GONNA LET YOU SIGN IN WITH MY LUCKY STYLUS!
FIFTY-FIVE PERCENT OF INTERVIEWEES WHO'VE SIGNED IN WITH THIS STYLUS EVENTUALLY GOT HIRED! NOT A BAD TRACK RECORD, AM I RIGHT?
NOT BAD AT ALL.
OH, DEAR, I'M AFRAID I DON'T SEE YOU ON THE SCHEDULE. LET ME MAKE A CALL.
TAKE YOUR TIME. RESTROOM NEARBY?
DOWN THE HALL TO YOUR LEFT, MR.... uh, HORACEMAN.

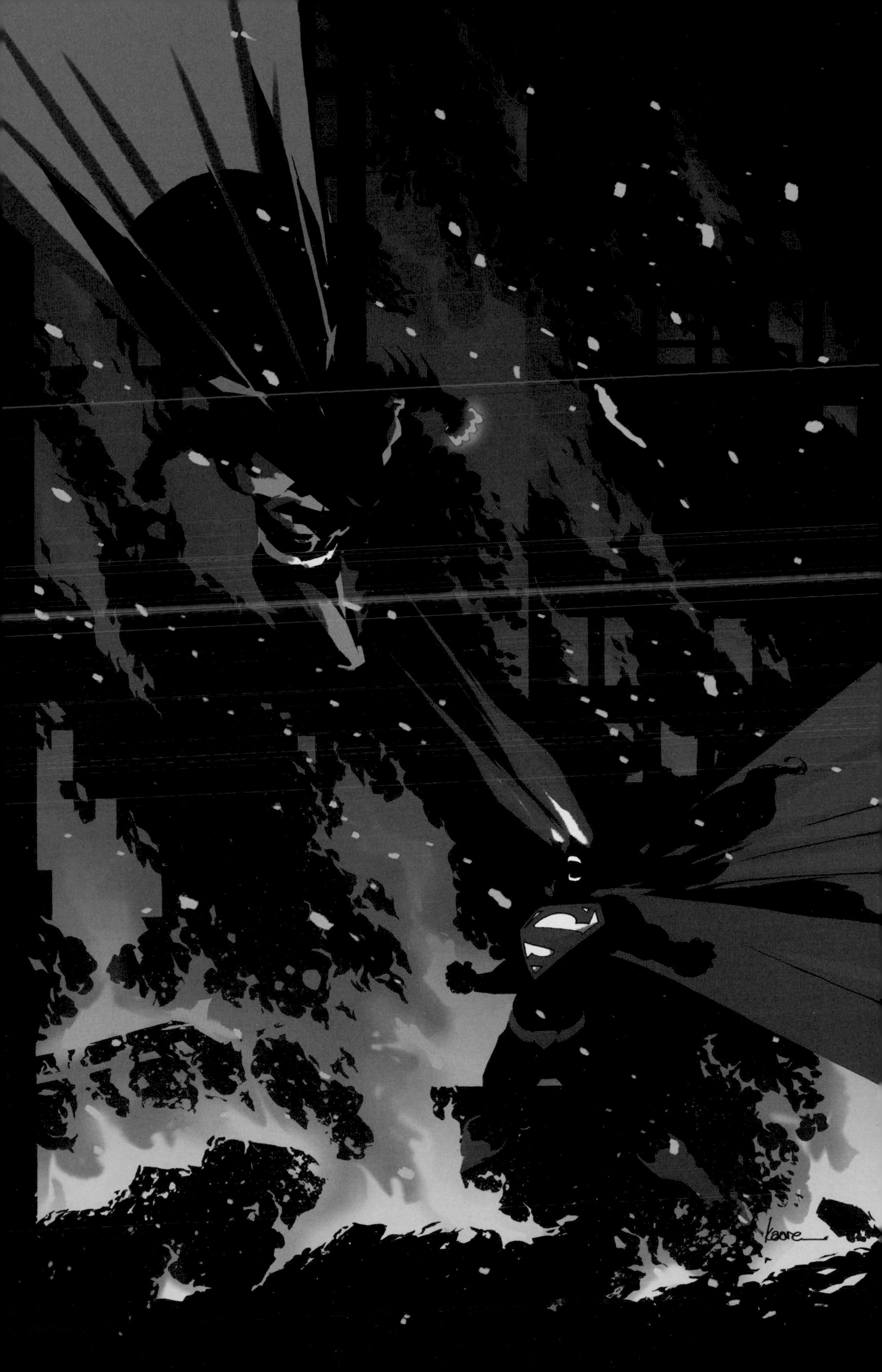

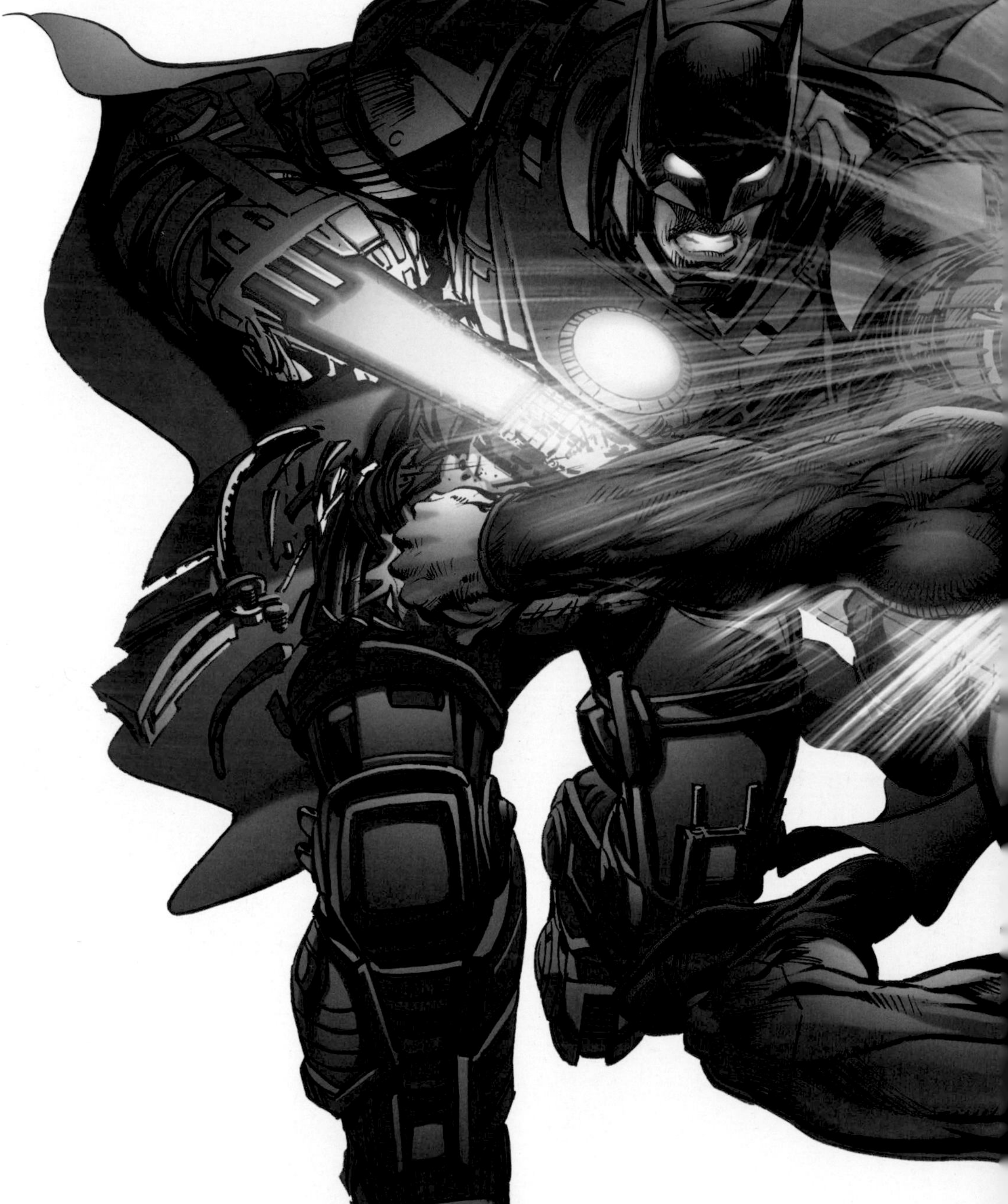

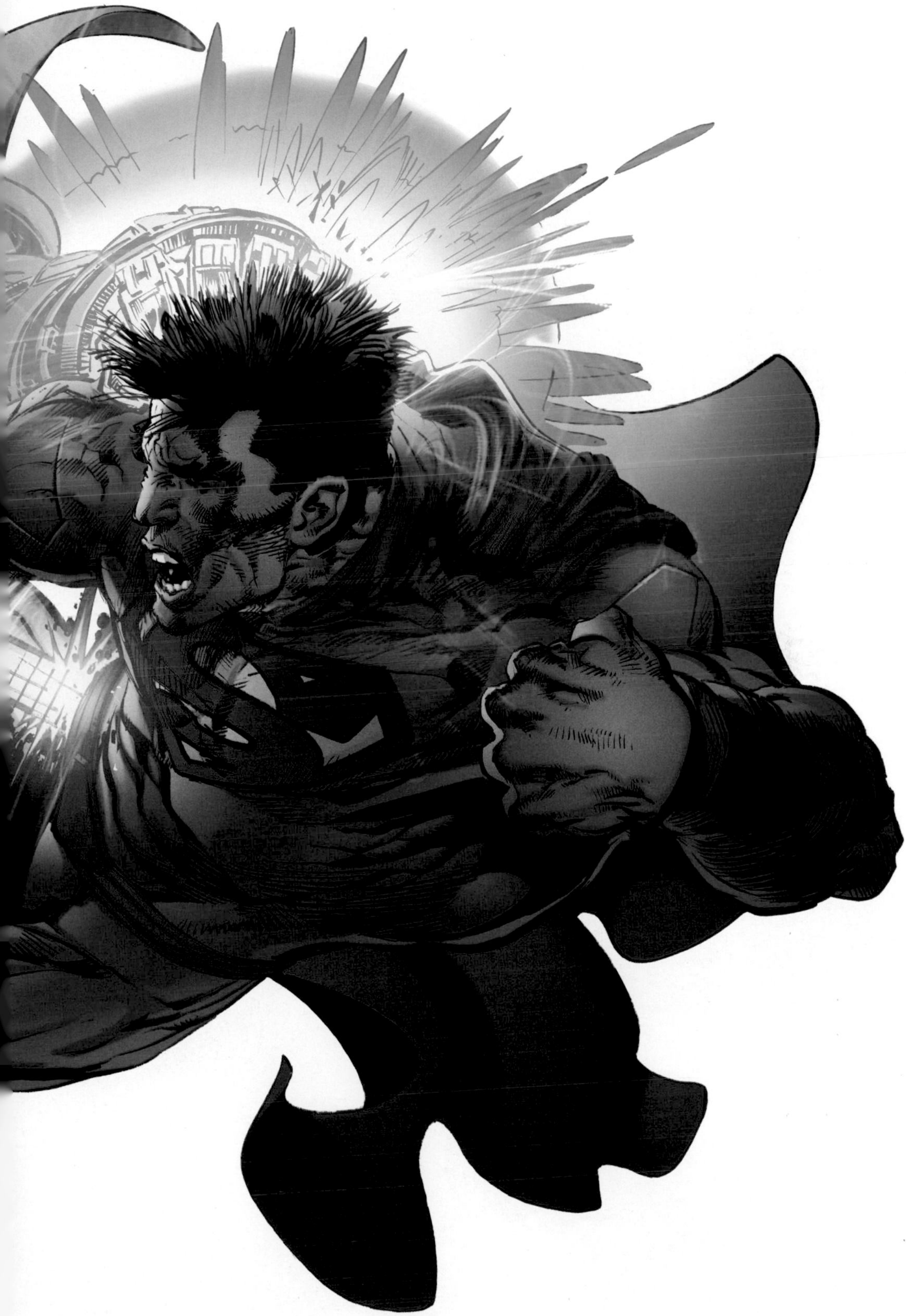

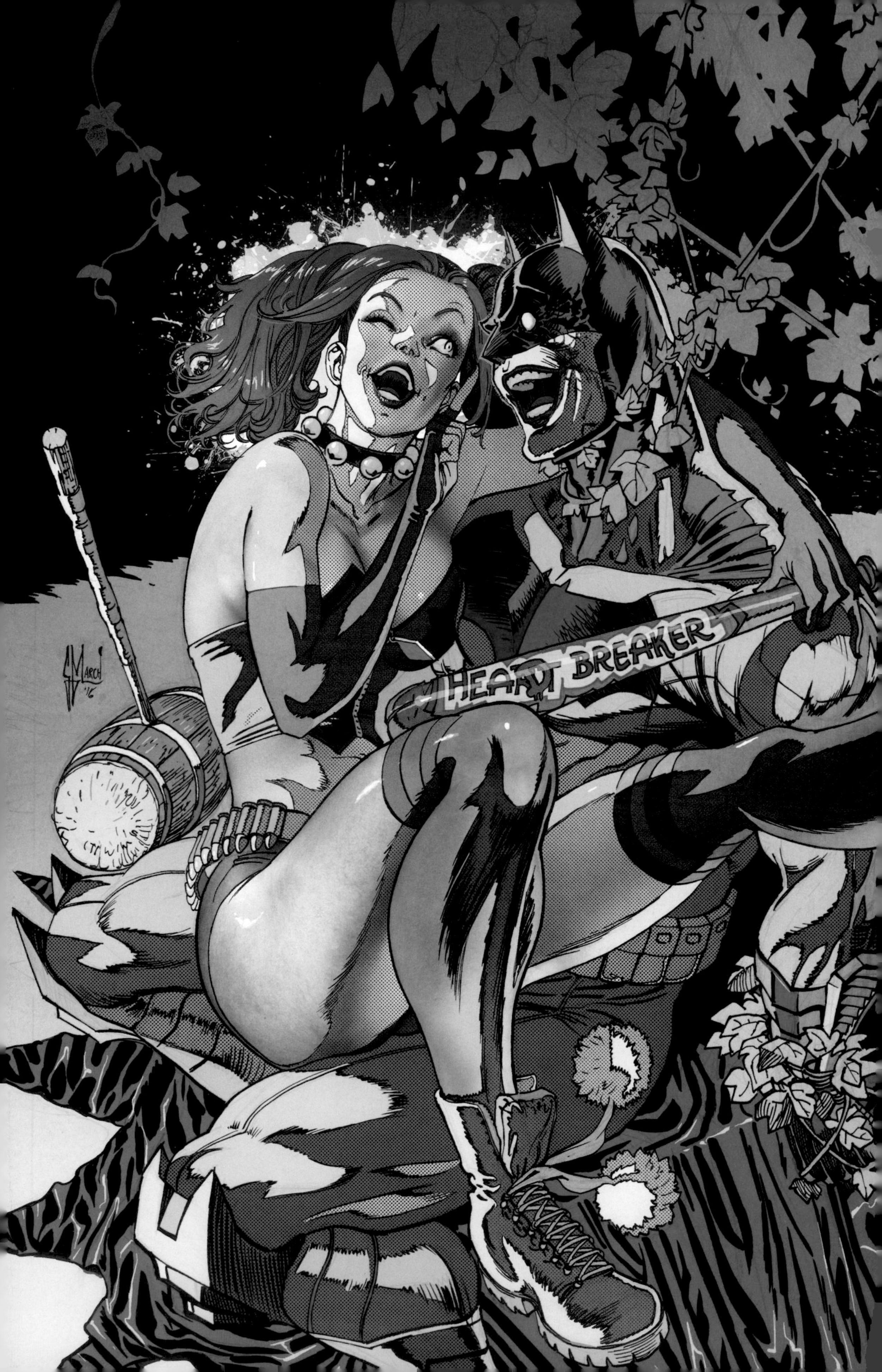
HEART BREAKER

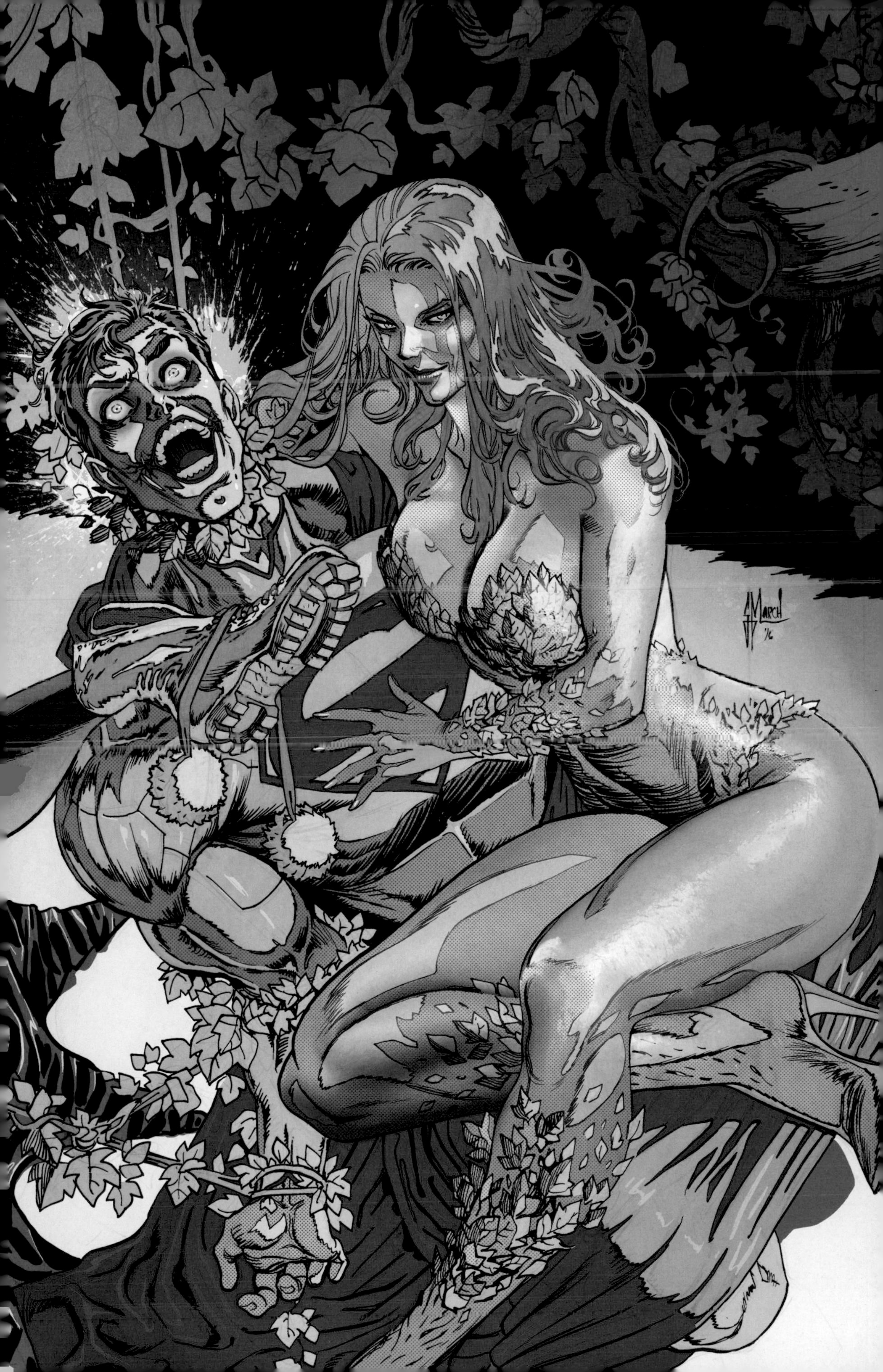

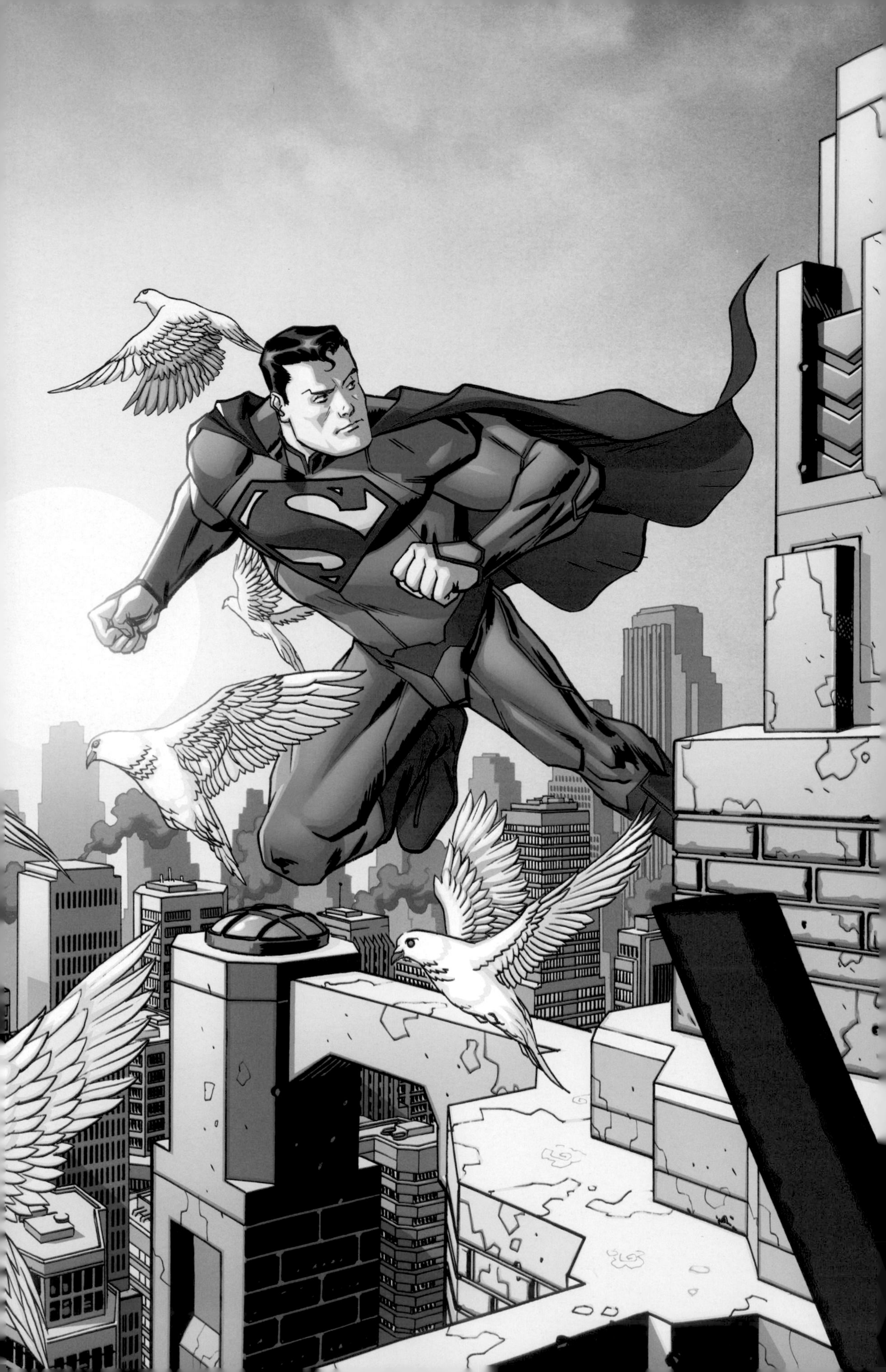

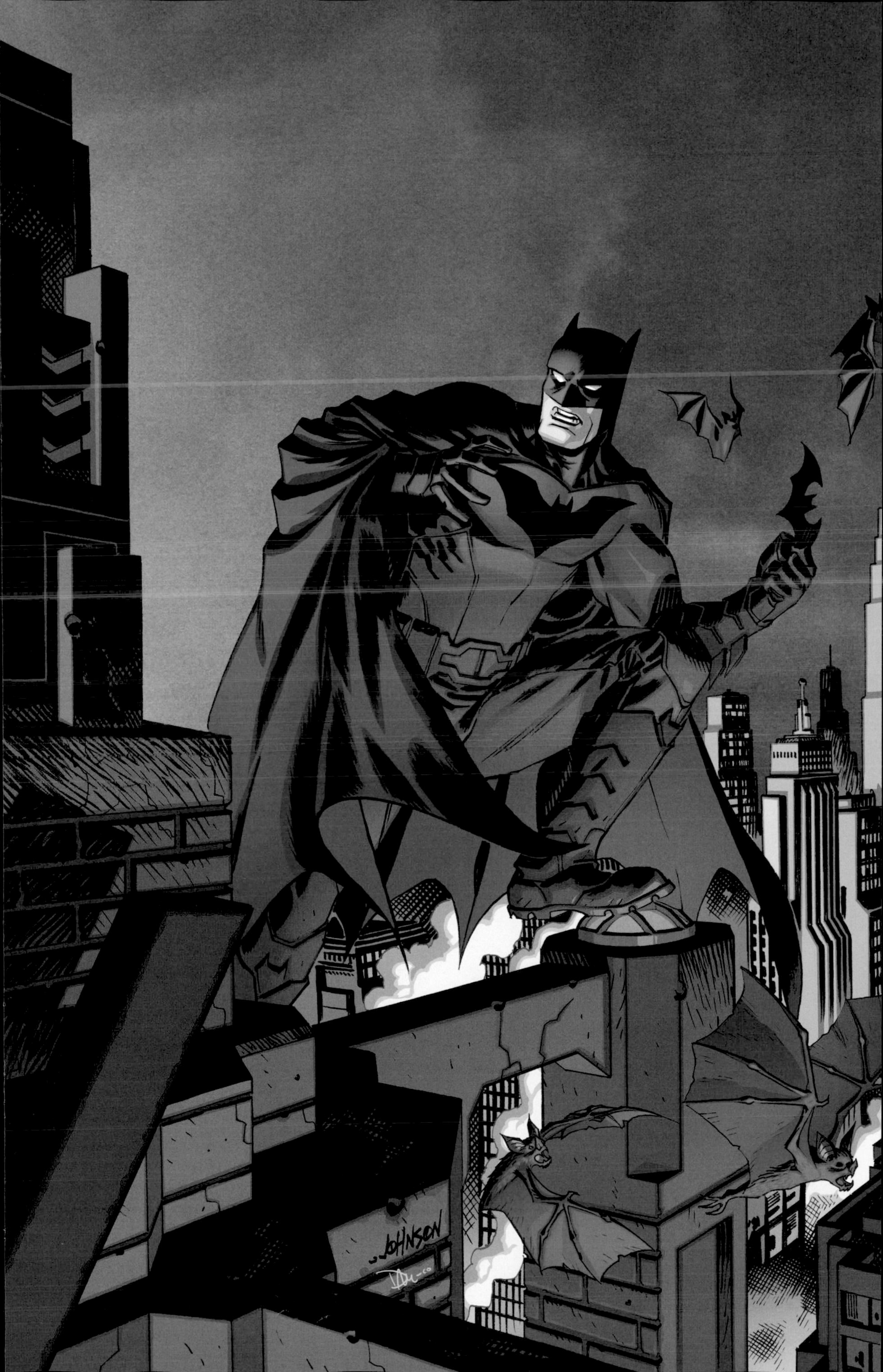
JOHNSON

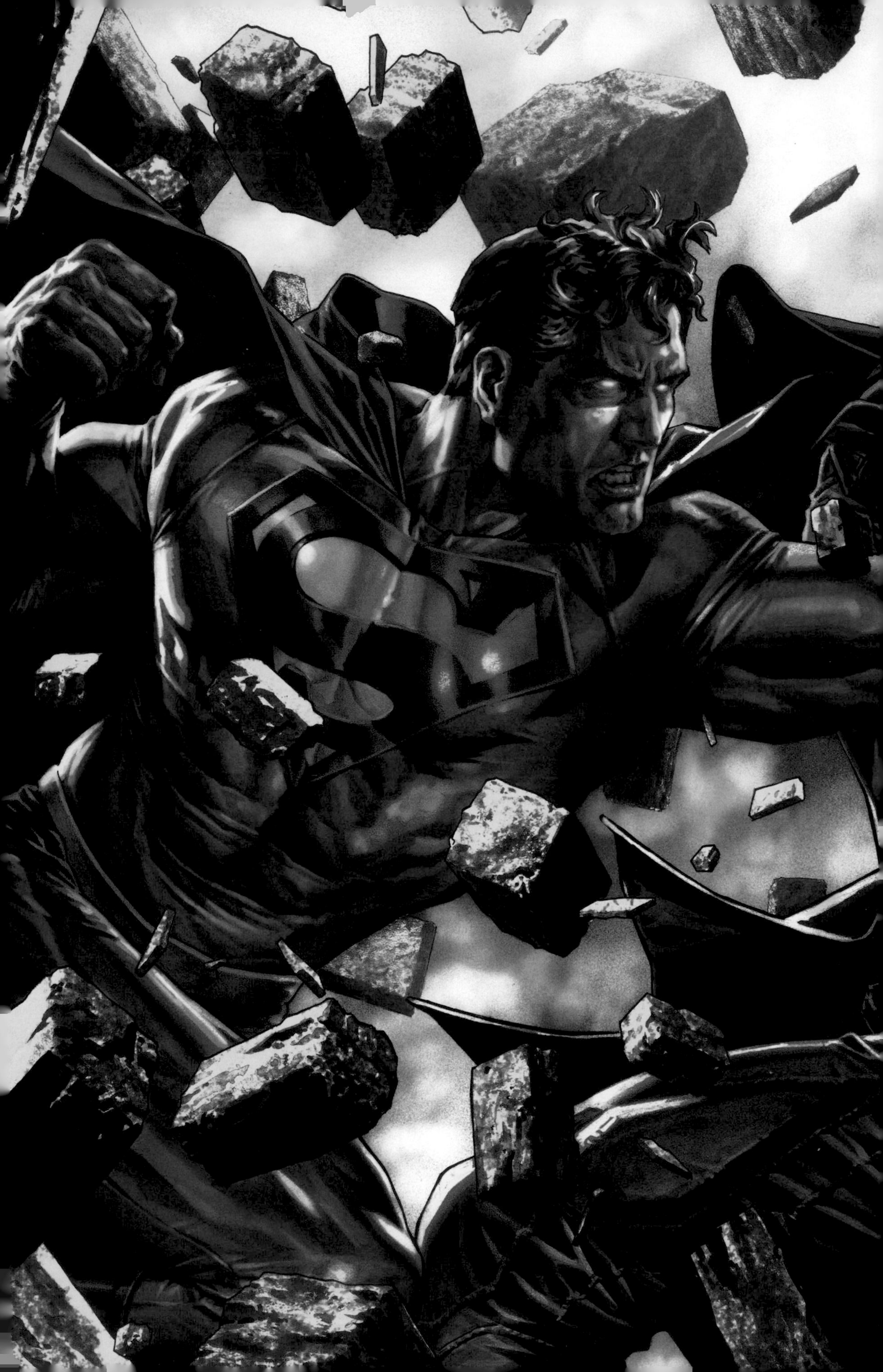

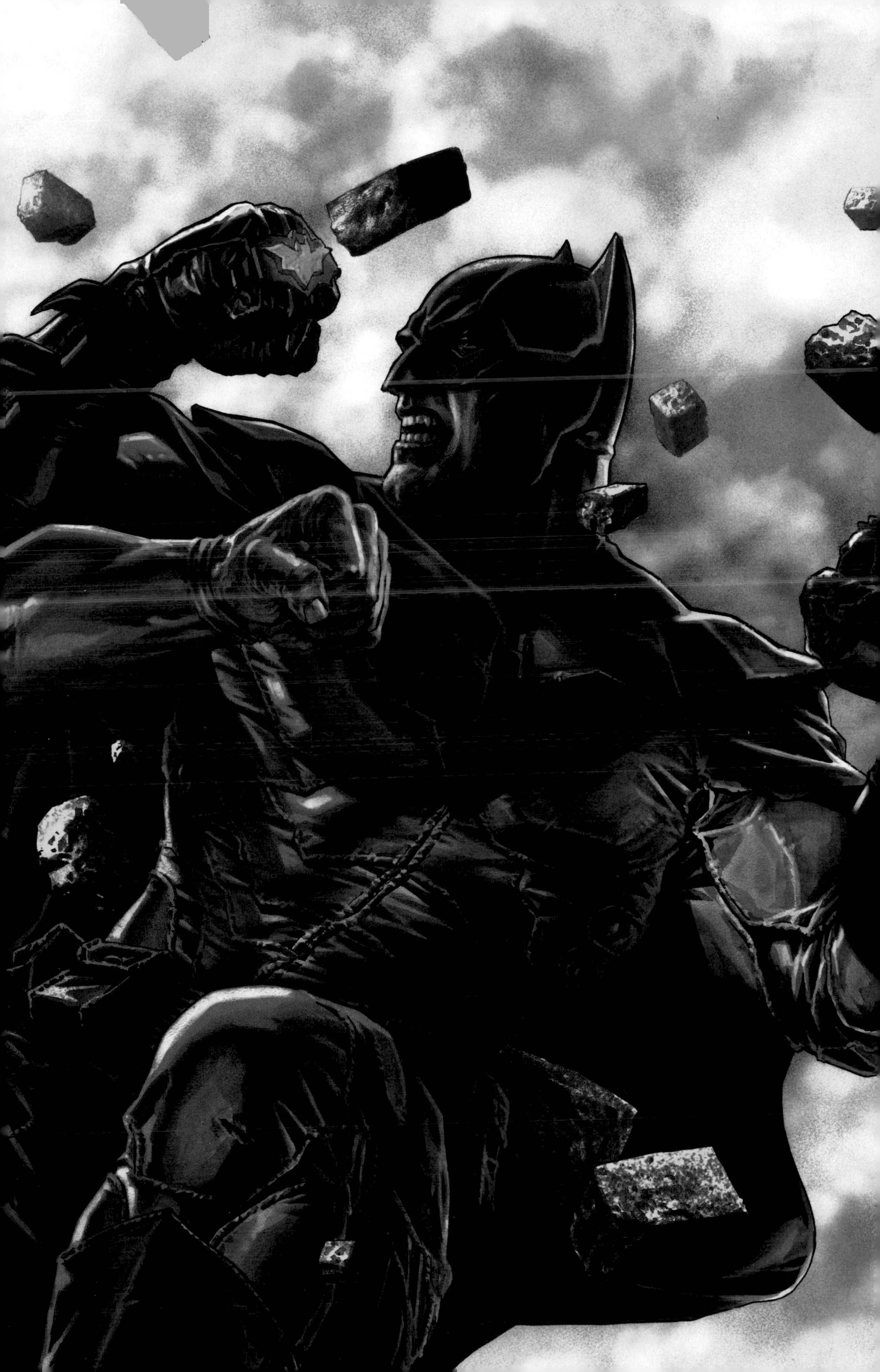

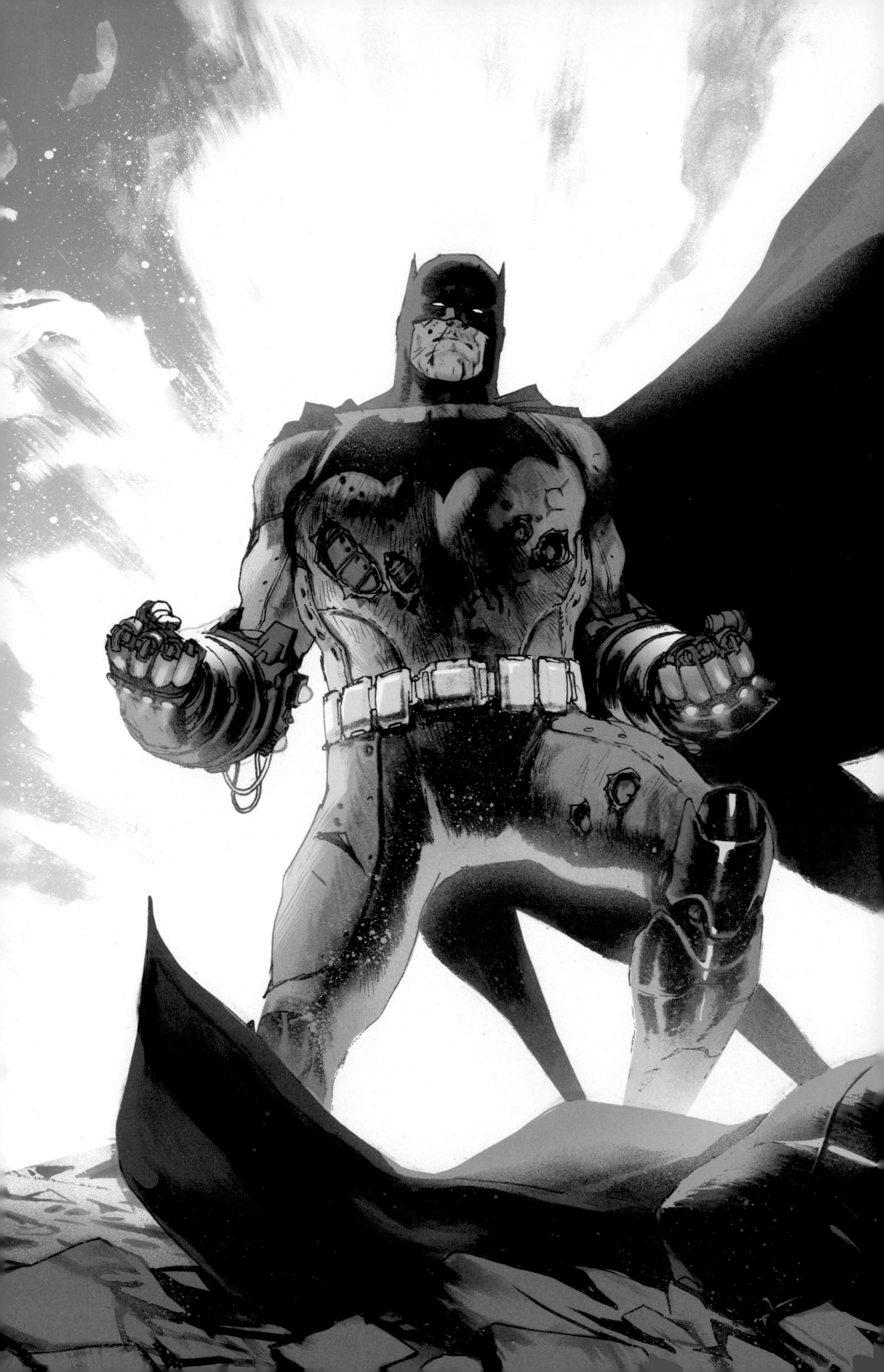

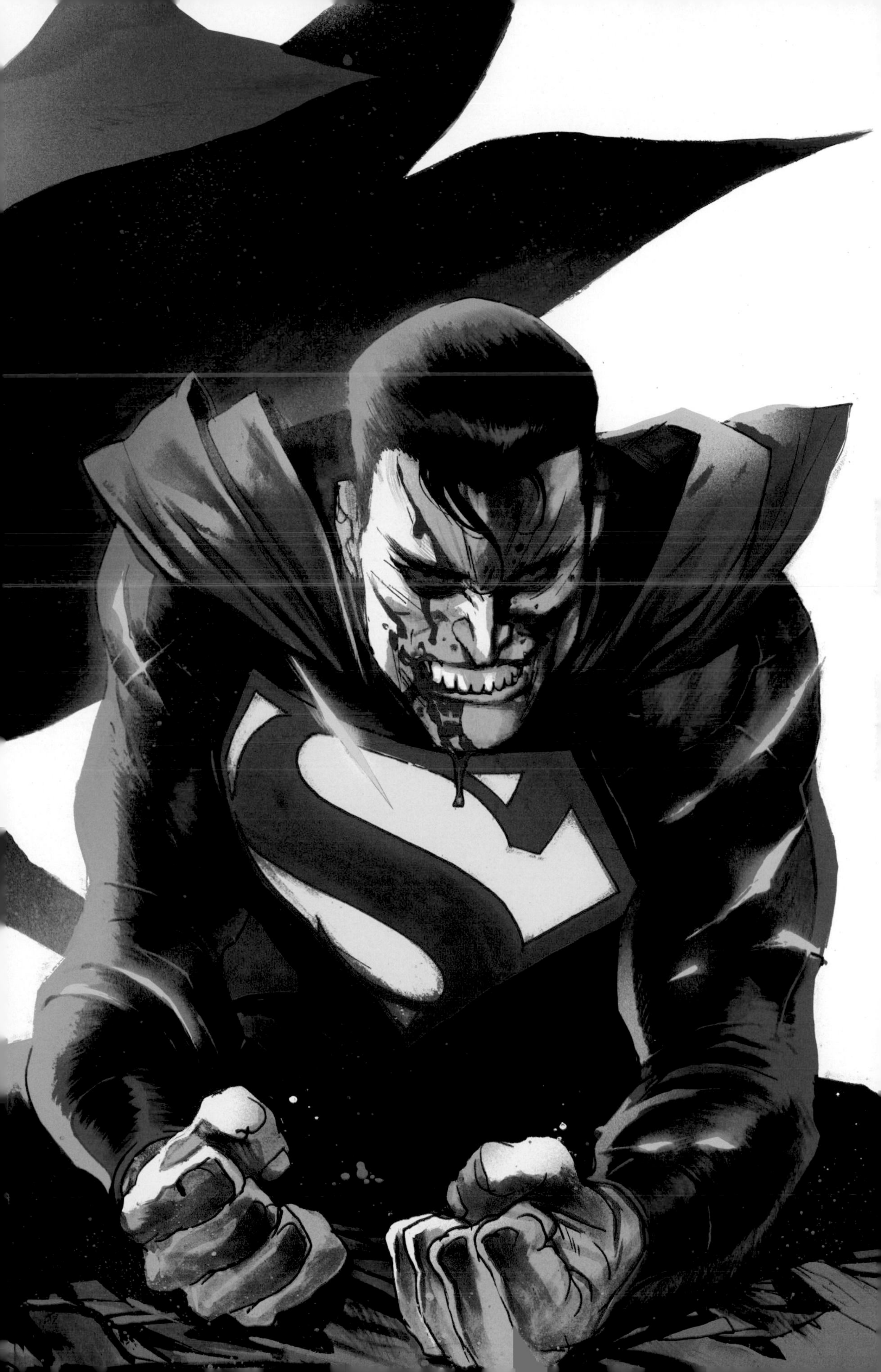

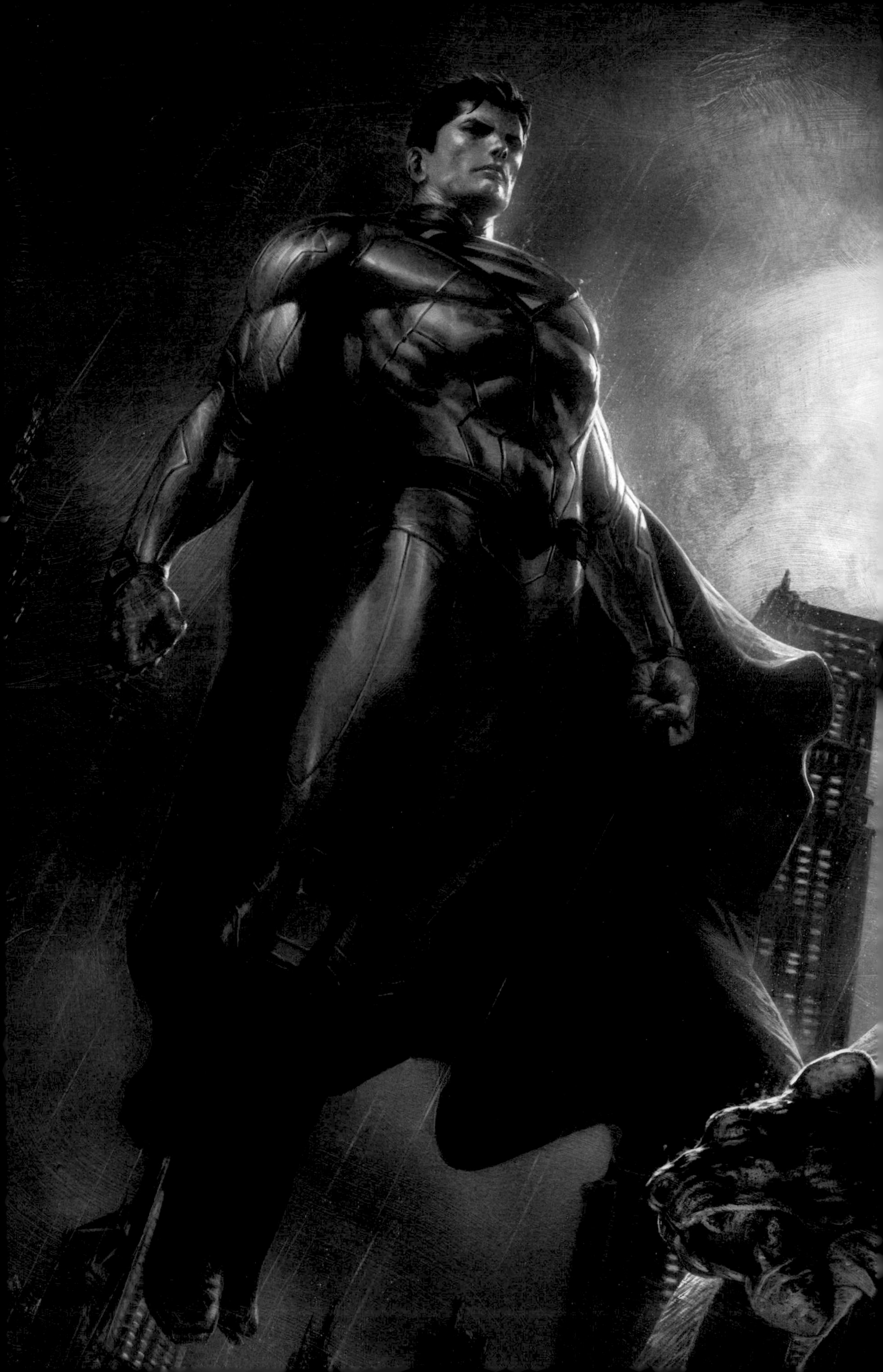

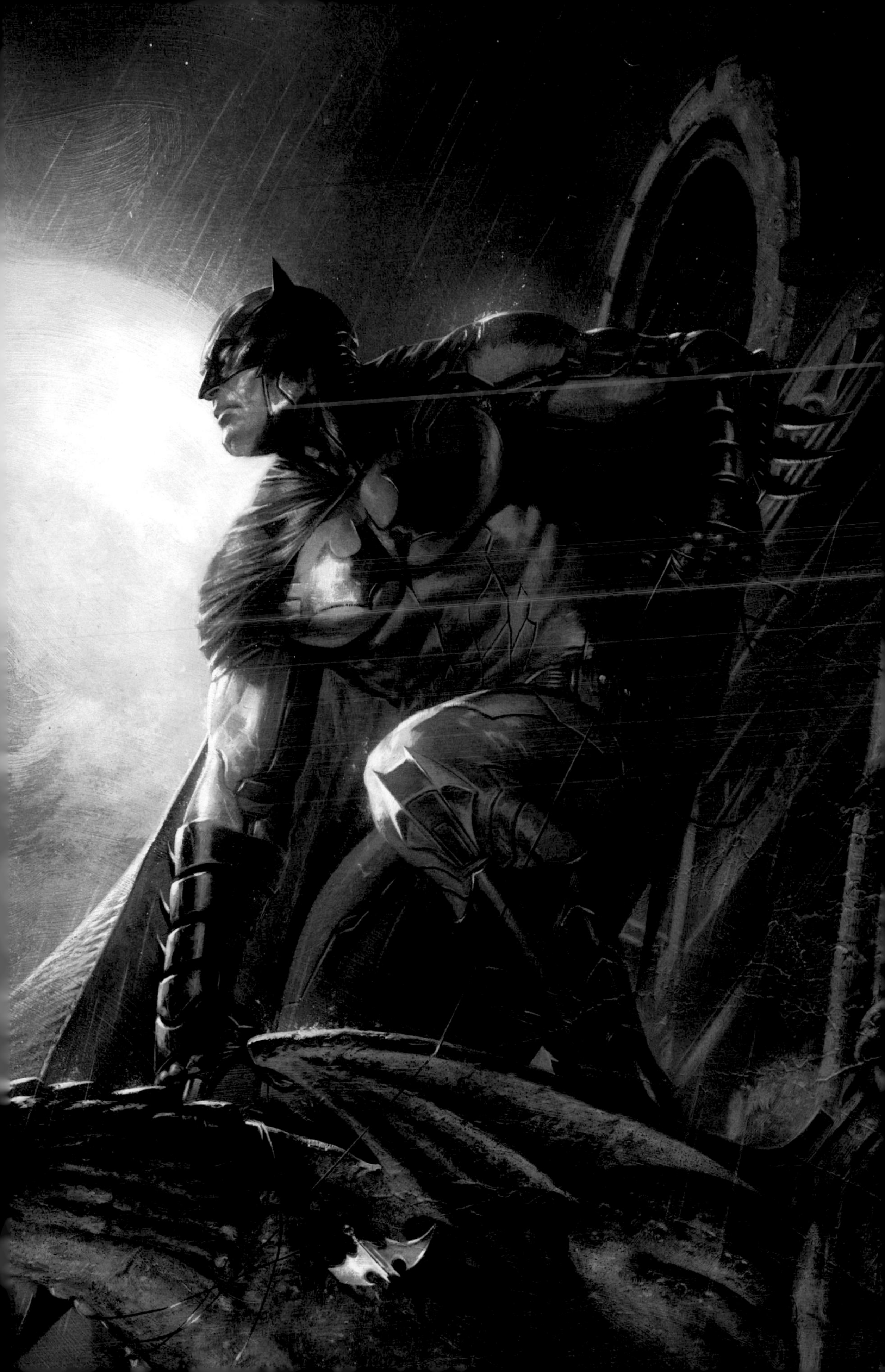

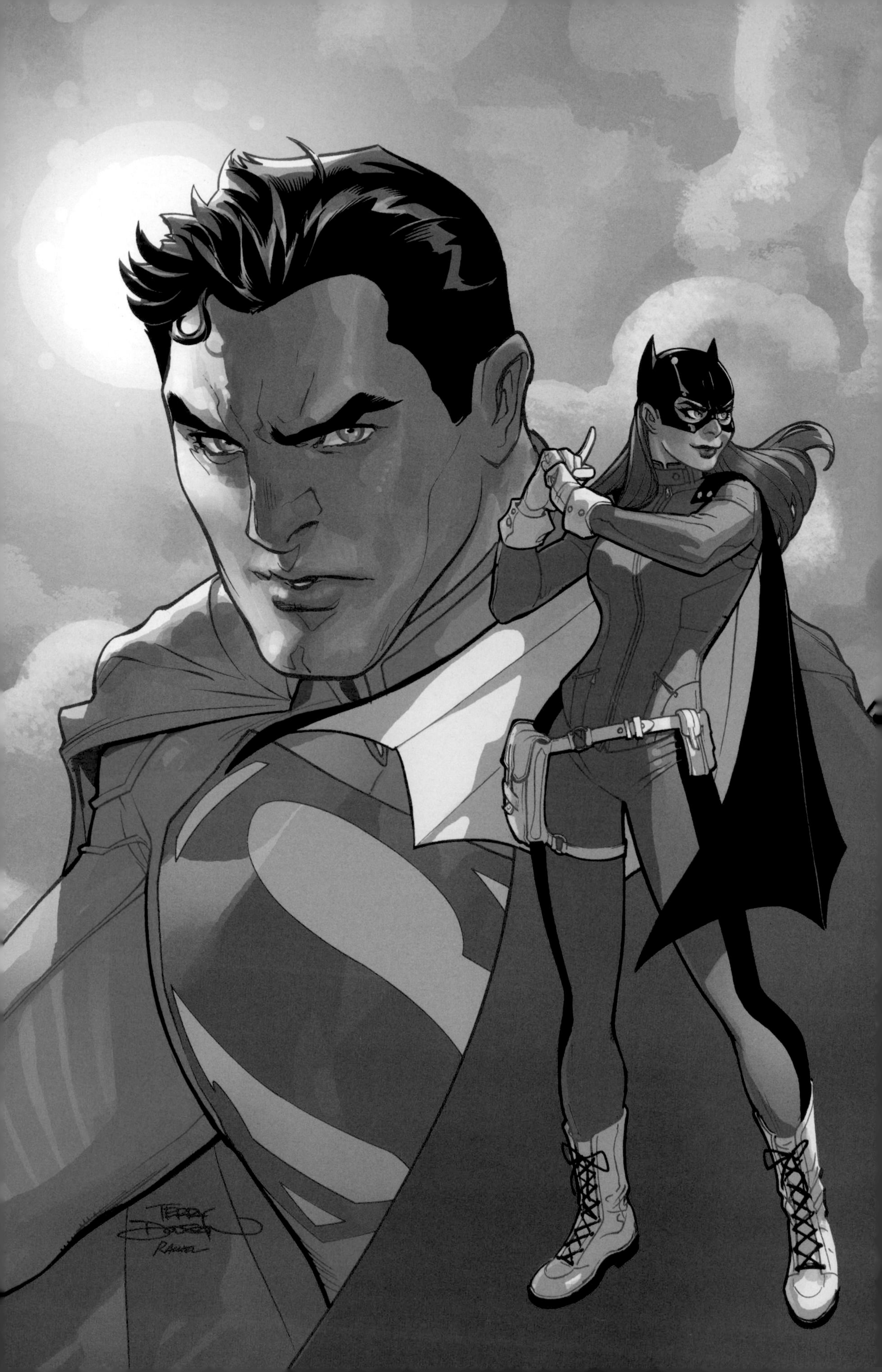

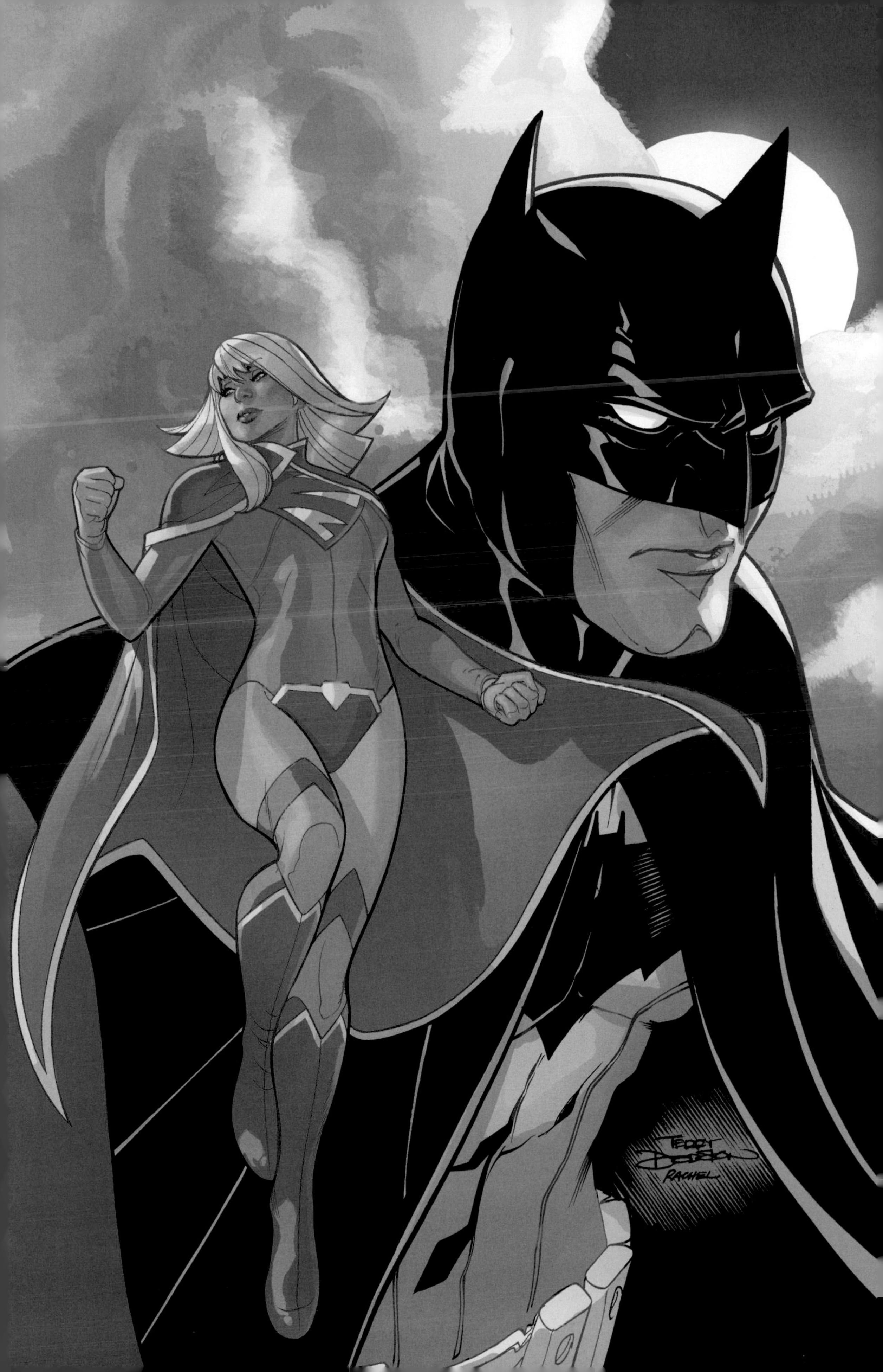

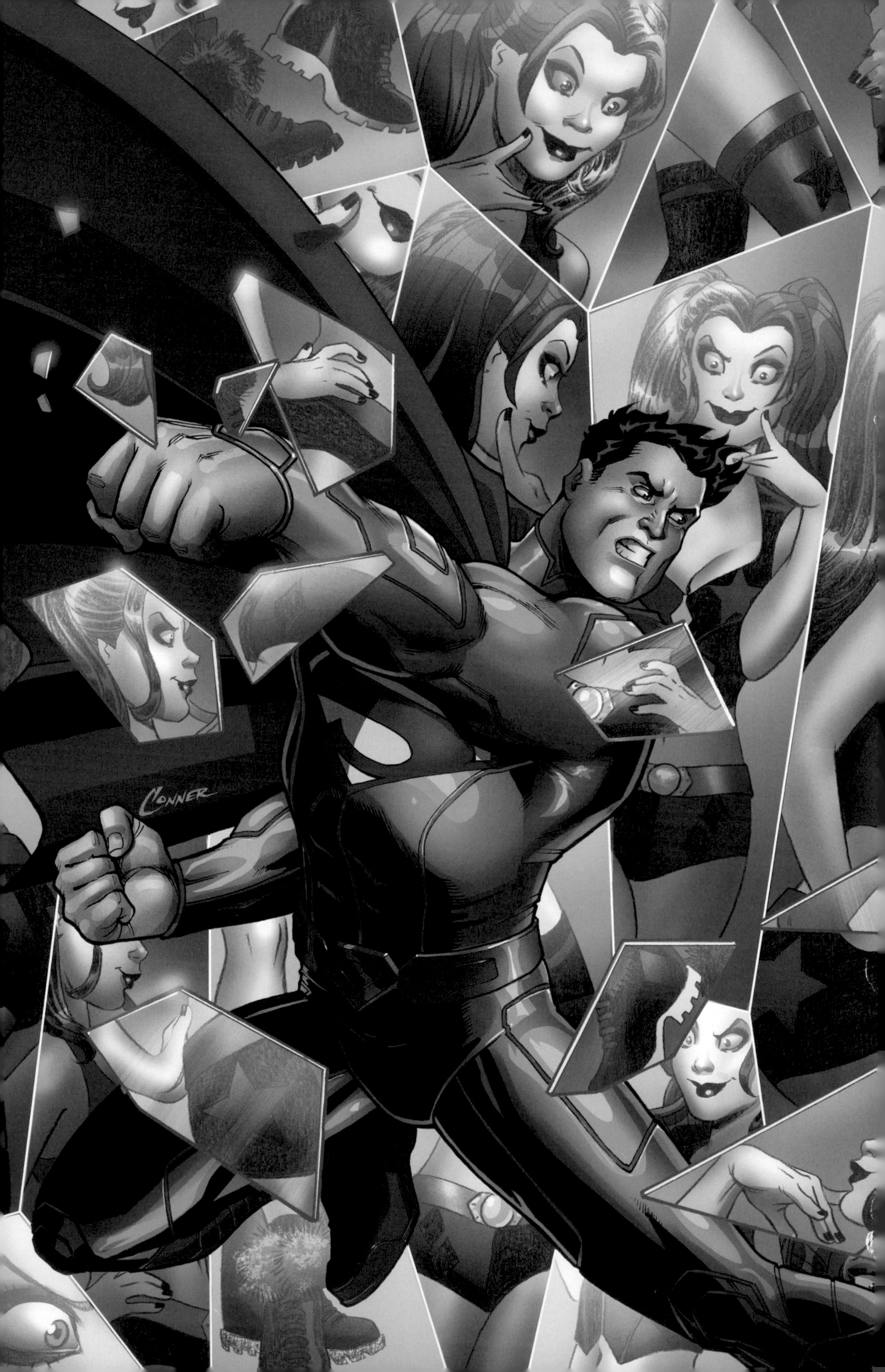
CONNER

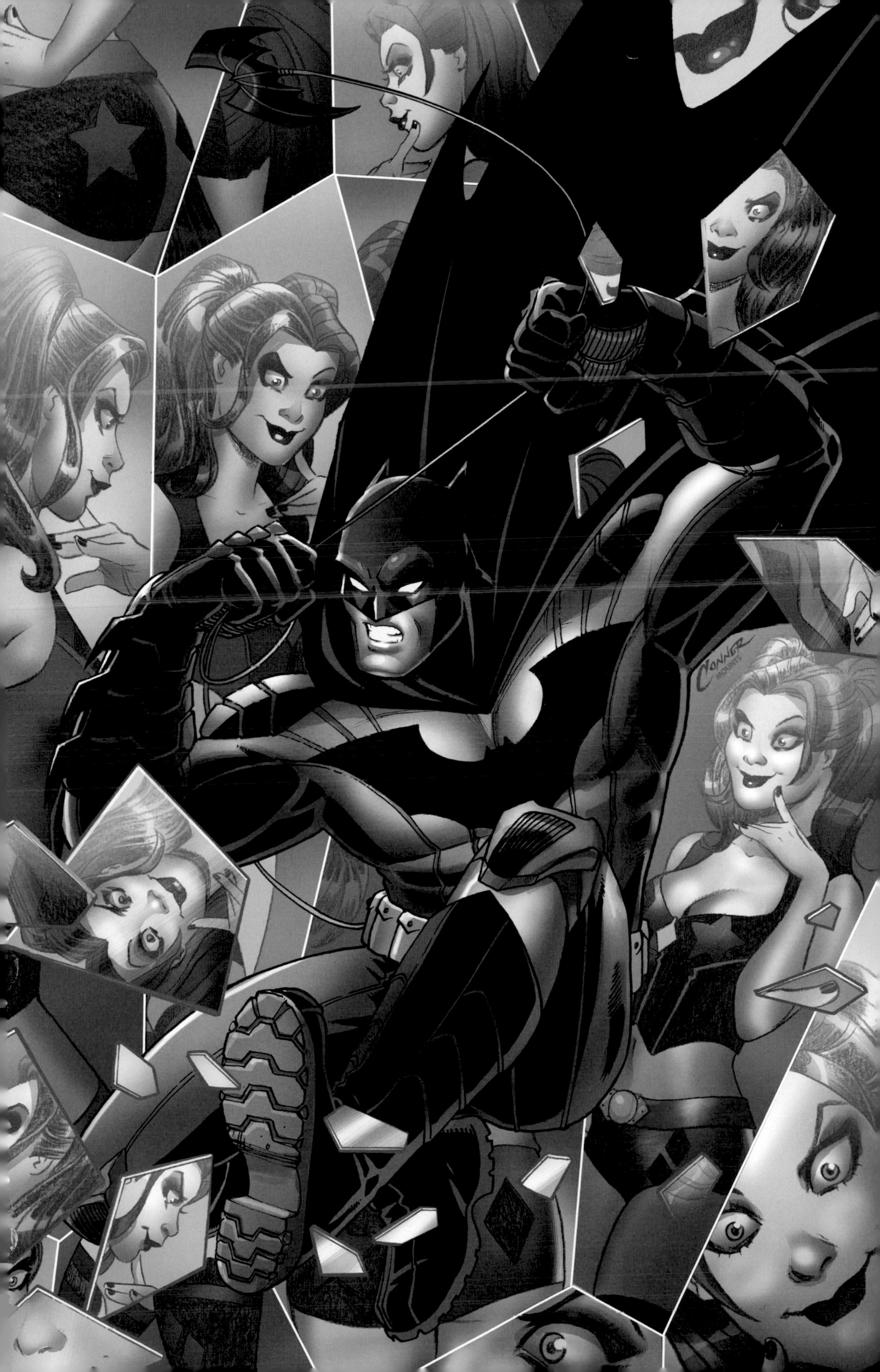

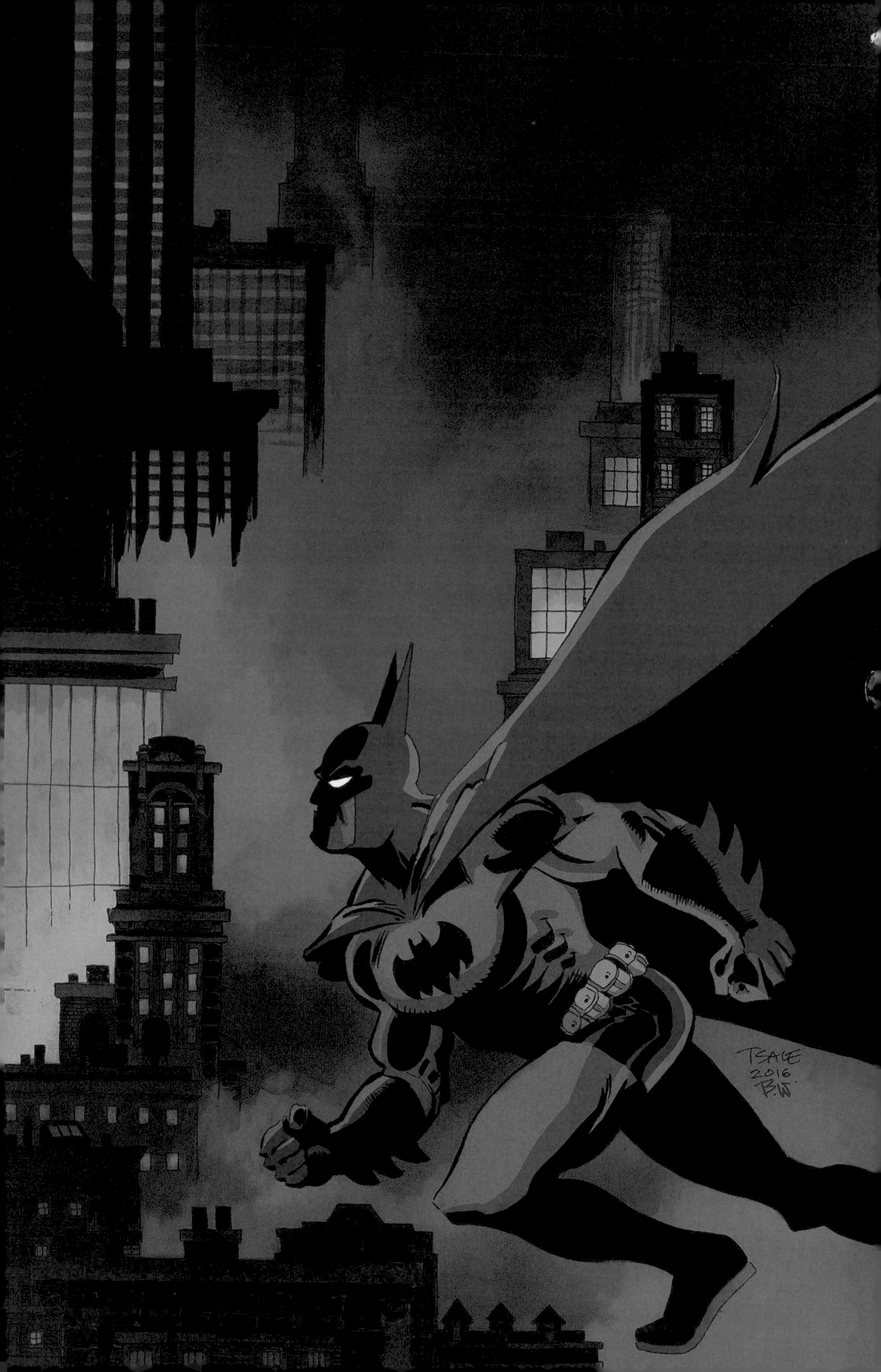
T SALE
2016
B.W.

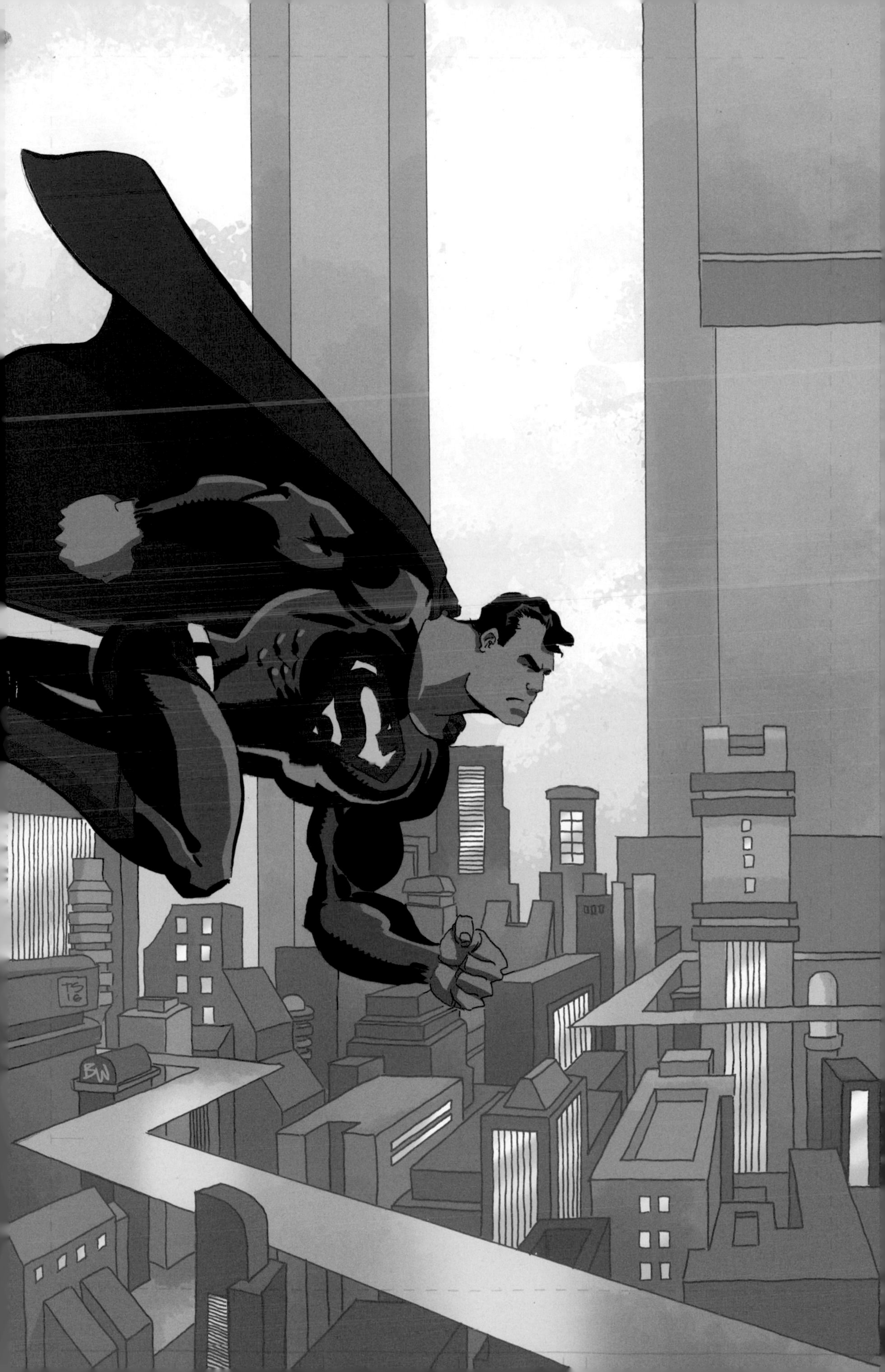
TS
16
BW

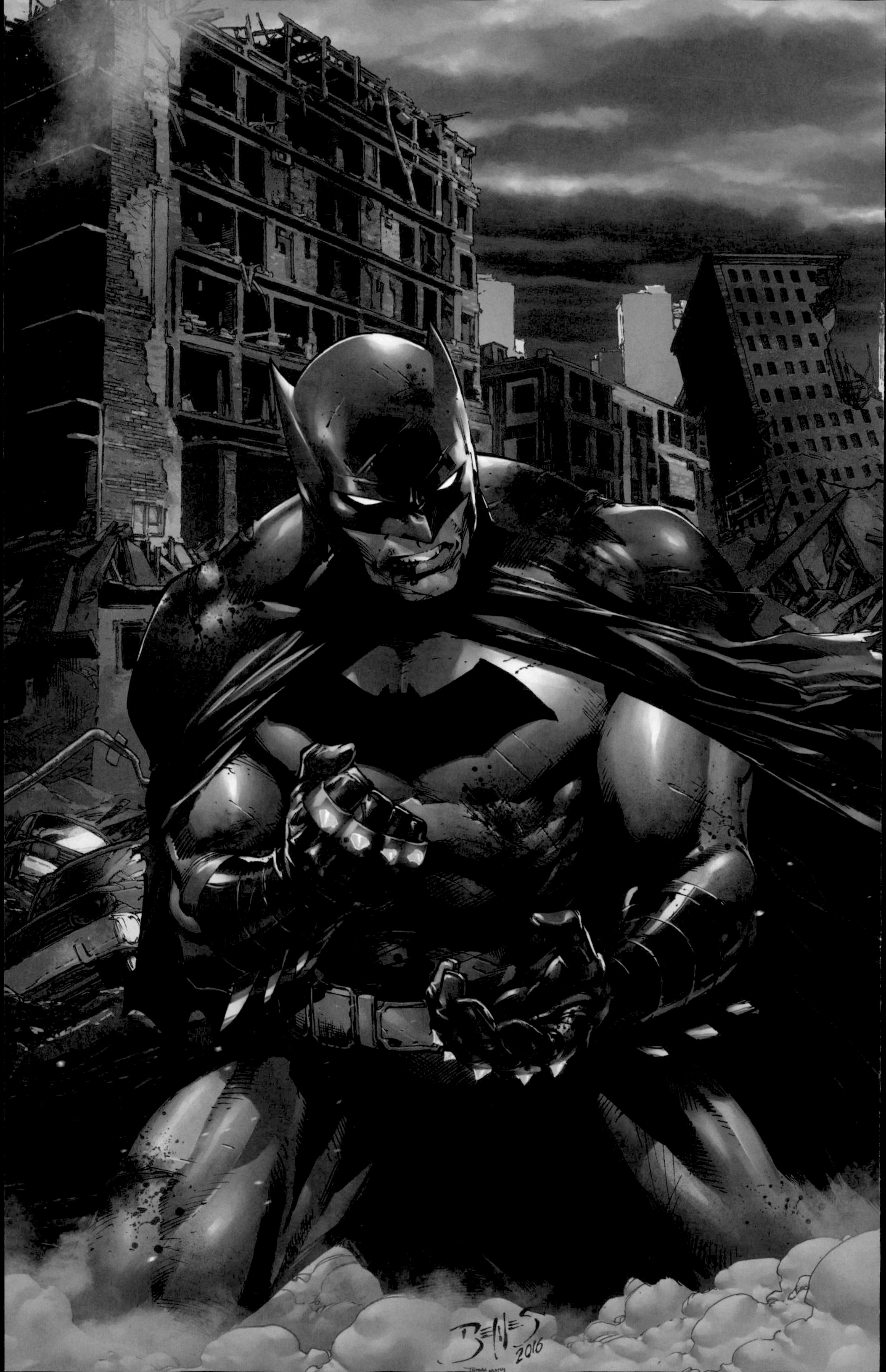
BENES
2016

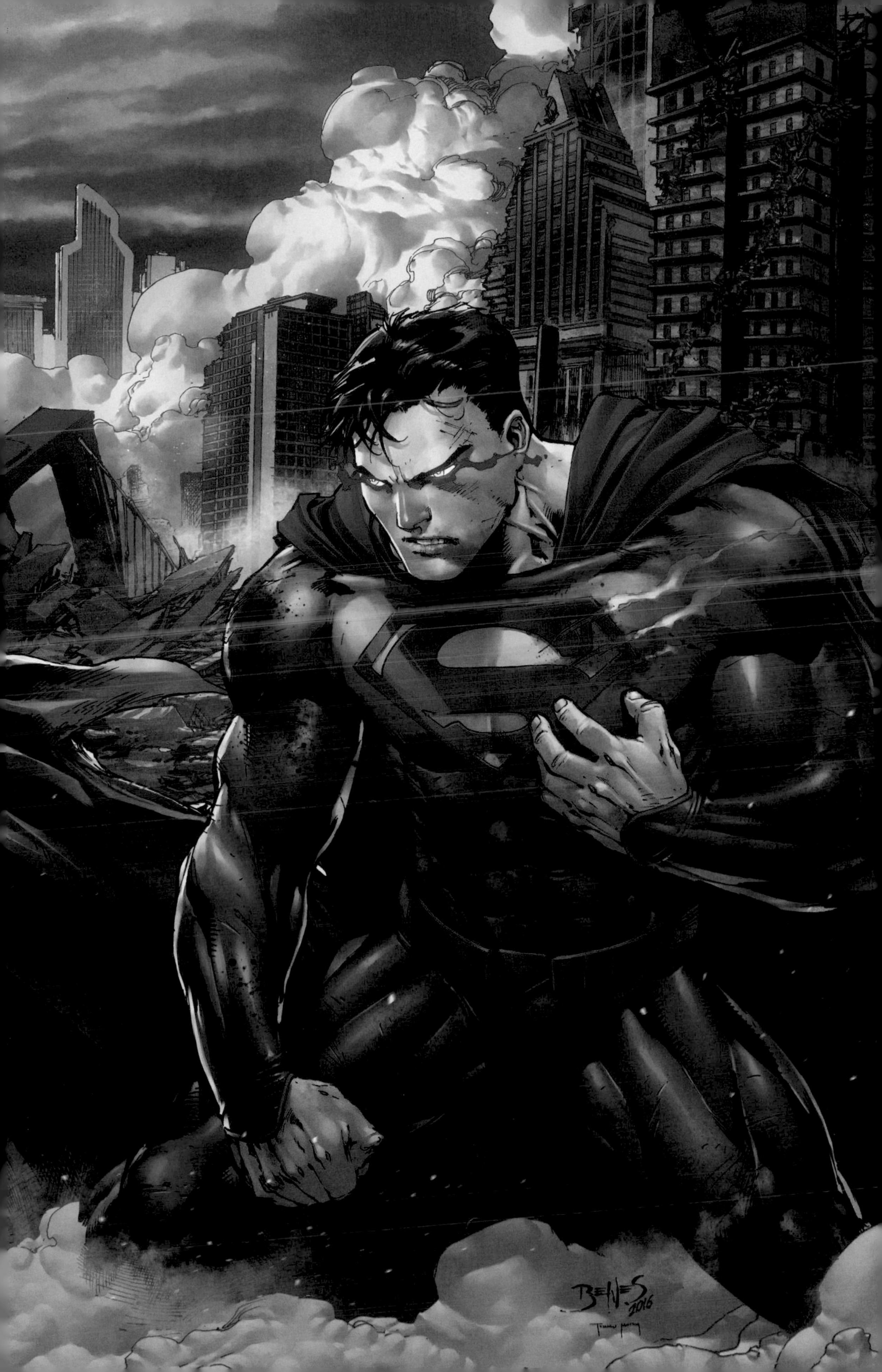
BENES
2016

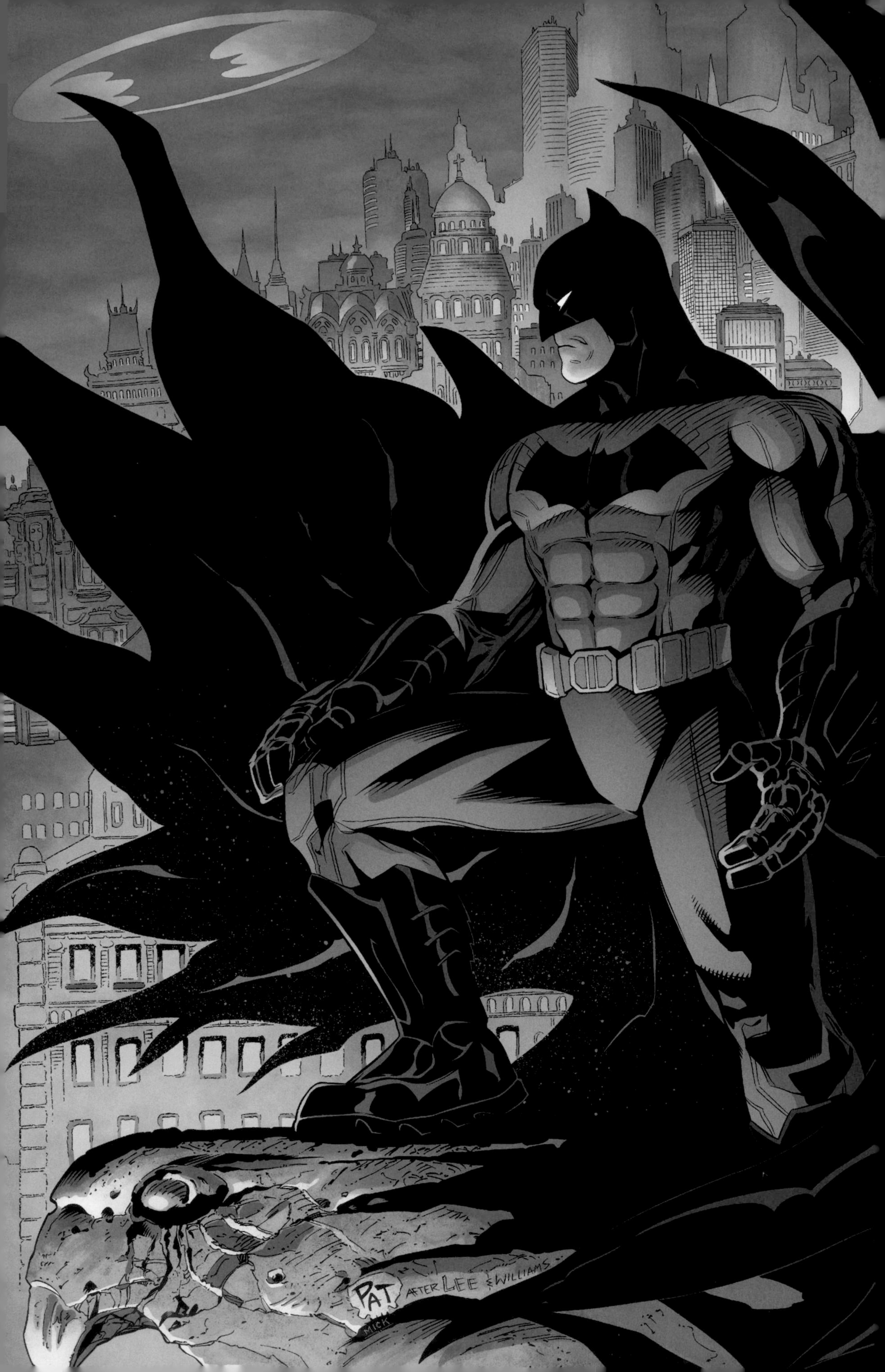
PAT AFTER LEE & WILLIAMS
MICK

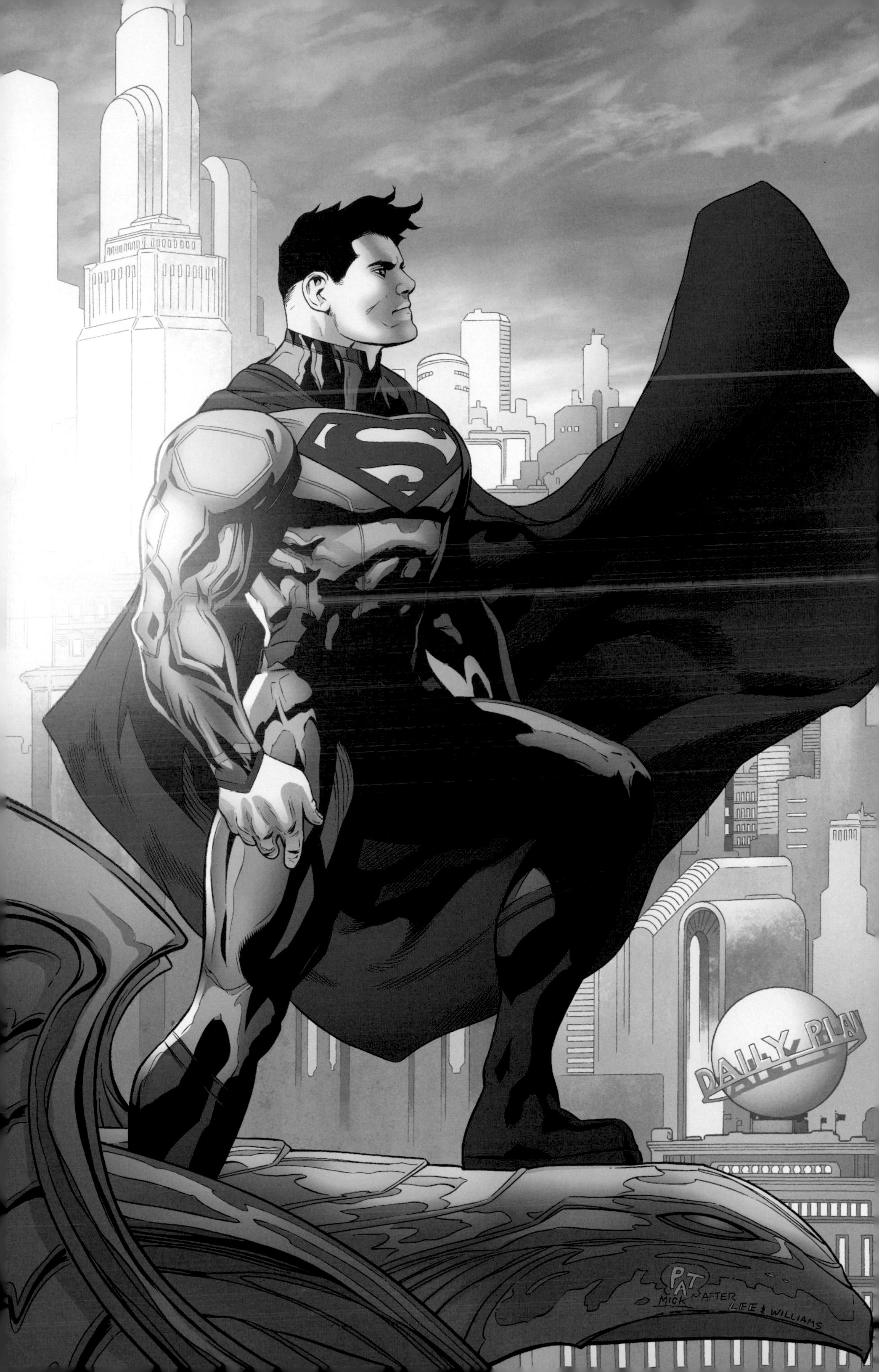
PAT MICK AFTER LEE & WILLIAMS

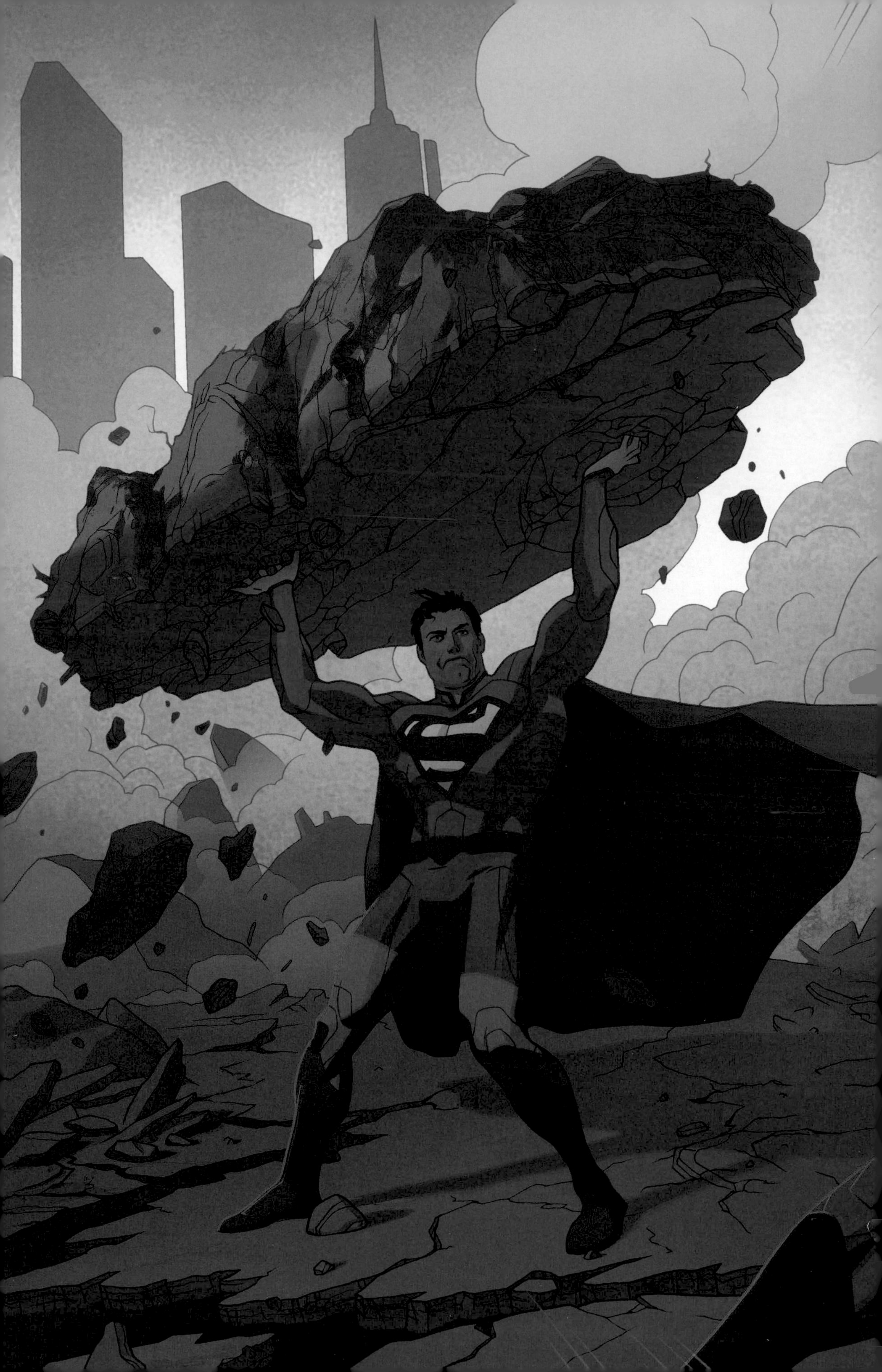

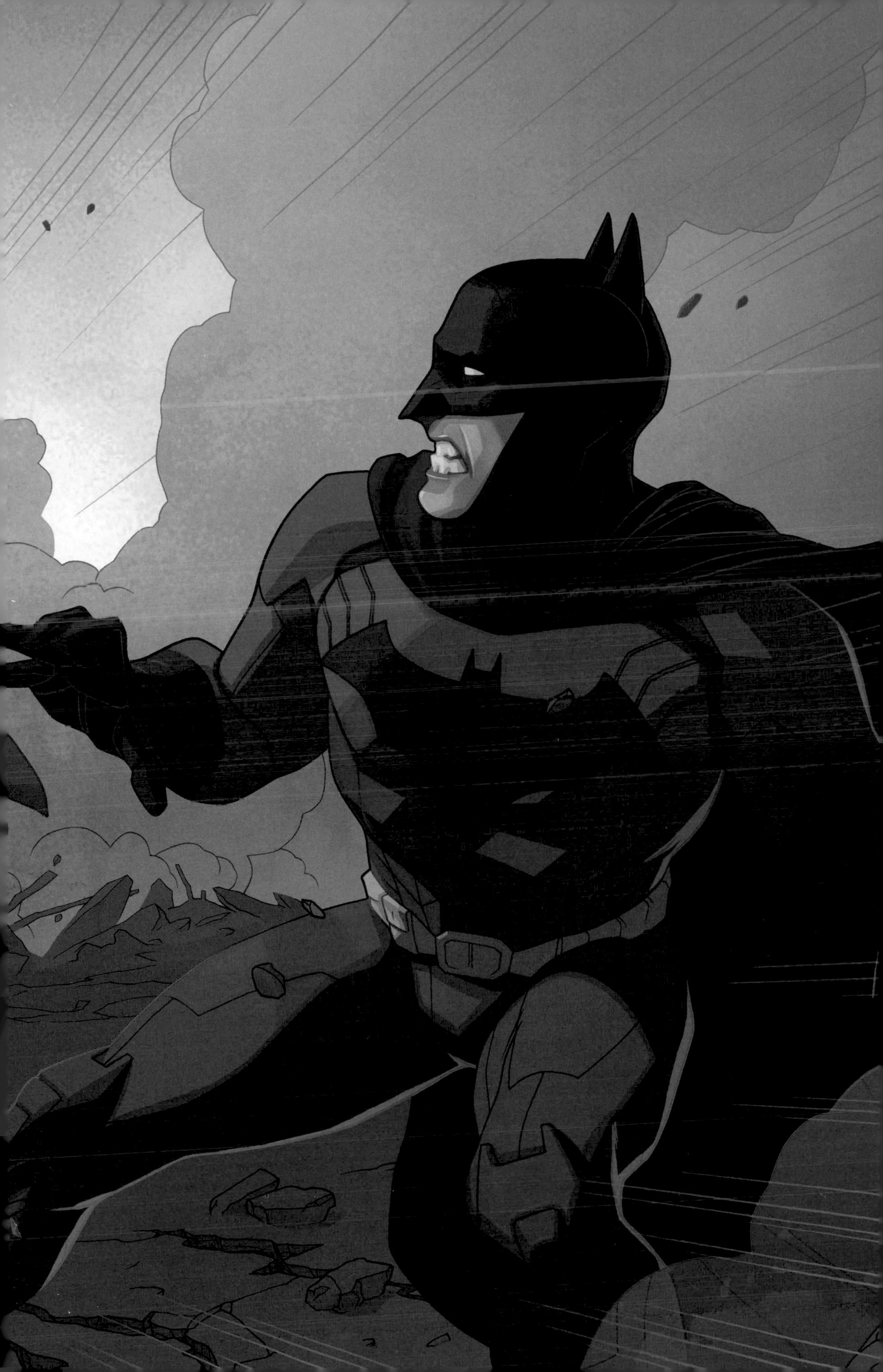

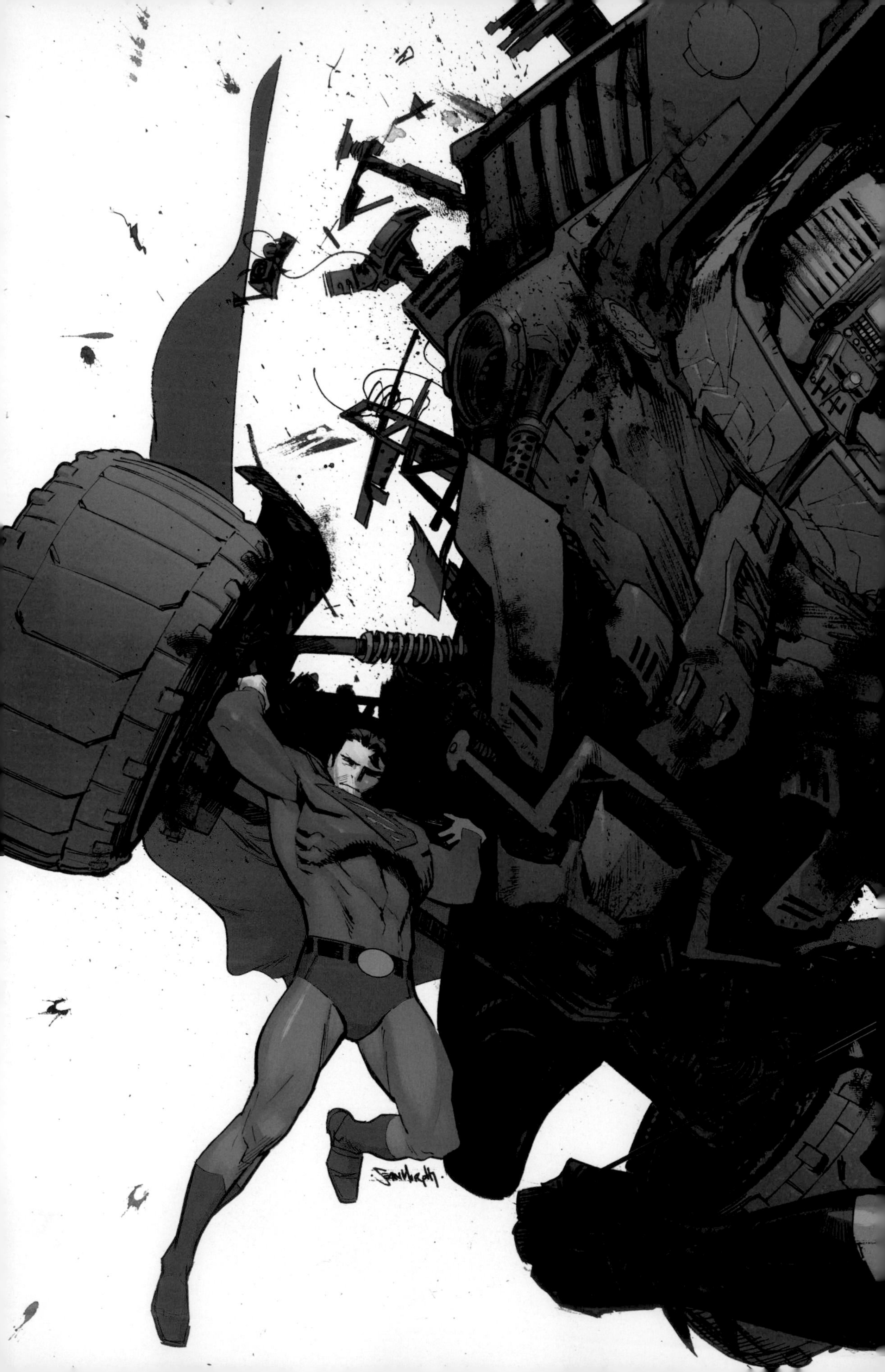

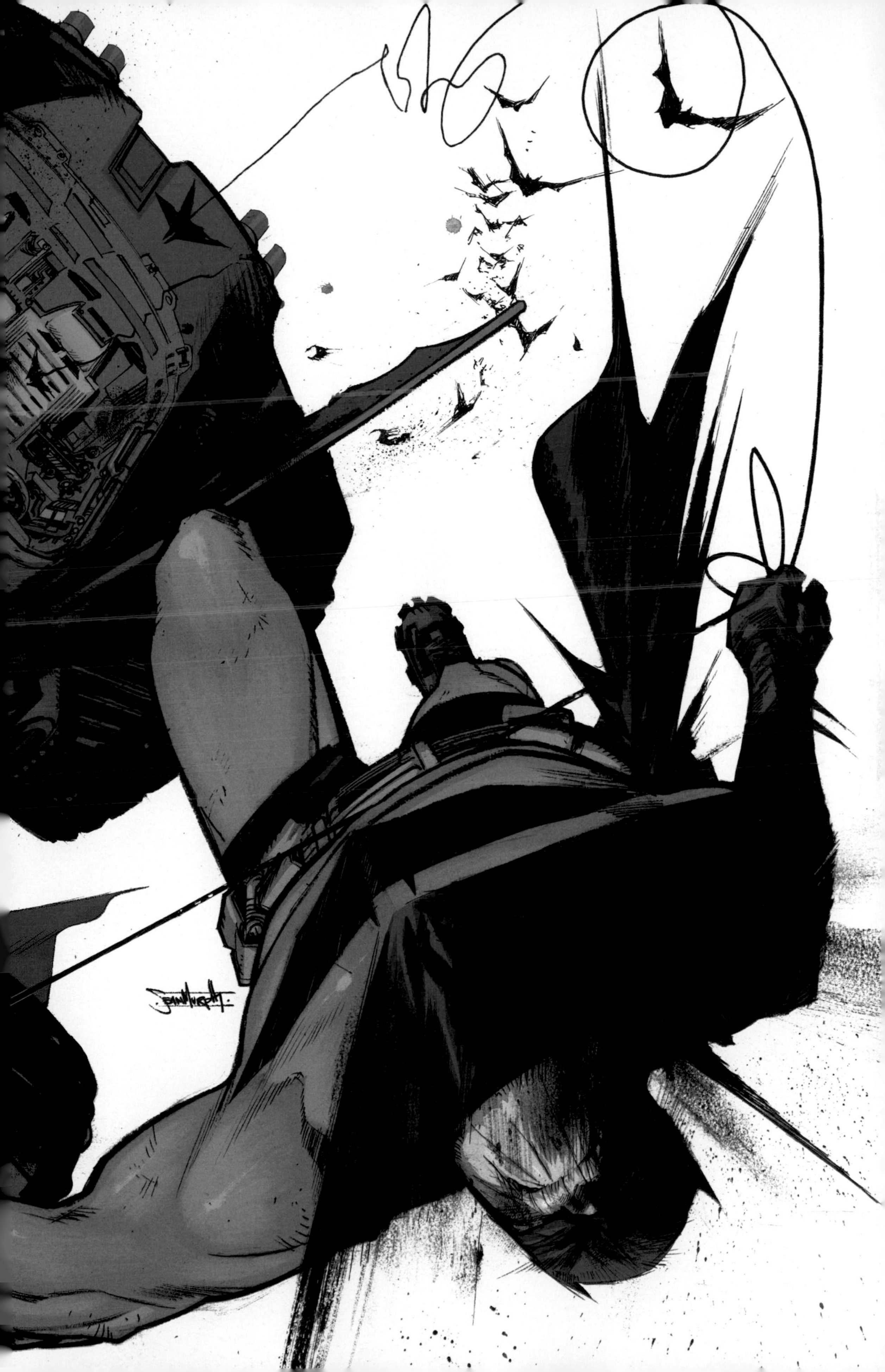

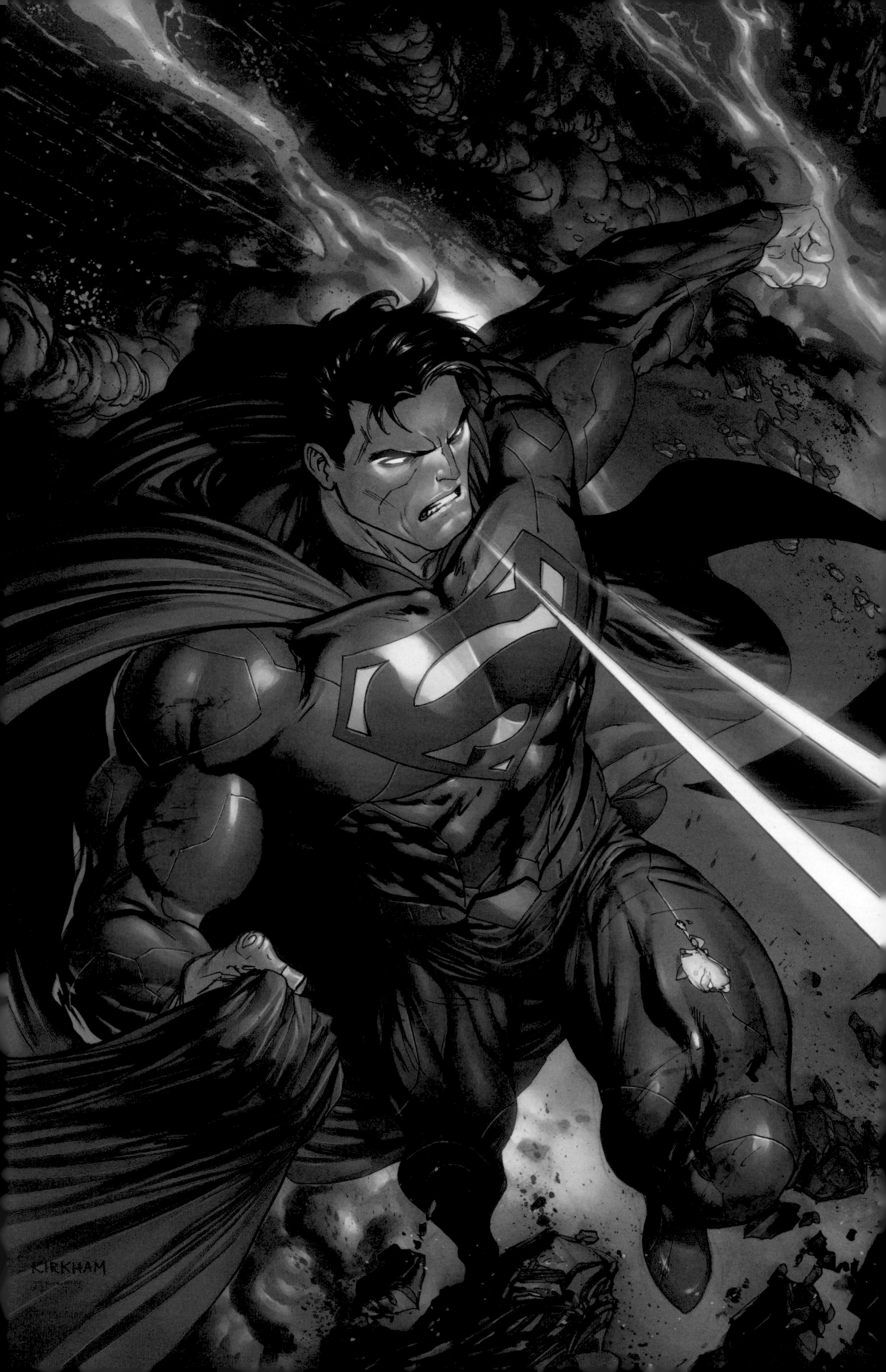
KIRKHAM

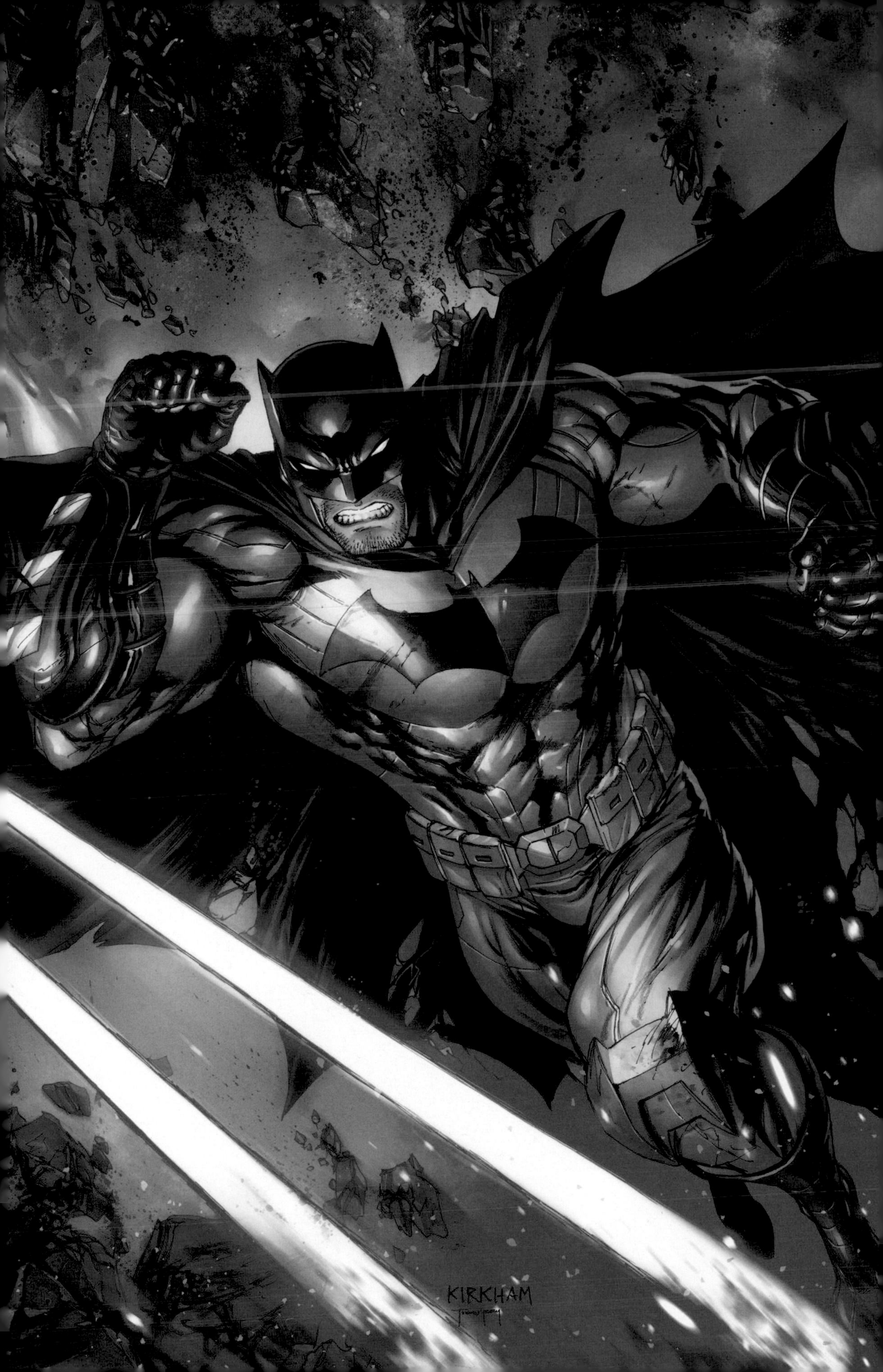
KIRKHAM

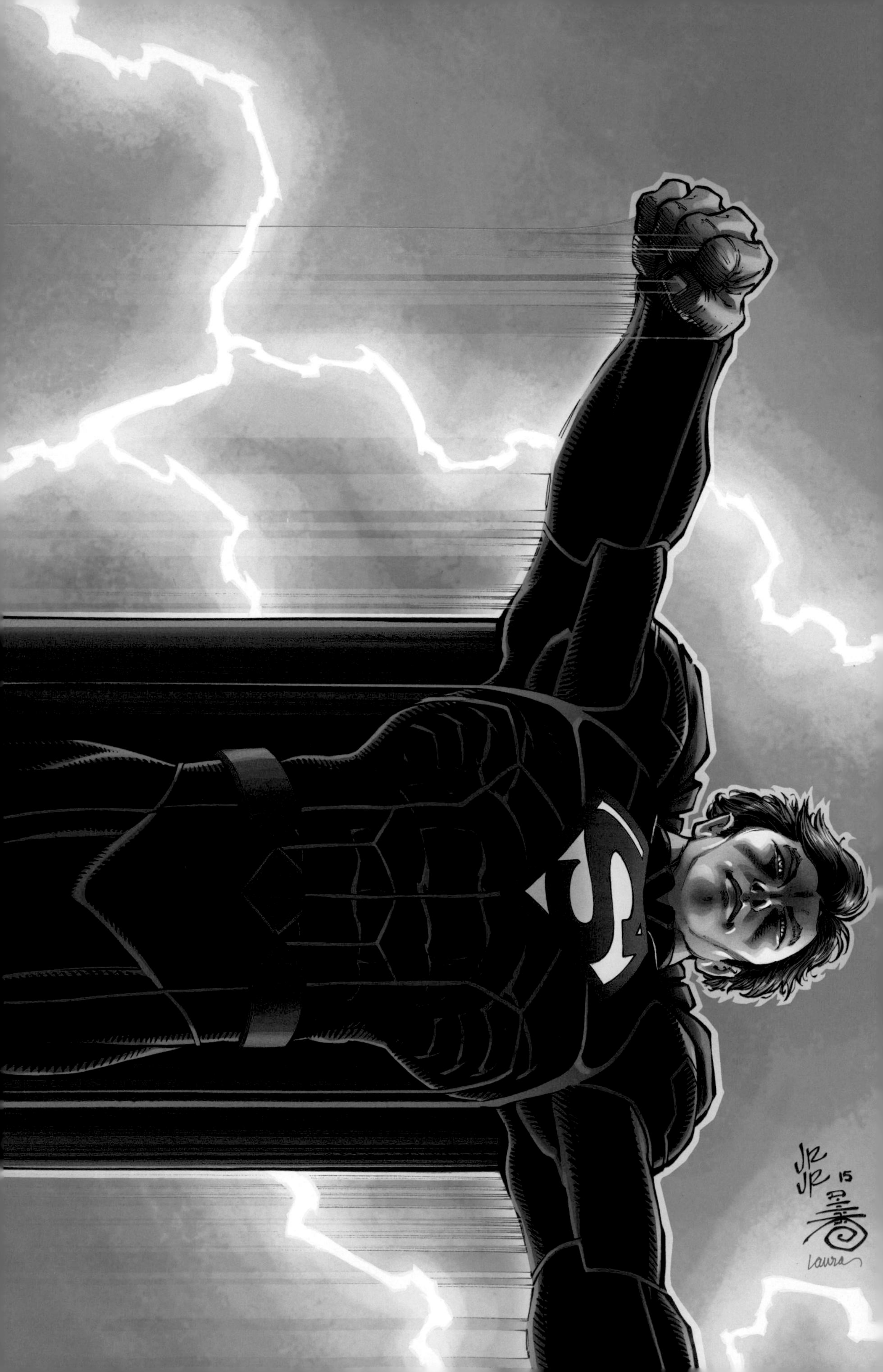

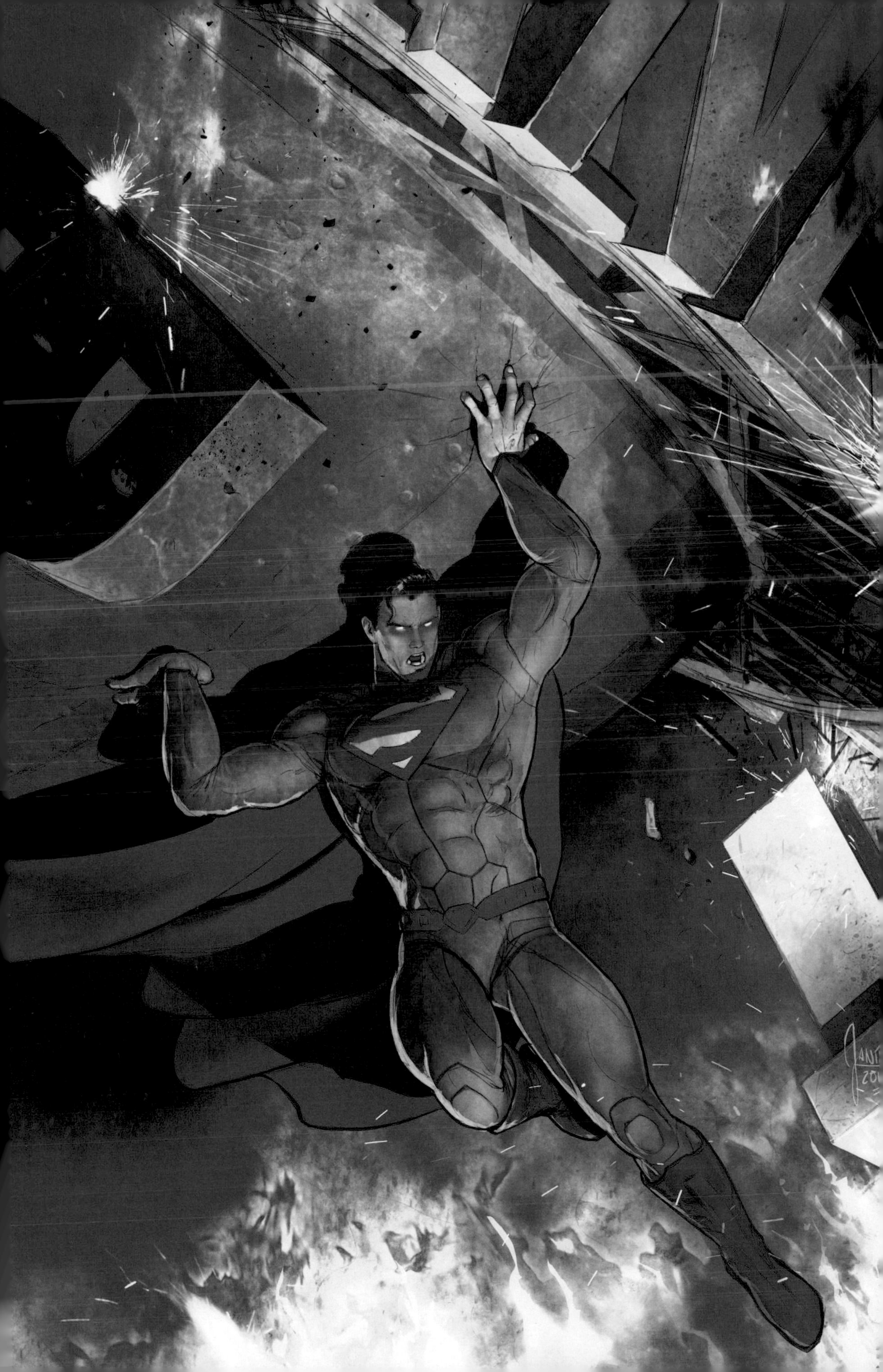

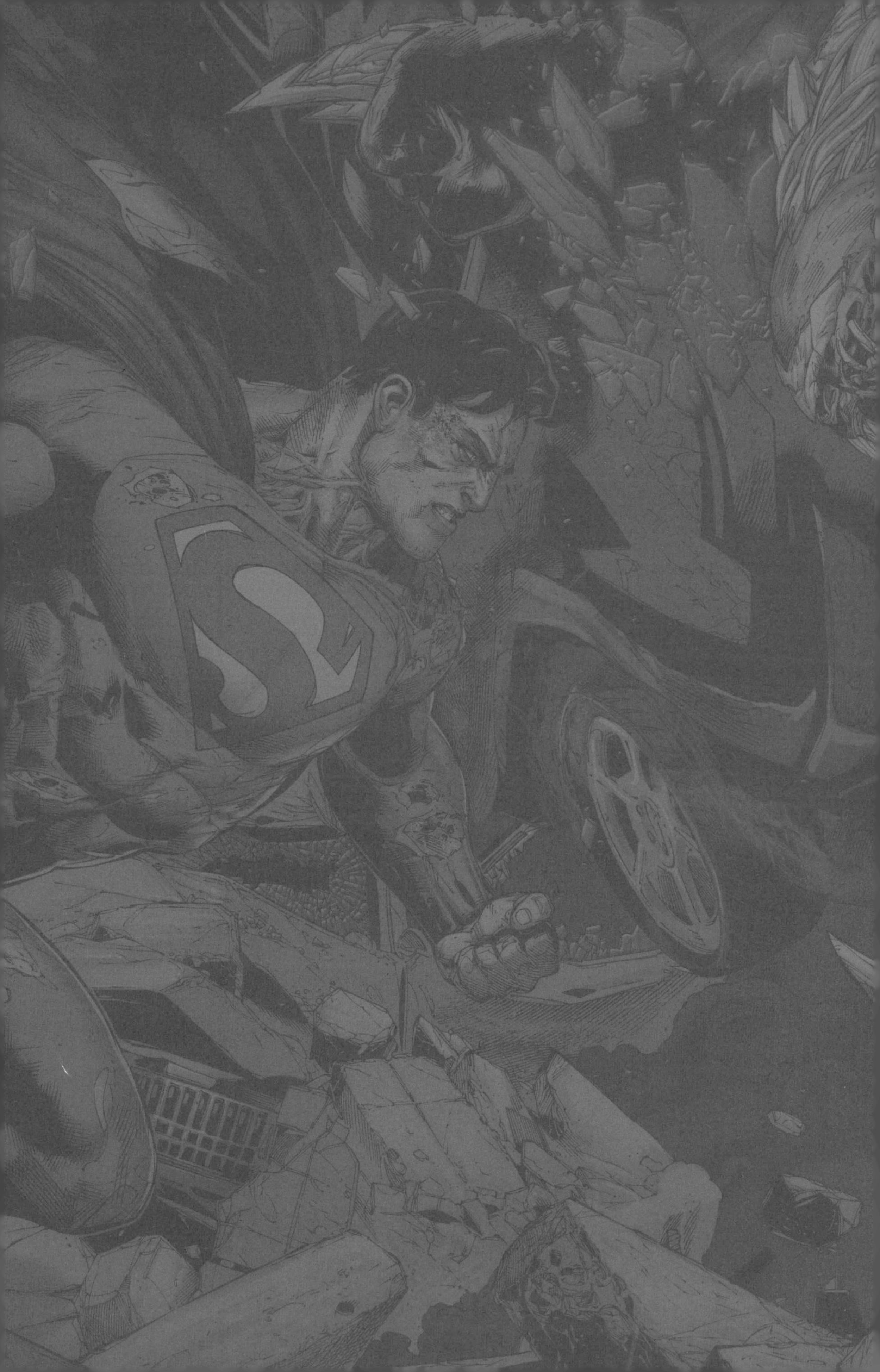

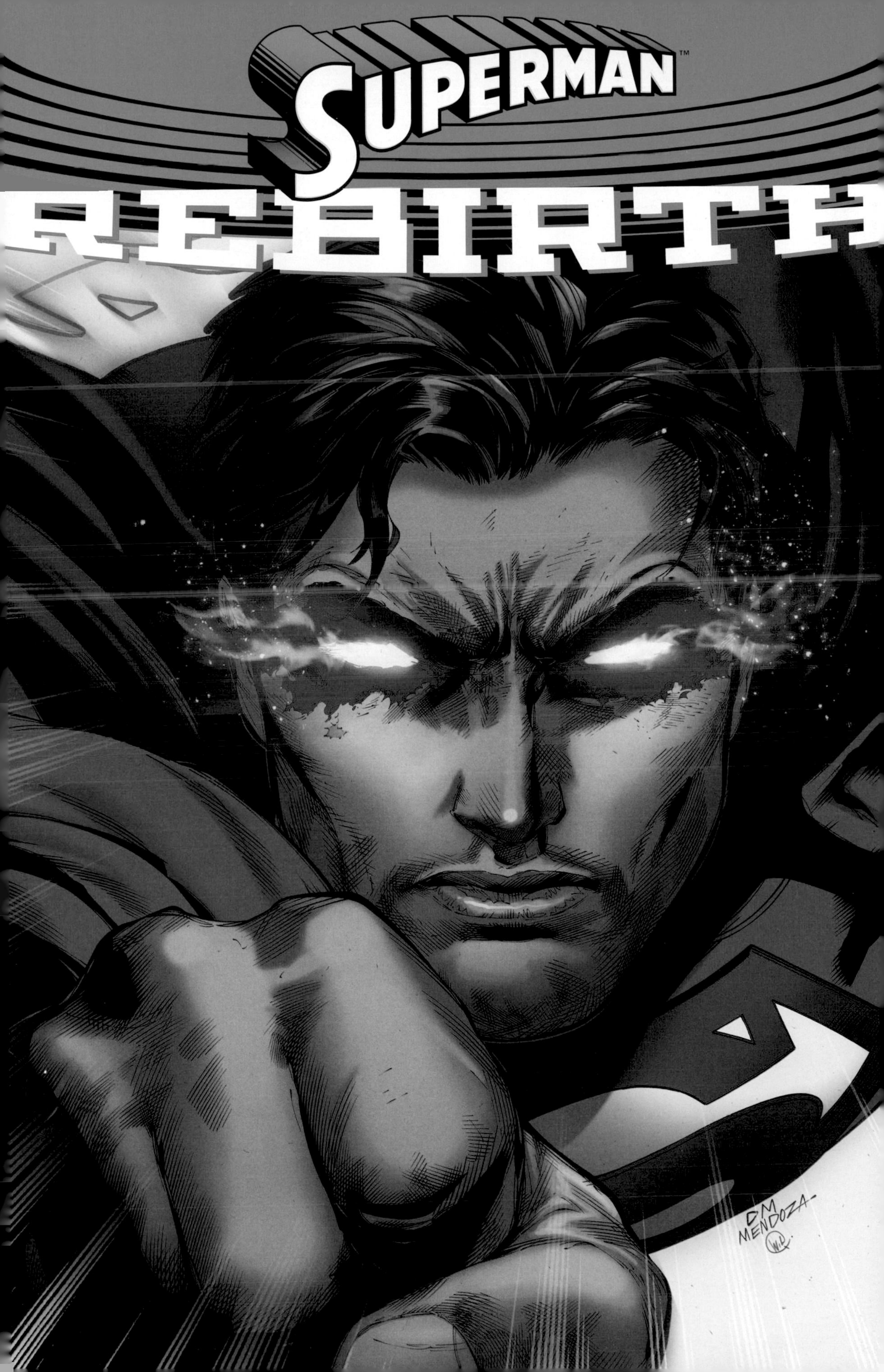
SUPERMAN
REBIRTH
DM
MENDOZA

The future (and past) of the DC Universe starts with DC UNIVERSE: REBIRTH!

Explore the changing world of SUPERMAN in this special bonus preview of **SUPERMAN: REBIRTH #1**!

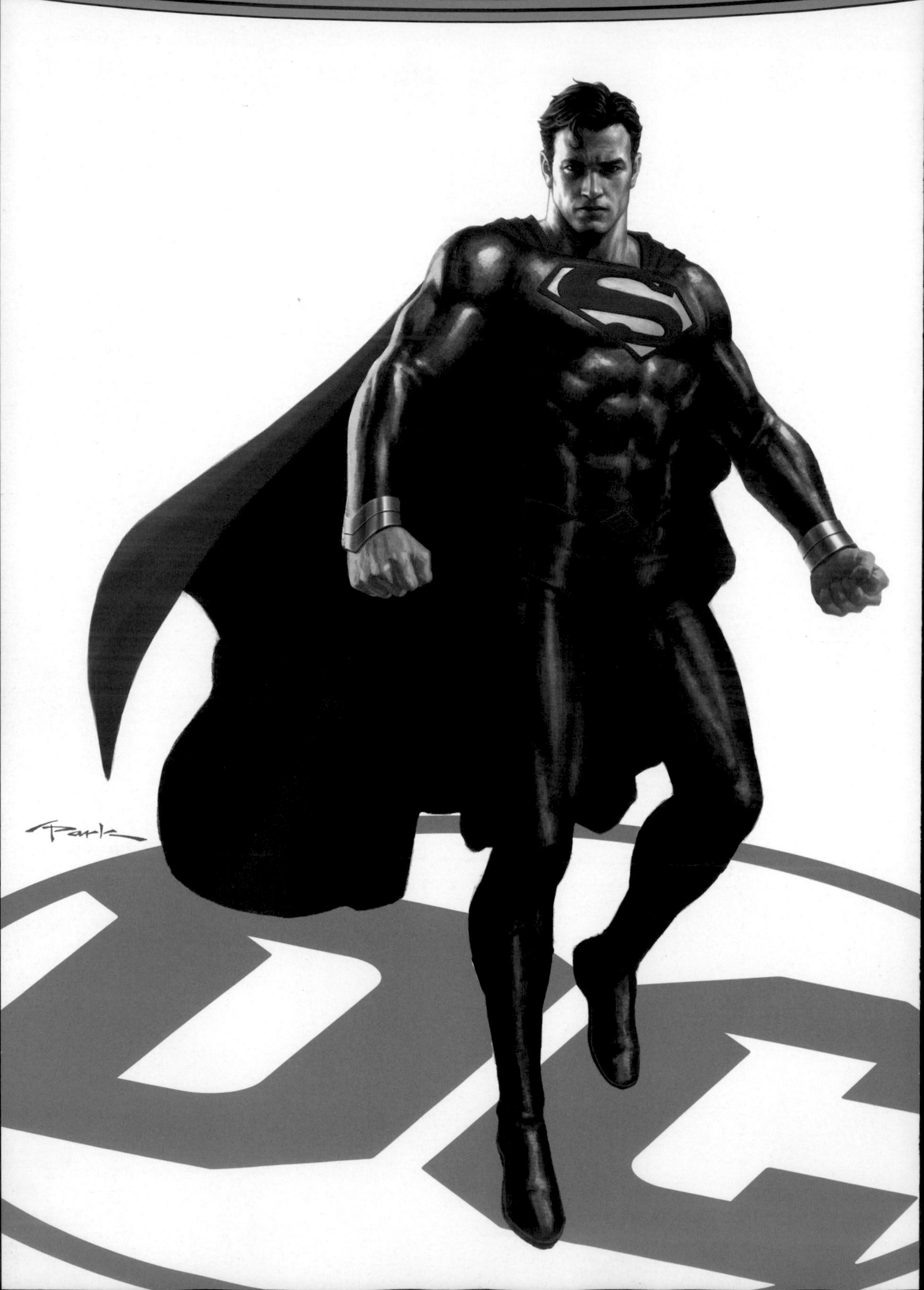

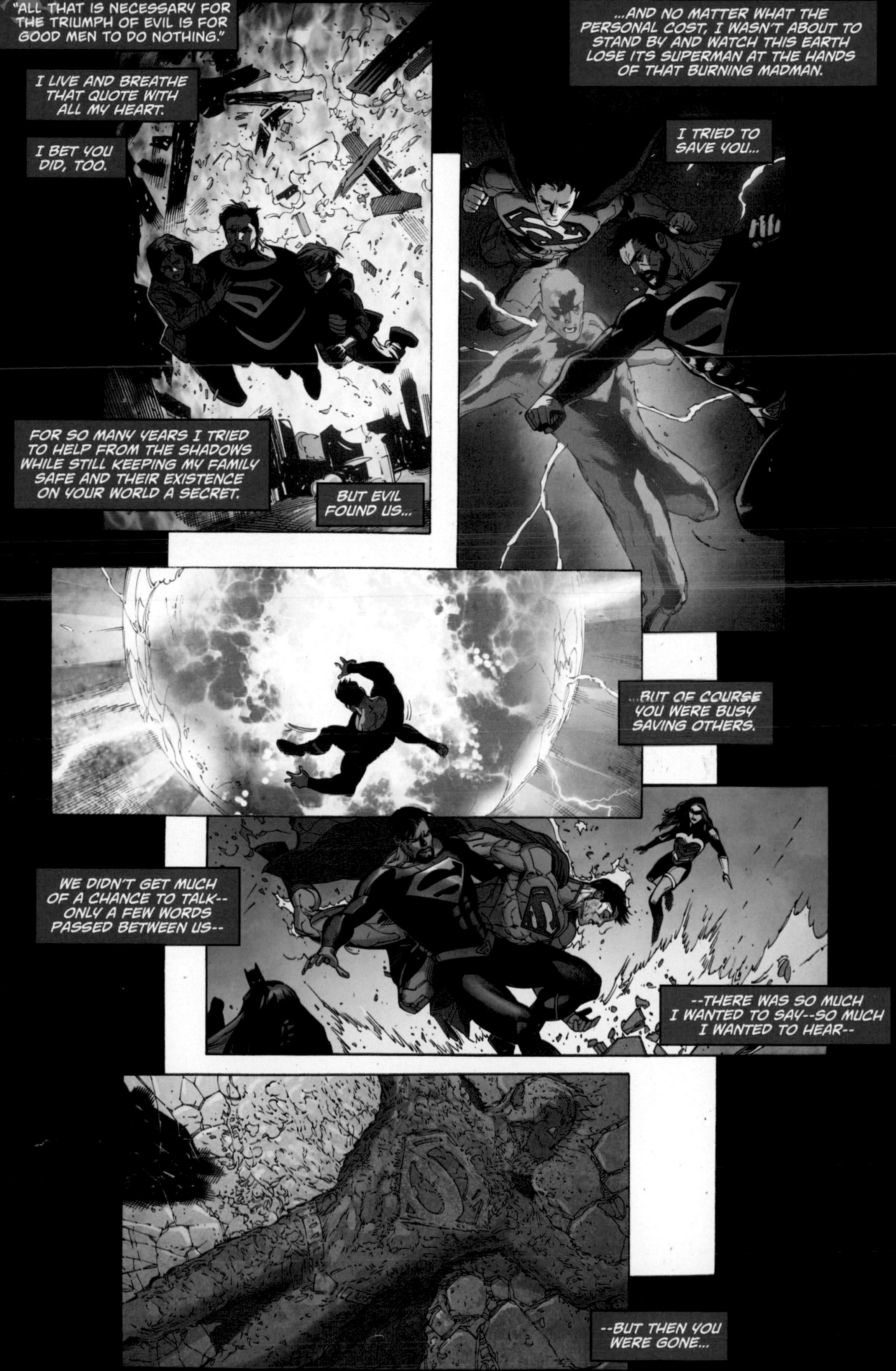
"ALL THAT IS NECESSARY FOR THE TRIUMPH OF EVIL IS FOR GOOD MEN TO DO NOTHING."
I LIVE AND BREATHE THAT QUOTE WITH ALL MY HEART.
I BET YOU DID, TOO.
FOR SO MANY YEARS I TRIED TO HELP FROM THE SHADOWS WHILE STILL KEEPING MY FAMILY SAFE AND THEIR EXISTENCE ON YOUR WORLD A SECRET.
BUT EVIL FOUND US...
...AND NO MATTER WHAT THE PERSONAL COST, I WASN'T ABOUT TO STAND BY AND WATCH THIS EARTH LOSE ITS SUPERMAN AT THE HANDS OF THAT BURNING MADMAN.
I TRIED TO SAVE YOU...
...BUT OF COURSE YOU WERE BUSY SAVING OTHERS.
WE DIDN'T GET MUCH OF A CHANCE TO TALK--ONLY A FEW WORDS PASSED BETWEEN US--
--THERE WAS SO MUCH I WANTED TO SAY--SO MUCH I WANTED TO HEAR--
--BUT THEN YOU WERE GONE...

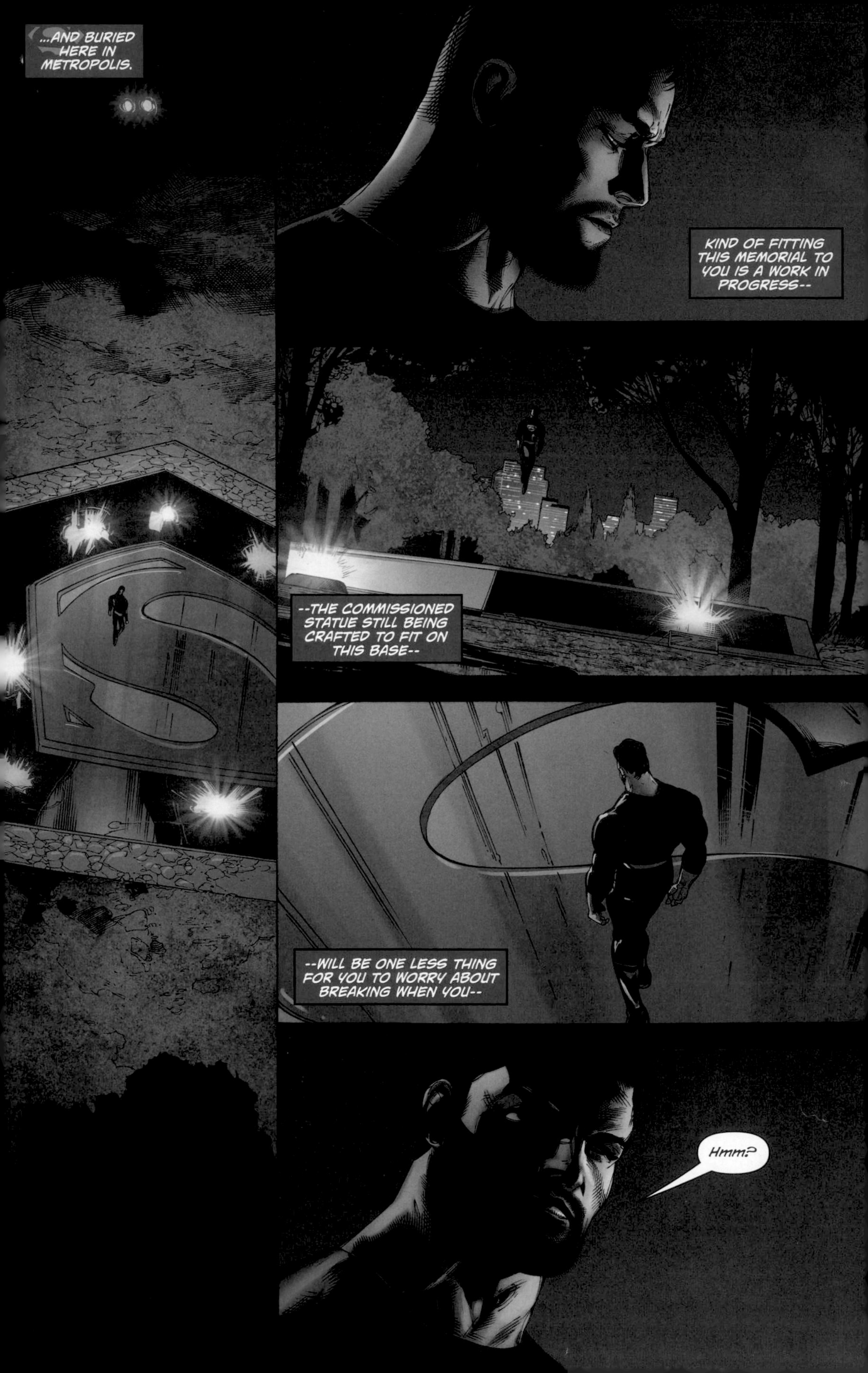
...AND BURIED HERE IN METROPOLIS.
KIND OF FITTING THIS MEMORIAL TO YOU IS A WORK IN PROGRESS--
--THE COMMISSIONED STATUE STILL BEING CRAFTED TO FIT ON THIS BASE--
--WILL BE ONE LESS THING FOR YOU TO WORRY ABOUT BREAKING WHEN YOU--
Hmm?

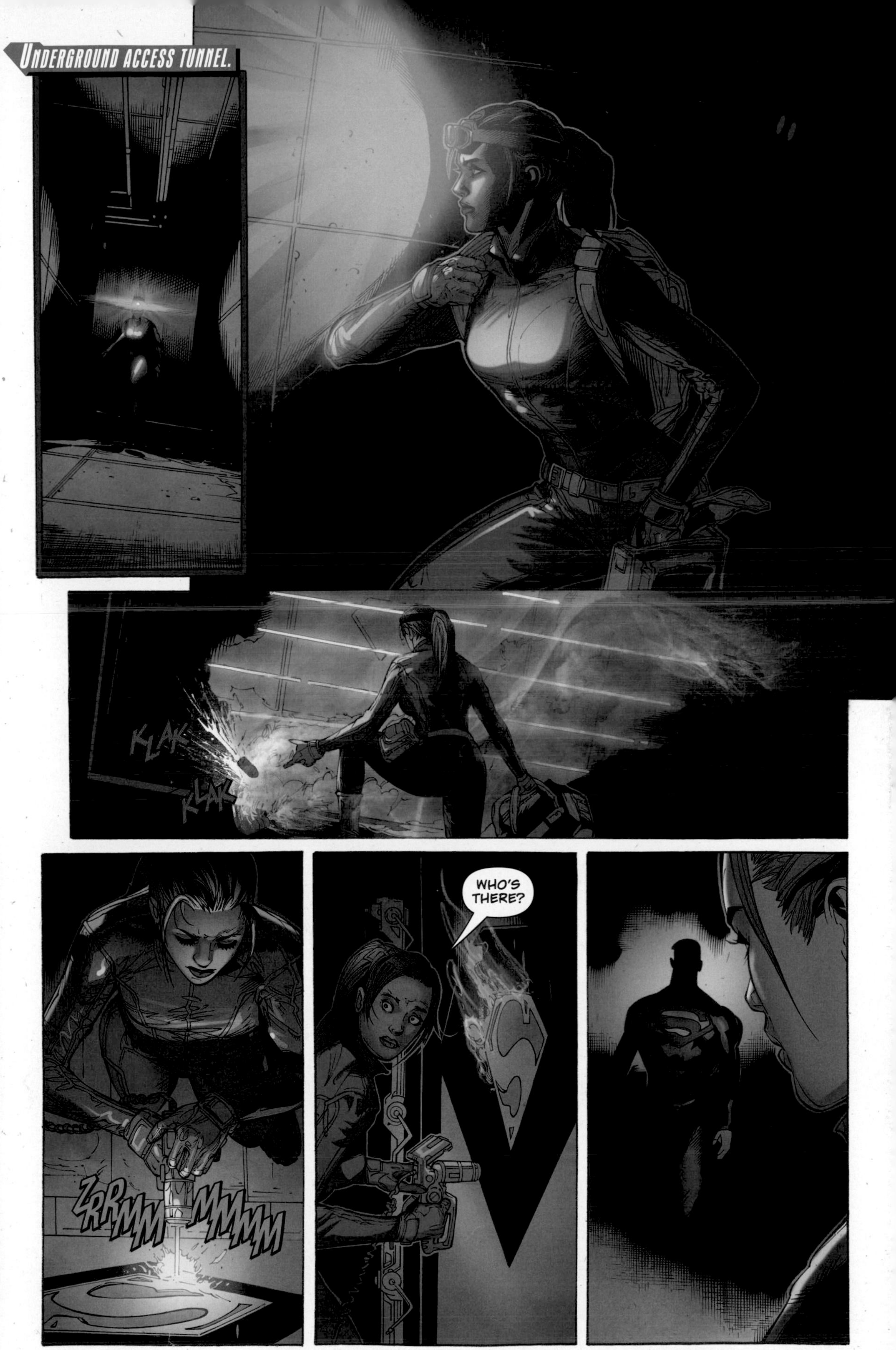
UNDERGROUND ACCESS TUNNEL.
KLAK
KLAK
ZRRMM MMMM
WHO'S THERE?

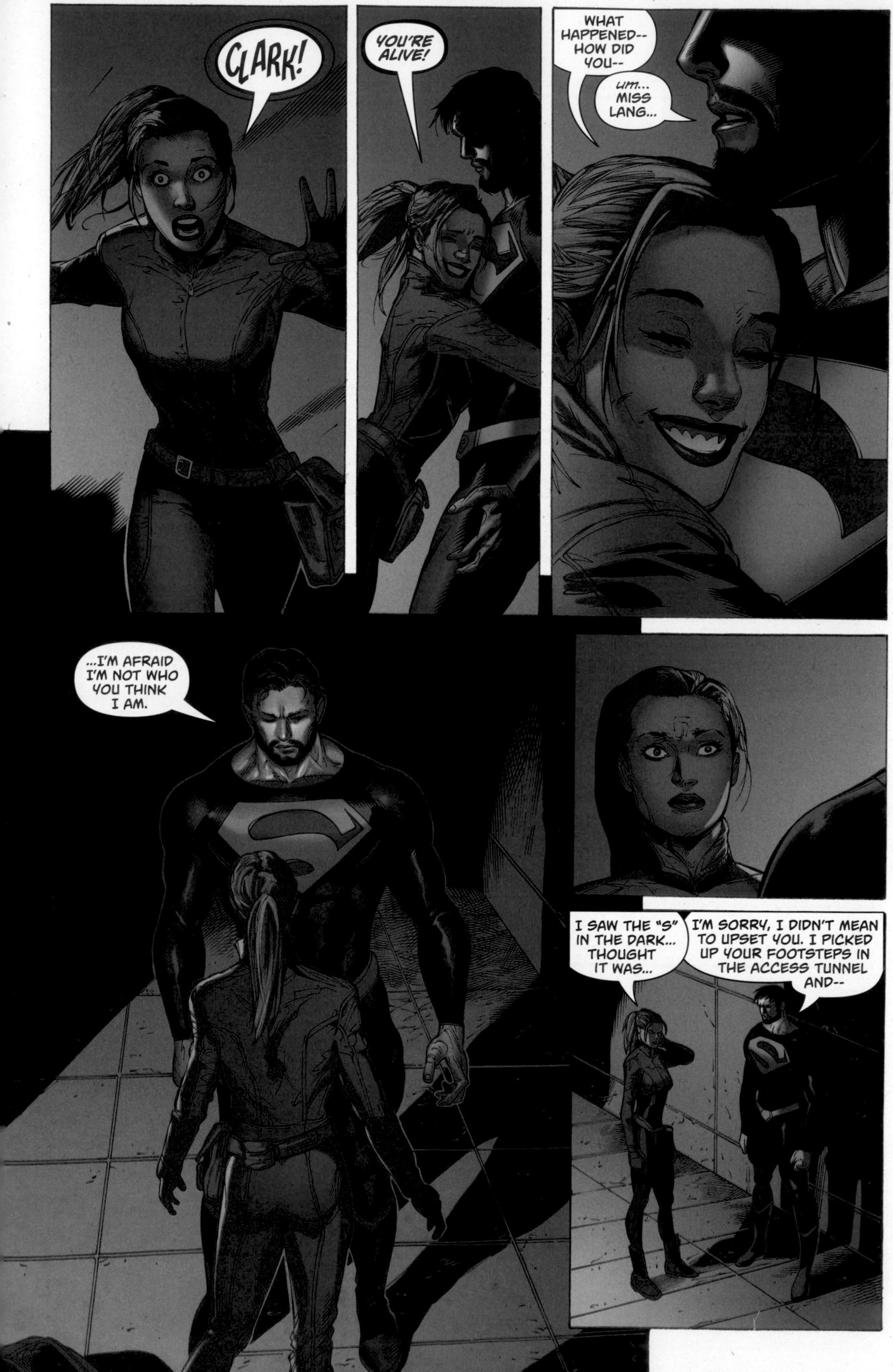
CLARK!
YOU'RE ALIVE!
WHAT HAPPENED-- HOW DID YOU--
UM... MISS LANG...
...I'M AFRAID I'M NOT WHO YOU THINK I AM.
I SAW THE "S" IN THE DARK... THOUGHT IT WAS...
I'M SORRY, I DIDN'T MEAN TO UPSET YOU. I PICKED UP YOUR FOOTSTEPS IN THE ACCESS TUNNEL AND--

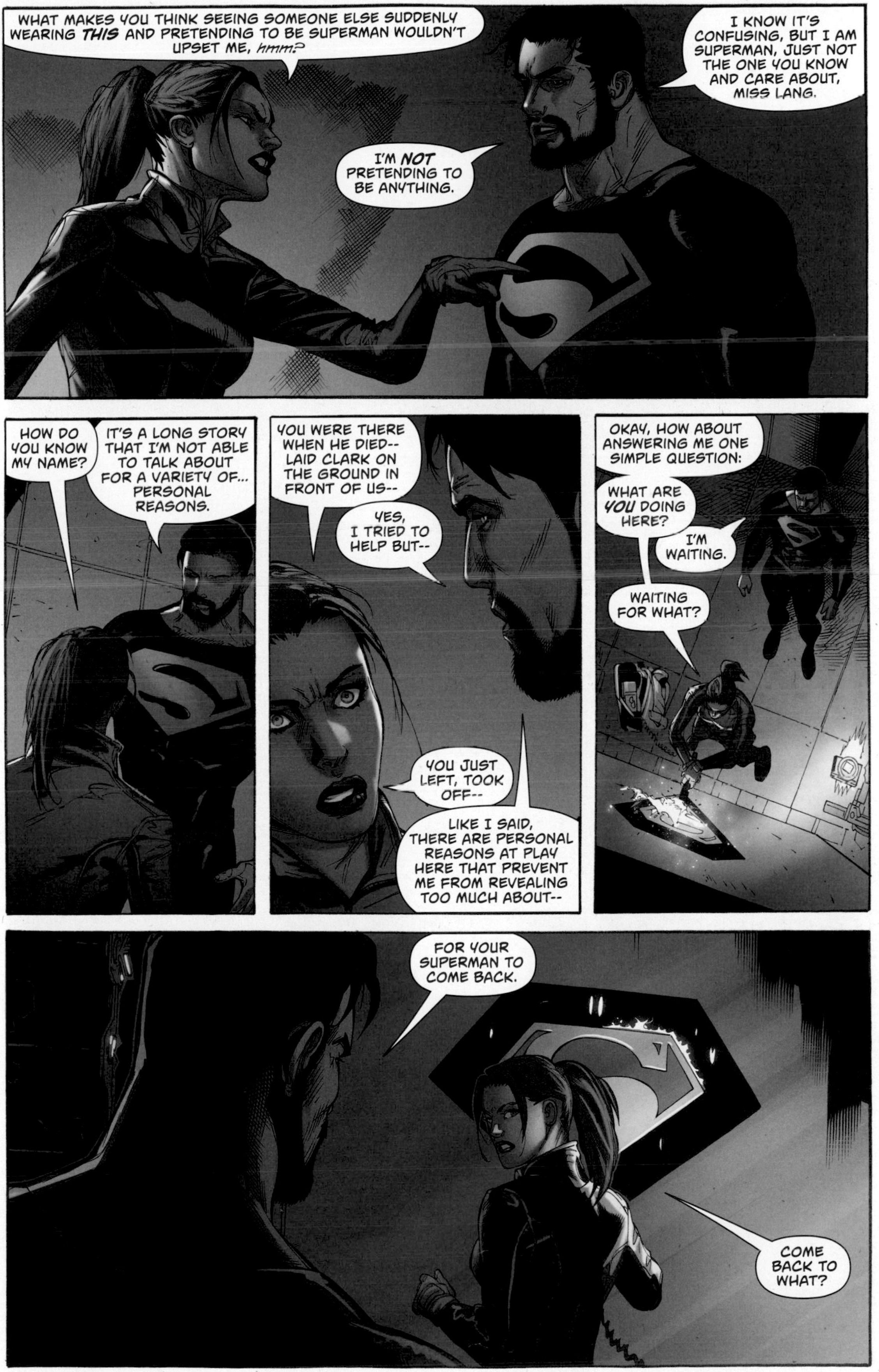
WHAT MAKES YOU THINK SEEING SOMEONE ELSE SUDDENLY WEARING THIS AND PRETENDING TO BE SUPERMAN WOULDN'T UPSET ME, hmm?
I'M NOT PRETENDING TO BE ANYTHING.
I KNOW IT'S CONFUSING, BUT I AM SUPERMAN, JUST NOT THE ONE YOU KNOW AND CARE ABOUT, MISS LANG.
HOW DO YOU KNOW MY NAME?
IT'S A LONG STORY THAT I'M NOT ABLE TO TALK ABOUT FOR A VARIETY OF... PERSONAL REASONS.
YOU WERE THERE WHEN HE DIED-- LAID CLARK ON THE GROUND IN FRONT OF US--
YES, I TRIED TO HELP BUT--
YOU JUST LEFT, TOOK OFF--
LIKE I SAID, THERE ARE PERSONAL REASONS AT PLAY HERE THAT PREVENT ME FROM REVEALING TOO MUCH ABOUT--
OKAY, HOW ABOUT ANSWERING ME ONE SIMPLE QUESTION:
WHAT ARE YOU DOING HERE?
I'M WAITING.
WAITING FOR WHAT?
FOR YOUR SUPERMAN TO COME BACK.
COME BACK TO WHAT?

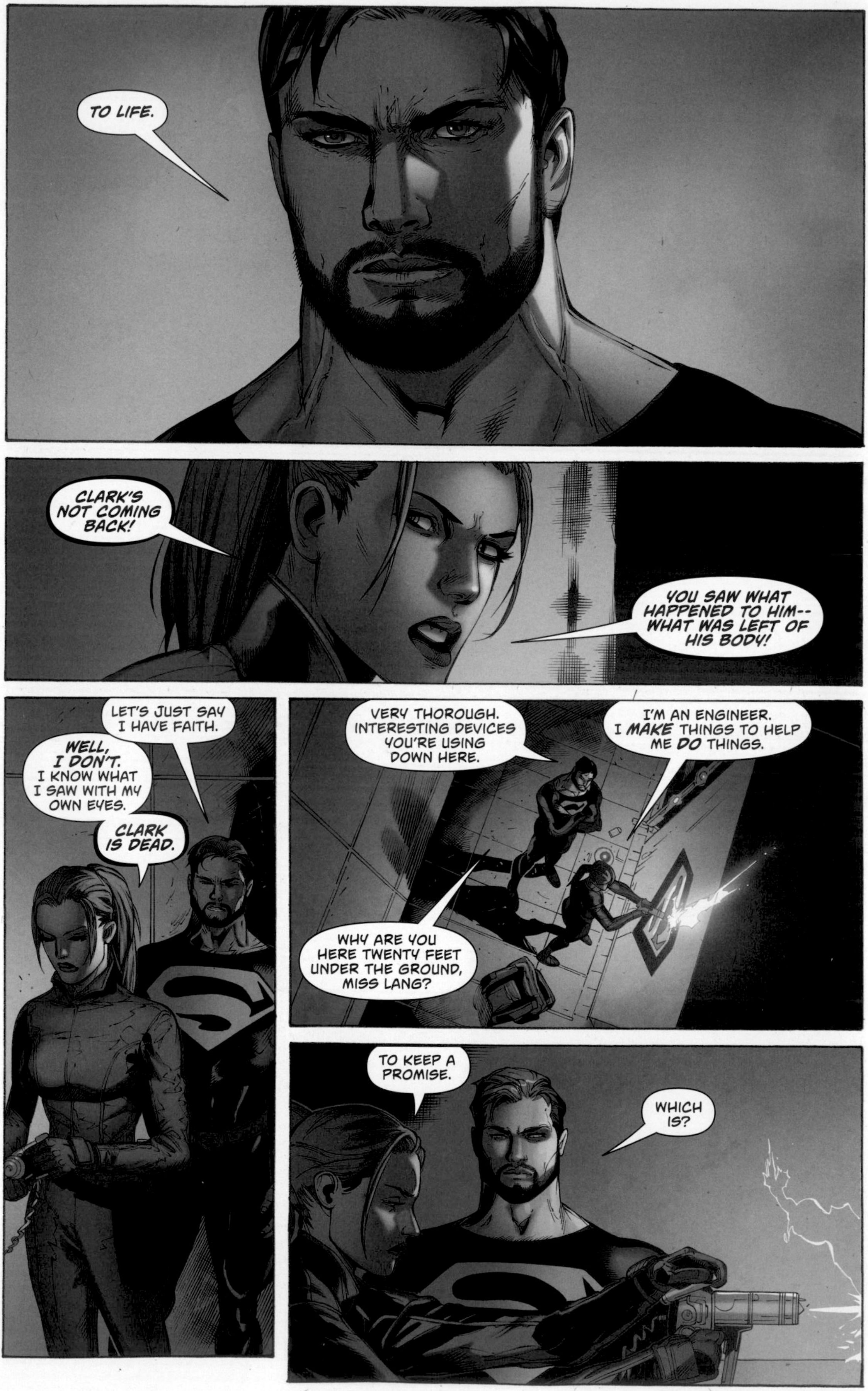
TO LIFE.
CLARK'S NOT COMING BACK!
YOU SAW WHAT HAPPENED TO HIM-- WHAT WAS LEFT OF HIS BODY!
LET'S JUST SAY I HAVE FAITH.
WELL, I DON'T. I KNOW WHAT I SAW WITH MY OWN EYES.
CLARK IS DEAD.
VERY THOROUGH. INTERESTING DEVICES YOU'RE USING DOWN HERE.
I'M AN ENGINEER. I MAKE THINGS TO HELP ME DO THINGS.
WHY ARE YOU HERE TWENTY FEET UNDER THE GROUND, MISS LANG?
TO KEEP A PROMISE.
WHICH IS?

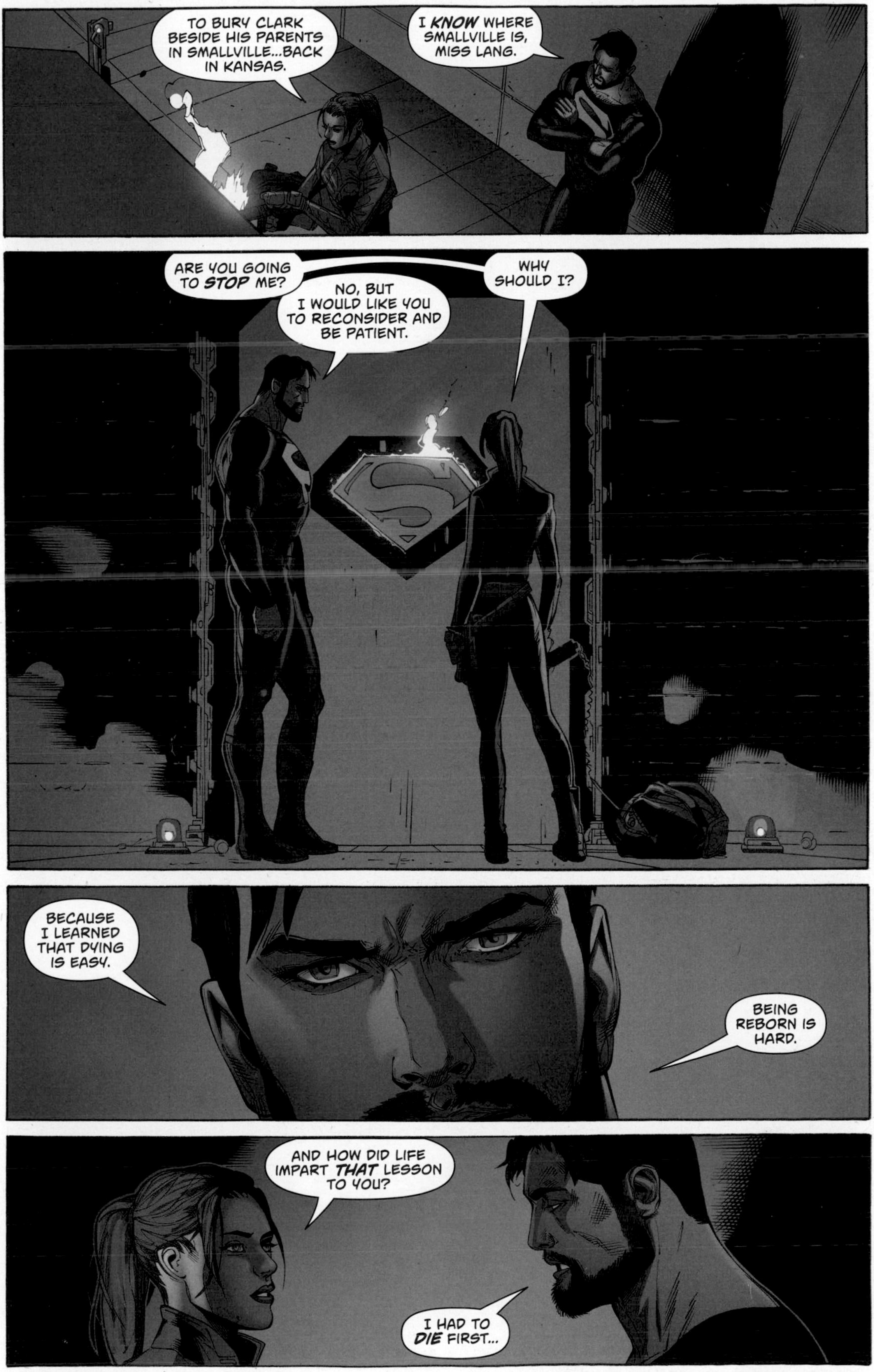
TO BURY CLARK BESIDE HIS PARENTS IN SMALLVILLE...BACK IN KANSAS.
I KNOW WHERE SMALLVILLE IS, MISS LANG.
ARE YOU GOING TO STOP ME?
NO, BUT I WOULD LIKE YOU TO RECONSIDER AND BE PATIENT.
WHY SHOULD I?
BECAUSE I LEARNED THAT DYING IS EASY.
BEING REBORN IS HARD.
AND HOW DID LIFE IMPART THAT LESSON TO YOU?
I HAD TO DIE FIRST...

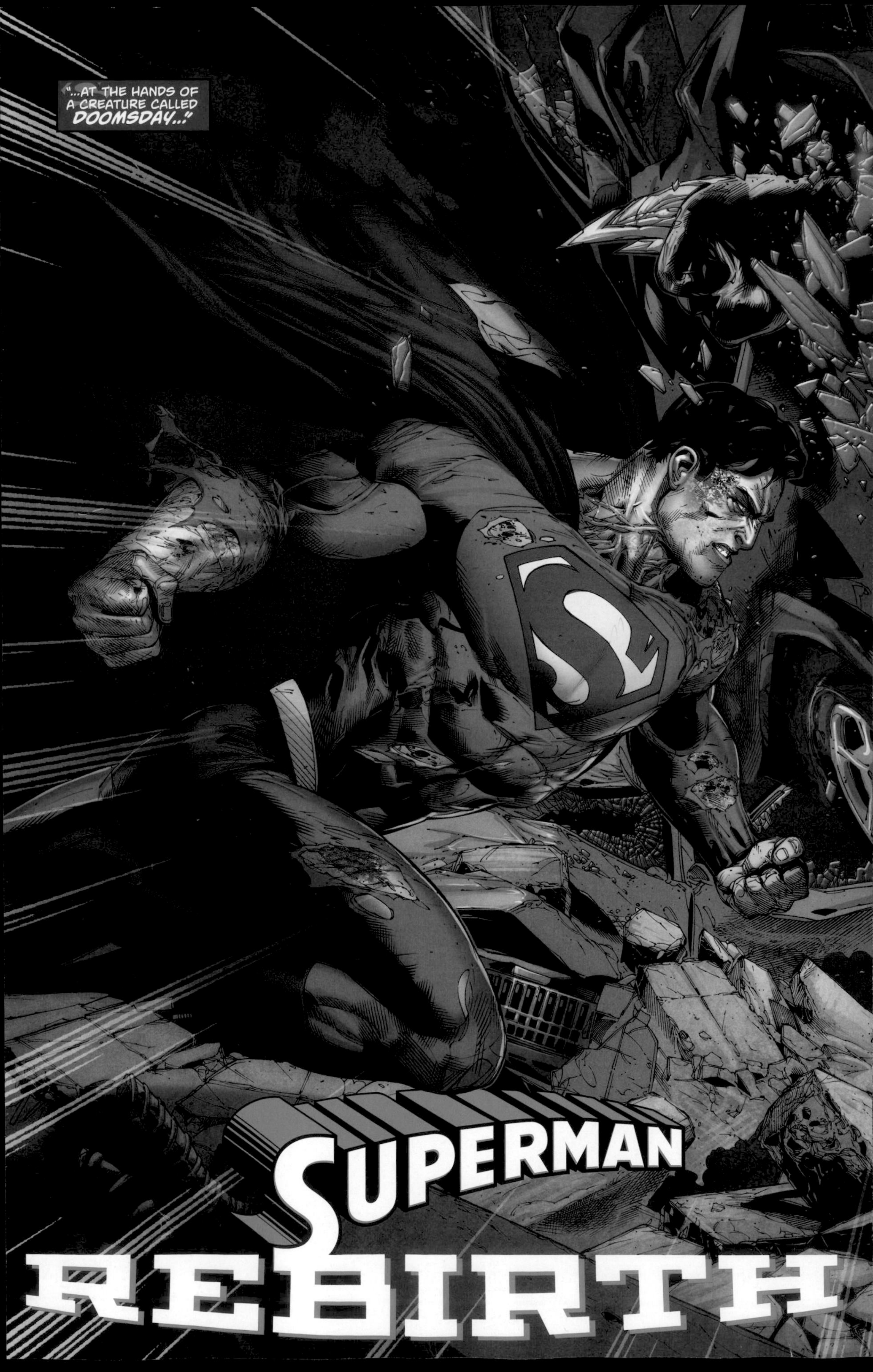
"...AT THE HANDS OF A CREATURE CALLED DOOMSDAY..."
SUPERMAN
REBIRTH

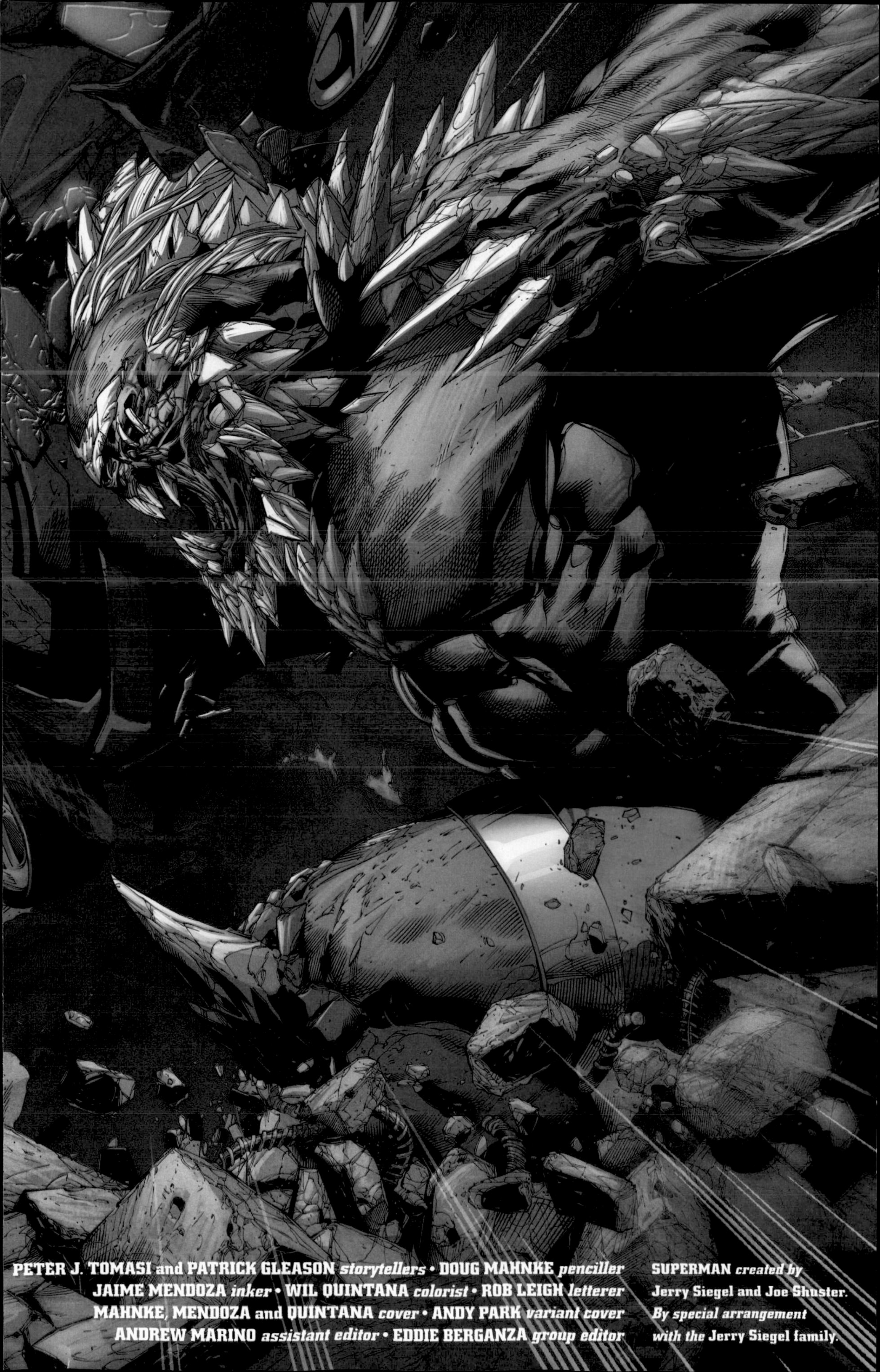

PETER J. TOMASI and **PATRICK GLEASON** *storytellers* • **DOUG MAHNKE** *penciller*
JAIME MENDOZA *inker* • **WIL QUINTANA** *colorist* • **ROB LEIGH** *letterer*
MAHNKE, MENDOZA and **QUINTANA** *cover* • **ANDY PARK** *variant cover*
ANDREW MARINO *assistant editor* • **EDDIE BERGANZA** *group editor*

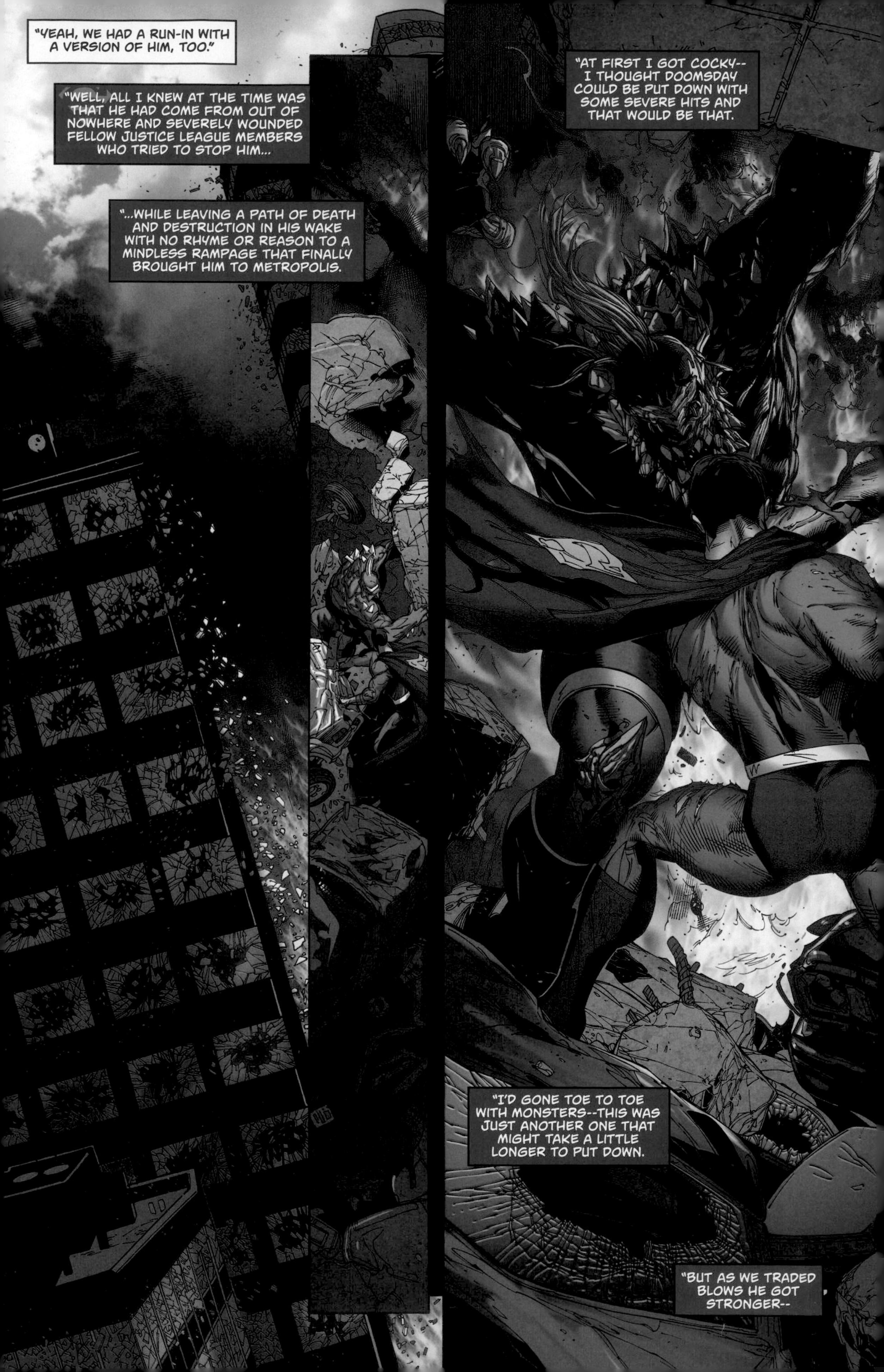
"YEAH, WE HAD A RUN-IN WITH A VERSION OF HIM, TOO."
"WELL, ALL I KNEW AT THE TIME WAS THAT HE HAD COME FROM OUT OF NOWHERE AND SEVERELY WOUNDED FELLOW JUSTICE LEAGUE MEMBERS WHO TRIED TO STOP HIM...
"...WHILE LEAVING A PATH OF DEATH AND DESTRUCTION IN HIS WAKE WITH NO RHYME OR REASON TO A MINDLESS RAMPAGE THAT FINALLY BROUGHT HIM TO METROPOLIS.
"AT FIRST I GOT COCKY-- I THOUGHT DOOMSDAY COULD BE PUT DOWN WITH SOME SEVERE HITS AND THAT WOULD BE THAT.
"I'D GONE TOE TO TOE WITH MONSTERS--THIS WAS JUST ANOTHER ONE THAT MIGHT TAKE A LITTLE LONGER TO PUT DOWN.
"BUT AS WE TRADED BLOWS HE GOT STRONGER--

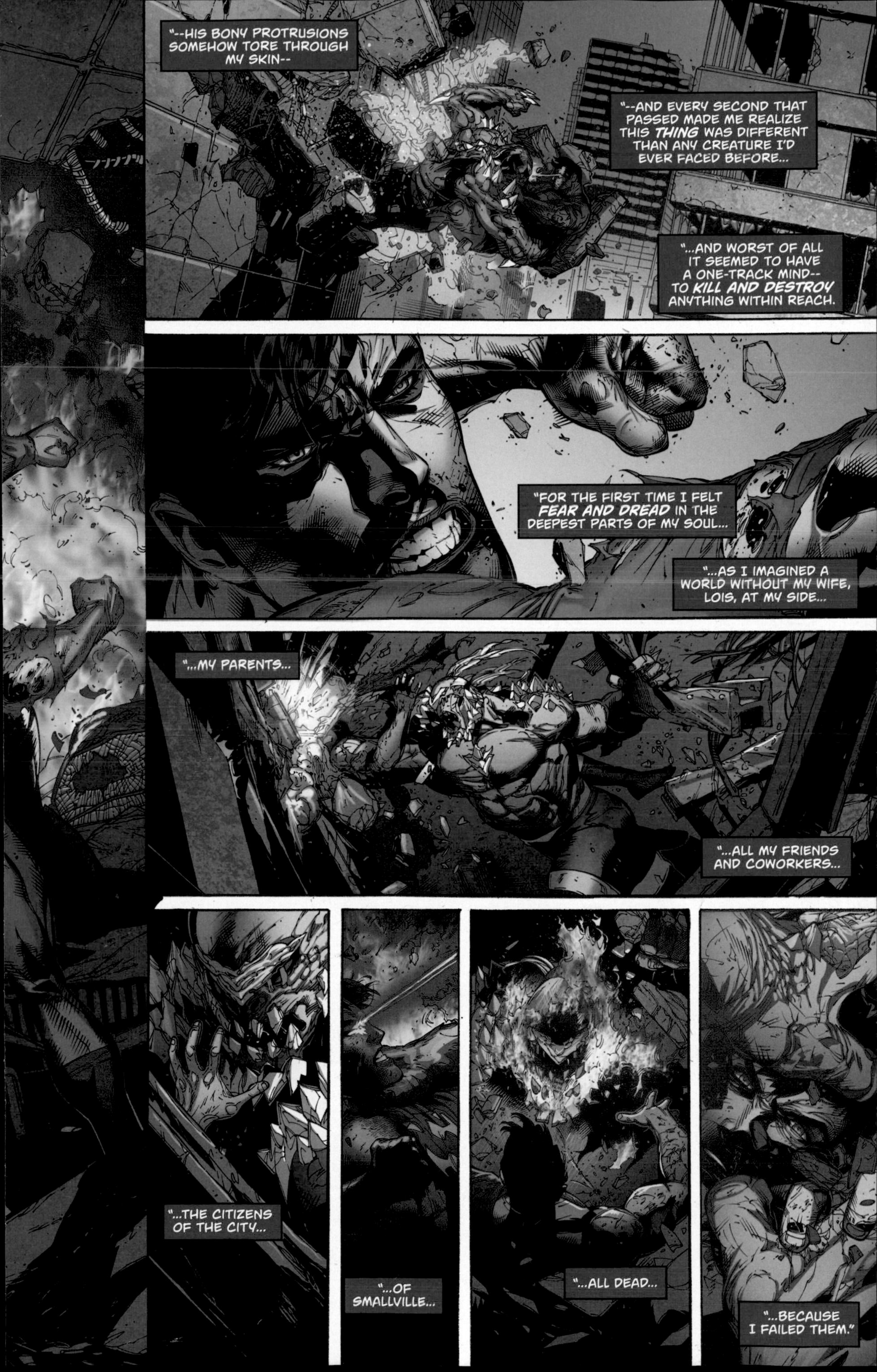
"--HIS BONY PROTRUSIONS SOMEHOW TORE THROUGH MY SKIN--
"--AND EVERY SECOND THAT PASSED MADE ME REALIZE THIS THING WAS DIFFERENT THAN ANY CREATURE I'D EVER FACED BEFORE...
"...AND WORST OF ALL IT SEEMED TO HAVE A ONE-TRACK MIND--TO KILL AND DESTROY ANYTHING WITHIN REACH.
"FOR THE FIRST TIME I FELT FEAR AND DREAD IN THE DEEPEST PARTS OF MY SOUL...
"...AS I IMAGINED A WORLD WITHOUT MY WIFE, LOIS, AT MY SIDE...
"...MY PARENTS...
"...ALL MY FRIENDS AND COWORKERS...
"...THE CITIZENS OF THE CITY...
"...OF SMALLVILLE...
"...ALL DEAD...
"...BECAUSE I FAILED THEM."

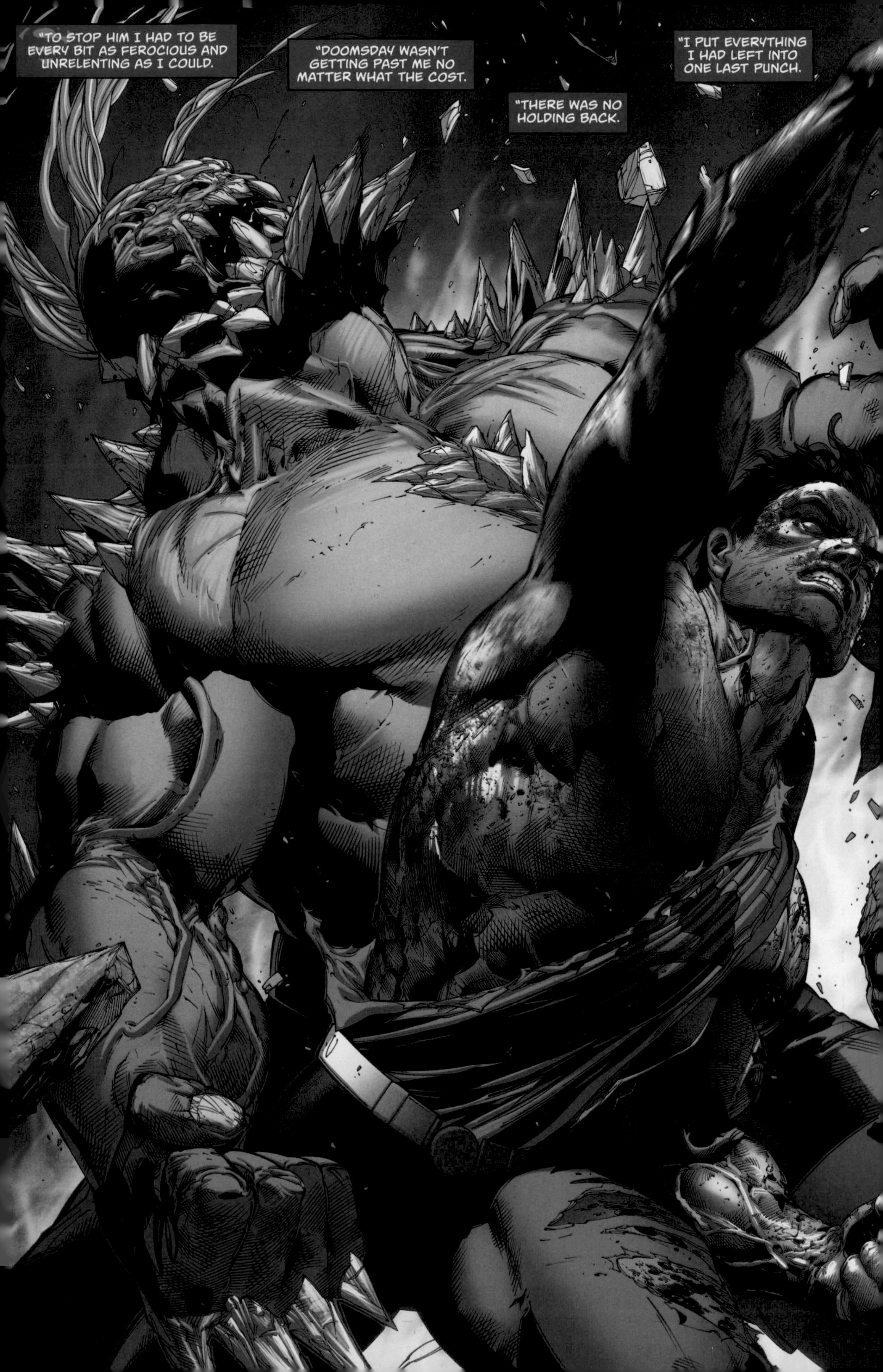
"TO STOP HIM I HAD TO BE EVERY BIT AS FEROCIOUS AND UNRELENTING AS I COULD.
"DOOMSDAY WASN'T GETTING PAST ME NO MATTER WHAT THE COST.
"THERE WAS NO HOLDING BACK.
"I PUT EVERYTHING I HAD LEFT INTO ONE LAST PUNCH.

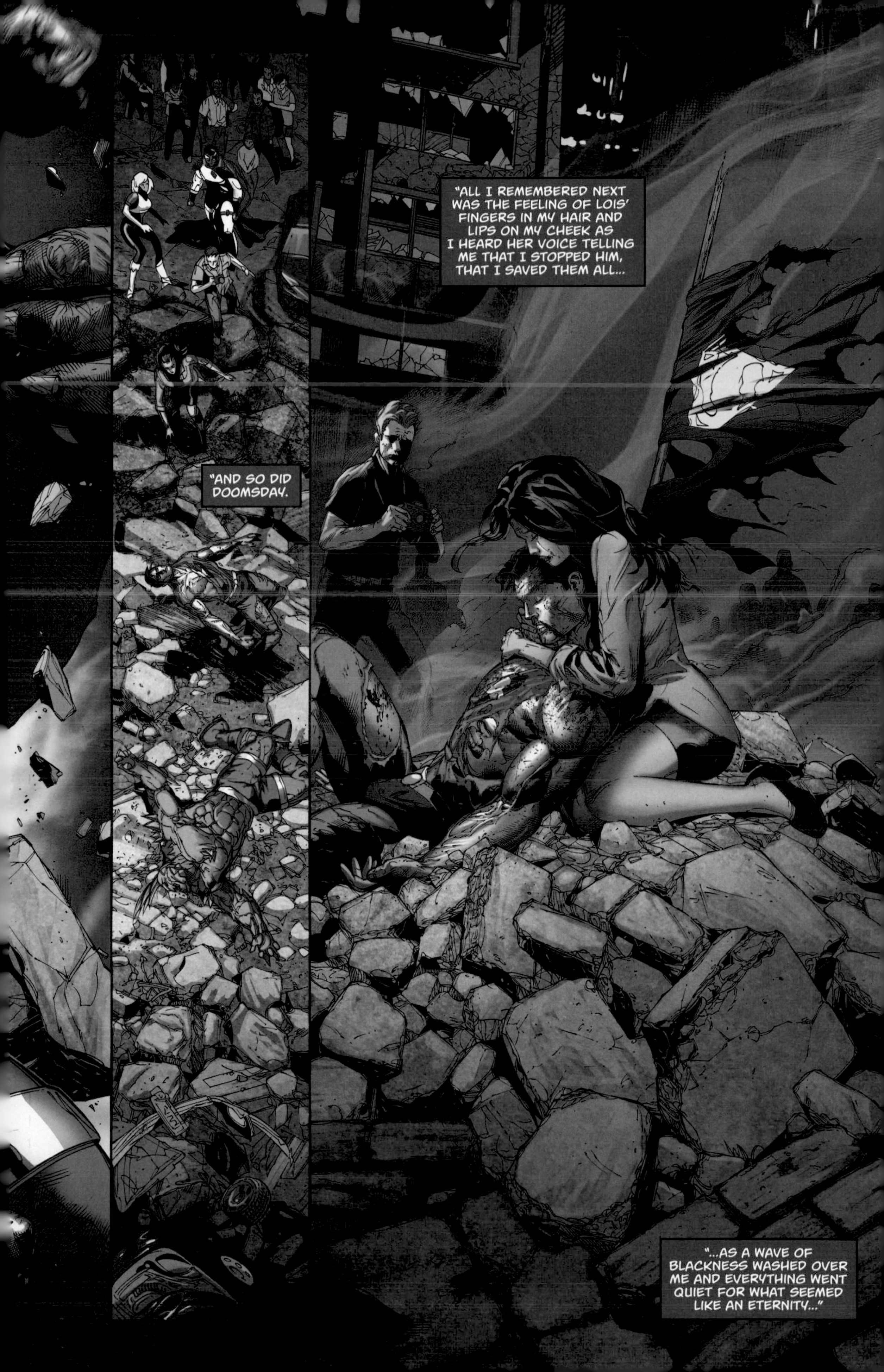
"AND SO DID DOOMSDAY.
"ALL I REMEMBERED NEXT WAS THE FEELING OF LOIS' FINGERS IN MY HAIR AND LIPS ON MY CHEEK AS I HEARD HER VOICE TELLING ME THAT I STOPPED HIM, THAT I SAVED THEM ALL...
"...AS A WAVE OF BLACKNESS WASHED OVER ME AND EVERYTHING WENT QUIET FOR WHAT SEEMED LIKE AN ETERNITY..."

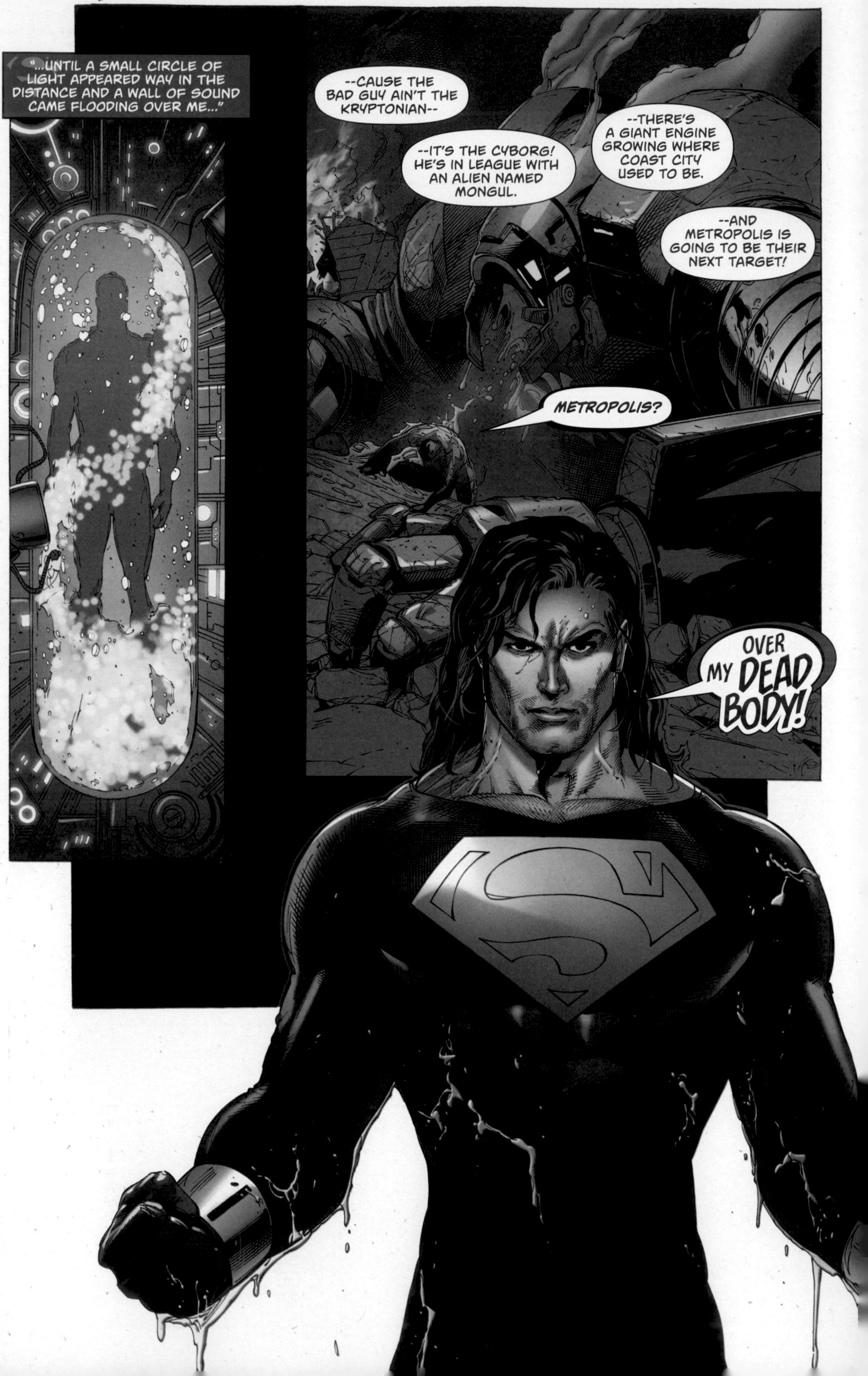
"...UNTIL A SMALL CIRCLE OF LIGHT APPEARED WAY IN THE DISTANCE AND A WALL OF SOUND CAME FLOODING OVER ME..."
--CAUSE THE BAD GUY AIN'T THE KRYPTONIAN--
--IT'S THE CYBORG! HE'S IN LEAGUE WITH AN ALIEN NAMED MONGUL.
--THERE'S A GIANT ENGINE GROWING WHERE COAST CITY USED TO BE.
--AND METROPOLIS IS GOING TO BE THEIR NEXT TARGET!
METROPOLIS?
OVER MY DEAD BODY!

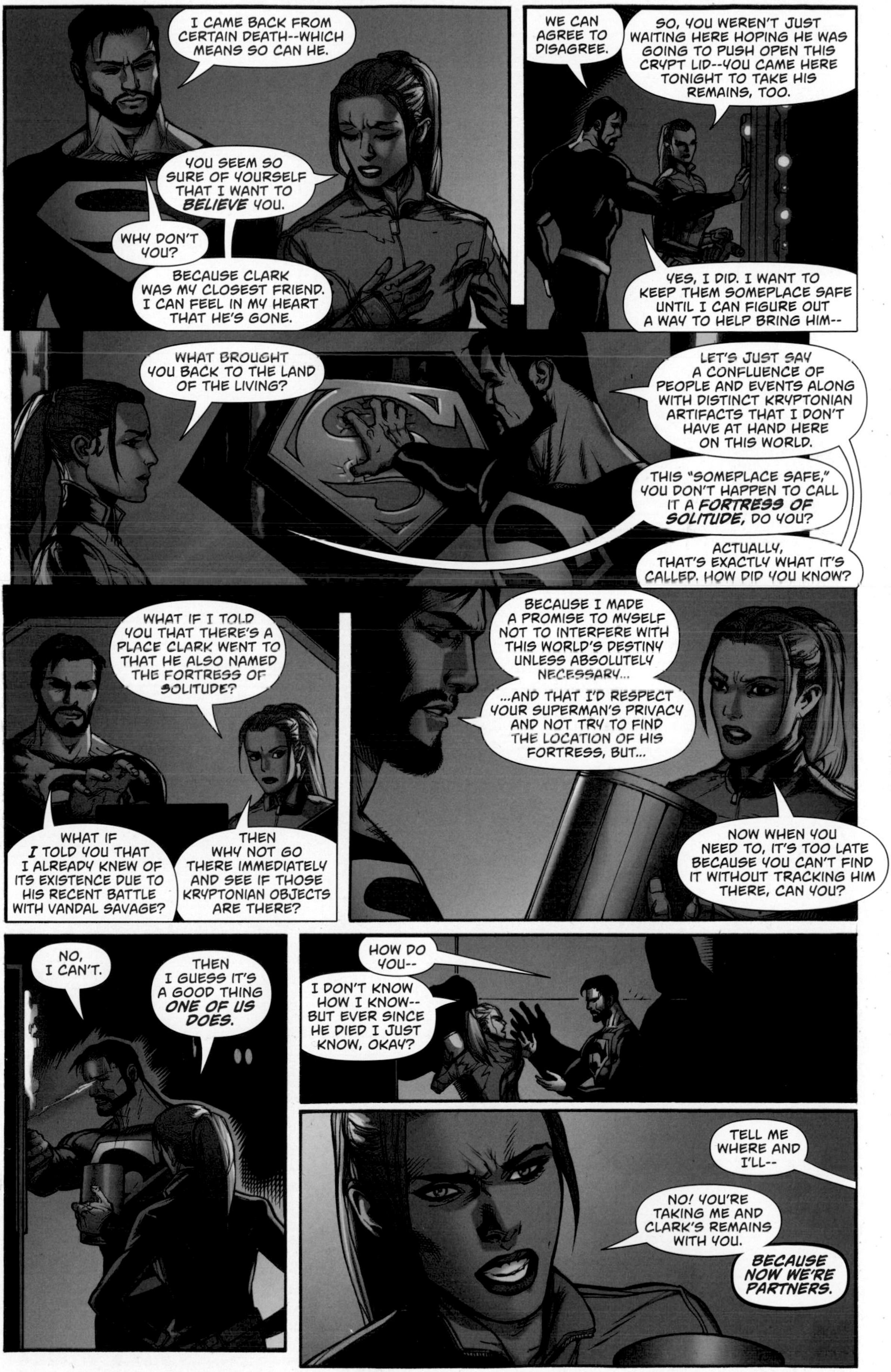
I CAME BACK FROM CERTAIN DEATH--WHICH MEANS SO CAN HE.
YOU SEEM SO SURE OF YOURSELF THAT I WANT TO BELIEVE YOU.
WHY DON'T YOU?
BECAUSE CLARK WAS MY CLOSEST FRIEND. I CAN FEEL IN MY HEART THAT HE'S GONE.
WE CAN AGREE TO DISAGREE.
SO, YOU WEREN'T JUST WAITING HERE HOPING HE WAS GOING TO PUSH OPEN THIS CRYPT LID--YOU CAME HERE TONIGHT TO TAKE HIS REMAINS, TOO.
YES, I DID. I WANT TO KEEP THEM SOMEPLACE SAFE UNTIL I CAN FIGURE OUT A WAY TO HELP BRING HIM--
WHAT BROUGHT YOU BACK TO THE LAND OF THE LIVING?
LET'S JUST SAY A CONFLUENCE OF PEOPLE AND EVENTS ALONG WITH DISTINCT KRYPTONIAN ARTIFACTS THAT I DON'T HAVE AT HAND HERE ON THIS WORLD.
THIS "SOMEPLACE SAFE," YOU DON'T HAPPEN TO CALL IT A FORTRESS OF SOLITUDE, DO YOU?
ACTUALLY, THAT'S EXACTLY WHAT IT'S CALLED. HOW DID YOU KNOW?
WHAT IF I TOLD YOU THAT THERE'S A PLACE CLARK WENT TO THAT HE ALSO NAMED THE FORTRESS OF SOLITUDE?
WHAT IF I TOLD YOU THAT I ALREADY KNEW OF ITS EXISTENCE DUE TO HIS RECENT BATTLE WITH VANDAL SAVAGE?
THEN WHY NOT GO THERE IMMEDIATELY AND SEE IF THOSE KRYPTONIAN OBJECTS ARE THERE?
BECAUSE I MADE A PROMISE TO MYSELF NOT TO INTERFERE WITH THIS WORLD'S DESTINY UNLESS ABSOLUTELY NECESSARY...
...AND THAT I'D RESPECT YOUR SUPERMAN'S PRIVACY AND NOT TRY TO FIND THE LOCATION OF HIS FORTRESS, BUT...
NOW WHEN YOU NEED TO, IT'S TOO LATE BECAUSE YOU CAN'T FIND IT WITHOUT TRACKING HIM THERE, CAN YOU?
NO, I CAN'T.
THEN I GUESS IT'S A GOOD THING ONE OF US DOES.
HOW DO YOU--
I DON'T KNOW HOW I KNOW--BUT EVER SINCE HE DIED I JUST KNOW, OKAY?
TELL ME WHERE AND I'LL--
NO! YOU'RE TAKING ME AND CLARK'S REMAINS WITH YOU.
BECAUSE NOW WE'RE PARTNERS.

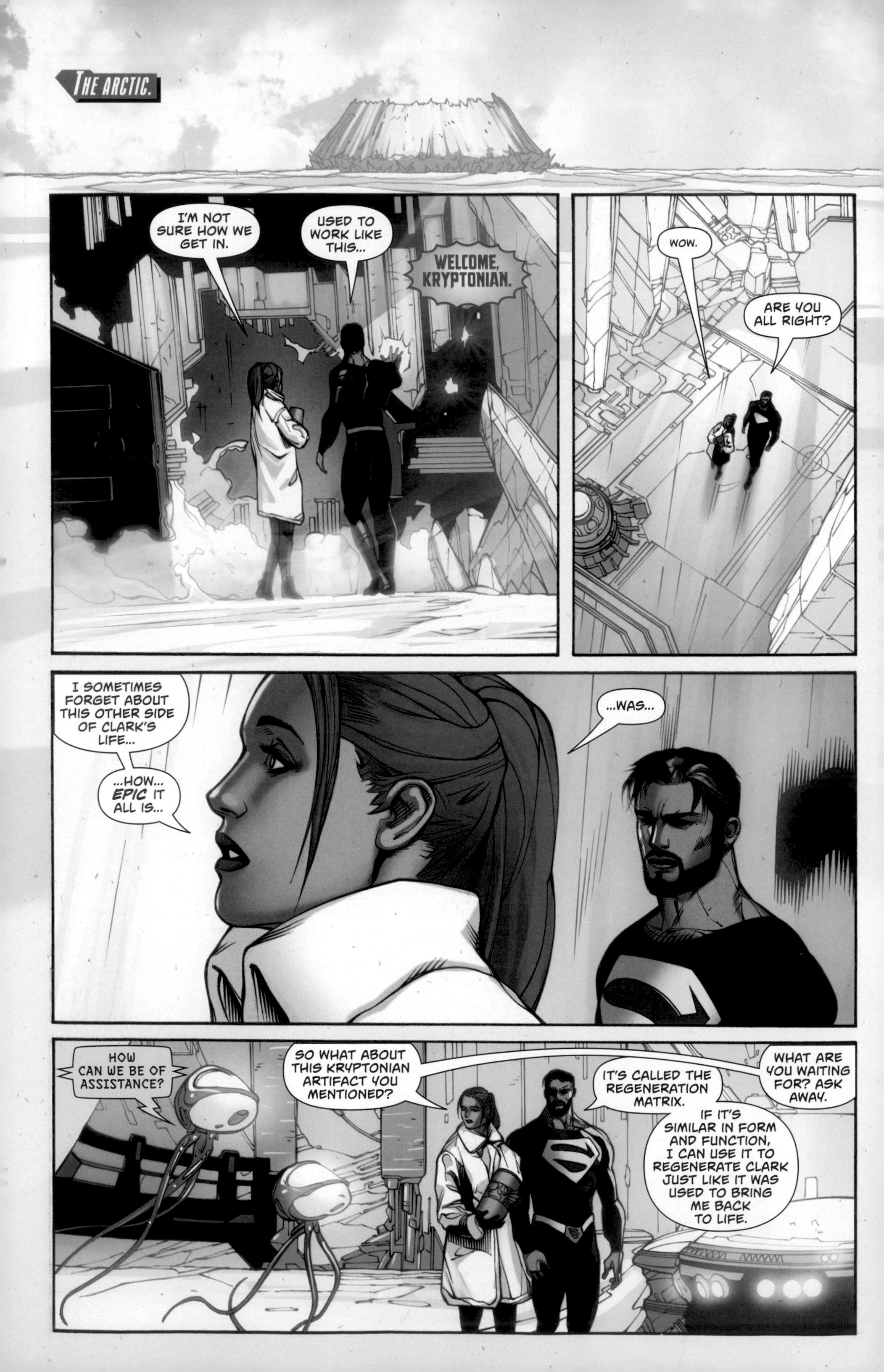
THE ARCTIC.
I'M NOT SURE HOW WE GET IN.
USED TO WORK LIKE THIS...
WELCOME, KRYPTONIAN.
WOW.
ARE YOU ALL RIGHT?
I SOMETIMES FORGET ABOUT THIS OTHER SIDE OF CLARK'S LIFE...
...HOW... EPIC IT ALL IS...
...WAS...
HOW CAN WE BE OF ASSISTANCE?
SO WHAT ABOUT THIS KRYPTONIAN ARTIFACT YOU MENTIONED?
WHAT ARE YOU WAITING FOR? ASK AWAY.
IT'S CALLED THE REGENERATION MATRIX.
IF IT'S SIMILAR IN FORM AND FUNCTION, I CAN USE IT TO REGENERATE CLARK JUST LIKE IT WAS USED TO BRING ME BACK TO LIFE.

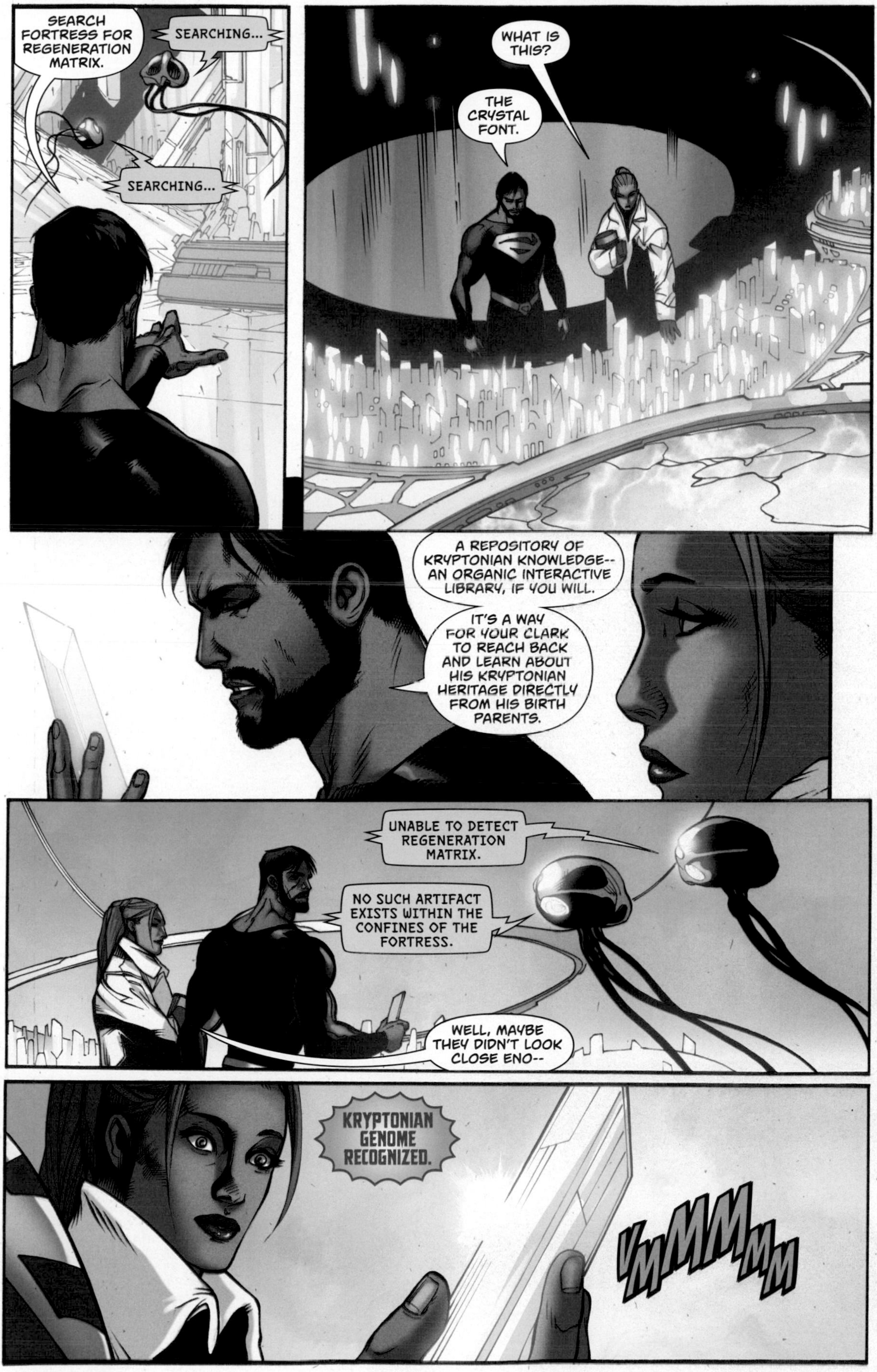
SEARCH FORTRESS FOR REGENERATION MATRIX.
SEARCHING...
SEARCHING...
WHAT IS THIS?
THE CRYSTAL FONT.
A REPOSITORY OF KRYPTONIAN KNOWLEDGE--AN ORGANIC INTERACTIVE LIBRARY, IF YOU WILL.
IT'S A WAY FOR YOUR CLARK TO REACH BACK AND LEARN ABOUT HIS KRYPTONIAN HERITAGE DIRECTLY FROM HIS BIRTH PARENTS.
UNABLE TO DETECT REGENERATION MATRIX.
NO SUCH ARTIFACT EXISTS WITHIN THE CONFINES OF THE FORTRESS.
WELL, MAYBE THEY DIDN'T LOOK CLOSE ENO--
KRYPTONIAN GENOME RECOGNIZED.
VMMMMMM

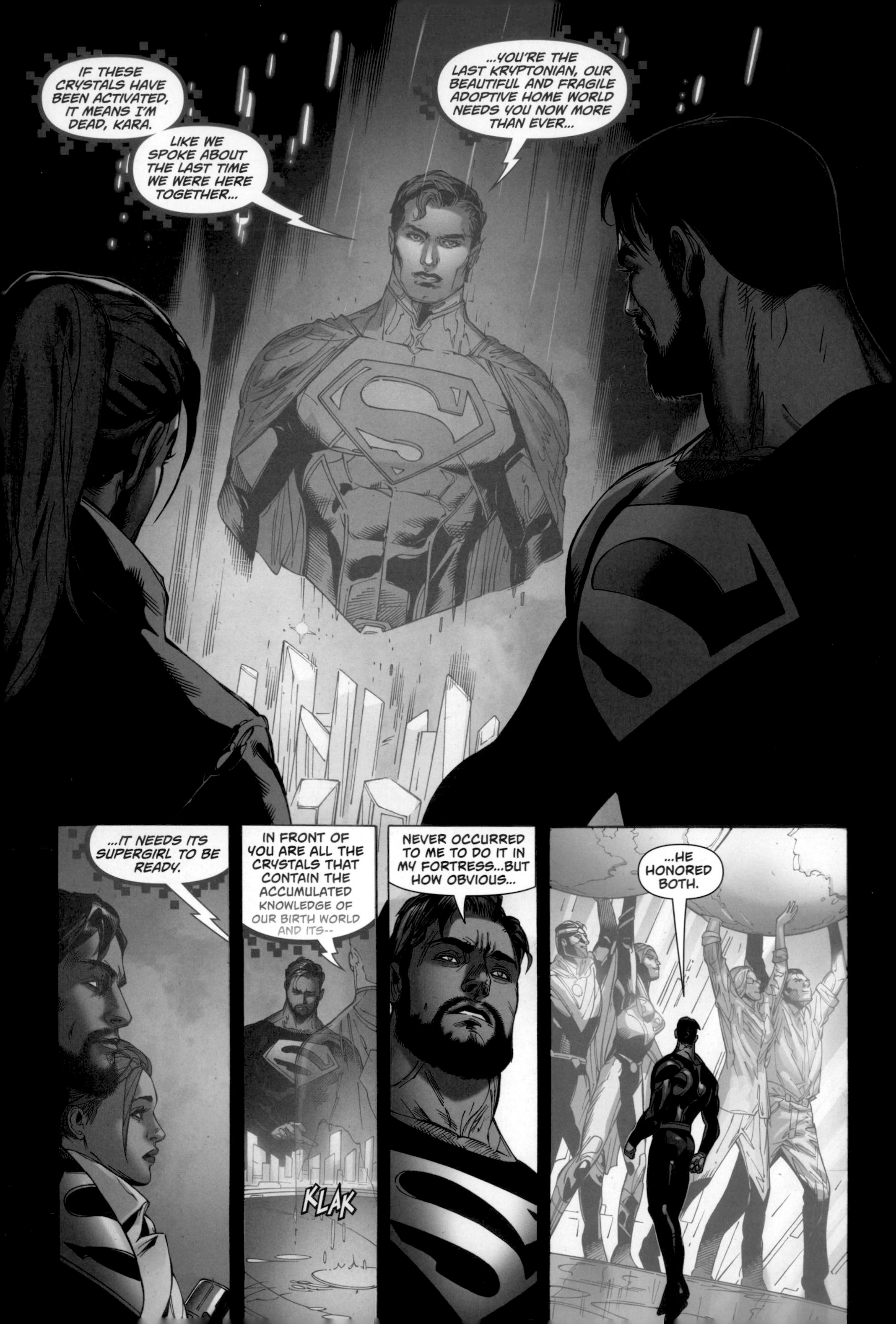
IF THESE CRYSTALS HAVE BEEN ACTIVATED, IT MEANS I'M DEAD, KARA.
LIKE WE SPOKE ABOUT THE LAST TIME WE WERE HERE TOGETHER...
...YOU'RE THE LAST KRYPTONIAN, OUR BEAUTIFUL AND FRAGILE ADOPTIVE HOME WORLD NEEDS YOU NOW MORE THAN EVER...
...IT NEEDS ITS SUPERGIRL TO BE READY.
IN FRONT OF YOU ARE ALL THE CRYSTALS THAT CONTAIN THE ACCUMULATED KNOWLEDGE OF OUR BIRTH WORLD AND ITS--
KLAK
NEVER OCCURRED TO ME TO DO IT IN MY FORTRESS...BUT HOW OBVIOUS...
...HE HONORED BOTH.

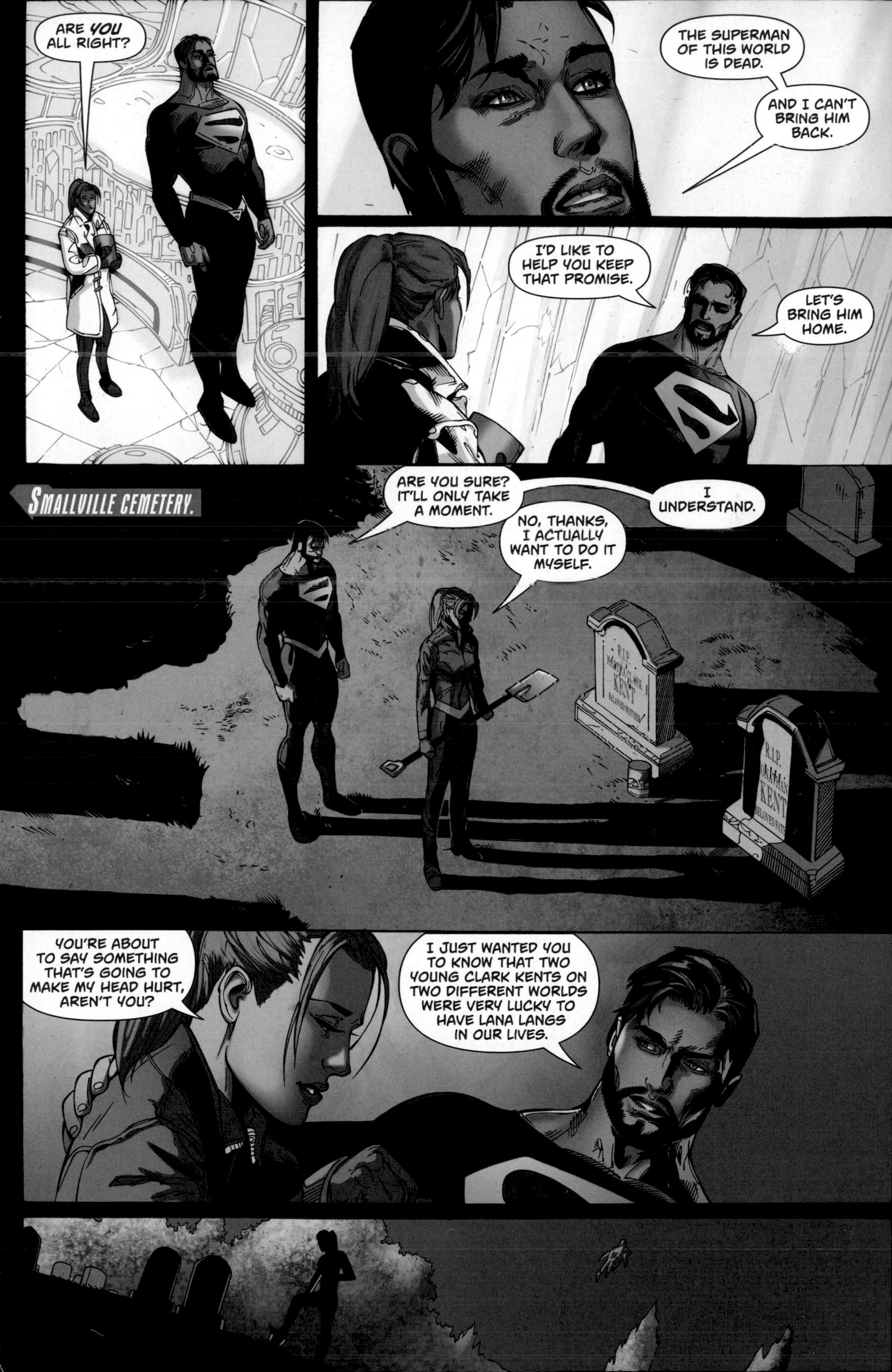
ARE YOU ALL RIGHT?
THE SUPERMAN OF THIS WORLD IS DEAD.
AND I CAN'T BRING HIM BACK.
I'D LIKE TO HELP YOU KEEP THAT PROMISE.
LET'S BRING HIM HOME.
SMALLVILLE CEMETERY.
ARE YOU SURE? IT'LL ONLY TAKE A MOMENT.
NO, THANKS, I ACTUALLY WANT TO DO IT MYSELF.
I UNDERSTAND.
R.I.P. MARTHA CLARK KENT BELOVED MOTHER
R.I.P. JONATHAN KENT BELOVED FATHER
YOU'RE ABOUT TO SAY SOMETHING THAT'S GOING TO MAKE MY HEAD HURT, AREN'T YOU?
I JUST WANTED YOU TO KNOW THAT TWO YOUNG CLARK KENTS ON TWO DIFFERENT WORLDS WERE VERY LUCKY TO HAVE LANA LANGS IN OUR LIVES.

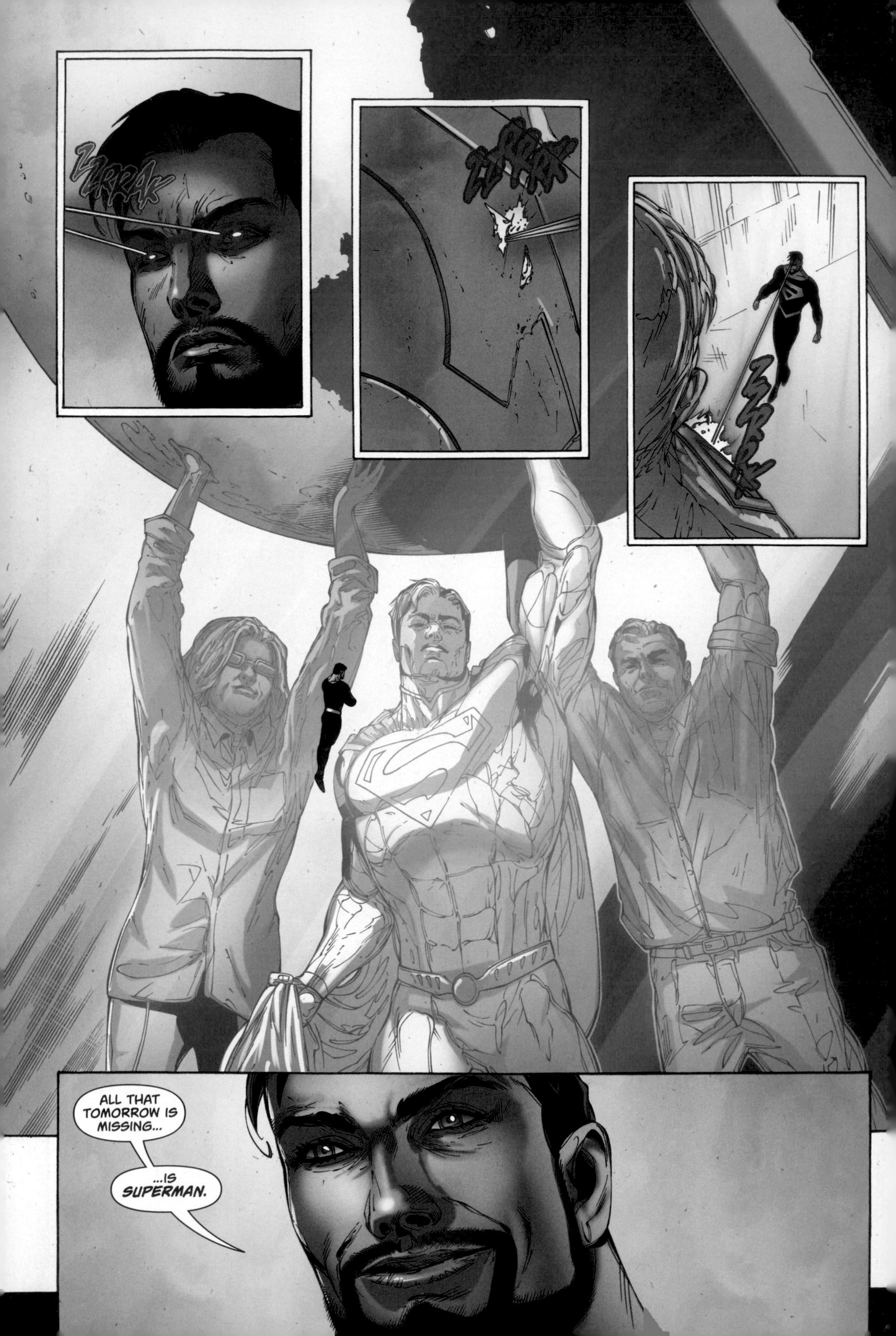

ALL THAT TOMORROW IS MISSING...
...IS SUPERMAN.

"ACTION COMICS has successfully carved its own territory and continued exploring Morrison's familiar themes about heroism and ideas."—IGN

"Casts the character in a new light, opens up fresh storytelling possibilities, and pushes it all forward with dynamic Rags Morales art. I loved it."—THE ONION/AV CLUB

START AT THE BEGINNING!

SUPERMAN: ACTION COMICS VOLUME 1:
SUPERMAN AND THE MEN OF STEEL

SUPERMAN: ACTION COMICS VOL. 2: BULLETPROOF

with GRANT MORRISON and RAGS MORALES

SUPERMAN: ACTION COMICS VOL. 3: AT THE END OF DAYS

with GRANT MORRISON and RAGS MORALES

SUPERBOY VOL. 1: INCUBATION

THE NEW 52!

DC COMICS™

SUPERMAN
ACTION
COMICS

VOLUME 1
SUPERMAN AND
THE MEN OF
STEEL

"BELIEVE THE HYPE: GRANT MORRISON WENT AND WROTE THE SINGLE BEST ISSUE OF SUPERMAN THESE EYES HAVE EVER READ."
— USA TODAY

GRANT **MORRISON** RAGS **MORALES** ANDY **KUBERT**

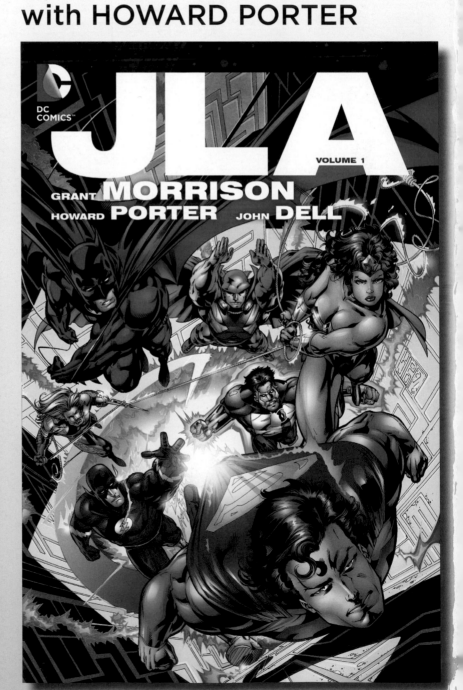

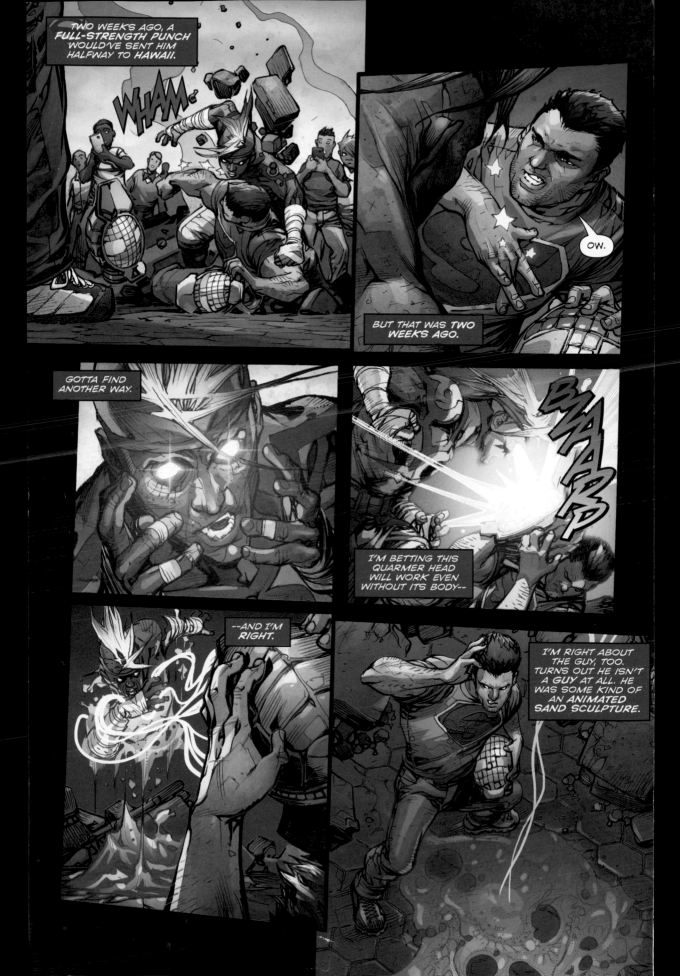

OH, GIVE IT A REST, HAEMOSU!

YEEEAH!!

'ZZRAKKT

BRAWL! BRAWL!! BRAWL!!

SO MYTHBRAWL IS SOME KIND OF SUPERPOWERED FIGHT CLUB, WHERE METAHUMANS USE THEIR GIFTS FOR SPECTACLE.

TO BEAT ON EACH OTHER FOR MONEY.

POP WOULDN'T APPROVE.

I NEED TO GET MY ANSWERS AND GET OUT OF HERE.

YOU DON'T TALK TO THE QUEEN UNLESS THE QUEEN TALKS TO YOU.

GET RID OF HIM, CROW.

EXCUSE ME. SHAHRAZAD, RIGHT?

GLADLY.

KAW!

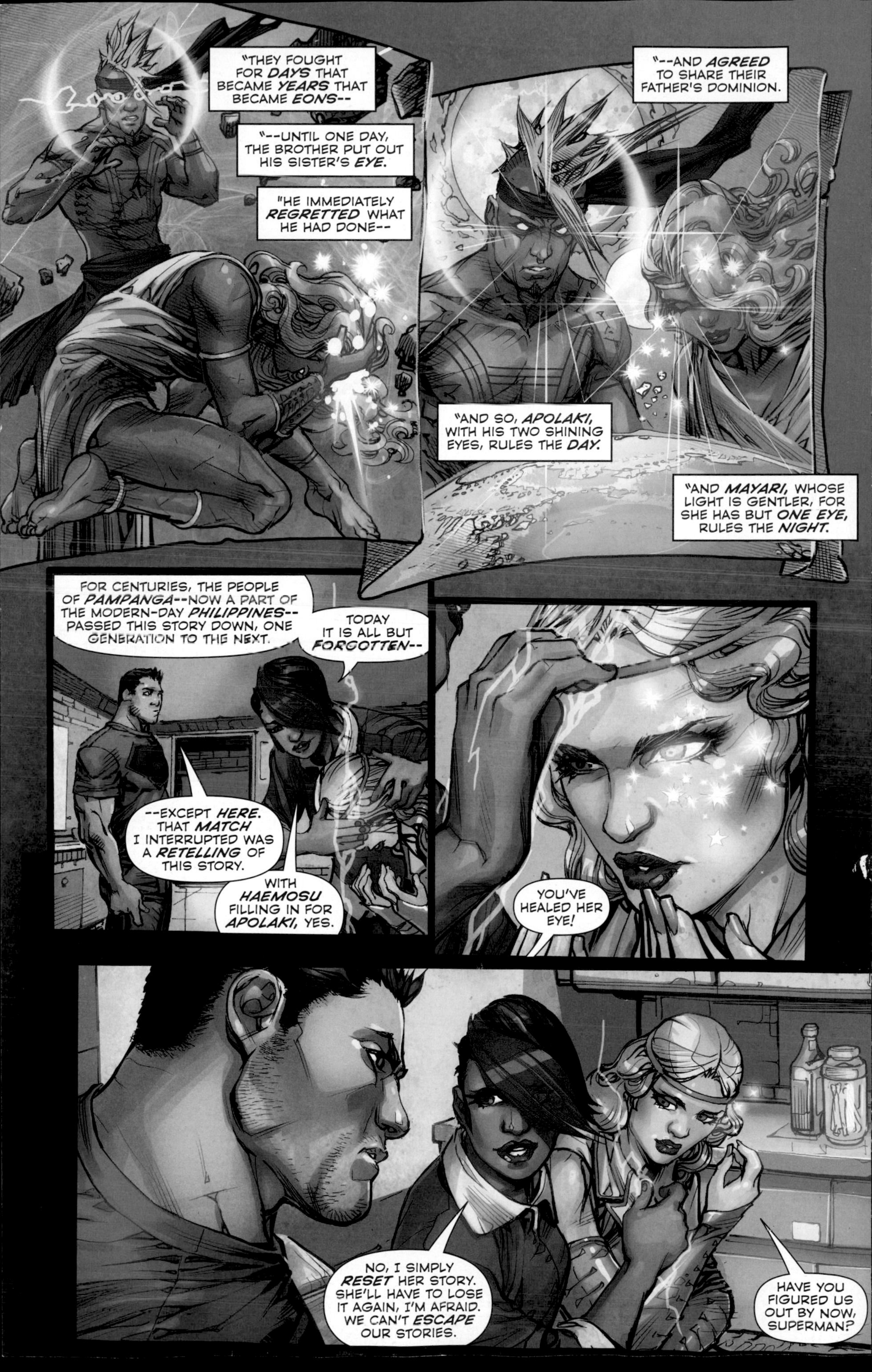
"THEY FOUGHT FOR DAYS THAT BECAME YEARS THAT BECAME EONS--
"--UNTIL ONE DAY, THE BROTHER PUT OUT HIS SISTER'S EYE.
"HE IMMEDIATELY REGRETTED WHAT HE HAD DONE--
"--AND AGREED TO SHARE THEIR FATHER'S DOMINION.
"AND SO, APOLAKI, WITH HIS TWO SHINING EYES, RULES THE DAY.
"AND MAYARI, WHOSE LIGHT IS GENTLER, FOR SHE HAS BUT ONE EYE, RULES THE NIGHT.
FOR CENTURIES, THE PEOPLE OF PAMPANGA--NOW A PART OF THE MODERN-DAY PHILIPPINES--PASSED THIS STORY DOWN, ONE GENERATION TO THE NEXT.
TODAY IT IS ALL BUT FORGOTTEN--
--EXCEPT HERE. THAT MATCH I INTERRUPTED WAS A RETELLING OF THIS STORY.
WITH HAEMOSU FILLING IN FOR APOLAKI, YES.
YOU'VE HEALED HER EYE!
NO, I SIMPLY RESET HER STORY. SHE'LL HAVE TO LOSE IT AGAIN, I'M AFRAID. WE CAN'T ESCAPE OUR STORIES.
HAVE YOU FIGURED US OUT BY NOW, SUPERMAN?

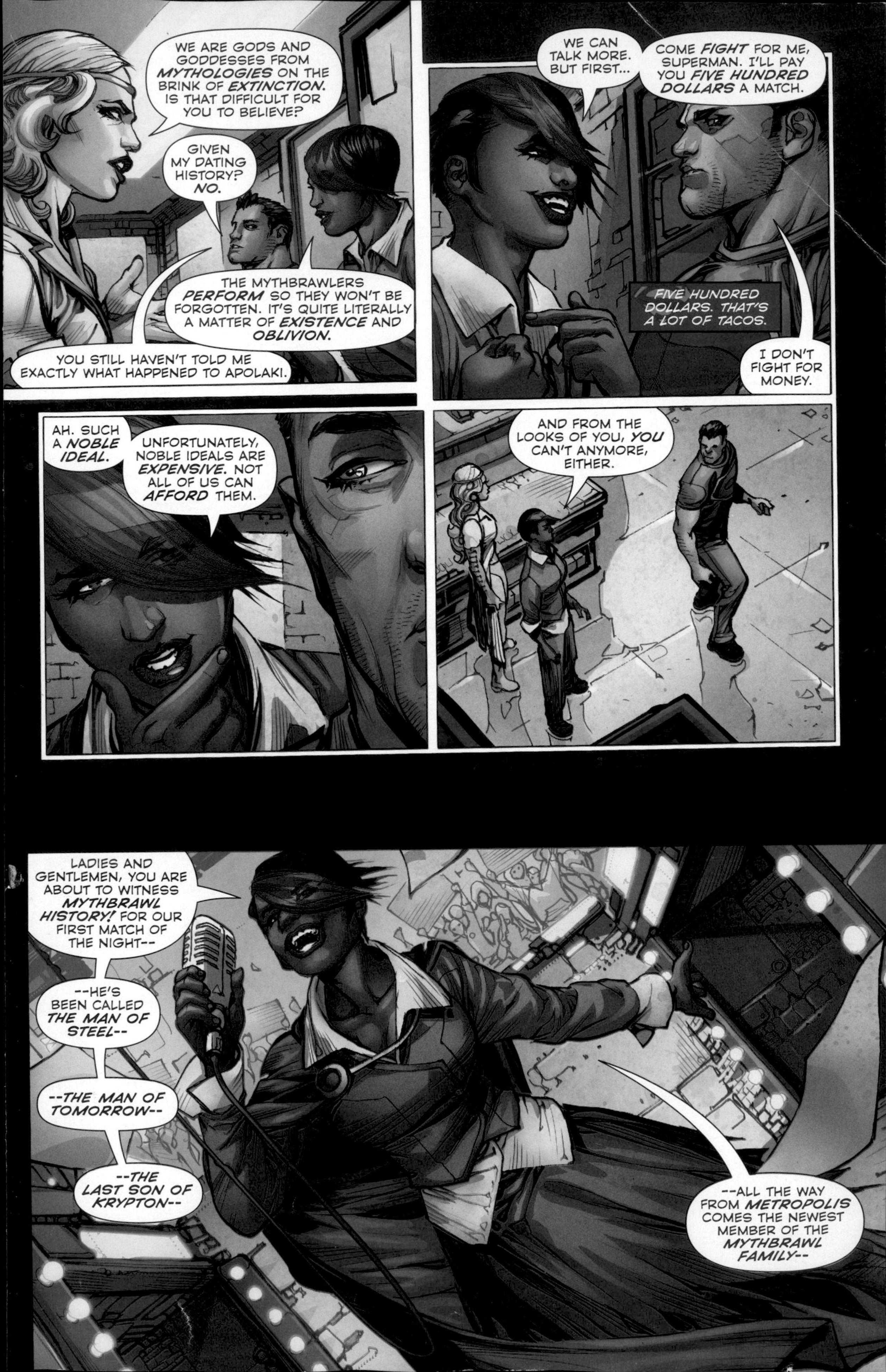
WE ARE GODS AND GODDESSES FROM MYTHOLOGIES ON THE BRINK OF EXTINCTION. IS THAT DIFFICULT FOR YOU TO BELIEVE?
GIVEN MY DATING HISTORY? NO.
THE MYTHBRAWLERS PERFORM SO THEY WON'T BE FORGOTTEN. IT'S QUITE LITERALLY A MATTER OF EXISTENCE AND OBLIVION.
YOU STILL HAVEN'T TOLD ME EXACTLY WHAT HAPPENED TO APOLAKI.
WE CAN TALK MORE. BUT FIRST...
COME FIGHT FOR ME, SUPERMAN. I'LL PAY YOU FIVE HUNDRED DOLLARS A MATCH.
FIVE HUNDRED DOLLARS. THAT'S A LOT OF TACOS.
I DON'T FIGHT FOR MONEY.
AH. SUCH A NOBLE IDEAL.
UNFORTUNATELY, NOBLE IDEALS ARE EXPENSIVE. NOT ALL OF US CAN AFFORD THEM.
AND FROM THE LOOKS OF YOU, YOU CAN'T ANYMORE, EITHER.
LADIES AND GENTLEMEN, YOU ARE ABOUT TO WITNESS MYTHBRAWL HISTORY! FOR OUR FIRST MATCH OF THE NIGHT--
--HE'S BEEN CALLED THE MAN OF STEEL--
--THE MAN OF TOMORROW--
--THE LAST SON OF KRYPTON--
--ALL THE WAY FROM METROPOLIS COMES THE NEWEST MEMBER OF THE MYTHBRAWL FAMILY--

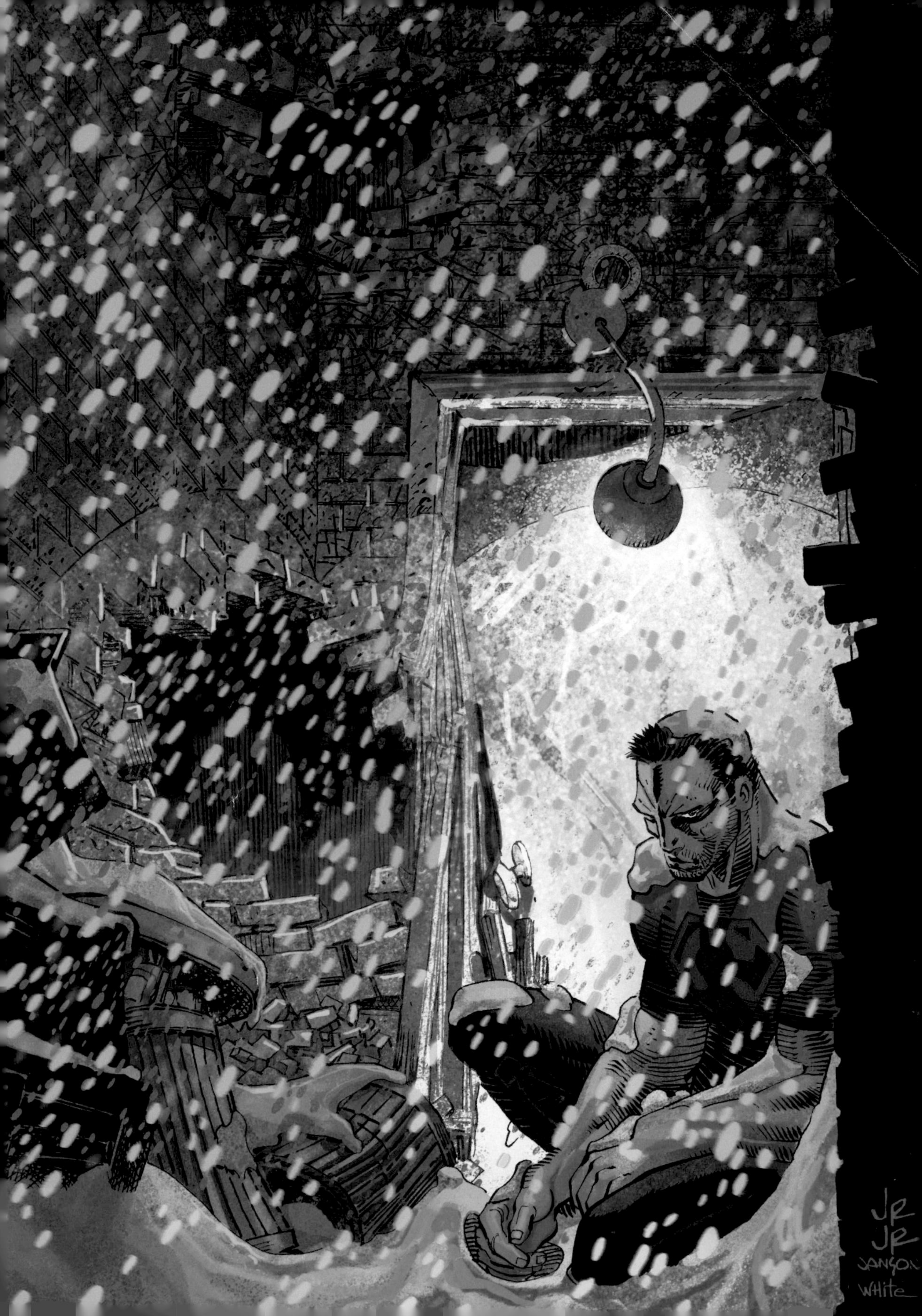
JR
JR
JANSON
WHITE

KNOCKED OUT!

GENE LUEN YANG writer   HOWARD PORTER artist   HI-FI colorist   ROB LEIGH letterer   JOHN ROMITA JR., KLAUS JANSON, DEAN WHITE cover

ANY LUCK, RED?

NOPE.

THE LADY AT THE COUNTER STOPPED TALKING TO ME AFTER I MENTIONED *SUPERMAN*.

XENOPHOBIC JERK.

I COULDN'T GET A THING OUT OF THE *TICKETING SYSTEM*, NEITHER. NO TICKETS HAVE BEEN ISSUED TO *CLARK KENT* IN THE LAST MONTH.

BUT MAYBE I AIN'T TALKING TO THE *RIGHT SYSTEM...*

01010011
01010101
01010000
01000101
01010011

01001111
01001011

KINDA WEIRD WHAT YOU CAN DO, BLUE. YOU'RE LIKE *AQUAMAN*, ONLY WITH *MACHINES* INSTEAD OF *FISH*.

...

I'MA TAKE THAT AS A *COMPLIMENT*, JIMMY.

PLEASE DO! I LIKE *AQUAMAN*!

AND *FISH*!

01000110
01001111
01010101
01001110
01000100

THERE IT IS. THE SECURITY SYSTEM'S SEEN HIM, ABOUT TWO WEEKS AGO. IT'S GONNA SEND ME A *PIC.*

THAT'S HIM RIGHT THERE.

WHAT IS HE *DOING*, CONDESA?!

LOOKS LIKE SUPERMAN FOLLOWED UP ON THE *LEAD* I GAVE HIM--

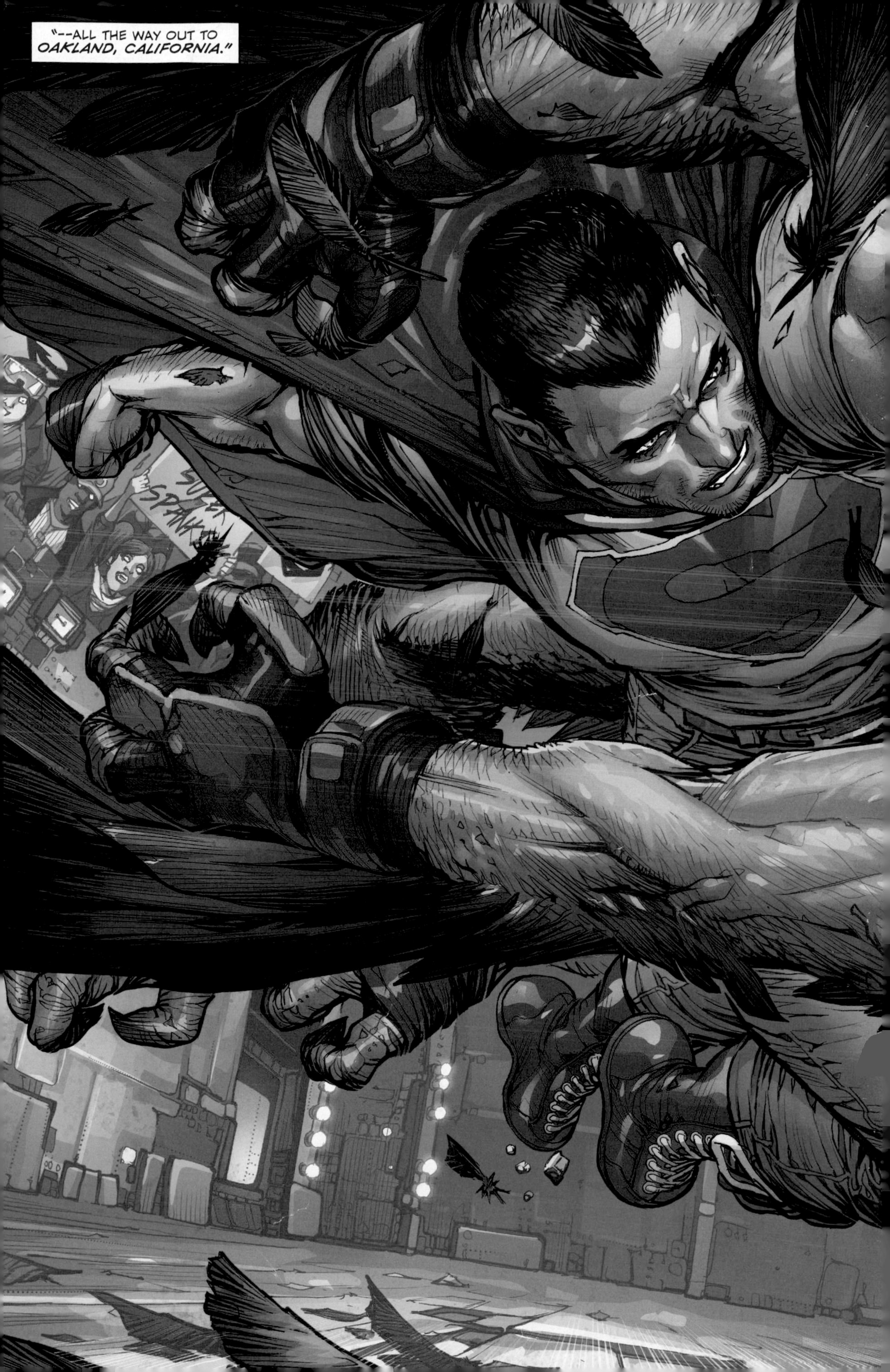
"--ALL THE WAY OUT TO
OAKLAND, CALIFORNIA."

CROW AND I ARE REENACTING AN OLD KOREAN MYTH:

CROW STEALS THE SUN, SO HAEMOSU, THE SUN GOD, HAS TO STEAL IT BACK.

THUD

SHAHRAZAD GAVE ME HAEMOSU'S ROLE TONIGHT. SAID HE NEEDED A BREAK.

STUNNING FINISH! NOW LET'S SEE HOW HE HANDLES HIS MONOLOGUE.

MY MONOLOGUE.

YES, OF COURSE, HAEMOSU. YOUR MONOLOGUE.

YOU THINK THAT'S REALLY HIM?

I DUNNO... MAYBE HE'S AN IMPERSONATOR!

PROBABLY BETTER THAT WAY-- HEARD THE REAL SUPERMAN'S LIKE A HUMAN TIME BOMB NOW!

ALL I KNOW? THIS DUDE IS AWESOME!

ONE FINAL BIT OF SCRIPTED BLUSTER AND WE'RE DONE.

CROW! AS YOU LIE THERE BROKEN, WATCHING ME TAKE BACK WHAT'S RIGHTFULLY MINE, I WANT YOU TO LISTEN TO ME!

AND I WANT YOU TO LISTEN GOOD!

NOBODY STEALS FROM SUPERMAN WITHOUT PAYING A PRICE!

NOBODY!

ENERGY RUNNING THROUGH ME...I HAVEN'T FELT THIS ALIVE IN A WHILE.

IT'S ENOUGH TO MAKE ME BELIEVE THE WORDS COMING OUT OF MY MOUTH.

SU-PER-MAN! SU-PER-MAN! SUPER-MAN! SU-PER-MAN!

THEY CHANT MY NAME LIKE IT MEANS SOMETHING TO THEM, LIKE THE LAST FEW WEEKS NEVER HAPPENED, LIKE I BELONG AMONG THESE GODS--

--LIKE MYTHBRAWL IS ALL THERE IS.

SQUEEEE--

KLANK

SU-PER-MAN! SU-PER-MAN! SU-PER-MAN!

HANGING OUT WITH THE OTHER *MYTHBRAWLERS* GIVES ME A *TASTE* OF WHAT LIFE MIGHT'VE BEEN LIKE HAD THINGS WORKED OUT WITH *DIANA.*

I DO MY *BEST* TO NOT DWELL ON IT. ON *HER.*

SUPERMAN, COME HERE. LET ME TEND TO THAT *BRUISE* ON YOUR CHEEK.

DON'T BOTHER, SHAHRAZAD. IT'S *NOTHING.*

SUPES, YOUR *MIC* WORK AT THE END... MAN, YOU'RE A *NATURAL!*

AND THAT *LAST PUNCH!* HA HA! POOR *CROW!*

WHAT?! *BARELY* FELT IT.

BUT, *uh,* MAYBE NEXT TIME YOU COULD LEAVE THOSE *RED WRAPPINGS* OFF YOUR KNUCKLES?

YOU GOT IT, BUDDY.

I PREFER TO KEEP THE FACE OF MYTHBRAWL'S NEWEST *SUPERSTAR* AS *PRISTINE* AS POSSIBLE. *SIT.*

"THERE, HE WAS ADOPTED BY *KINDLY PARENTS* AND DEVELOPED THE MOST *REMARKABLE POWERS.*"

GIVE ME A SECOND...LET ME FIND YOUR *STORY.*

Ah. THERE IT IS.

ONCE UPON A TIME, A *BABY BOY* WAS SENT TO A *FOREIGN WORLD* TO SAVE HIM FROM *DOOM.*

"EVEN SO, DEEP DOWN INSIDE, HE ALWAYS FELT *OUT OF PLACE.*"

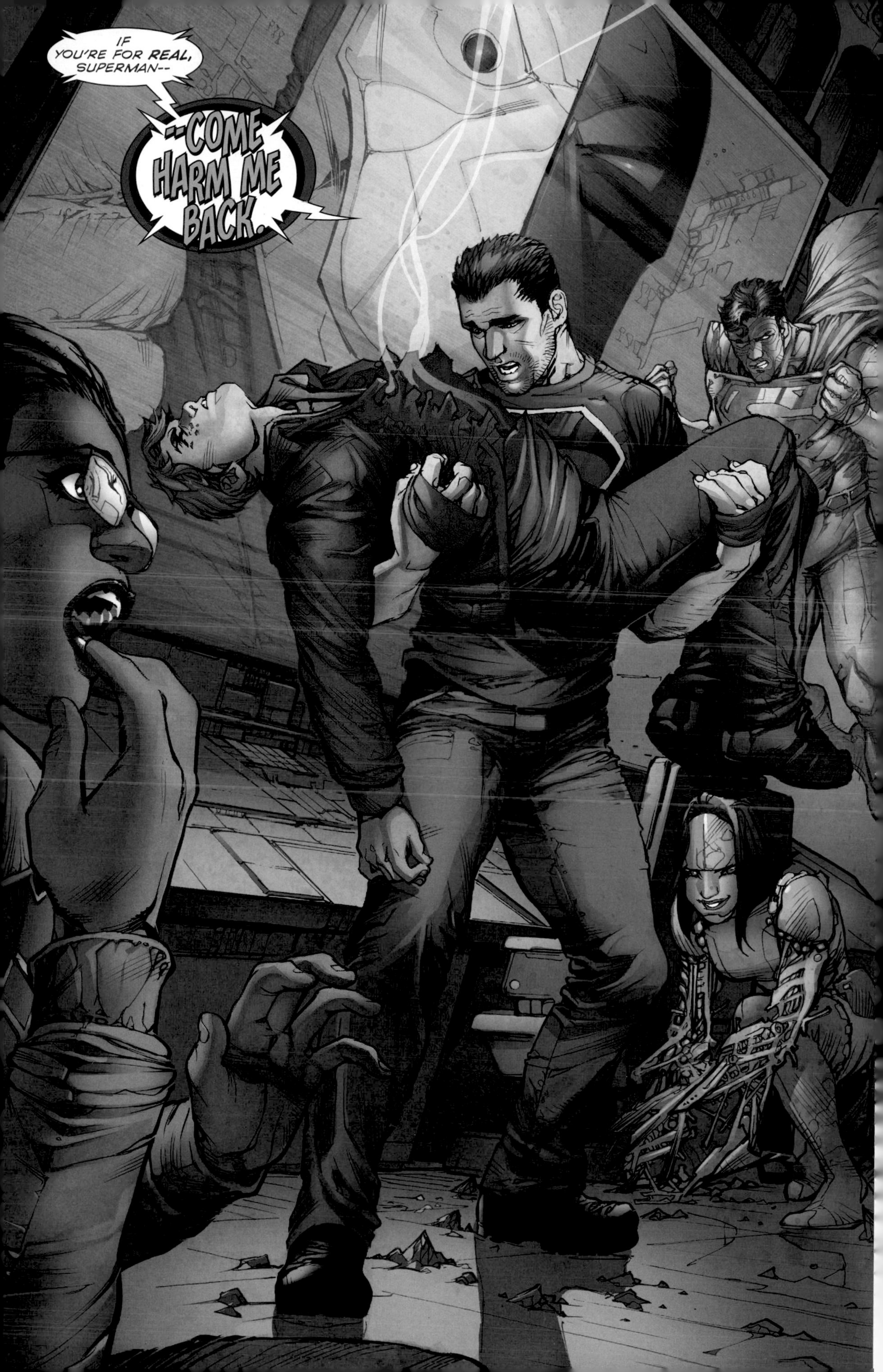
IF YOU'RE FOR REAL, SUPERMAN--
--COME HARM ME BACK.

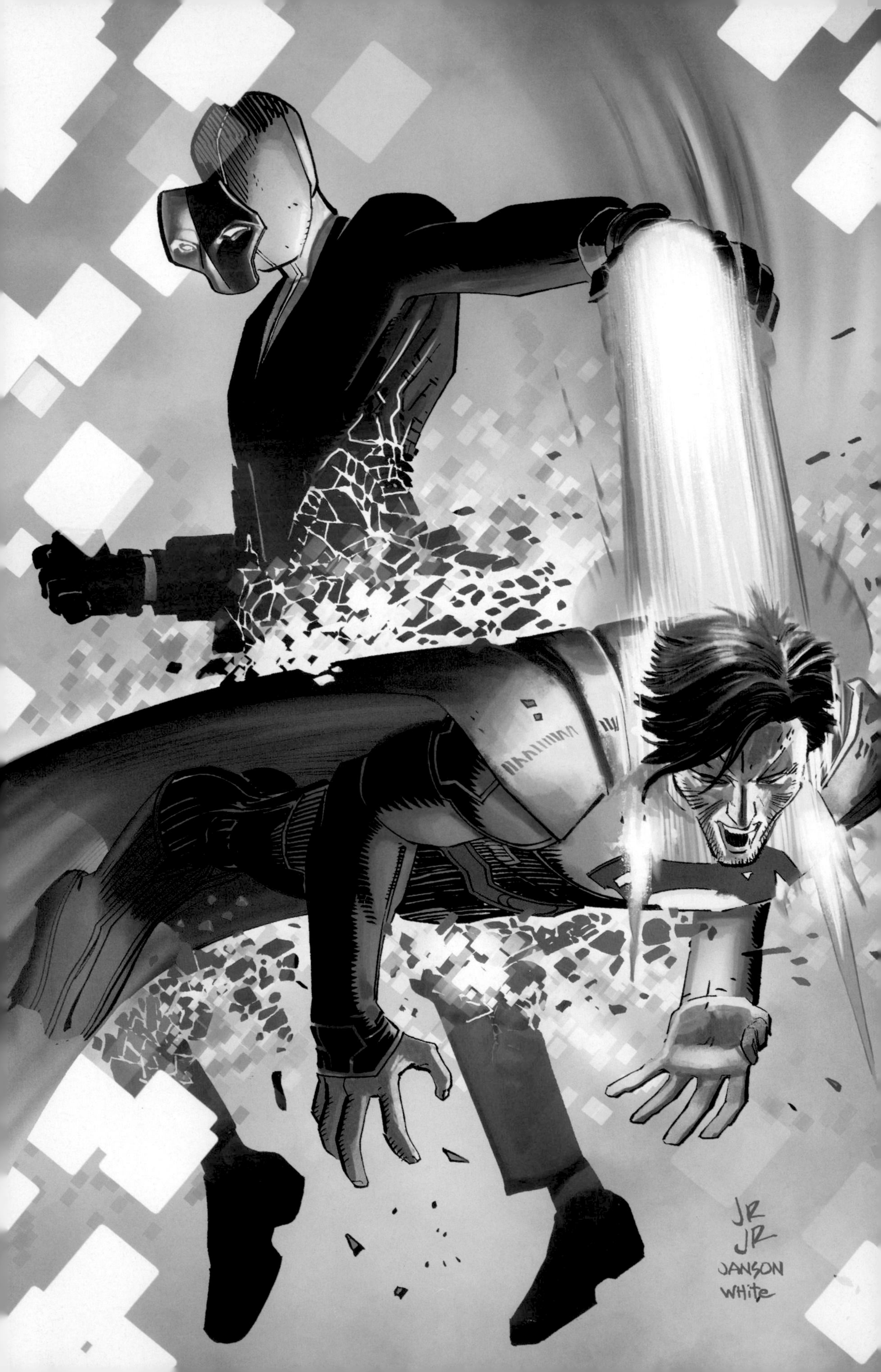
JR JR
JANSON
WHITE

INFILTRATED

GENE LUEN YANG writer **HOWARD PORTER, RAYMUND BERMUDEZ, TOM DERENICK** artists **HI-FI, LEE LOUGHRIDGE** colorists **ROB LEIGH** letterer
JOHN ROMITA JR., KLAUS JANSON, DEAN WHITE cover

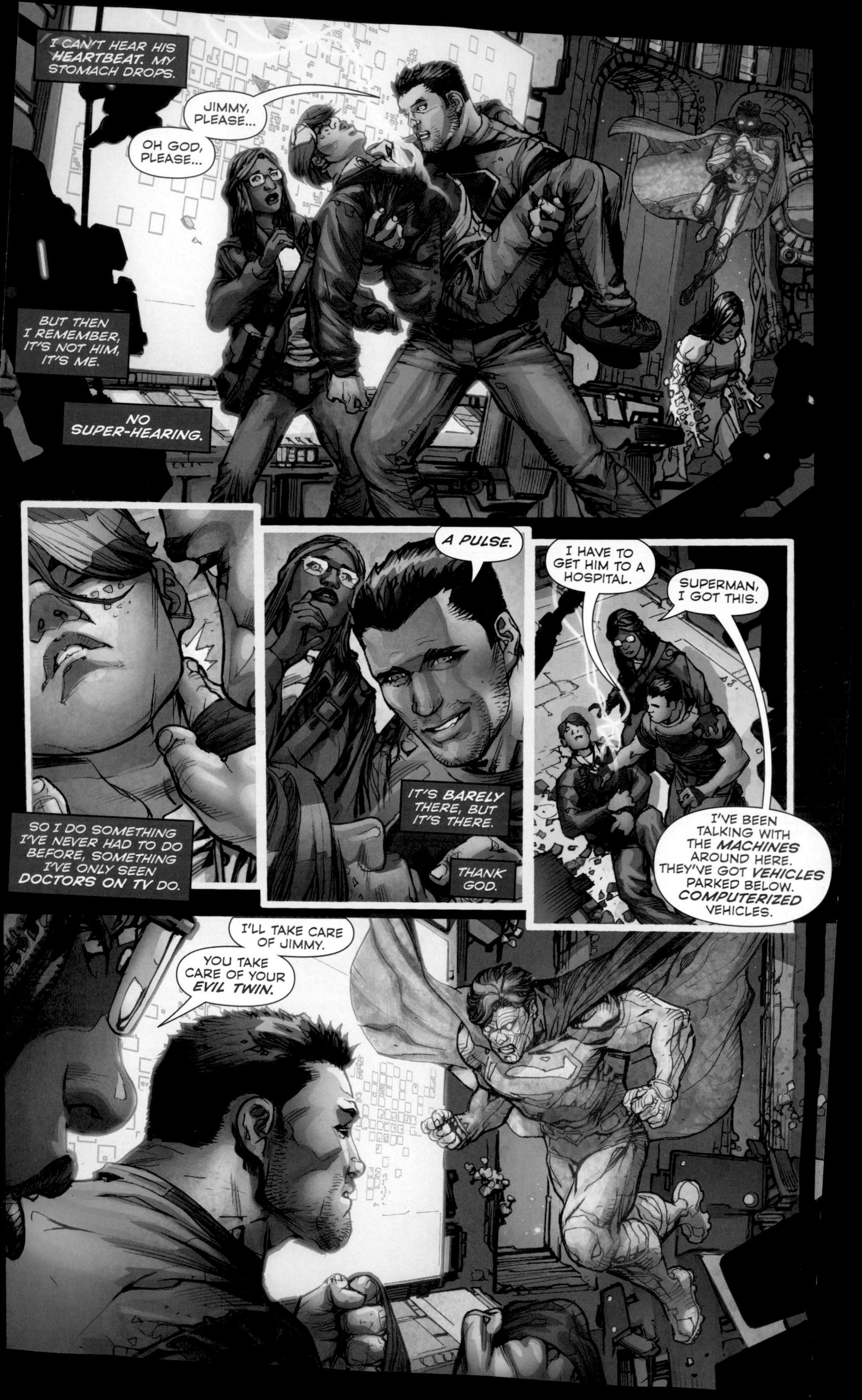
I CAN'T HEAR HIS HEARTBEAT. MY STOMACH DROPS.
JIMMY, PLEASE...
OH GOD, PLEASE...
BUT THEN I REMEMBER, IT'S NOT HIM, IT'S ME.
NO SUPER-HEARING.
SO I DO SOMETHING I'VE NEVER HAD TO DO BEFORE, SOMETHING I'VE ONLY SEEN DOCTORS ON TV DO.
A PULSE.
IT'S BARELY THERE, BUT IT'S THERE.
THANK GOD.
I HAVE TO GET HIM TO A HOSPITAL.
SUPERMAN, I GOT THIS.
I'VE BEEN TALKING WITH THE MACHINES AROUND HERE. THEY'VE GOT VEHICLES PARKED BELOW. COMPUTERIZED VEHICLES.
I'LL TAKE CARE OF JIMMY.
YOU TAKE CARE OF YOUR EVIL TWIN.

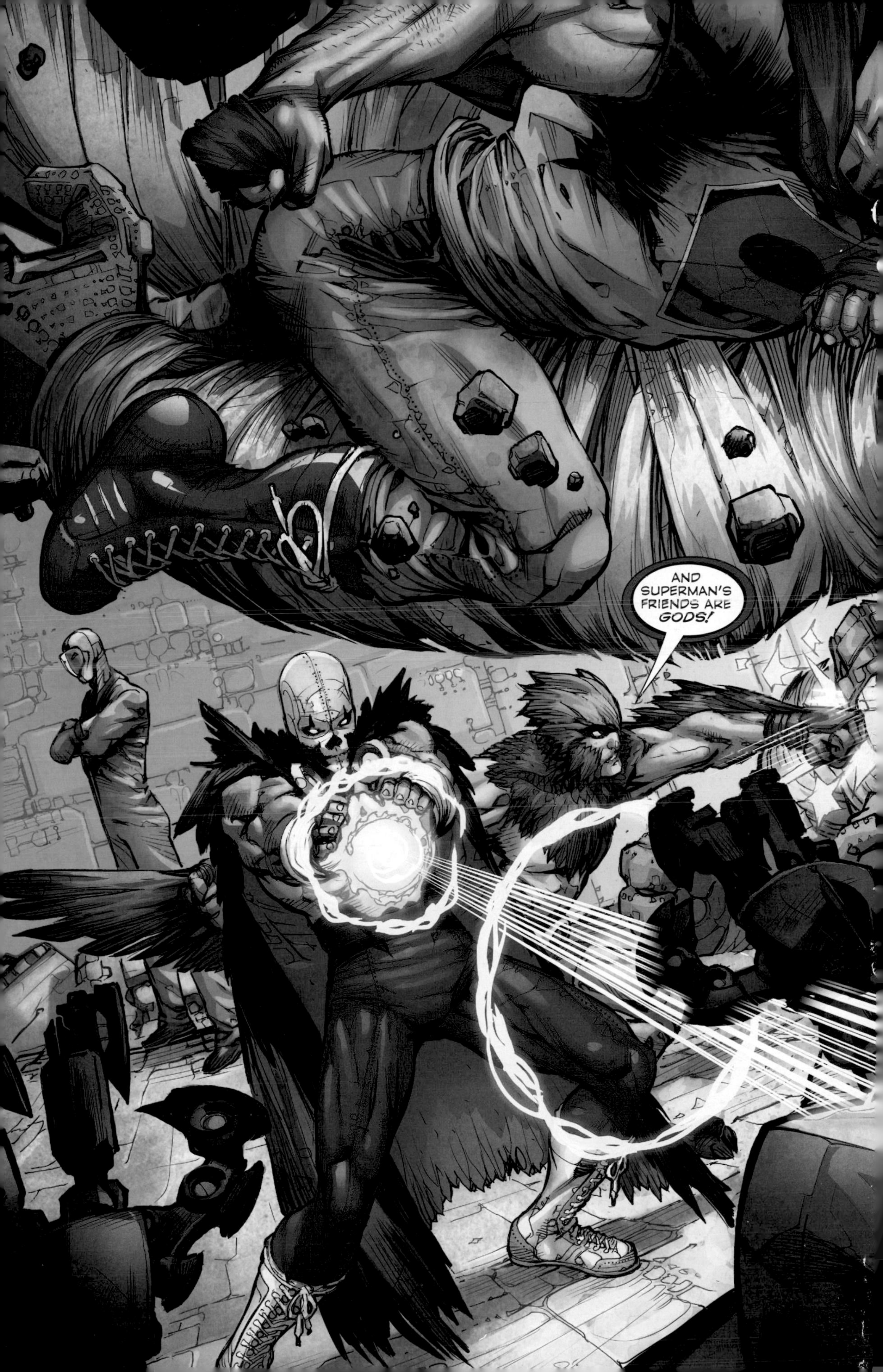
AND SUPERMAN'S FRIENDS ARE GODS!

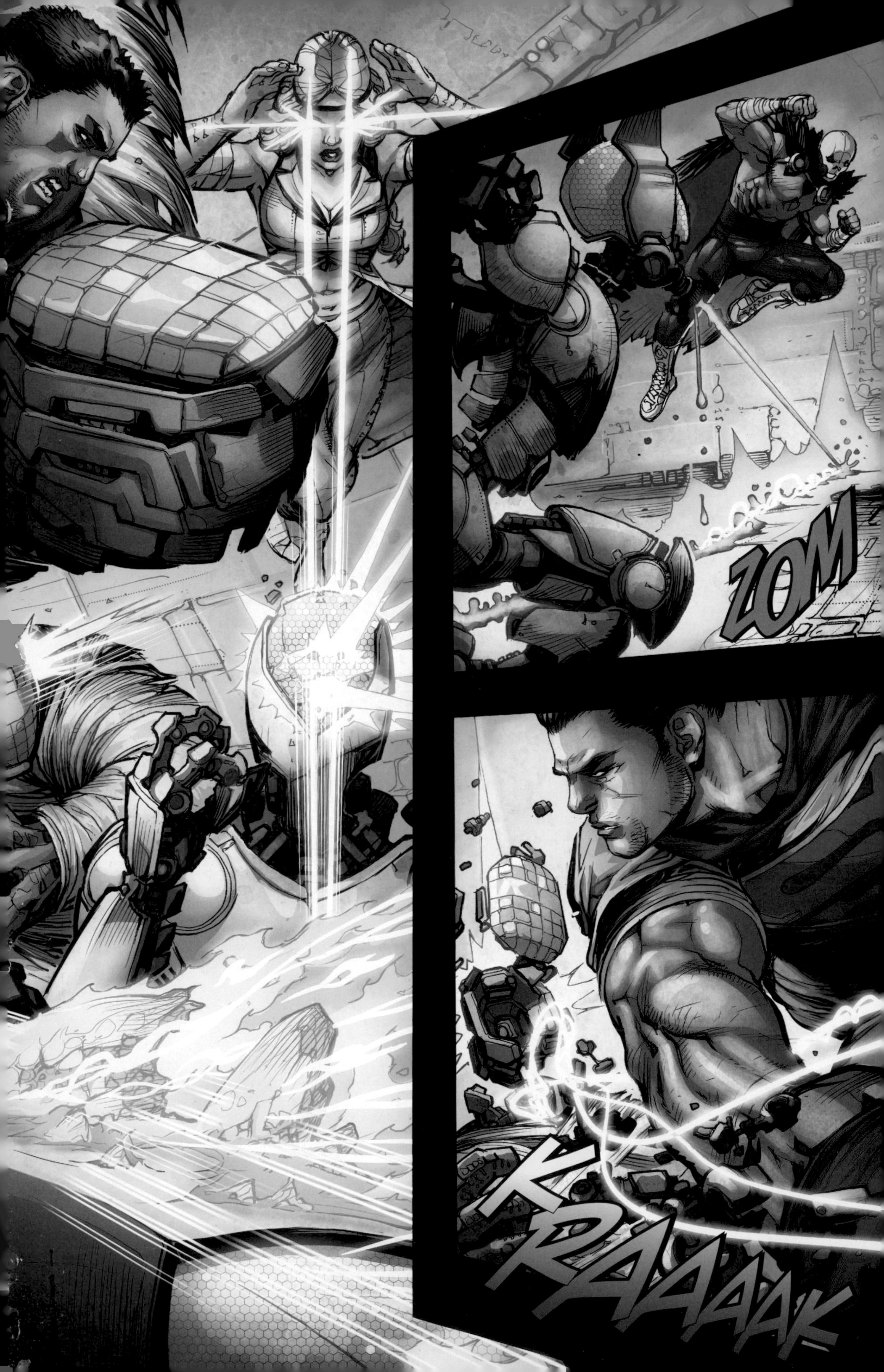
ZOM
KRAAAAK

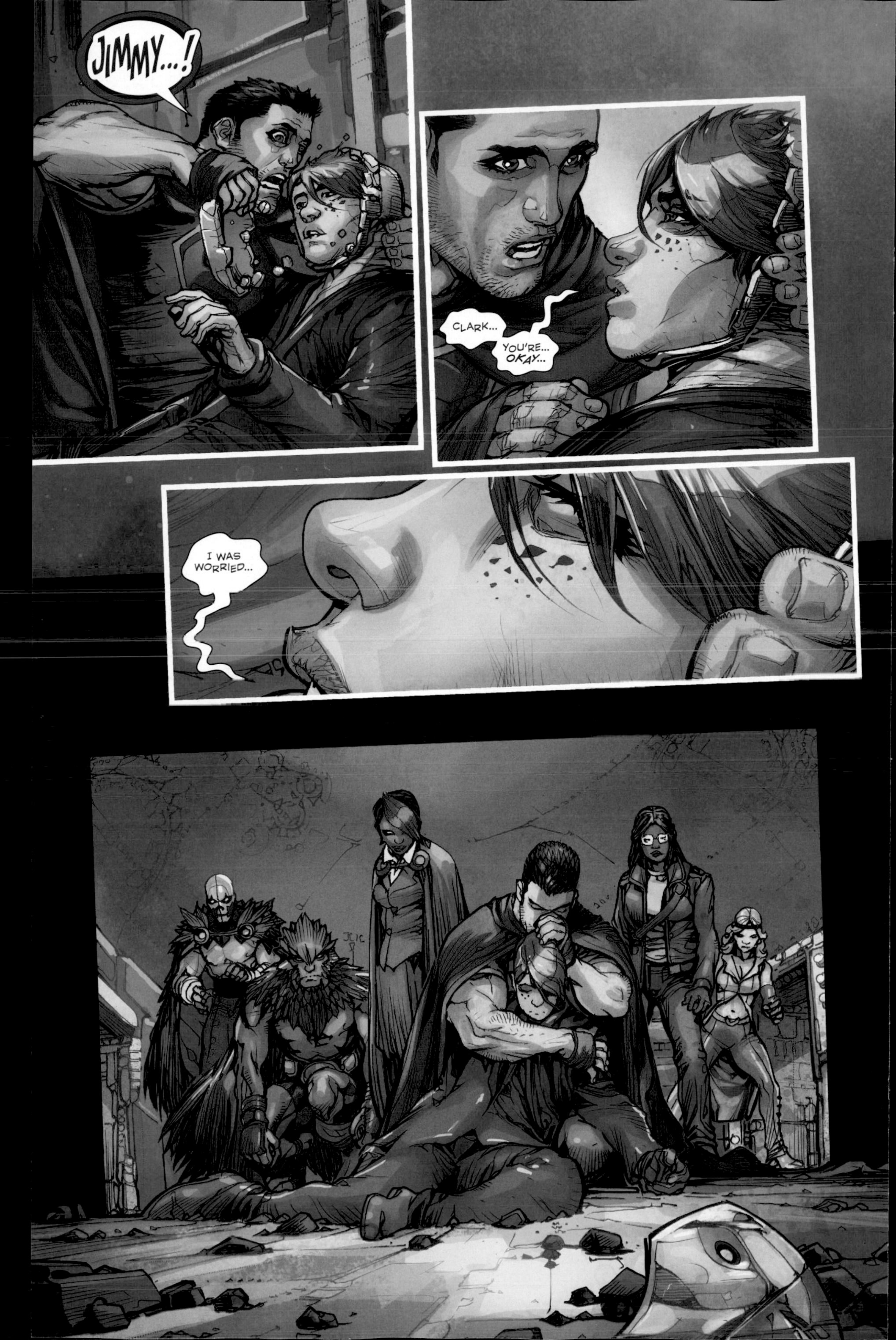
JIMMY...!
CLARK...
YOU'RE... OKAY...
I WAS WORRIED...

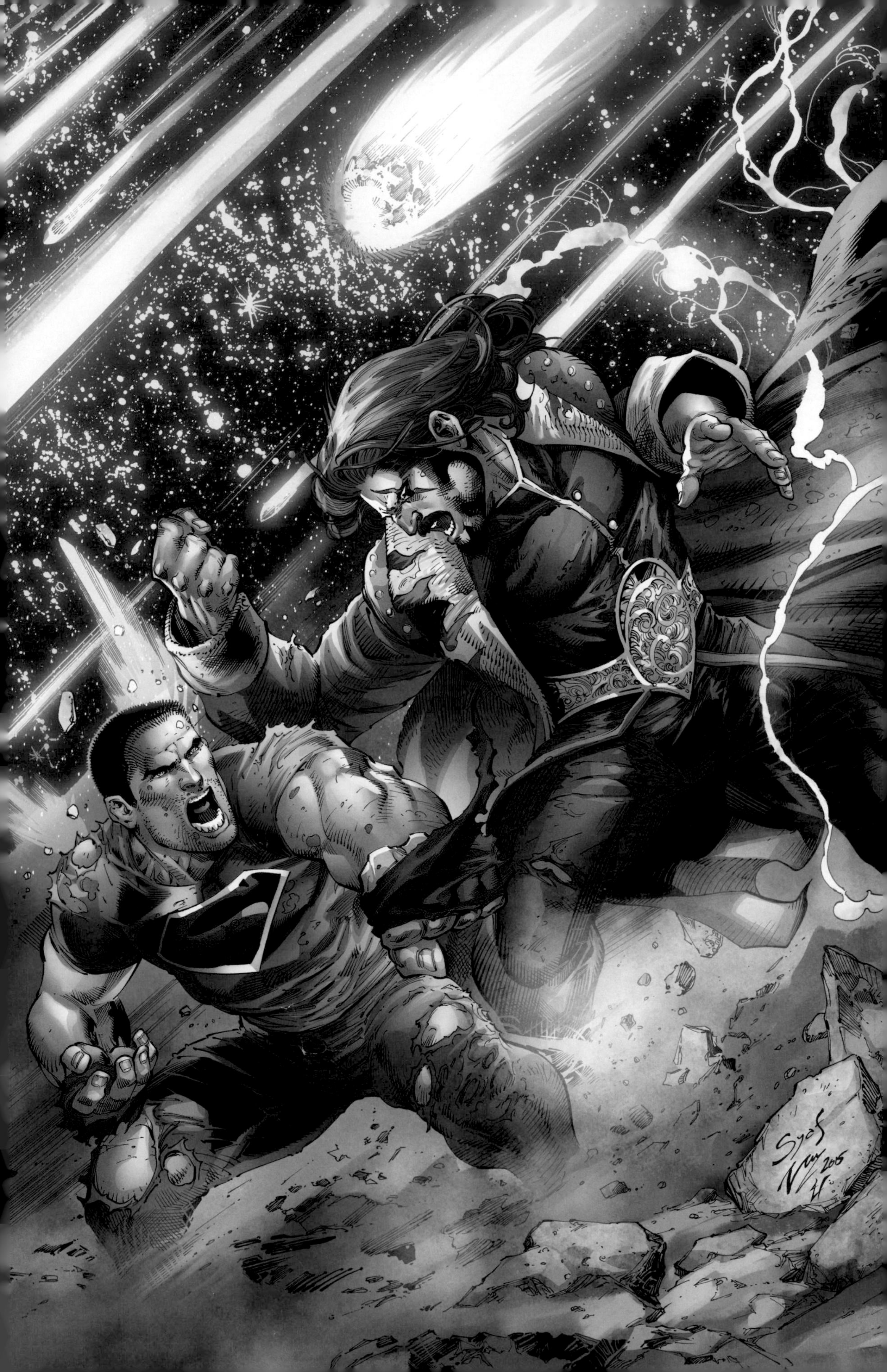

SAVAGE DAWN

GREG PAK, GENE LUEN YANG, PETER J. TOMASI, AARON HUDER writers DAN JURGENS, RAFA SANDOVAL, BEN OLIVER pencillers BILL SIENKIEWICZ, BEN OLIVER inkers TRISH MULVIHILL, LEE LOUGHRIDGE, TOMEU MOREY, BEN OLIVER colorists A LARGER WORLD STUDIOS letterer ARDIAN SYAF, VICENTE CIFUENTES, ULISES ARREOLA cover

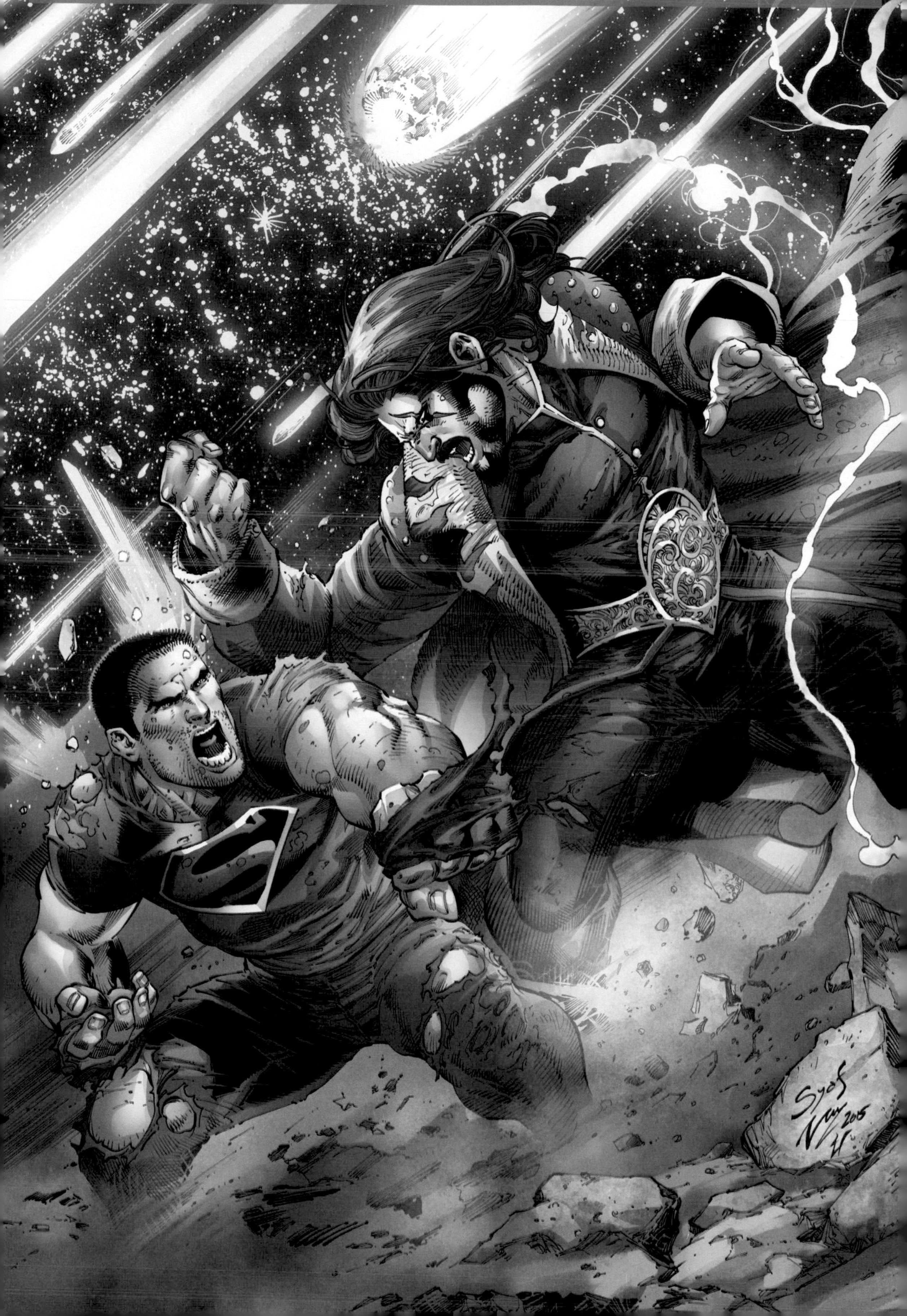

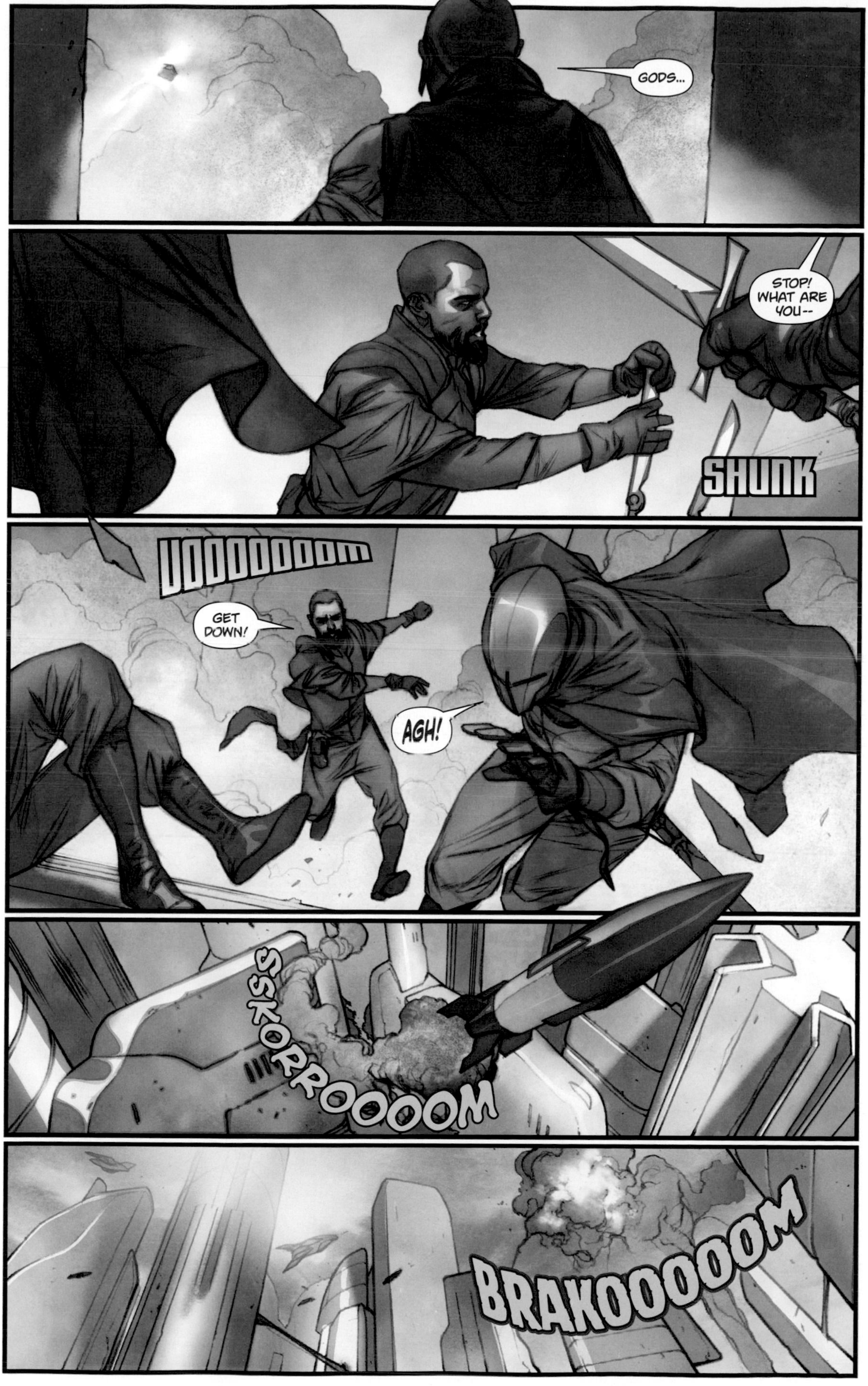
GODS...
STOP! WHAT ARE YOU--
SHUNK
VOOOOOOOM
GET DOWN!
AGH!
SSKORROOOOM
BRAKOOOOOM

WHEN I HEARD ABOUT THE HAN DYNASTY, I WAS INTRIGUED.

HOW COULD A SMALL FAMILY OF HUMANS, AS TEMPORARY AS ALL THE OTHERS, MAINTAIN CONTROL OVER SUCH A MASSIVE POPULATION?

I HAD TO COME SEE FOR MYSELF.

I'VE BEEN CALLED "SAVAGE" OFTEN ENOUGH THAT I'VE EMBRACED IT AS MY NAME. HERE, IT'S BEEN SHORTENED TO A SINGLE SYLLABLE: SHA.

〈THERE, GENERAL SHA! THAT'S THE LEADER OF THE REBELLION!〉*

*TRANSLATED FROM CLASSICAL CHINESE

OVER THE CENTURIES, I HAVE CONQUERED, THEN RULED, AND THEN BEEN DEPOSED COUNTLESS TIMES. AND EACH TIME, MY FRUSTRATION GREW.

LONG AGO, LIFETIMES AGO, I DECLARED THAT I WOULD CREATE THE STRONGEST CLAN FOREVER.

SO FAR, I HAVE NOT SUCCEEDED.

WITHOUT IMMORTAL POWER, IMMORTAL LIFE IS NOTHING MORE THAN AN ENDLESS CHAIN OF FAILURES.

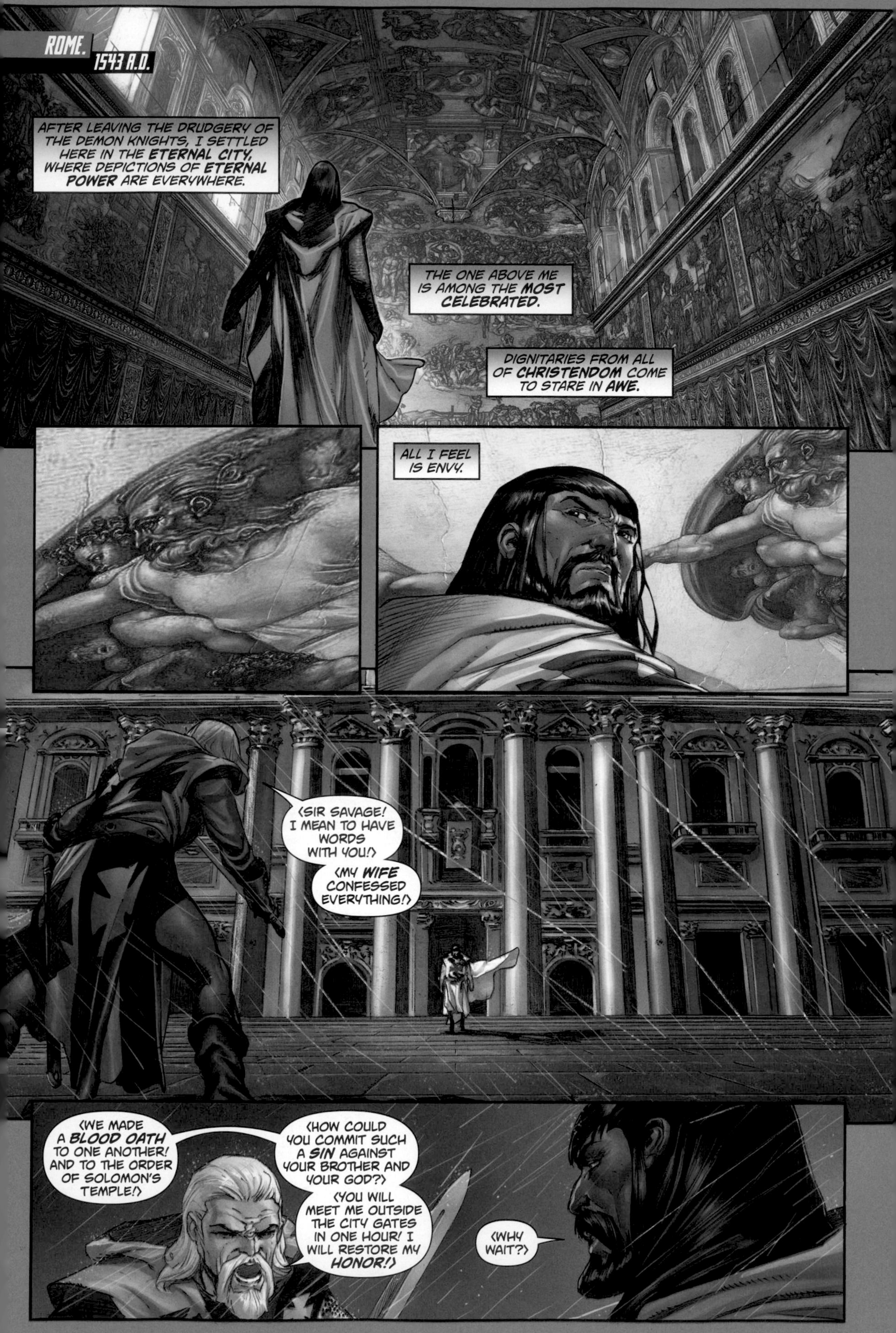
ROME.
1543 A.D.
AFTER LEAVING THE DRUDGERY OF THE DEMON KNIGHTS, I SETTLED HERE IN THE ETERNAL CITY, WHERE DEPICTIONS OF ETERNAL POWER ARE EVERYWHERE.
THE ONE ABOVE ME IS AMONG THE MOST CELEBRATED.
DIGNITARIES FROM ALL OF CHRISTENDOM COME TO STARE IN AWE.
ALL I FEEL IS ENVY.
‹SIR SAVAGE! I MEAN TO HAVE WORDS WITH YOU!›
‹MY WIFE CONFESSED EVERYTHING!›
‹WE MADE A BLOOD OATH TO ONE ANOTHER! AND TO THE ORDER OF SOLOMON'S TEMPLE!›
‹HOW COULD YOU COMMIT SUCH A SIN AGAINST YOUR BROTHER AND YOUR GOD?›
‹YOU WILL MEET ME OUTSIDE THE CITY GATES IN ONE HOUR! I WILL RESTORE MY HONOR!›
‹WHY WAIT?›

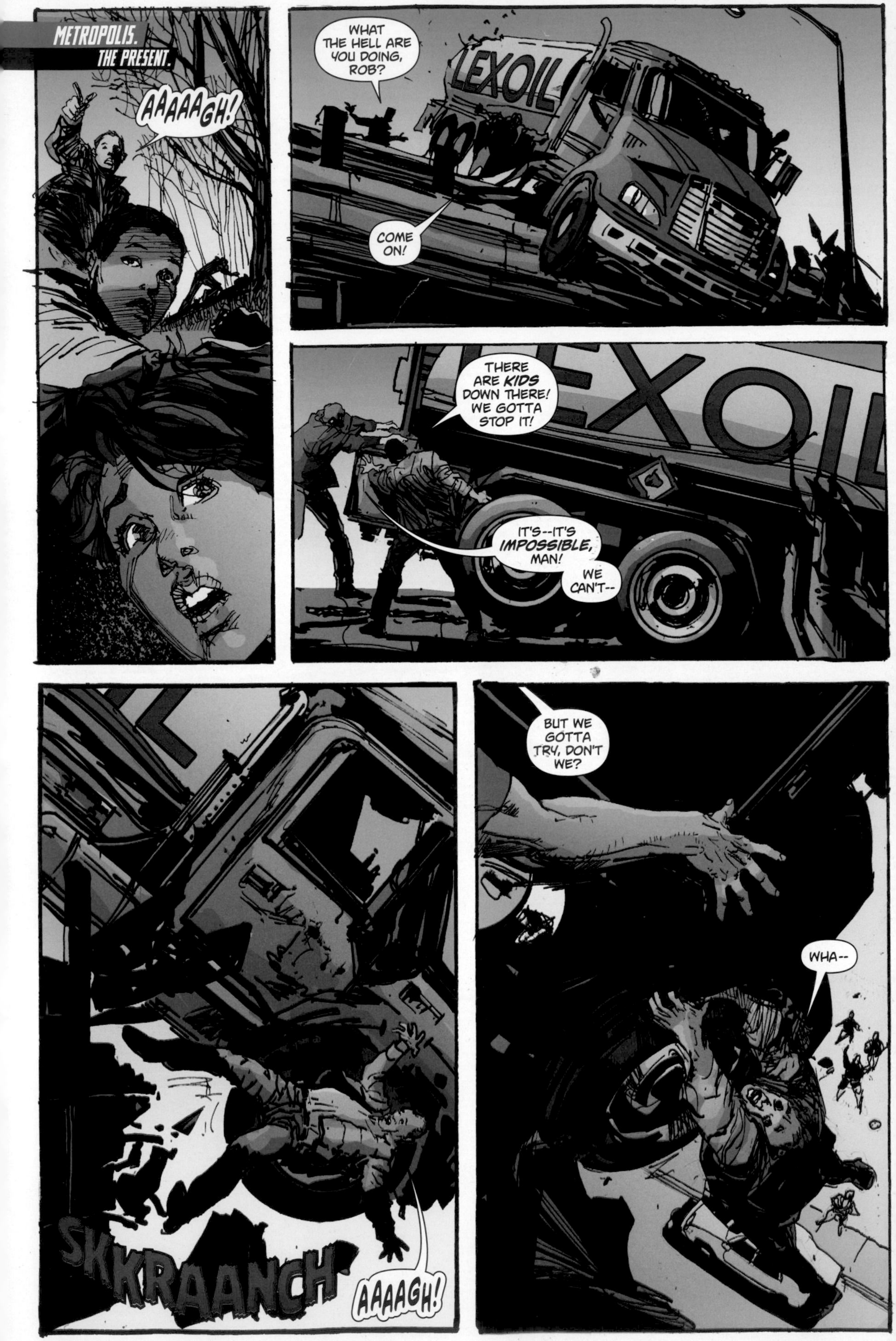
METROPOLIS. THE PRESENT.
AAAAAGH!
WHAT THE HELL ARE YOU DOING, ROB?
COME ON!
LEXOIL
THERE ARE KIDS DOWN THERE! WE GOTTA STOP IT!
IT'S--IT'S IMPOSSIBLE, MAN!
WE CAN'T--
SKKRAANCH
AAAAGH!
BUT WE GOTTA TRY, DON'T WE?
WHA--

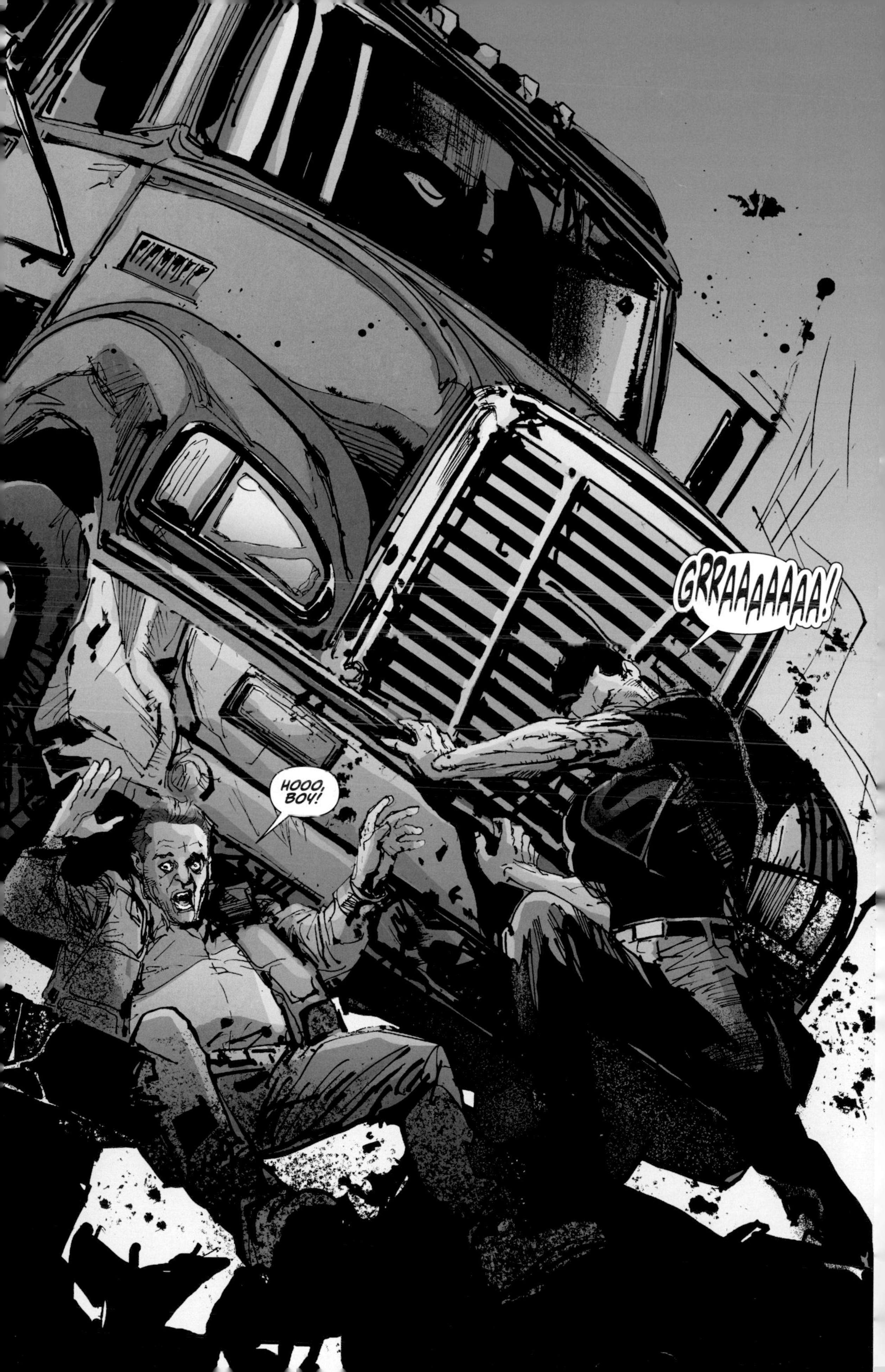
GRRAAAAAAA!
HOOO, BOY!

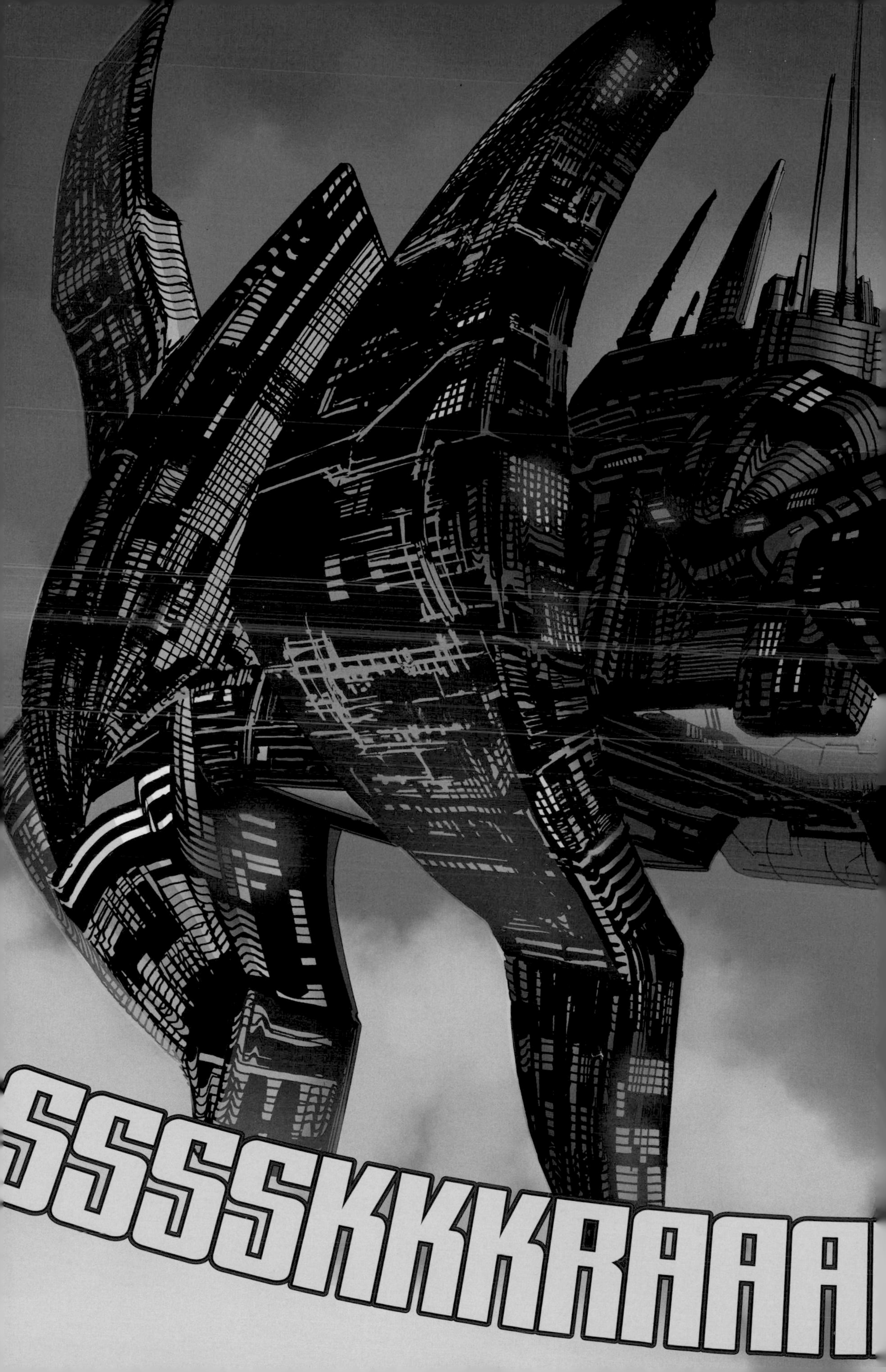
SSSSKKKRAAA

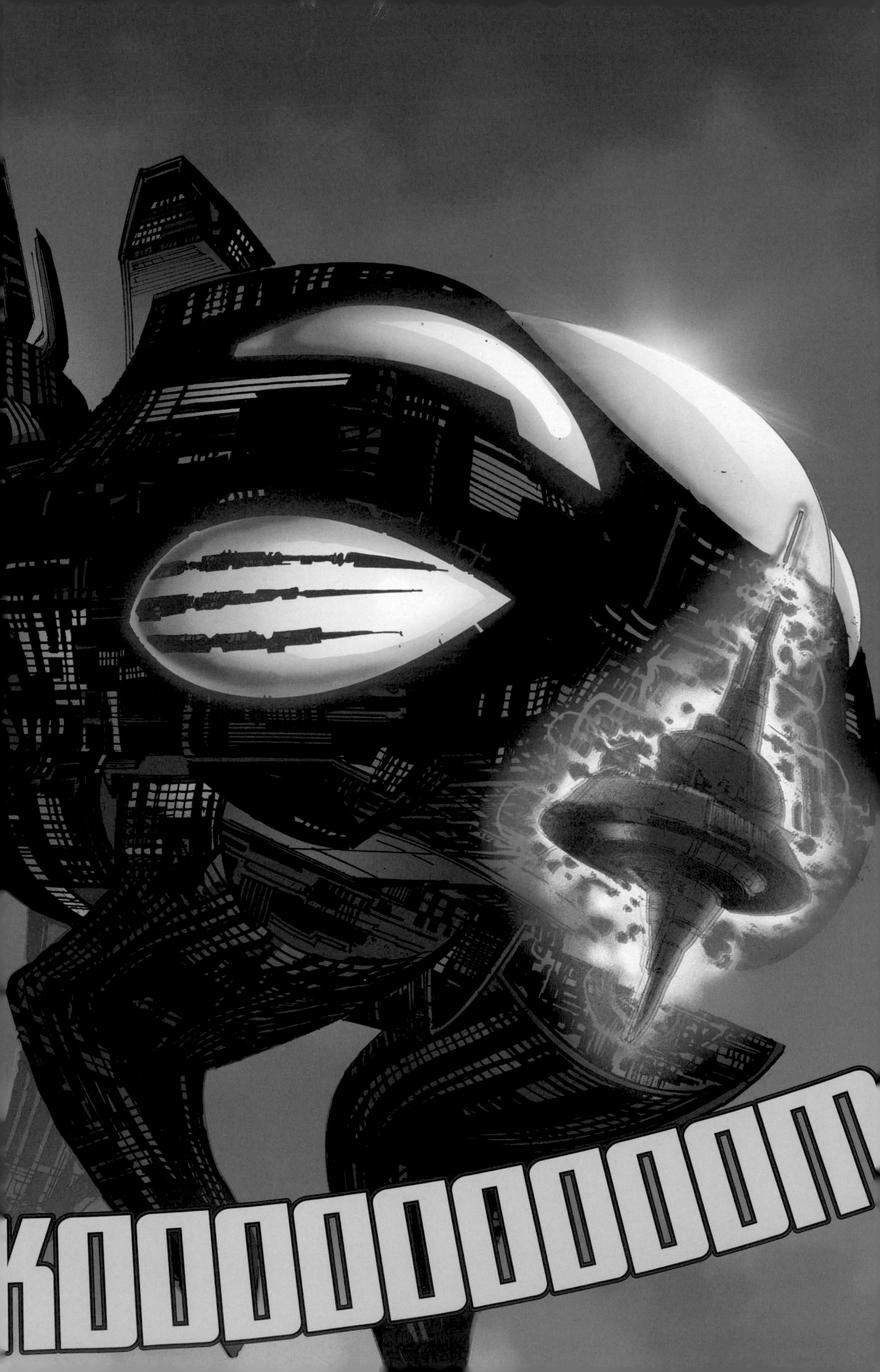
KOOOOOOOOOM

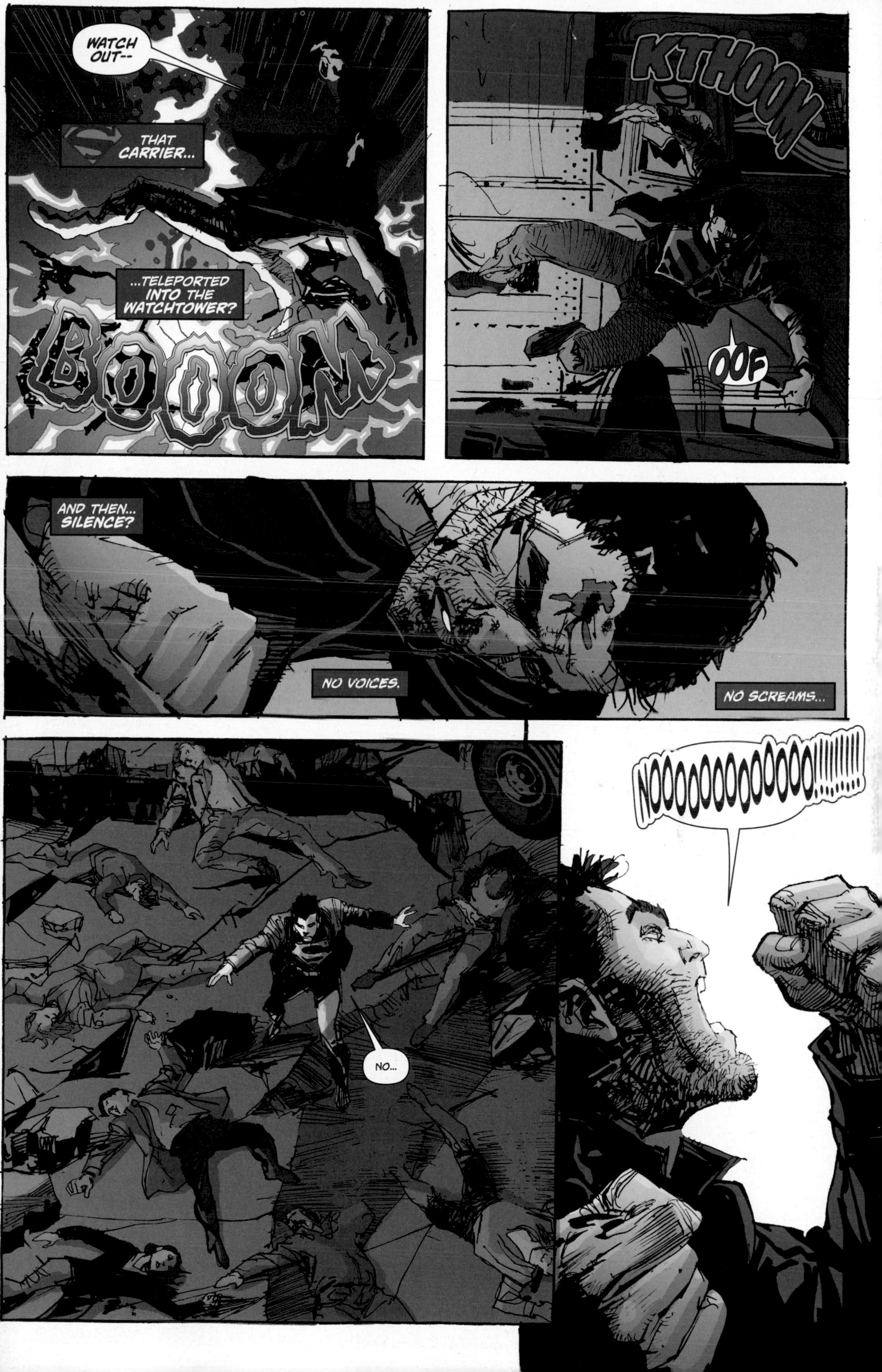
WATCH OUT--
THAT CARRIER...
...TELEPORTED INTO THE WATCHTOWER?
BOOOM
KTHOOM
OOF
AND THEN... SILENCE?
NO VOICES.
NO SCREAMS...
NO...
NOOOOOOOOOOOO!!!!!!!!

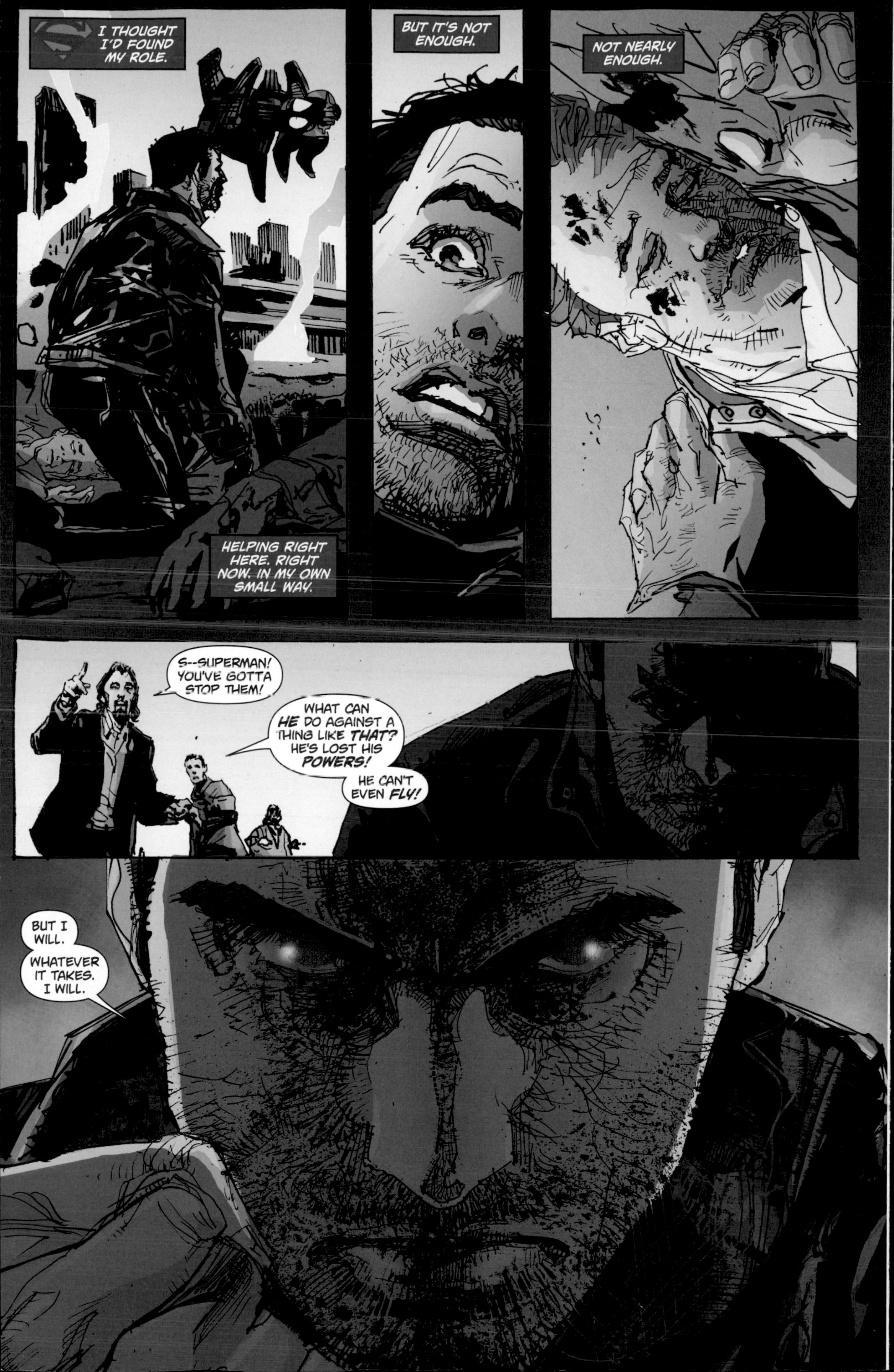
I THOUGHT I'D FOUND MY ROLE.
HELPING RIGHT HERE. RIGHT NOW. IN MY OWN SMALL WAY.
BUT IT'S NOT ENOUGH.
NOT NEARLY ENOUGH.
S--SUPERMAN! YOU'VE GOTTA STOP THEM!
WHAT CAN HE DO AGAINST A THING LIKE THAT? HE'S LOST HIS POWERS!
HE CAN'T EVEN FLY!
BUT I WILL.
WHATEVER IT TAKES. I WILL.

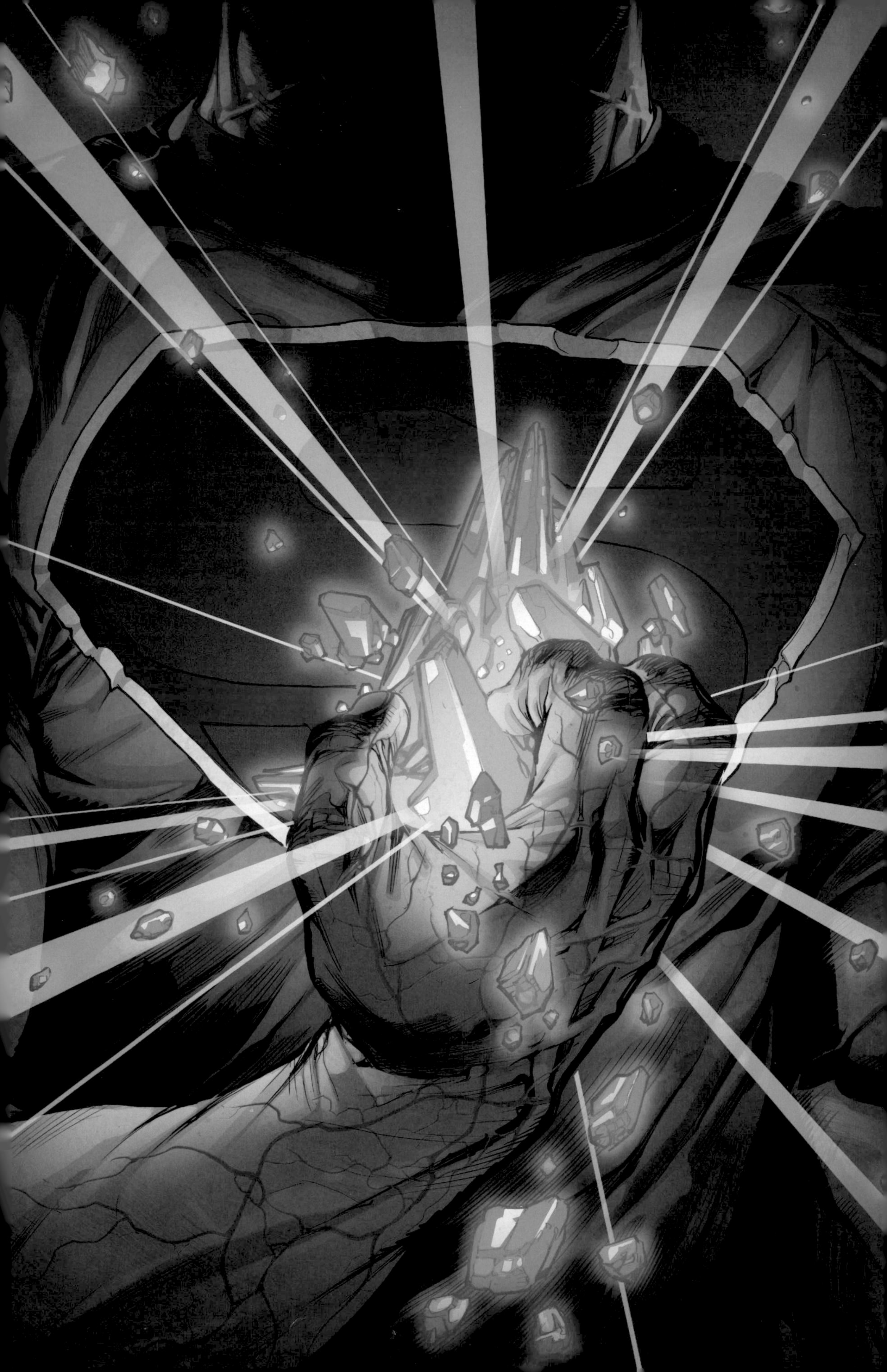

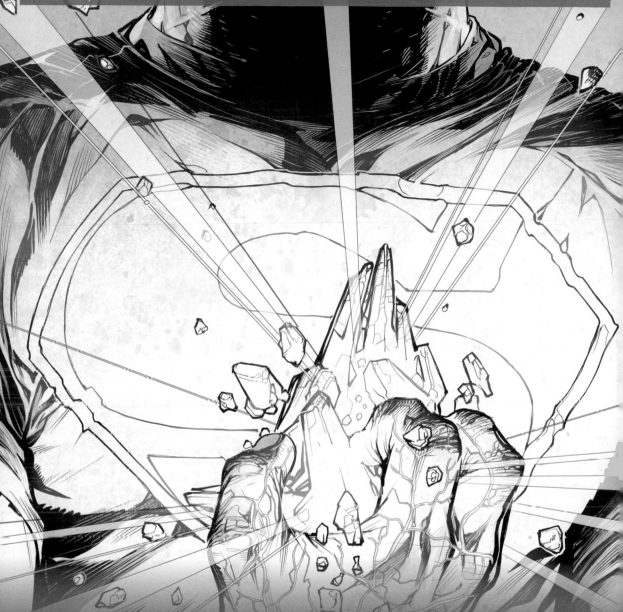

TREATMENT
GENE LUEN YANG writer **HOWARD PORTER, ARDIAN SYAF** pencillers **HOWARD PORTER, DON HO, JEROME K. MOORE** inkers **HI-FI** colorist **ROB LEIGH** letterer
HOWARD PORTER, HI-FI cover

Previously, in SUPERMAN: SAVAGE DAWN ...

Having successfully merged the Justice League Watchtower with the Stormwatch Carrier, Vandal Savage and his army have defeated the Justice League. As Savage siphons the imprisoned League members' powers for his own use, a desperate Superman, aided by Steel and members of the Justice League United, temporarily finds renewed strength through charging his cells inside Metallo's original Kryptonite-powered armor. The move almost proves fatal – after freeing Wonder Woman, the Man of Steel lays motionless while Savage's forces capture the remaining Leaguers and power up his spacecraft for the next step of the immortal's grand design.

Diana, fearing the man she loves has breathed his last, brings Superman to the Greek Gods in the hopes they will bestow the Gift of Healing. After putting Superman's spiritual form through an emotionally grueling series of tests to determine his worthiness, they agree to heal him – and in doing so, make him completely and fully mortal...

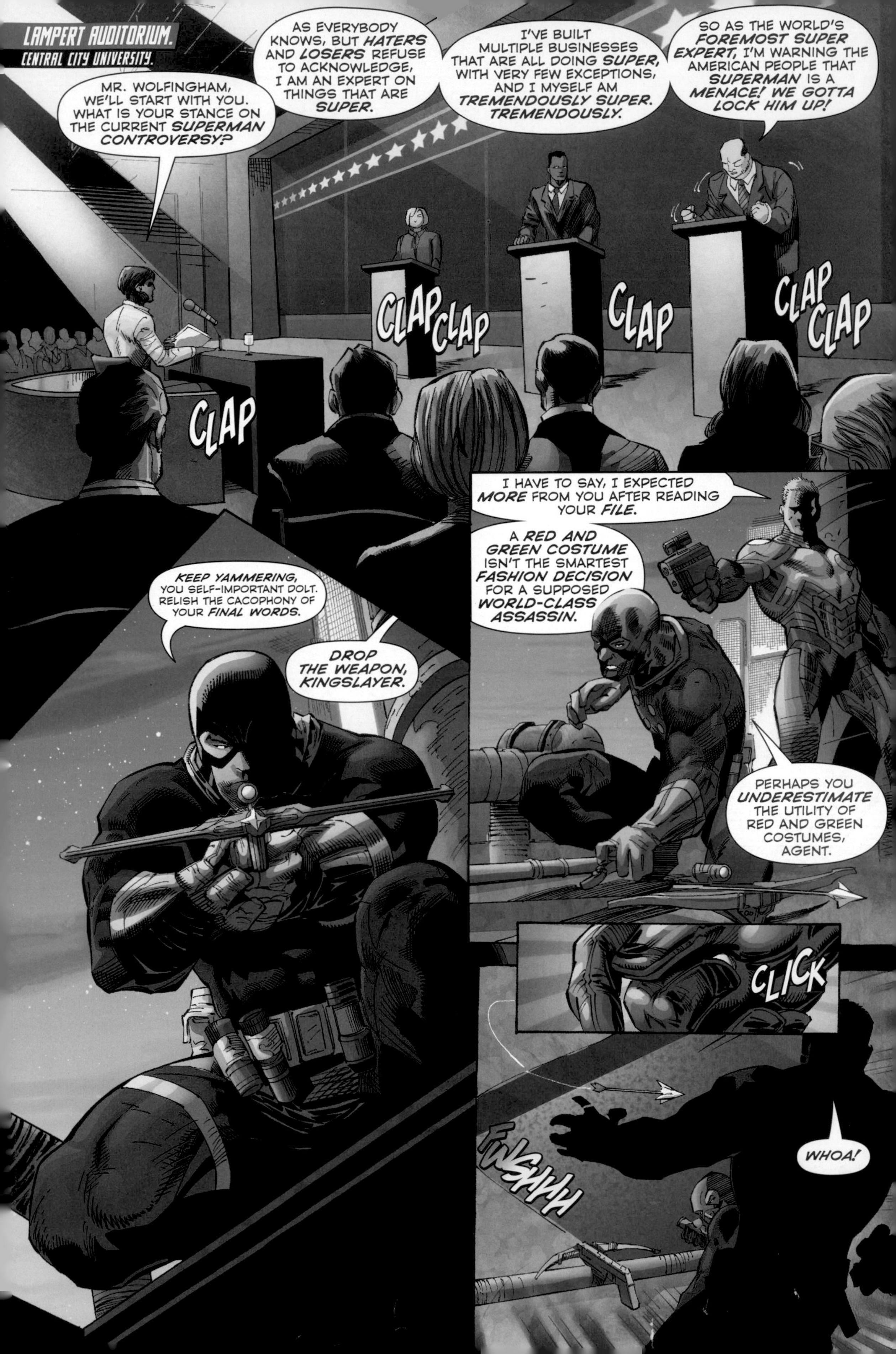
LAMPERT AUDITORIUM.
CENTRAL CITY UNIVERSITY.
MR. WOLFINGHAM, WE'LL START WITH YOU. WHAT IS YOUR STANCE ON THE CURRENT SUPERMAN CONTROVERSY?
AS EVERYBODY KNOWS, BUT HATERS AND LOSERS REFUSE TO ACKNOWLEDGE, I AM AN EXPERT ON THINGS THAT ARE SUPER.
I'VE BUILT MULTIPLE BUSINESSES THAT ARE ALL DOING SUPER, WITH VERY FEW EXCEPTIONS, AND I MYSELF AM TREMENDOUSLY SUPER. TREMENDOUSLY.
SO AS THE WORLD'S FOREMOST SUPER EXPERT, I'M WARNING THE AMERICAN PEOPLE THAT SUPERMAN IS A MENACE! WE GOTTA LOCK HIM UP!
CLAP CLAP
CLAP
CLAP CLAP
CLAP
KEEP YAMMERING, YOU SELF-IMPORTANT DOLT. RELISH THE CACOPHONY OF YOUR FINAL WORDS.
DROP THE WEAPON, KINGSLAYER.
I HAVE TO SAY, I EXPECTED MORE FROM YOU AFTER READING YOUR FILE.
A RED AND GREEN COSTUME ISN'T THE SMARTEST FASHION DECISION FOR A SUPPOSED WORLD-CLASS ASSASSIN.
PERHAPS YOU UNDERESTIMATE THE UTILITY OF RED AND GREEN COSTUMES, AGENT.
CLICK
FWSHHH
WHOA!

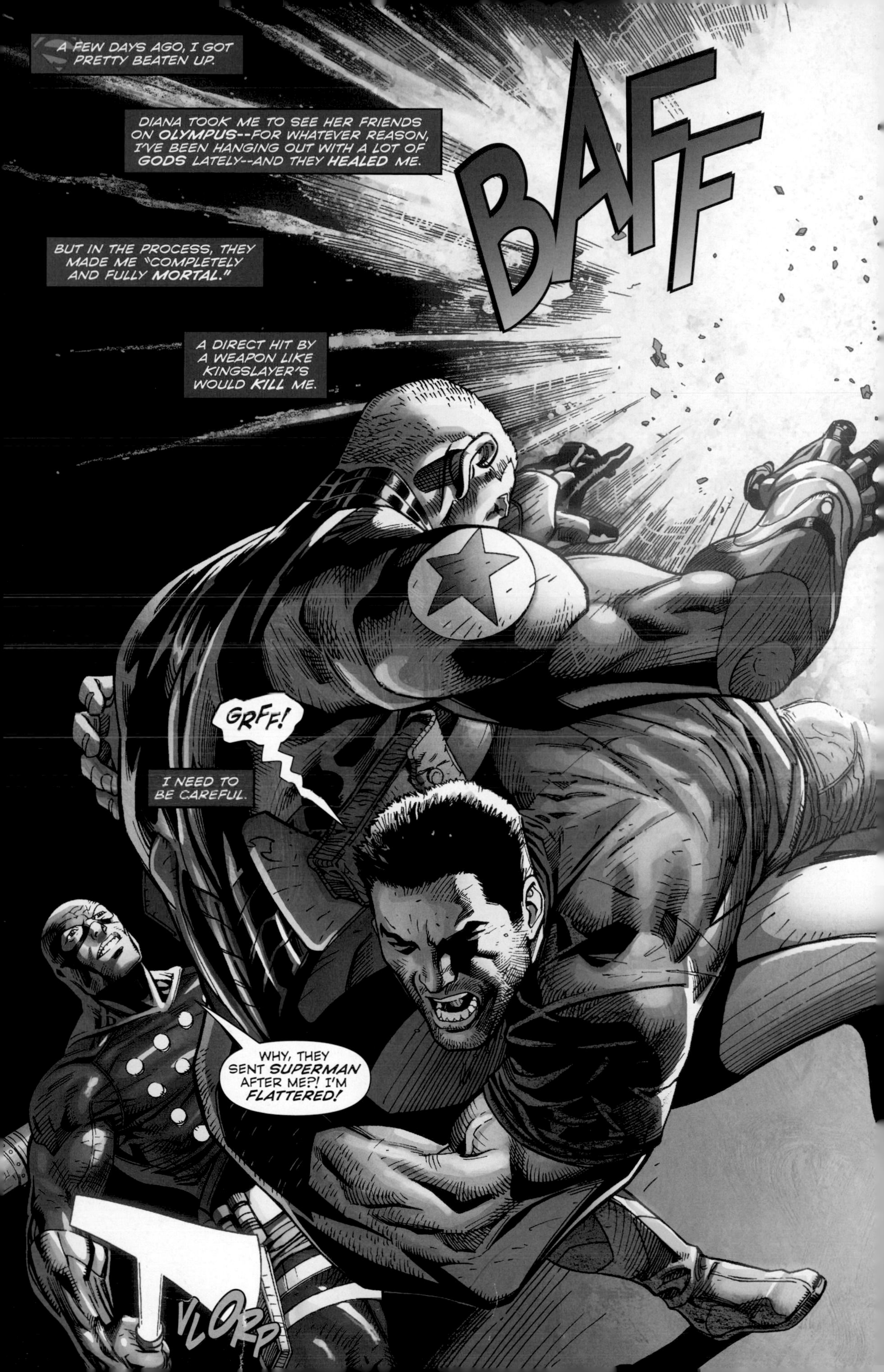
A FEW DAYS AGO, I GOT PRETTY BEATEN UP.
DIANA TOOK ME TO SEE HER FRIENDS ON OLYMPUS--FOR WHATEVER REASON, I'VE BEEN HANGING OUT WITH A LOT OF GODS LATELY--AND THEY HEALED ME.
BAFF
BUT IN THE PROCESS, THEY MADE ME "COMPLETELY AND FULLY MORTAL."
A DIRECT HIT BY A WEAPON LIKE KINGSLAYER'S WOULD KILL ME.
GRFF!
I NEED TO BE CAREFUL.
WHY, THEY SENT SUPERMAN AFTER ME?! I'M FLATTERED!
VLORP

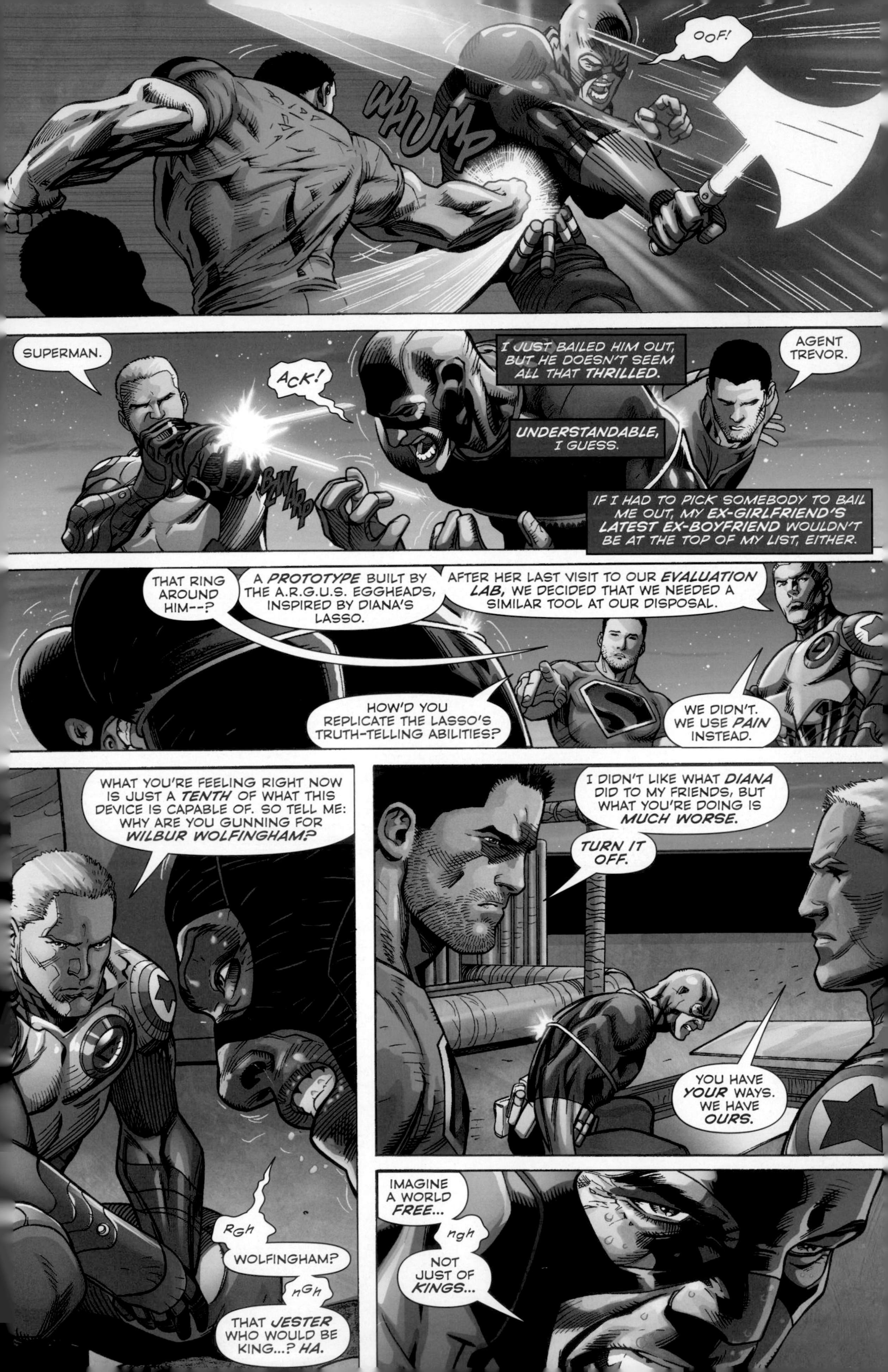
OOF!
WHUMP
SUPERMAN.
ACK!
BZWARP
I JUST BAILED HIM OUT, BUT HE DOESN'T SEEM ALL THAT THRILLED.
UNDERSTANDABLE, I GUESS.
AGENT TREVOR.
IF I HAD TO PICK SOMEBODY TO BAIL ME OUT, MY EX-GIRLFRIEND'S LATEST EX-BOYFRIEND WOULDN'T BE AT THE TOP OF MY LIST, EITHER.
THAT RING AROUND HIM--?
A PROTOTYPE BUILT BY THE A.R.G.U.S. EGGHEADS, INSPIRED BY DIANA'S LASSO.
AFTER HER LAST VISIT TO OUR EVALUATION LAB, WE DECIDED THAT WE NEEDED A SIMILAR TOOL AT OUR DISPOSAL.
HOW'D YOU REPLICATE THE LASSO'S TRUTH-TELLING ABILITIES?
WE DIDN'T. WE USE PAIN INSTEAD.
WHAT YOU'RE FEELING RIGHT NOW IS JUST A TENTH OF WHAT THIS DEVICE IS CAPABLE OF. SO TELL ME: WHY ARE YOU GUNNING FOR WILBUR WOLFINGHAM?
RGH
WOLFINGHAM?
NGH
THAT JESTER WHO WOULD BE KING...? HA.
I DIDN'T LIKE WHAT DIANA DID TO MY FRIENDS, BUT WHAT YOU'RE DOING IS MUCH WORSE.
TURN IT OFF.
YOU HAVE YOUR WAYS. WE HAVE OURS.
IMAGINE A WORLD FREE...
NGH
NOT JUST OF KINGS...

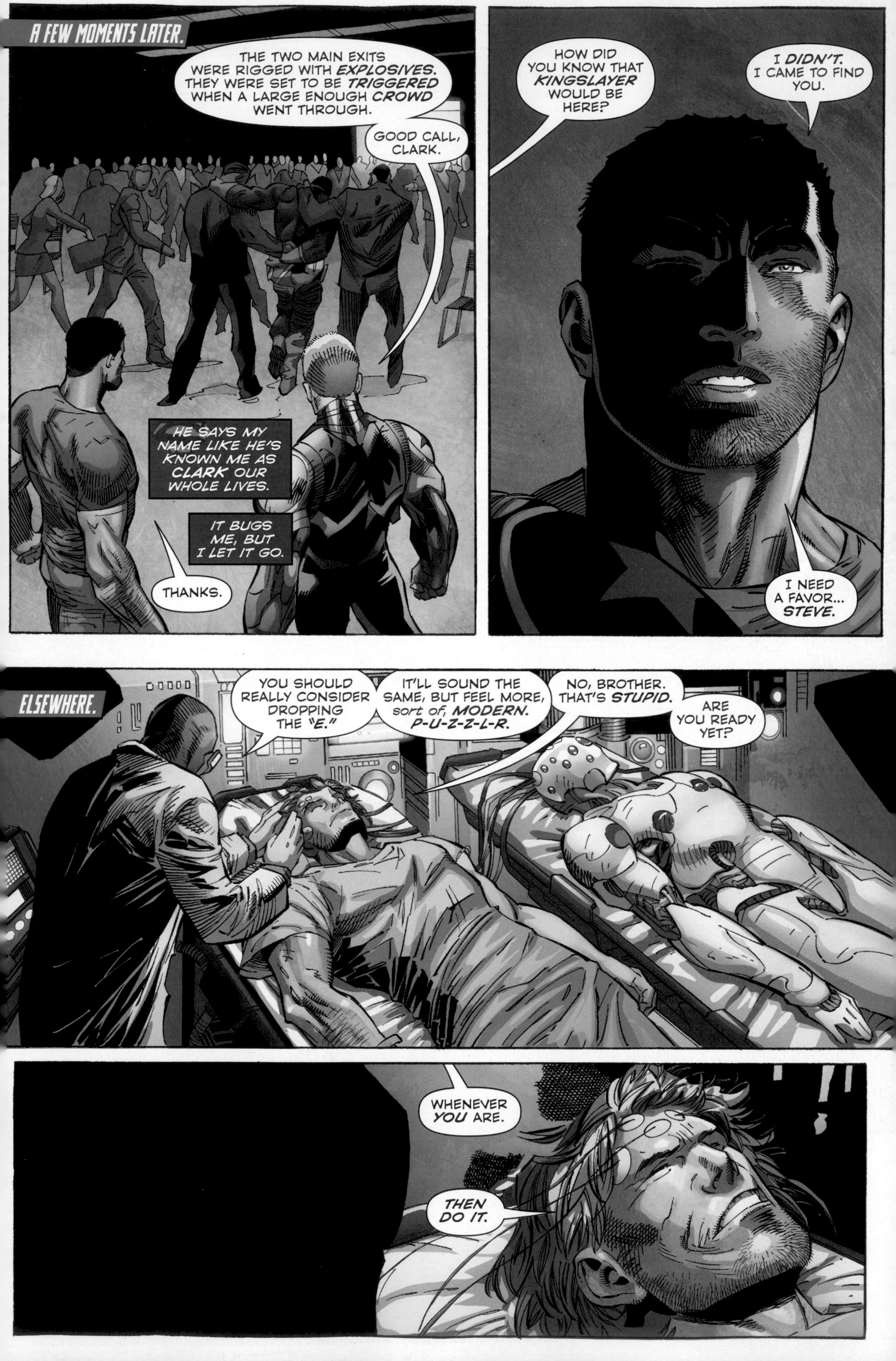
A FEW MOMENTS LATER.
THE TWO MAIN EXITS WERE RIGGED WITH EXPLOSIVES. THEY WERE SET TO BE TRIGGERED WHEN A LARGE ENOUGH CROWD WENT THROUGH.
GOOD CALL, CLARK.
HE SAYS MY NAME LIKE HE'S KNOWN ME AS CLARK OUR WHOLE LIVES.
IT BUGS ME, BUT I LET IT GO.
THANKS.
HOW DID YOU KNOW THAT KINGSLAYER WOULD BE HERE?
I DIDN'T. I CAME TO FIND YOU.
I NEED A FAVOR... STEVE.
ELSEWHERE.
YOU SHOULD REALLY CONSIDER DROPPING THE "E."
IT'LL SOUND THE SAME, BUT FEEL MORE, sort of, MODERN. P-U-Z-Z-L-R.
NO, BROTHER. THAT'S STUPID.
ARE YOU READY YET?
WHENEVER YOU ARE.
THEN DO IT.

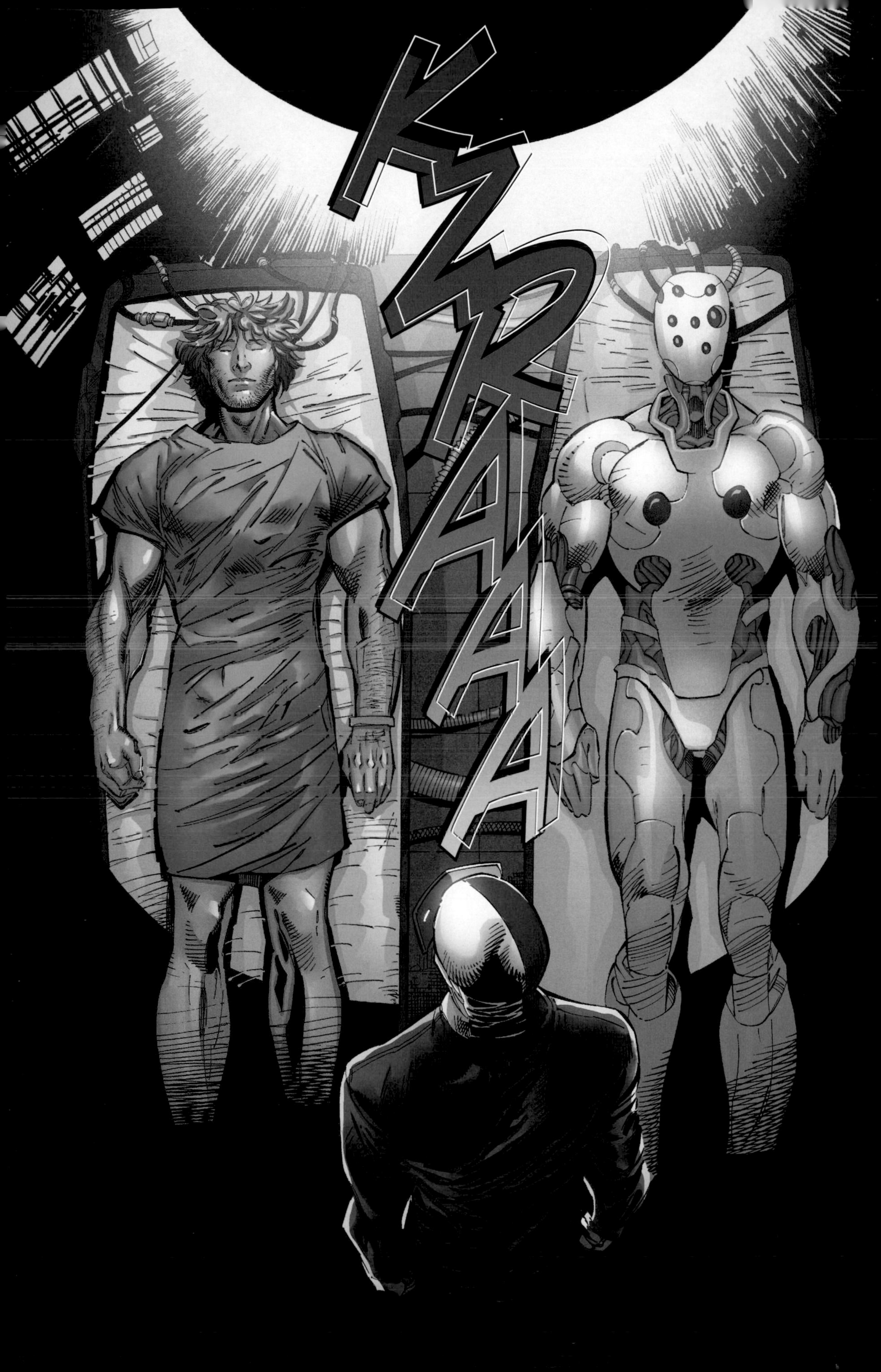
KRRAAAA

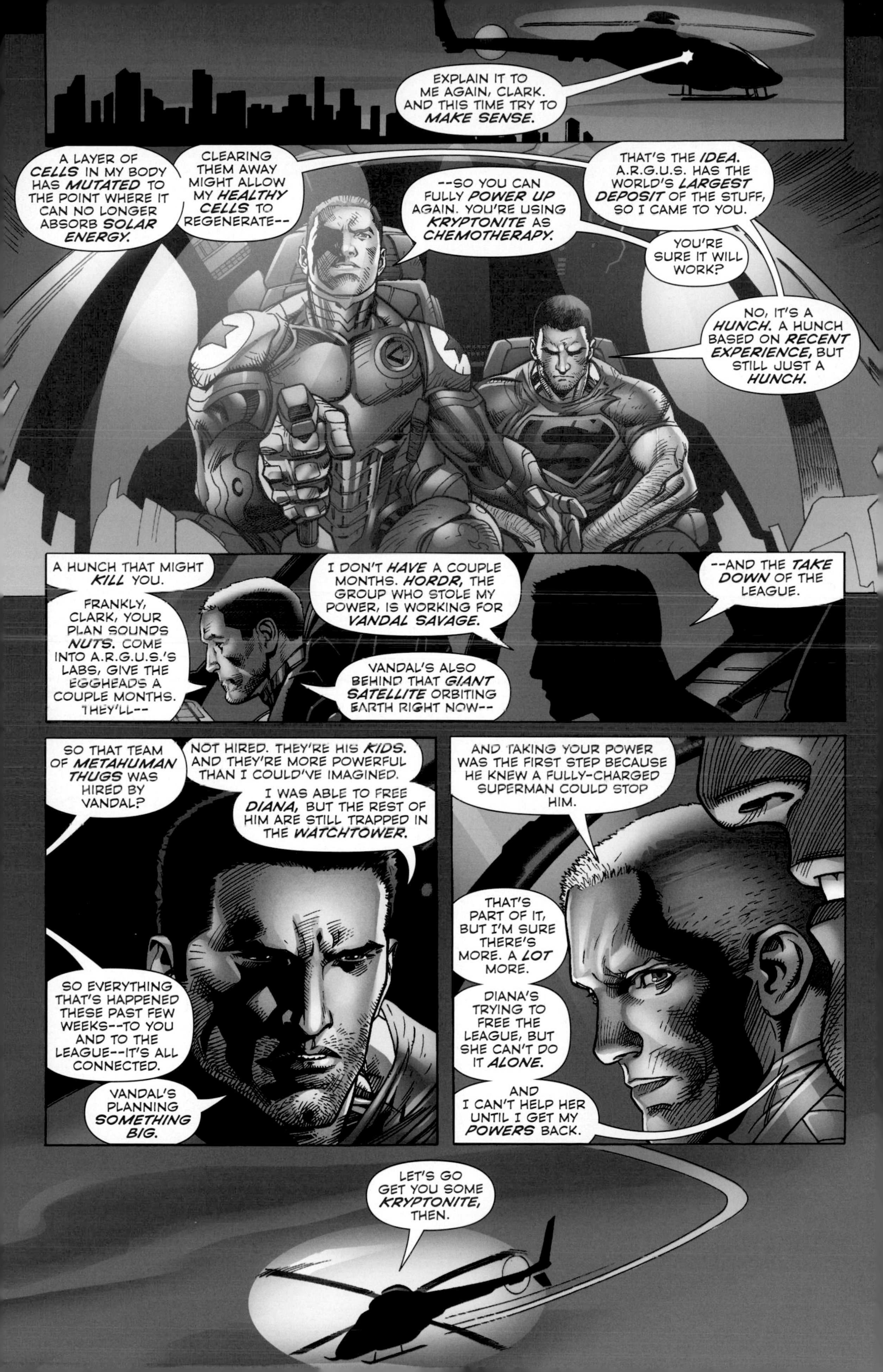
EXPLAIN IT TO ME AGAIN, CLARK. AND THIS TIME TRY TO MAKE SENSE.
A LAYER OF CELLS IN MY BODY HAS MUTATED TO THE POINT WHERE IT CAN NO LONGER ABSORB SOLAR ENERGY.
CLEARING THEM AWAY MIGHT ALLOW MY HEALTHY CELLS TO REGENERATE--
--SO YOU CAN FULLY POWER UP AGAIN. YOU'RE USING KRYPTONITE AS CHEMOTHERAPY.
THAT'S THE IDEA. A.R.G.U.S. HAS THE WORLD'S LARGEST DEPOSIT OF THE STUFF, SO I CAME TO YOU.
YOU'RE SURE IT WILL WORK?
NO, IT'S A HUNCH. A HUNCH BASED ON RECENT EXPERIENCE, BUT STILL JUST A HUNCH.
A HUNCH THAT MIGHT KILL YOU.
FRANKLY, CLARK, YOUR PLAN SOUNDS NUTS. COME INTO A.R.G.U.S.'S LABS, GIVE THE EGGHEADS A COUPLE MONTHS. THEY'LL--
I DON'T HAVE A COUPLE MONTHS. HORDR, THE GROUP WHO STOLE MY POWER, IS WORKING FOR VANDAL SAVAGE.
VANDAL'S ALSO BEHIND THAT GIANT SATELLITE ORBITING EARTH RIGHT NOW--
--AND THE TAKE DOWN OF THE LEAGUE.
SO THAT TEAM OF METAHUMAN THUGS WAS HIRED BY VANDAL?
NOT HIRED. THEY'RE HIS KIDS. AND THEY'RE MORE POWERFUL THAN I COULD'VE IMAGINED.
I WAS ABLE TO FREE DIANA, BUT THE REST OF HIM ARE STILL TRAPPED IN THE WATCHTOWER.
SO EVERYTHING THAT'S HAPPENED THESE PAST FEW WEEKS--TO YOU AND TO THE LEAGUE--IT'S ALL CONNECTED.
VANDAL'S PLANNING SOMETHING BIG.
AND TAKING YOUR POWER WAS THE FIRST STEP BECAUSE HE KNEW A FULLY-CHARGED SUPERMAN COULD STOP HIM.
THAT'S PART OF IT, BUT I'M SURE THERE'S MORE. A LOT MORE.
DIANA'S TRYING TO FREE THE LEAGUE, BUT SHE CAN'T DO IT ALONE.
AND I CAN'T HELP HER UNTIL I GET MY POWERS BACK.
LET'S GO GET YOU SOME KRYPTONITE, THEN.

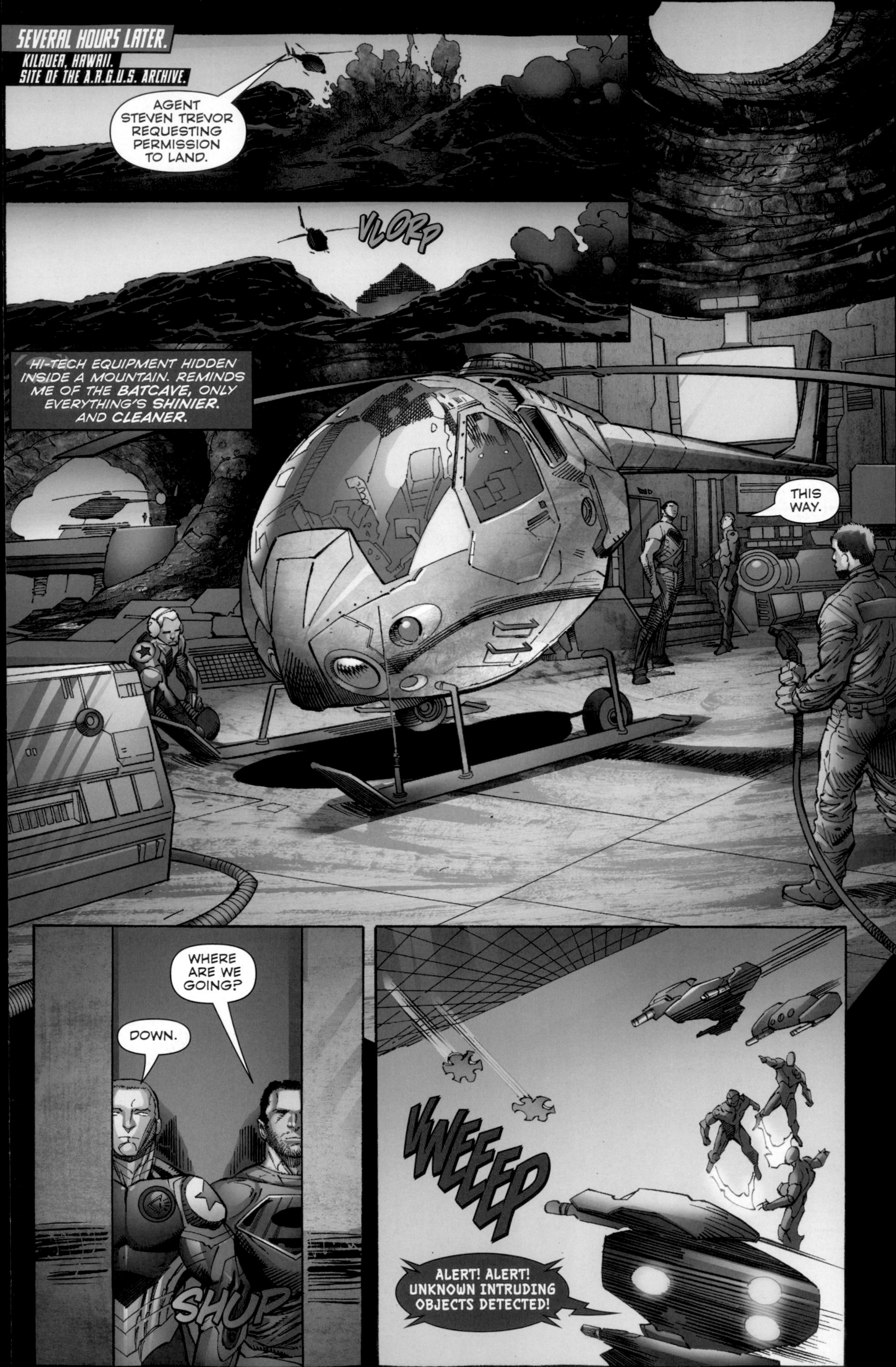
SEVERAL HOURS LATER.
KILAUEA, HAWAII.
SITE OF THE A.R.G.U.S. ARCHIVE.
AGENT STEVEN TREVOR REQUESTING PERMISSION TO LAND.
VLORP
HI-TECH EQUIPMENT HIDDEN INSIDE A MOUNTAIN. REMINDS ME OF THE BATCAVE, ONLY EVERYTHING'S SHINIER. AND CLEANER.
THIS WAY.
WHERE ARE WE GOING?
DOWN.
SHUP
VWEEEP
ALERT! ALERT! UNKNOWN INTRUDING OBJECTS DETECTED!

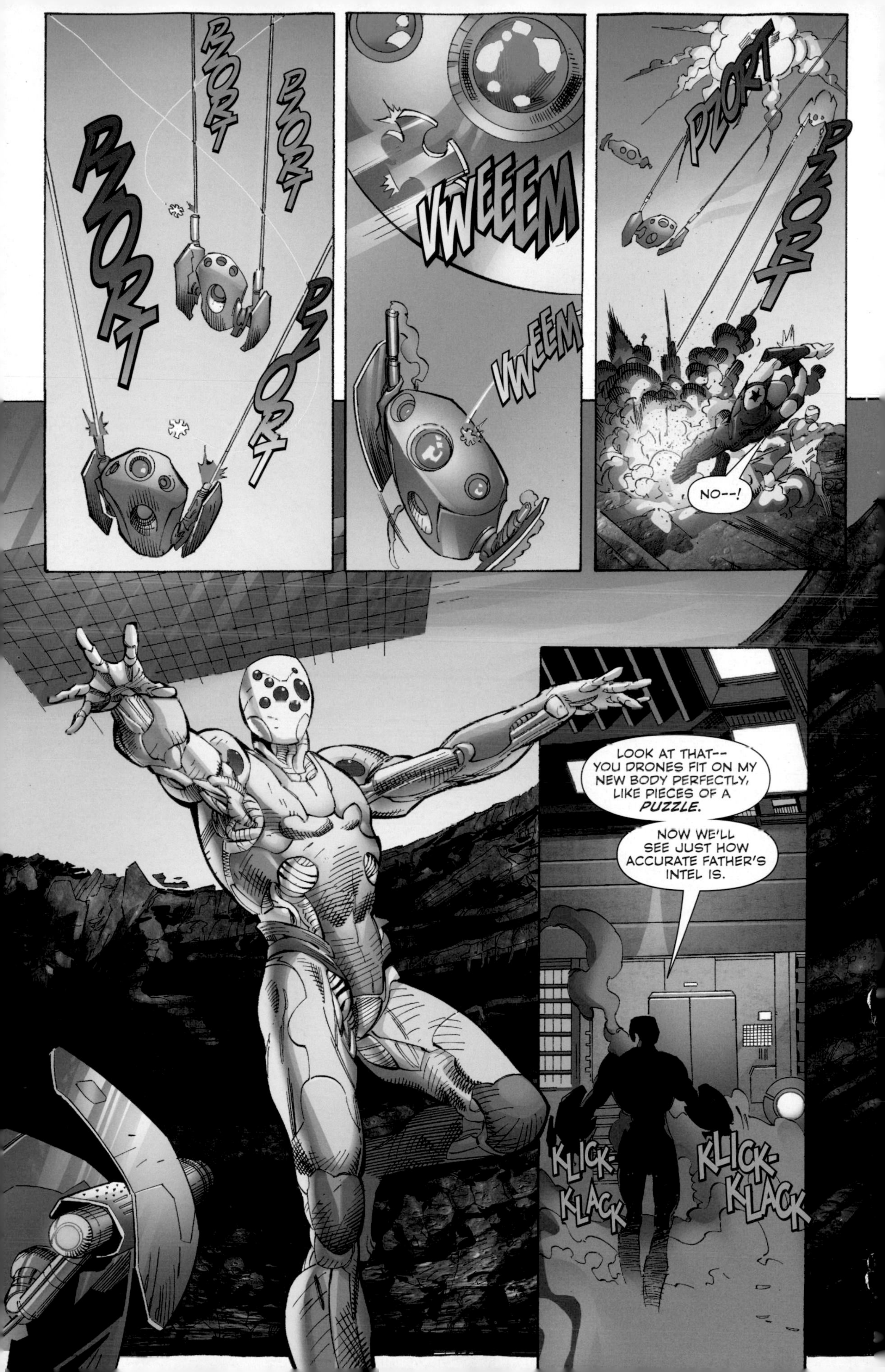
PZORT
PZORT
PZORT
PZORT
VWEEEM
VWEEM
PZORT
PZORT
NO--!
LOOK AT THAT-- YOU DRONES FIT ON MY NEW BODY PERFECTLY, LIKE PIECES OF A PUZZLE.
NOW WE'LL SEE JUST HOW ACCURATE FATHER'S INTEL IS.
KLICK-KLACK
KLICK-KLACK

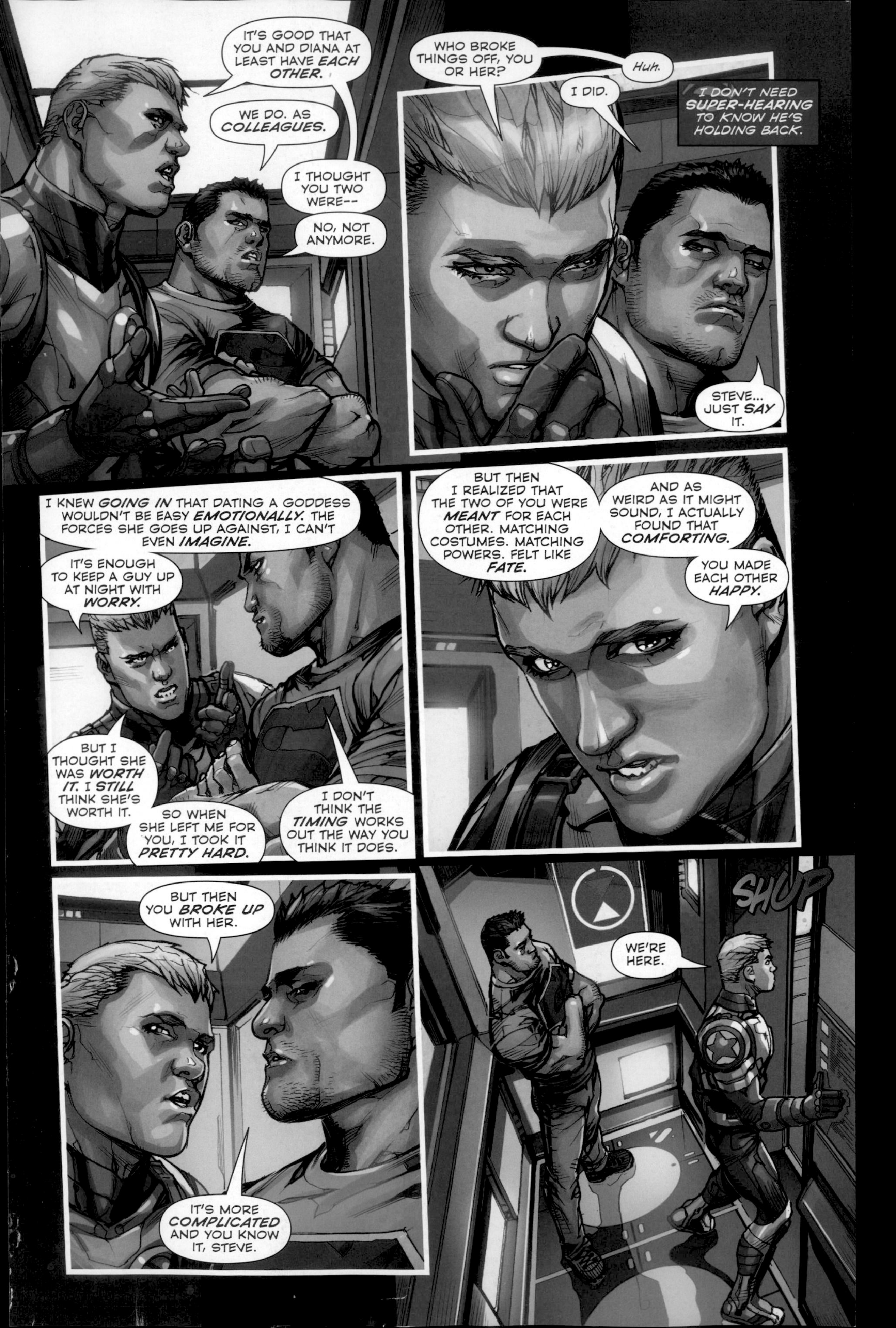
IT'S GOOD THAT YOU AND DIANA AT LEAST HAVE EACH OTHER.
WE DO. AS COLLEAGUES.
I THOUGHT YOU TWO WERE--
NO, NOT ANYMORE.
WHO BROKE THINGS OFF, YOU OR HER?
Huh.
I DID.
I DON'T NEED SUPER-HEARING TO KNOW HE'S HOLDING BACK.
STEVE... JUST SAY IT.
I KNEW GOING IN THAT DATING A GODDESS WOULDN'T BE EASY EMOTIONALLY. THE FORCES SHE GOES UP AGAINST, I CAN'T EVEN IMAGINE.
IT'S ENOUGH TO KEEP A GUY UP AT NIGHT WITH WORRY.
BUT I THOUGHT SHE WAS WORTH IT. I STILL THINK SHE'S WORTH IT.
SO WHEN SHE LEFT ME FOR YOU, I TOOK IT PRETTY HARD.
I DON'T THINK THE TIMING WORKS OUT THE WAY YOU THINK IT DOES.
BUT THEN I REALIZED THAT THE TWO OF YOU WERE MEANT FOR EACH OTHER. MATCHING COSTUMES. MATCHING POWERS. FELT LIKE FATE.
AND AS WEIRD AS IT MIGHT SOUND, I ACTUALLY FOUND THAT COMFORTING.
YOU MADE EACH OTHER HAPPY.
BUT THEN YOU BROKE UP WITH HER.
IT'S MORE COMPLICATED AND YOU KNOW IT, STEVE.
SHUP
WE'RE HERE.

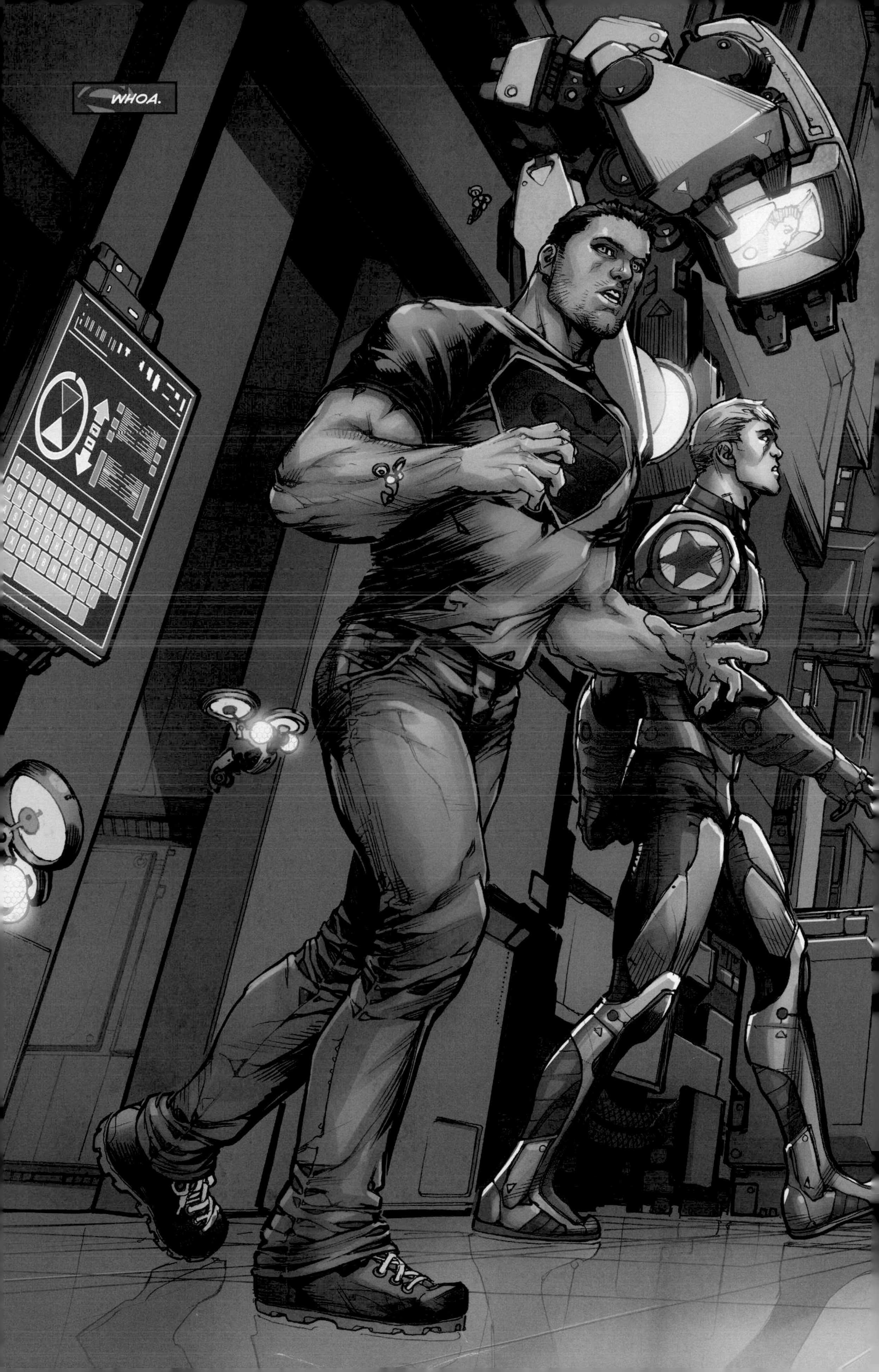
WHOA.

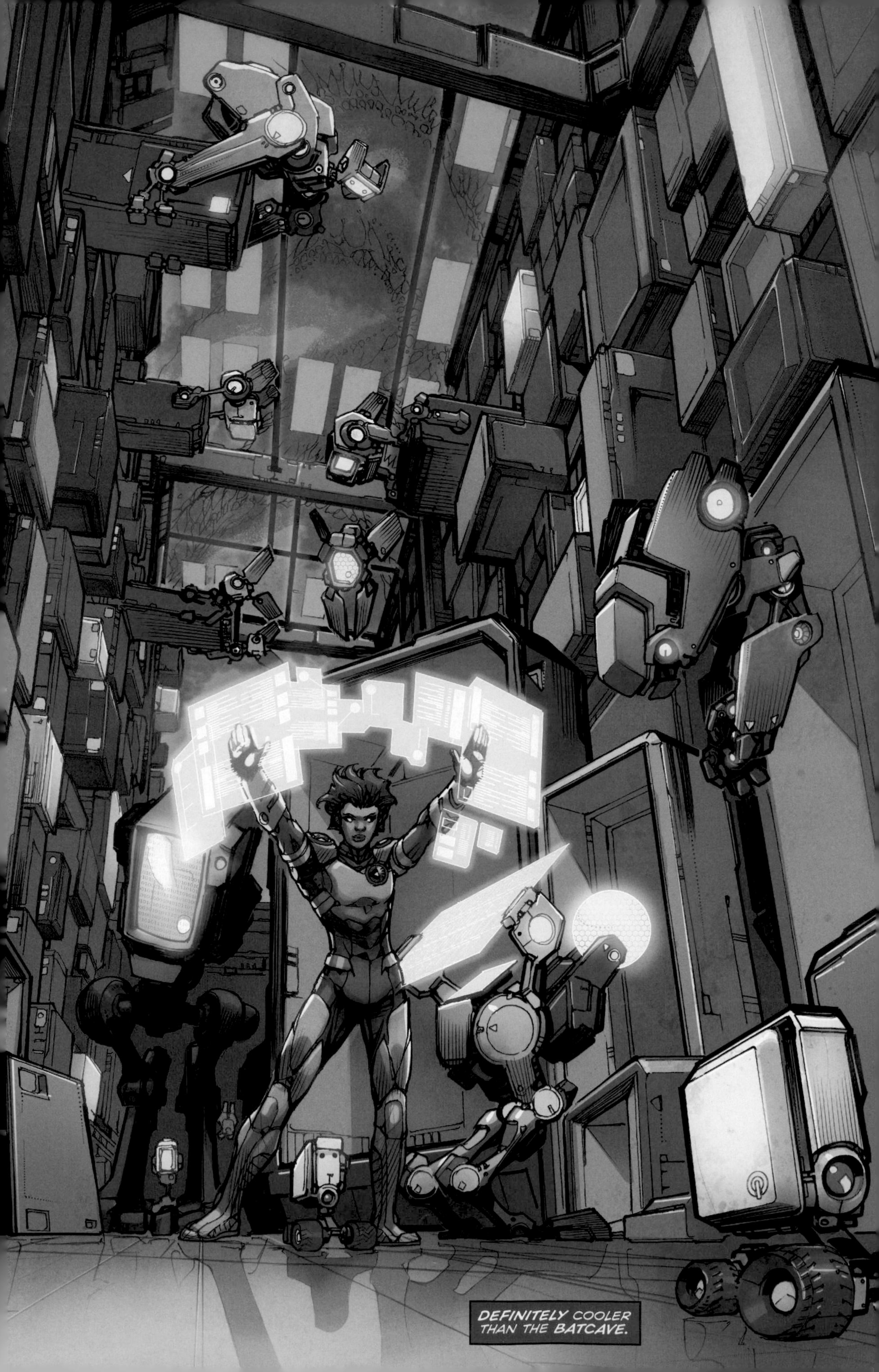
DEFINITELY COOLER THAN THE BATCAVE.

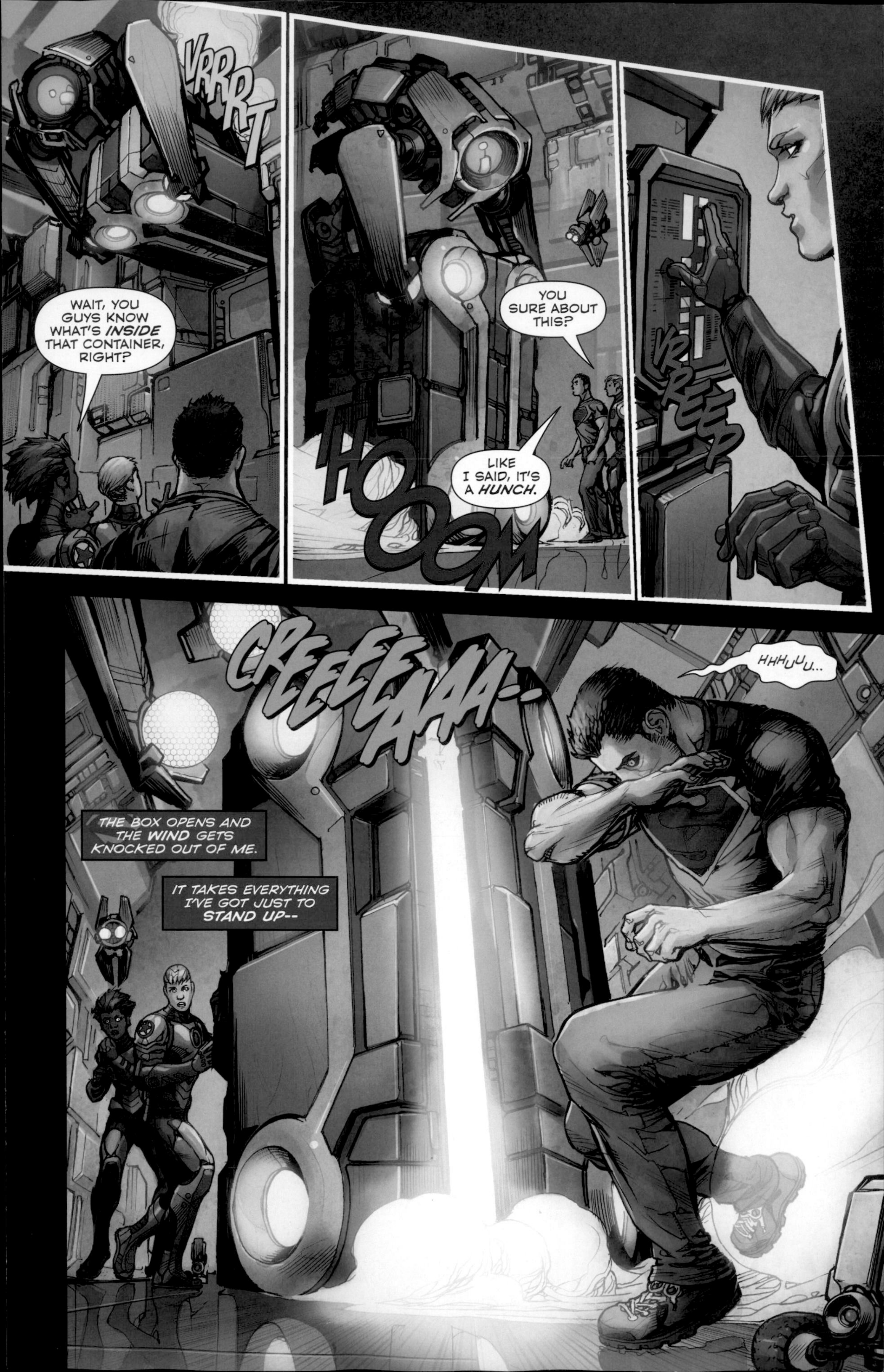
VRRRT
WAIT, YOU GUYS KNOW WHAT'S *INSIDE* THAT CONTAINER, RIGHT?
YOU SURE ABOUT THIS?
LIKE I SAID, IT'S A *HUNCH.*
THOOOOM
VRREEP
CREEEEAAAA--
HHHUUU...
THE BOX OPENS AND THE **WIND** GETS KNOCKED OUT OF ME.
IT TAKES EVERYTHING I'VE GOT JUST TO **STAND UP--**

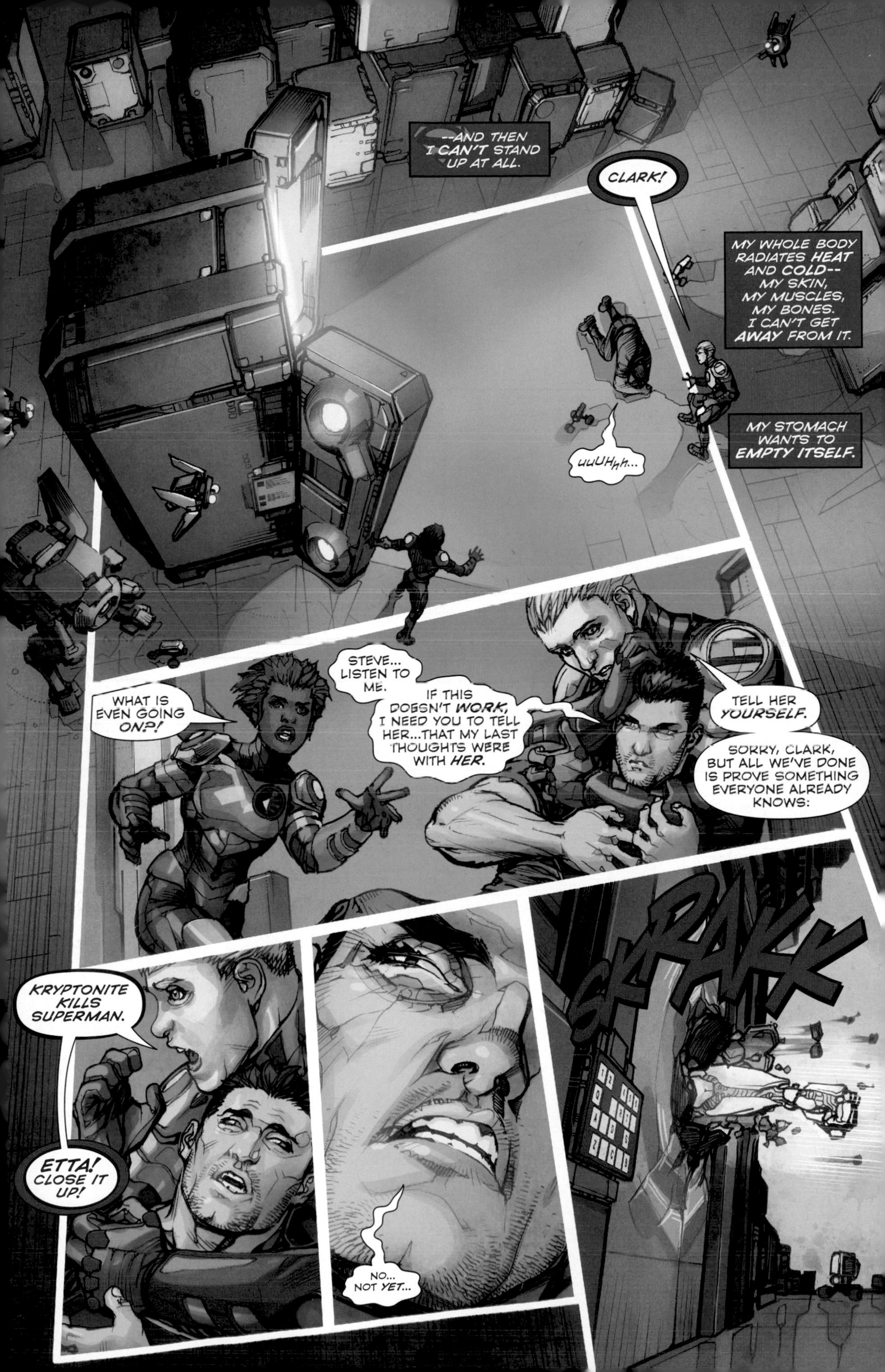

--AND THEN I CAN'T STAND UP AT ALL.
CLARK!
MY WHOLE BODY RADIATES HEAT AND COLD-- MY SKIN, MY MUSCLES, MY BONES. I CAN'T GET AWAY FROM IT.
uuUHhh...
MY STOMACH WANTS TO EMPTY ITSELF.
WHAT IS EVEN GOING ON?!
STEVE... LISTEN TO ME.
IF THIS DOESN'T WORK, I NEED YOU TO TELL HER...THAT MY LAST THOUGHTS WERE WITH HER.
TELL HER YOURSELF.
SORRY, CLARK, BUT ALL WE'VE DONE IS PROVE SOMETHING EVERYONE ALREADY KNOWS:
KRYPTONITE KILLS SUPERMAN.
ETTA! CLOSE IT UP!
NO... NOT YET...
SKRAKK

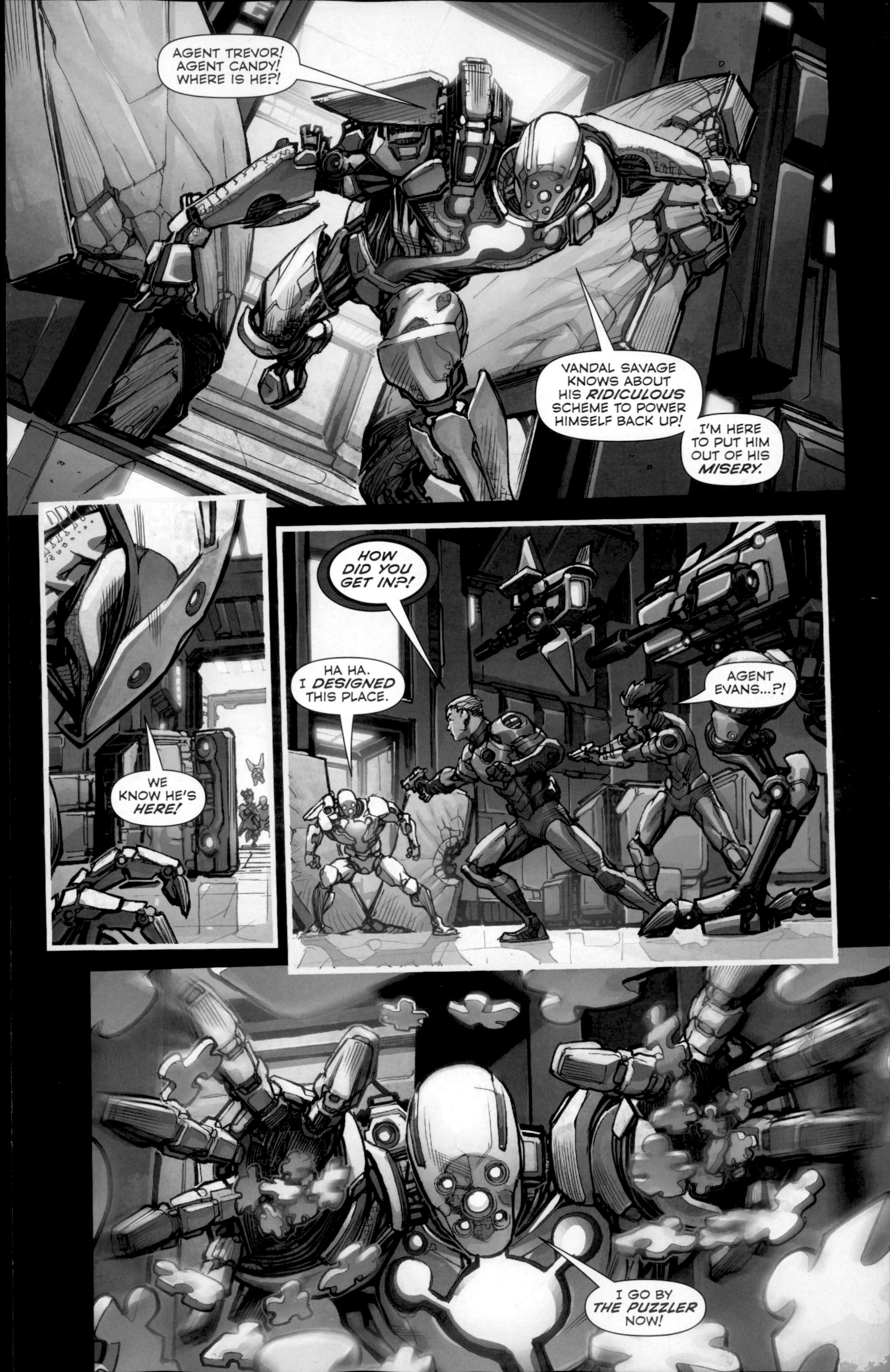
AGENT TREVOR! AGENT CANDY! WHERE IS HE?!
VANDAL SAVAGE KNOWS ABOUT HIS *RIDICULOUS* SCHEME TO POWER HIMSELF BACK UP!
I'M HERE TO PUT HIM OUT OF HIS *MISERY*.
WE KNOW HE'S *HERE!*
HOW DID YOU GET IN?!
HA HA. I *DESIGNED* THIS PLACE.
AGENT EVANS...?!
I GO BY *THE PUZZLER* NOW!

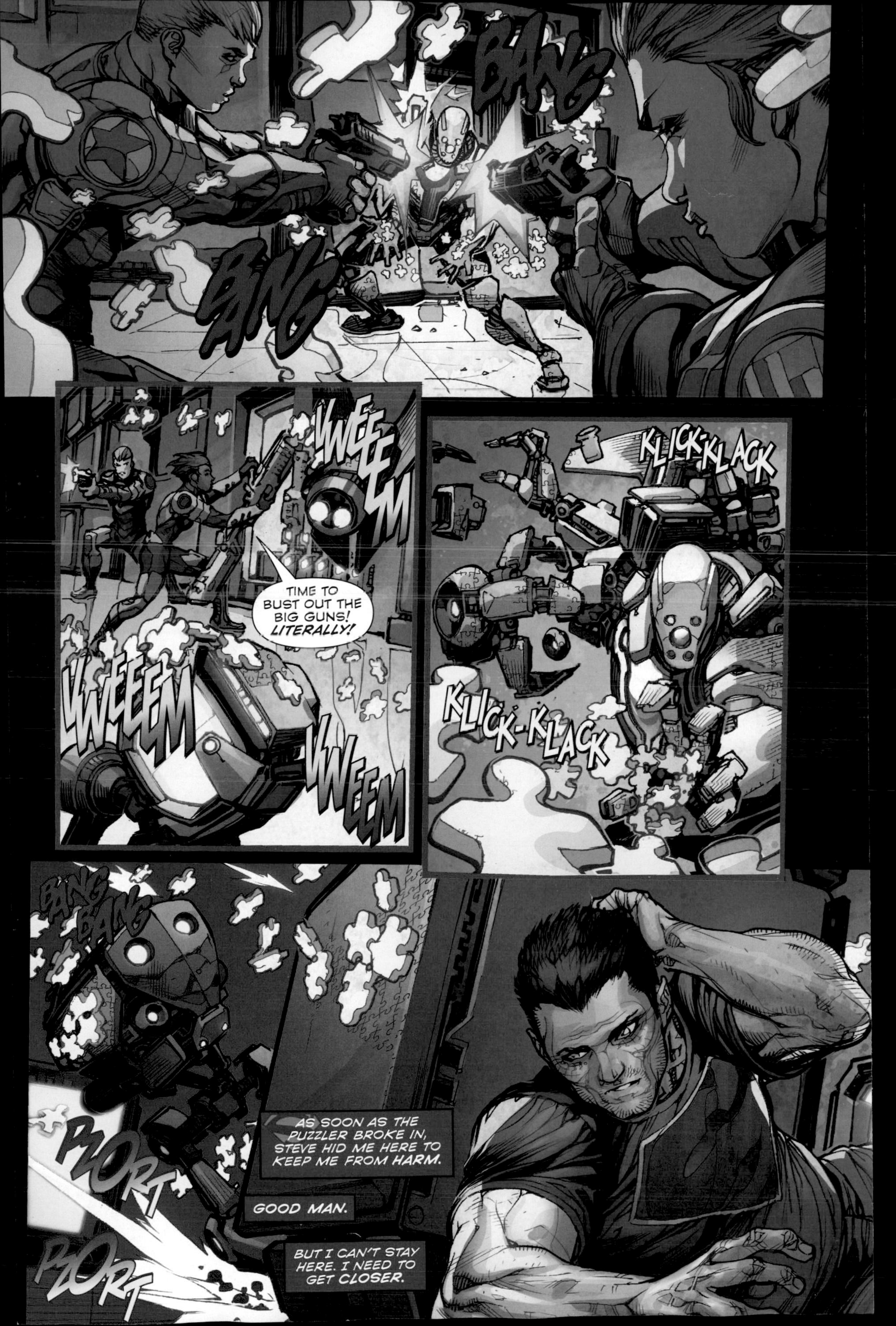
BANG
BANG
VWEEEM
TIME TO BUST OUT THE BIG GUNS! LITERALLY!
VWEEEM
VWEEM
KLICK-KLACK
KLICK-KLACK
BANG BANG
PLORT
PLORT
AS SOON AS THE PUZZLER BROKE IN, STEVE HID ME HERE TO KEEP ME FROM HARM.
GOOD MAN.
BUT I CAN'T STAY HERE. I NEED TO GET CLOSER.

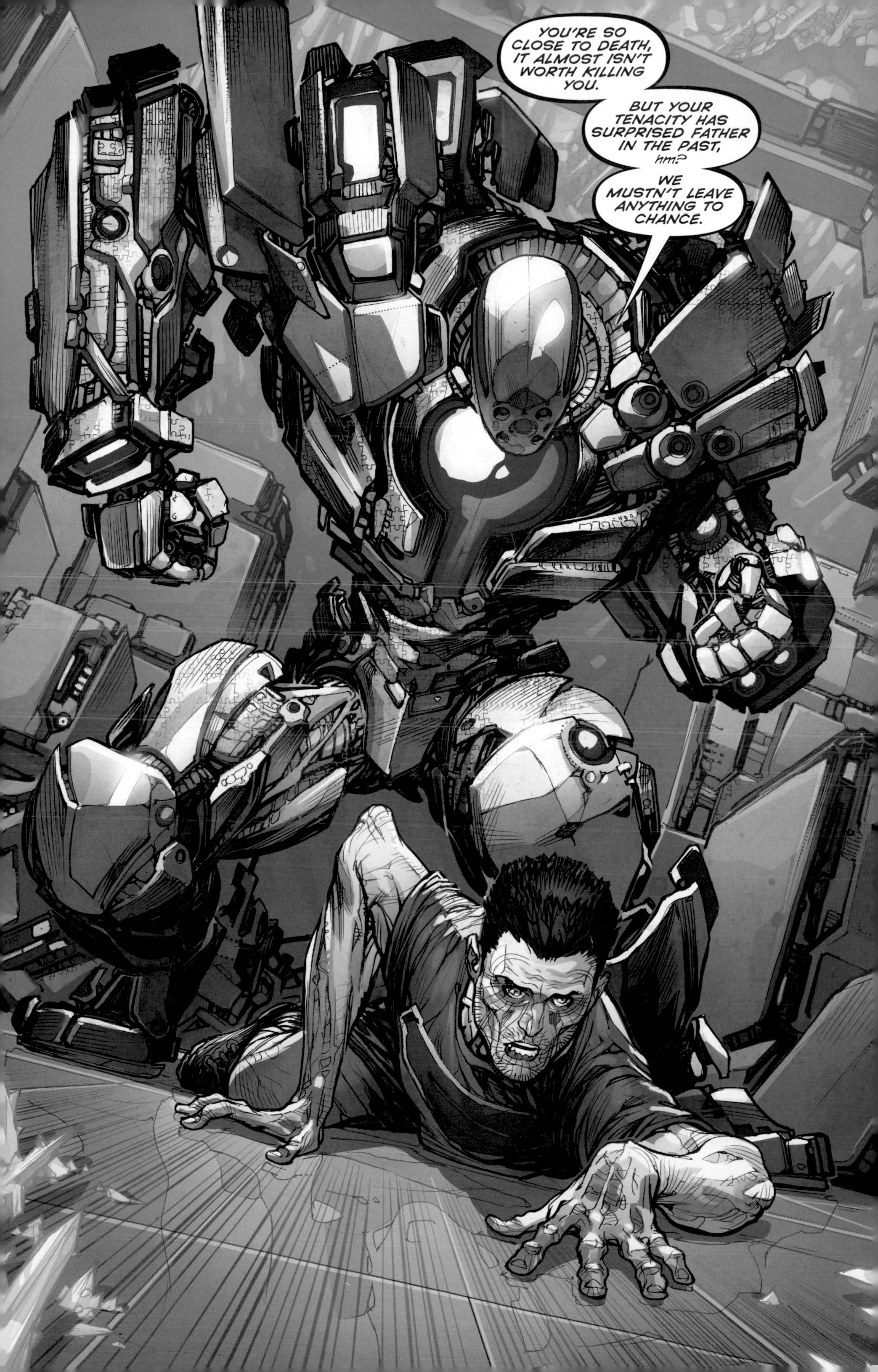
YOU'RE SO CLOSE TO DEATH, IT ALMOST ISN'T WORTH KILLING YOU.
BUT YOUR TENACITY HAS SURPRISED FATHER IN THE PAST, hm?
WE MUSTN'T LEAVE ANYTHING TO CHANCE.

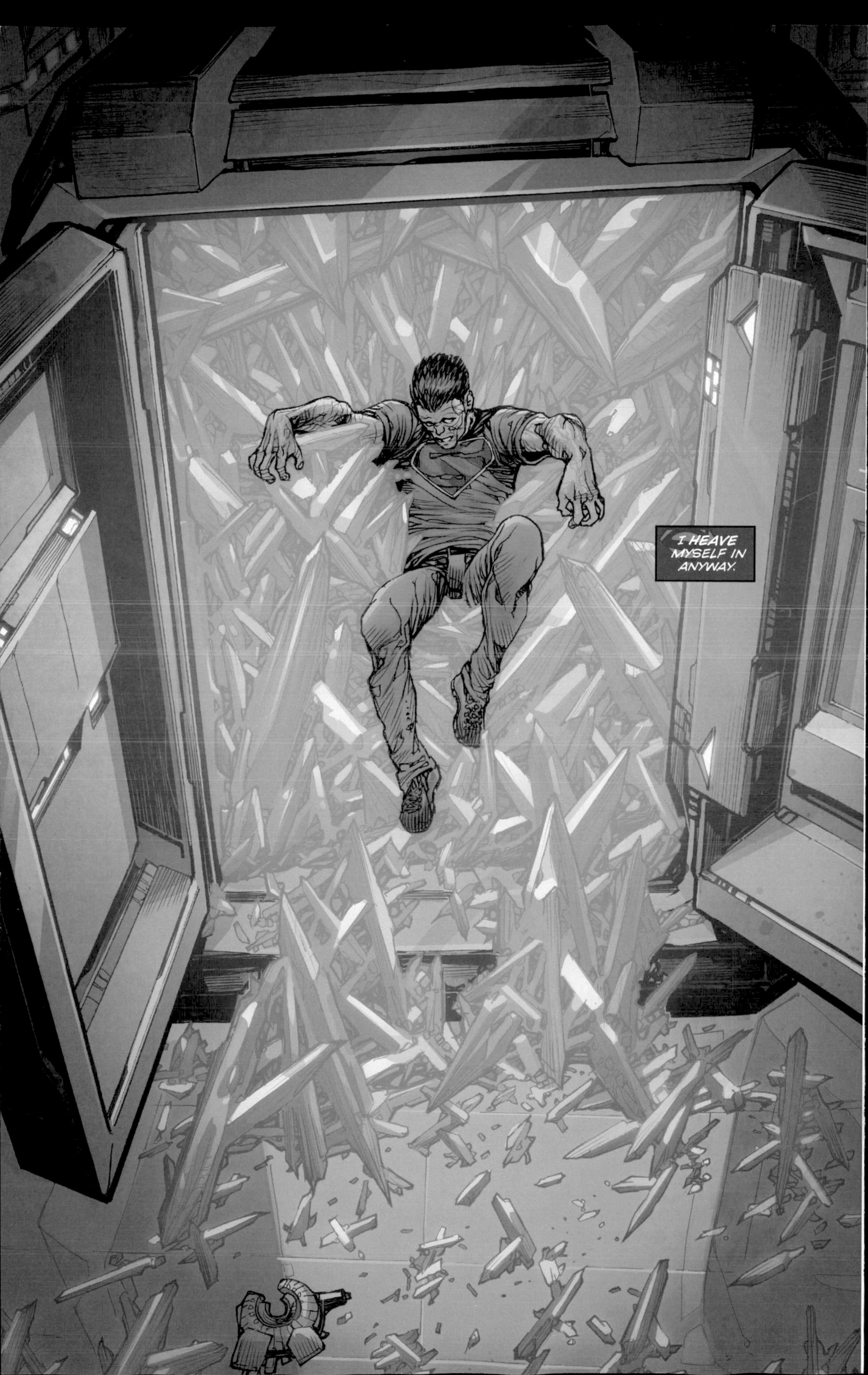
I HEAVE MYSELF IN ANYWAY.

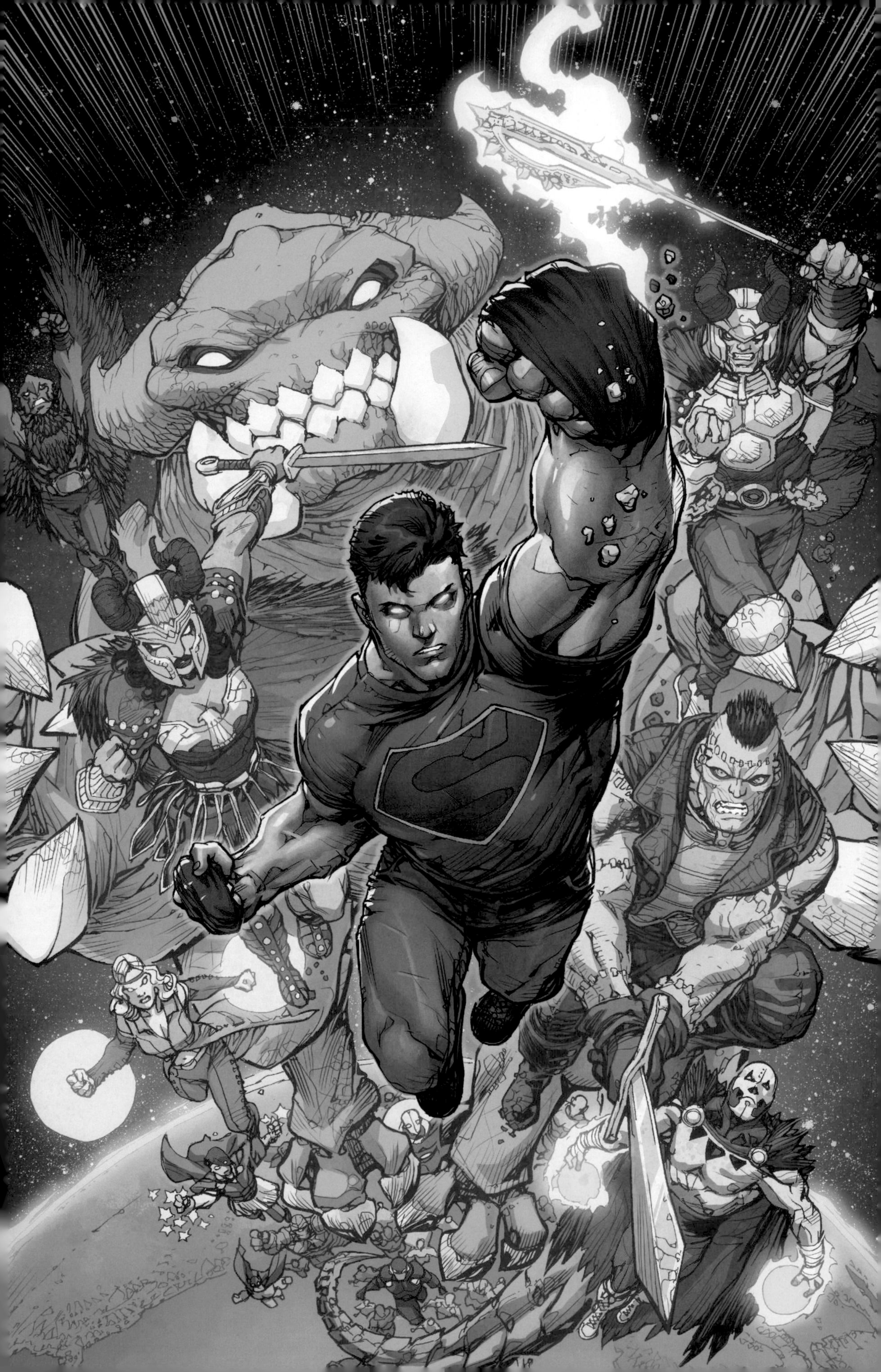

SACRIFICE
GENE LUEN YANG writer JACK HERBERT artist HI-FI, BLOND colorists STEVE WANDS letterer HOWARD PORTER, HI-FI cover

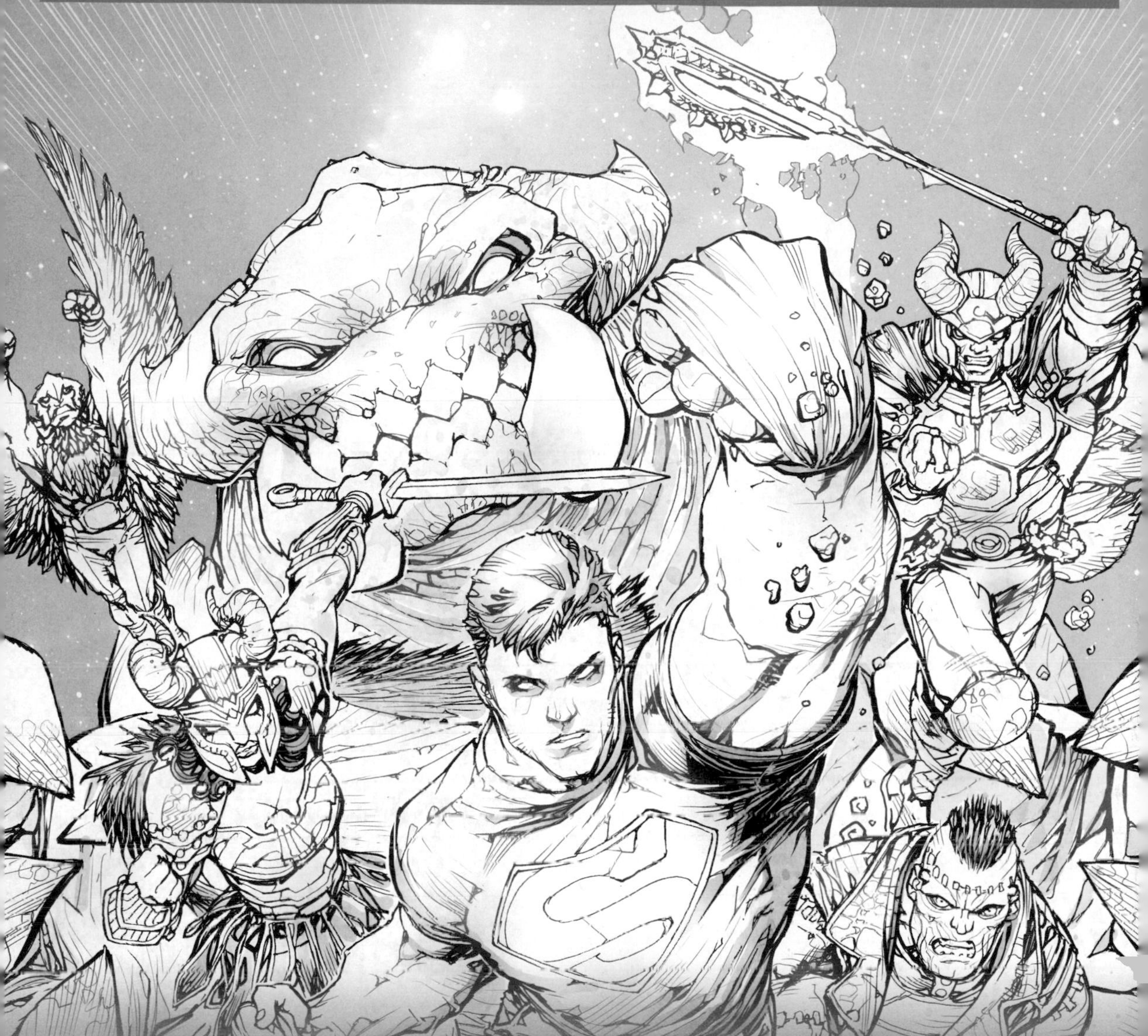

Previously, in SUPERMAN: SAVAGE DAWN ...

Heaving himself into a chamber of Kryptonite within the A.R.G.U.S. Archives, Superman's dangerous gamble pays off – sort of. The Kryptonite, while killing off his healthy cells, re-powers the Man of Steel in unpredictable ways and enables him to defeat the Puzzlerbot attacking A.R.G.U.S.

Joining Wonder Woman for a dual assault against Vandal Savage, Superman is instead distracted by the first of Savage's Black Mist-saturated "offspring": a young boy-turned-maddened behemoth called Salvaxe. The diversion proves costly, allowing Savage to realign Jupiter's moons and merge the Man of Steel's Fortress of Solitude with the already-fused Justice League Watchtower and Stormwatch Carrier.

As Wonder Woman rejoins Superman to aid him against more of Savage's super-powered progeny, the three structures, completely aligned and charged at maximum strength, create a tractor beam strong enough to draw toward Earth the comet that first granted Savage his immortality. The effort also nearly brings the bonded base down on Metropolis, until Superman makes a supreme effort to push it just outside the city – and unfortunately, right on top of him...

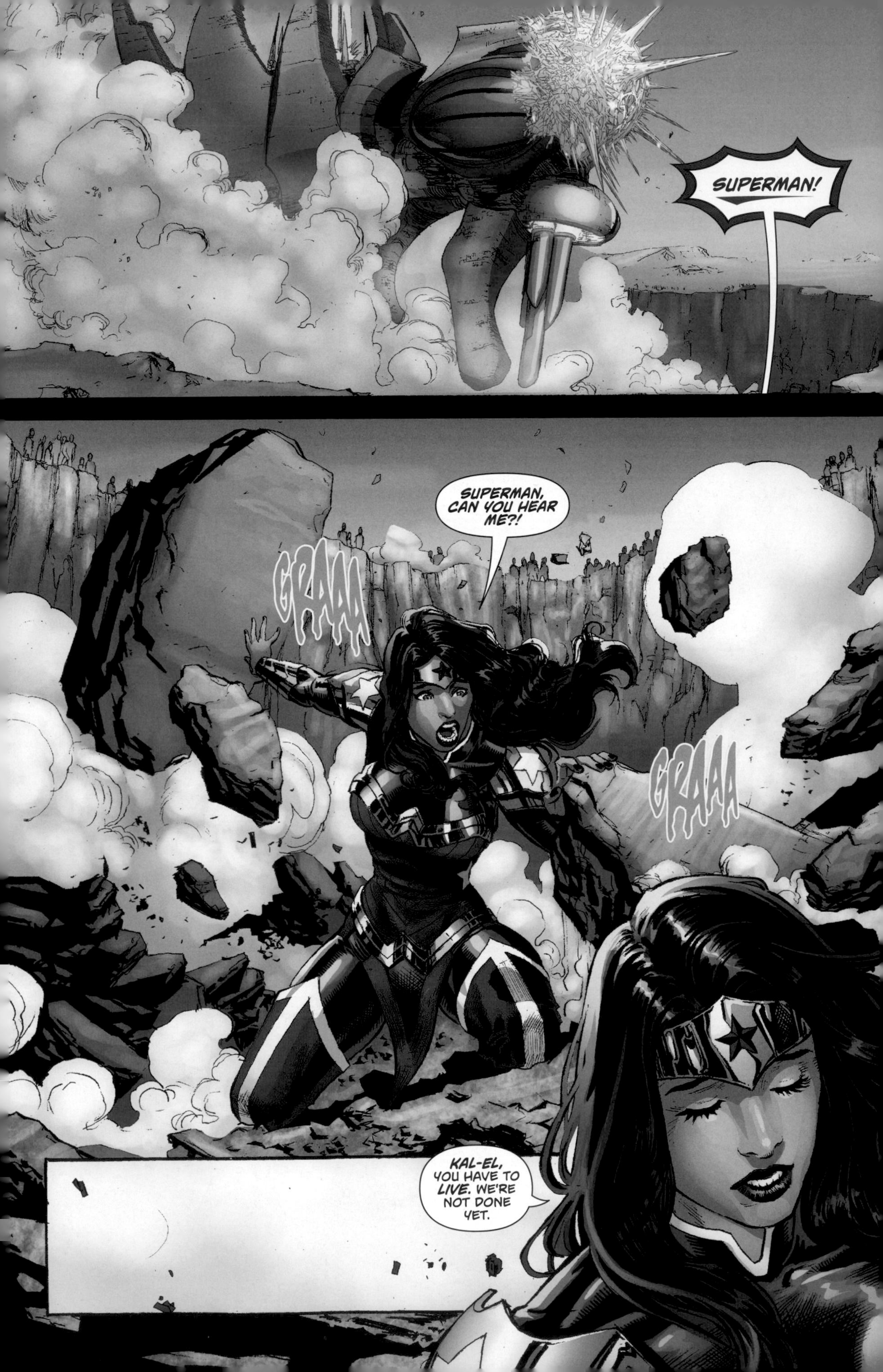
SUPERMAN!
SUPERMAN, CAN YOU HEAR ME?!
GRAAA
GRAAA
KAL-EL, YOU HAVE TO LIVE. WE'RE NOT DONE YET.

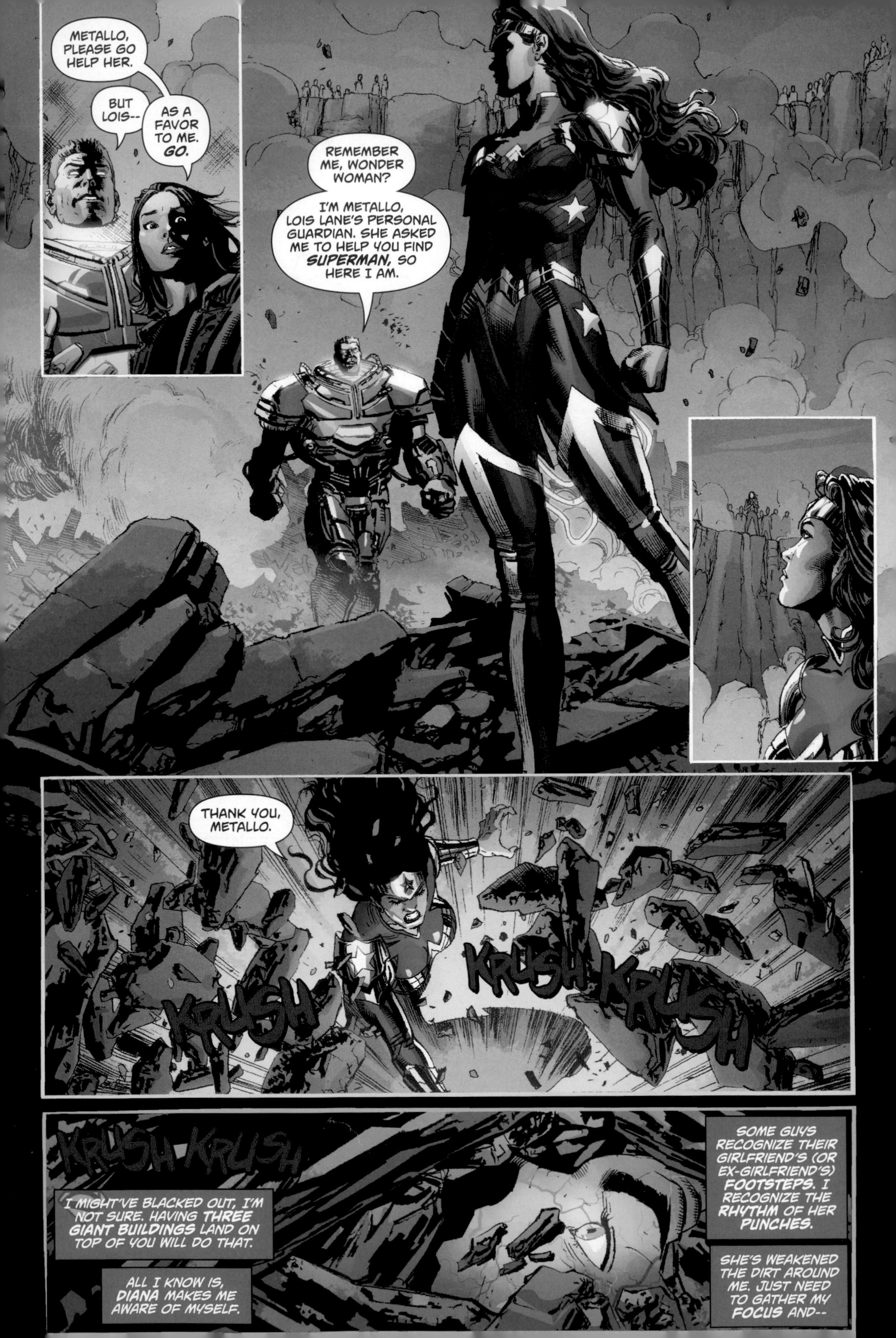
METALLO, PLEASE GO HELP HER.
BUT LOIS--
AS A FAVOR TO ME. GO.
REMEMBER ME, WONDER WOMAN?
I'M METALLO, LOIS LANE'S PERSONAL GUARDIAN. SHE ASKED ME TO HELP YOU FIND SUPERMAN, SO HERE I AM.
THANK YOU, METALLO.
KRUSH
KRUSH KRUSH
KRUSH KRUSH
I MIGHT'VE BLACKED OUT, I'M NOT SURE. HAVING THREE GIANT BUILDINGS LAND ON TOP OF YOU WILL DO THAT.
ALL I KNOW IS, DIANA MAKES ME AWARE OF MYSELF.
SOME GUYS RECOGNIZE THEIR GIRLFRIEND'S (OR EX-GIRLFRIEND'S) FOOTSTEPS. I RECOGNIZE THE RHYTHM OF HER PUNCHES.
SHE'S WEAKENED THE DIRT AROUND ME. JUST NEED TO GATHER MY FOCUS AND--

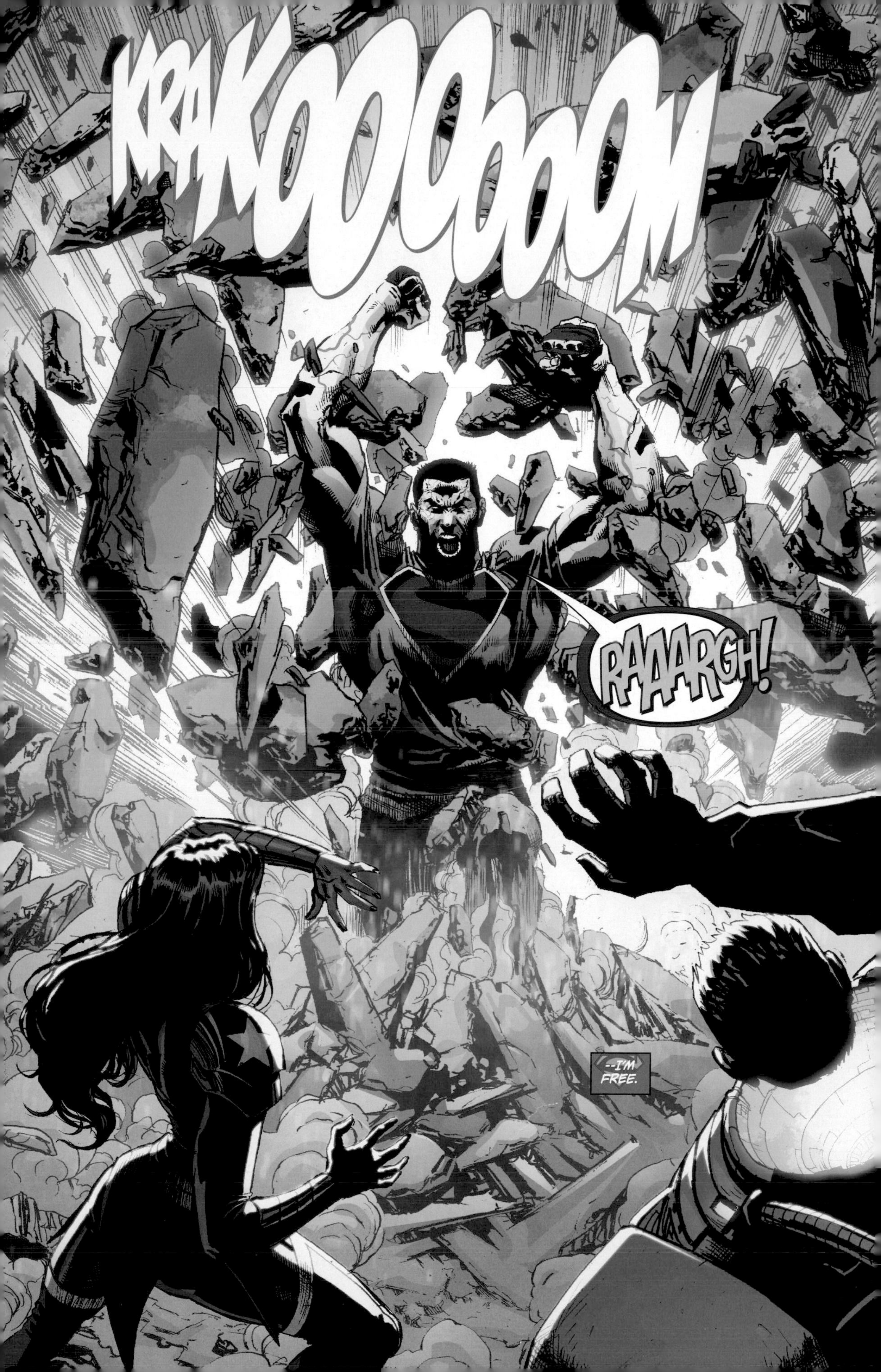
KRAKOOOOOOM
RAAARGH!
--I'M FREE.

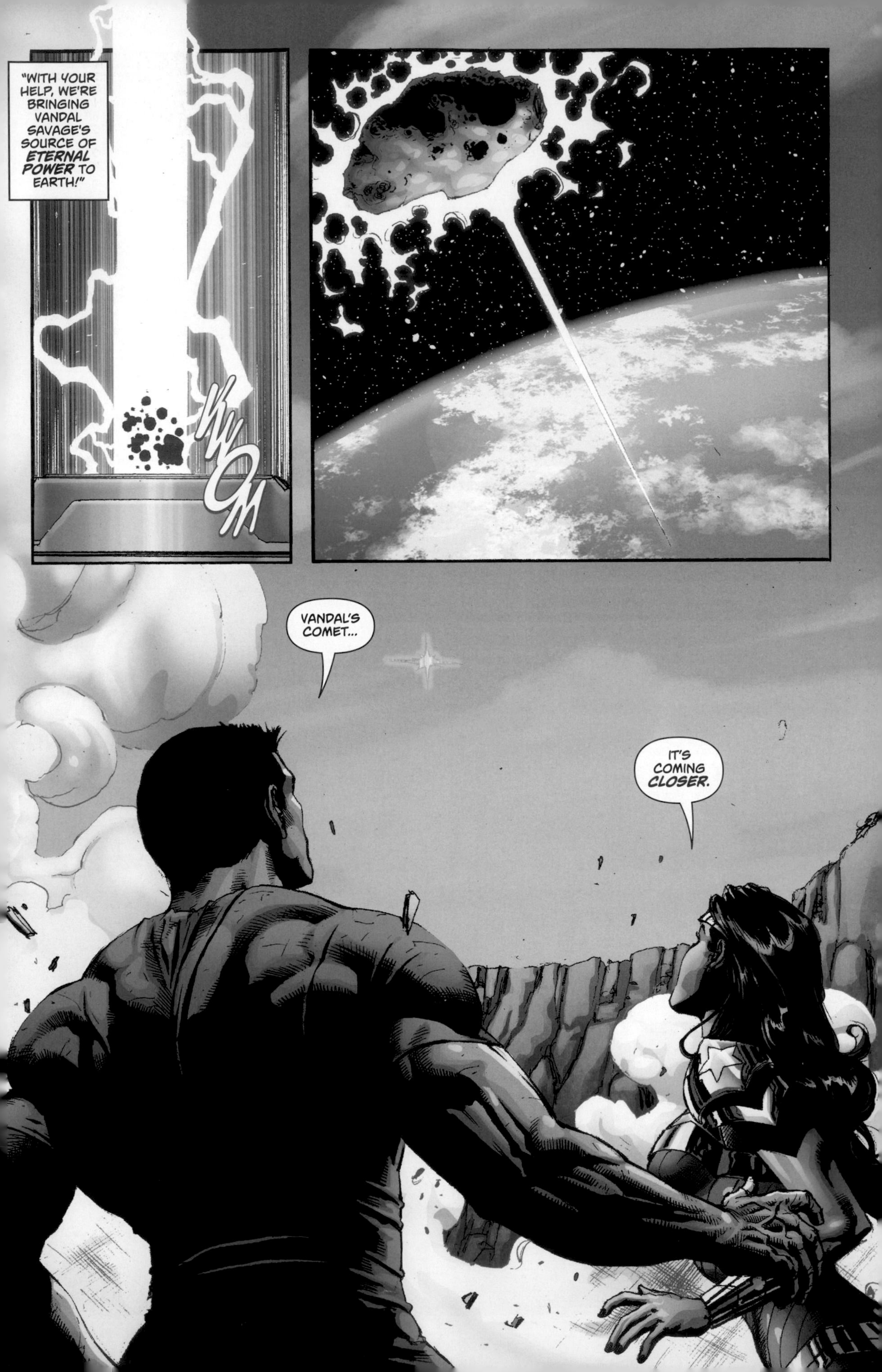
"WITH YOUR HELP, WE'RE BRINGING VANDAL SAVAGE'S SOURCE OF ETERNAL POWER TO EARTH!"
KWOM
VANDAL'S COMET...
IT'S COMING CLOSER.

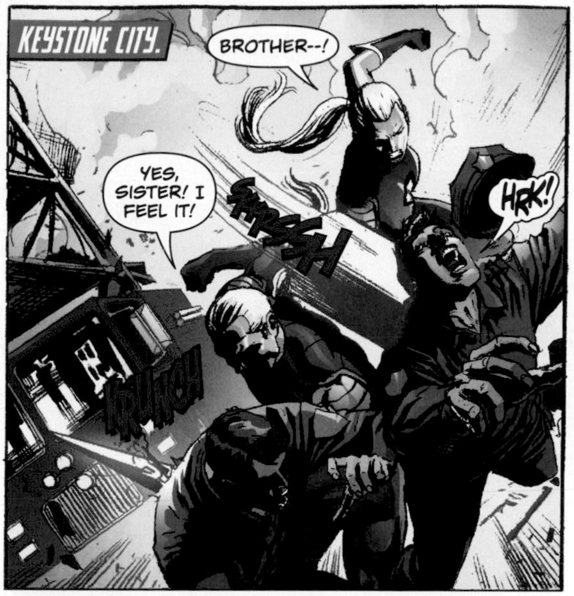
KEYSTONE CITY.
BROTHER--!
YES, SISTER! I FEEL IT!
HRK!

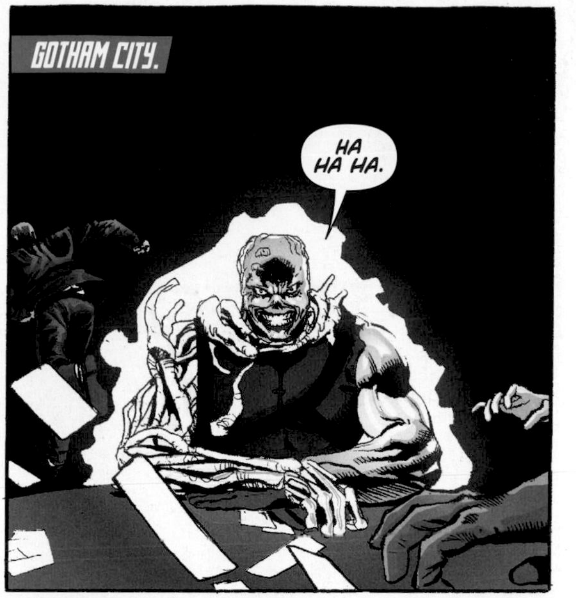
GOTHAM CITY.
HA HA HA.

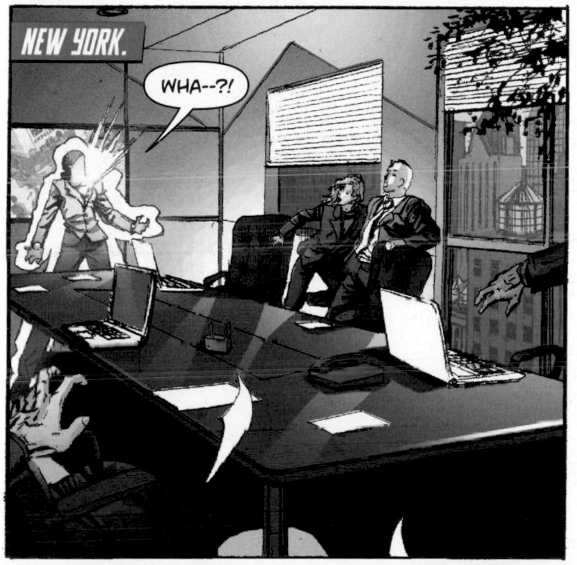
NEW YORK.
WHA--?!

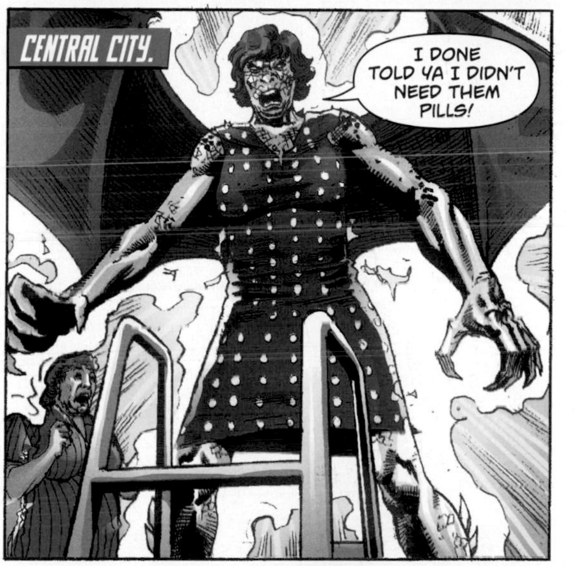
CENTRAL CITY.
I DONE TOLD YA I DIDN'T NEED THEM PILLS!

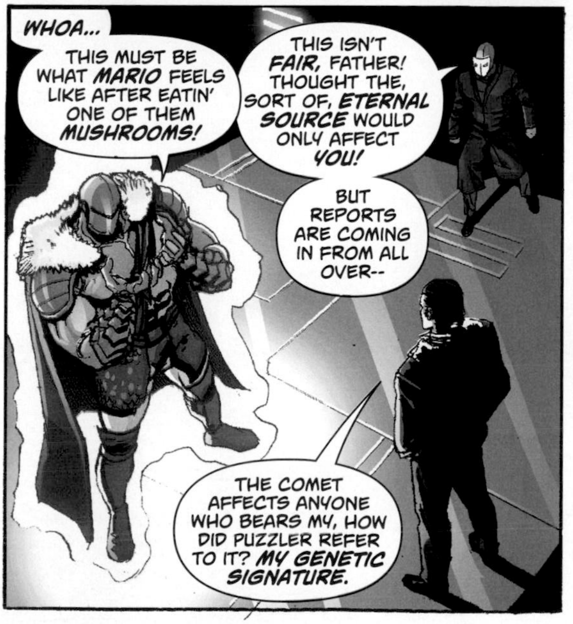
WHOA...
THIS MUST BE WHAT MARIO FEELS LIKE AFTER EATIN' ONE OF THEM MUSHROOMS!
THIS ISN'T FAIR, FATHER! THOUGHT THE, SORT OF, ETERNAL SOURCE WOULD ONLY AFFECT YOU!
BUT REPORTS ARE COMING IN FROM ALL OVER--
THE COMET AFFECTS ANYONE WHO BEARS MY, HOW DID PUZZLER REFER TO IT? MY GENETIC SIGNATURE.

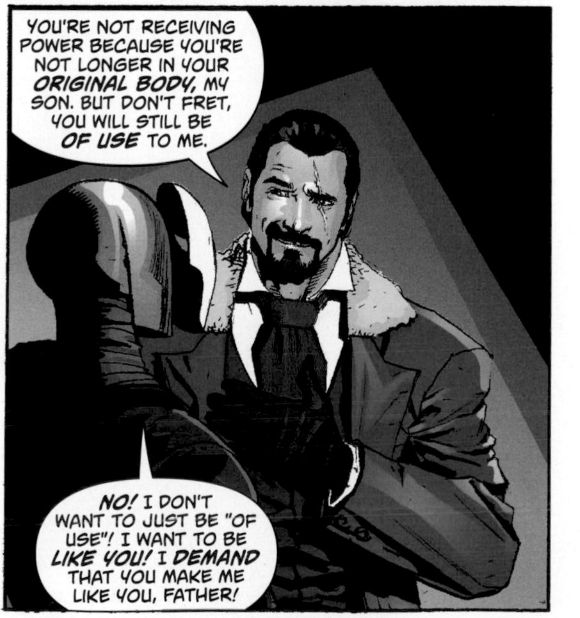
YOU'RE NOT RECEIVING POWER BECAUSE YOU'RE NOT LONGER IN YOUR ORIGINAL BODY, MY SON. BUT DON'T FRET, YOU WILL STILL BE OF USE TO ME.
NO! I DON'T WANT TO JUST BE "OF USE"! I WANT TO BE LIKE YOU! I DEMAND THAT YOU MAKE ME LIKE YOU, FATHER!

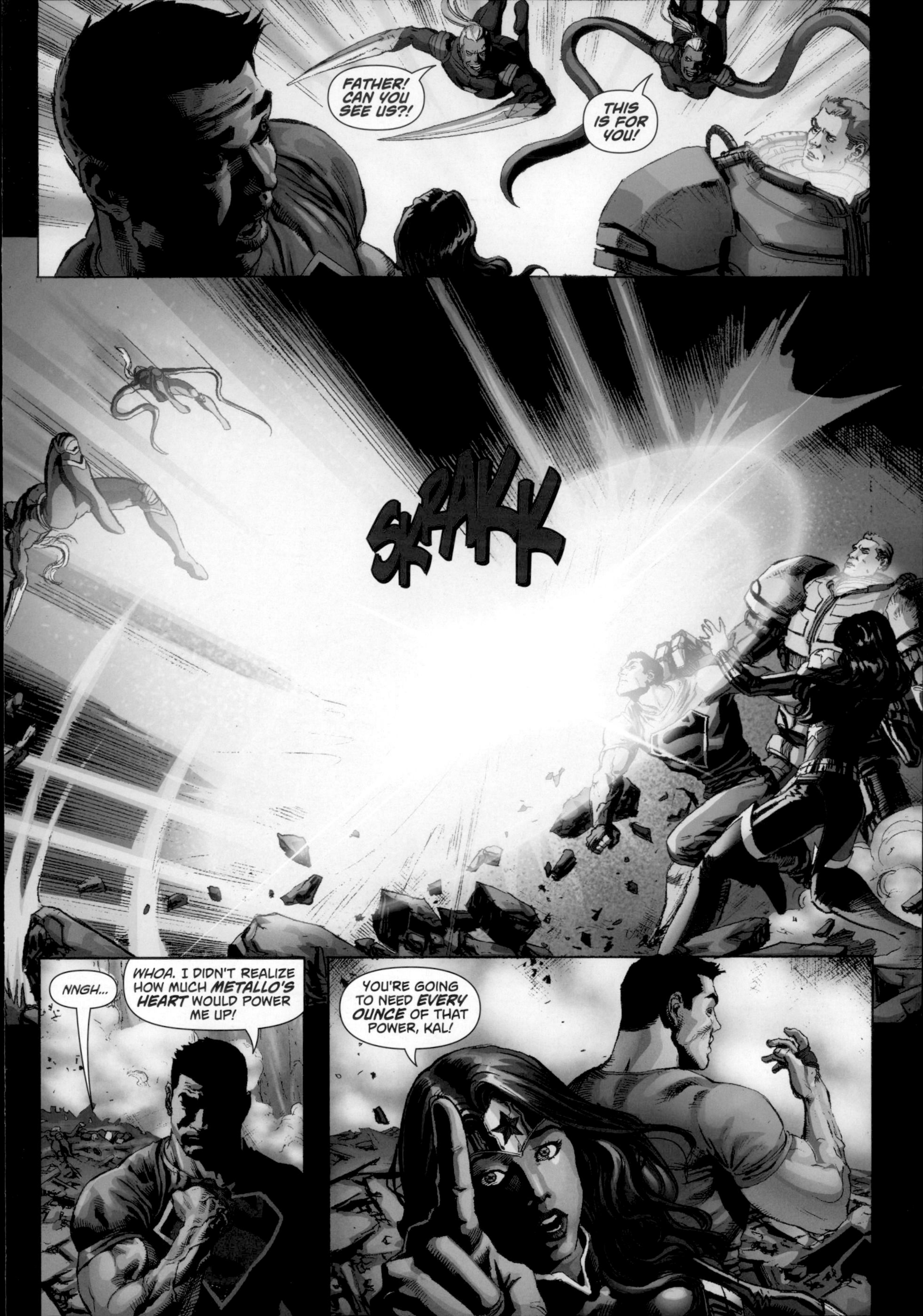
FATHER! CAN YOU SEE US?!
THIS IS FOR YOU!
SKRAKK
NNGH...
WHOA. I DIDN'T REALIZE HOW MUCH METALLO'S HEART WOULD POWER ME UP!
YOU'RE GOING TO NEED EVERY OUNCE OF THAT POWER, KAL!

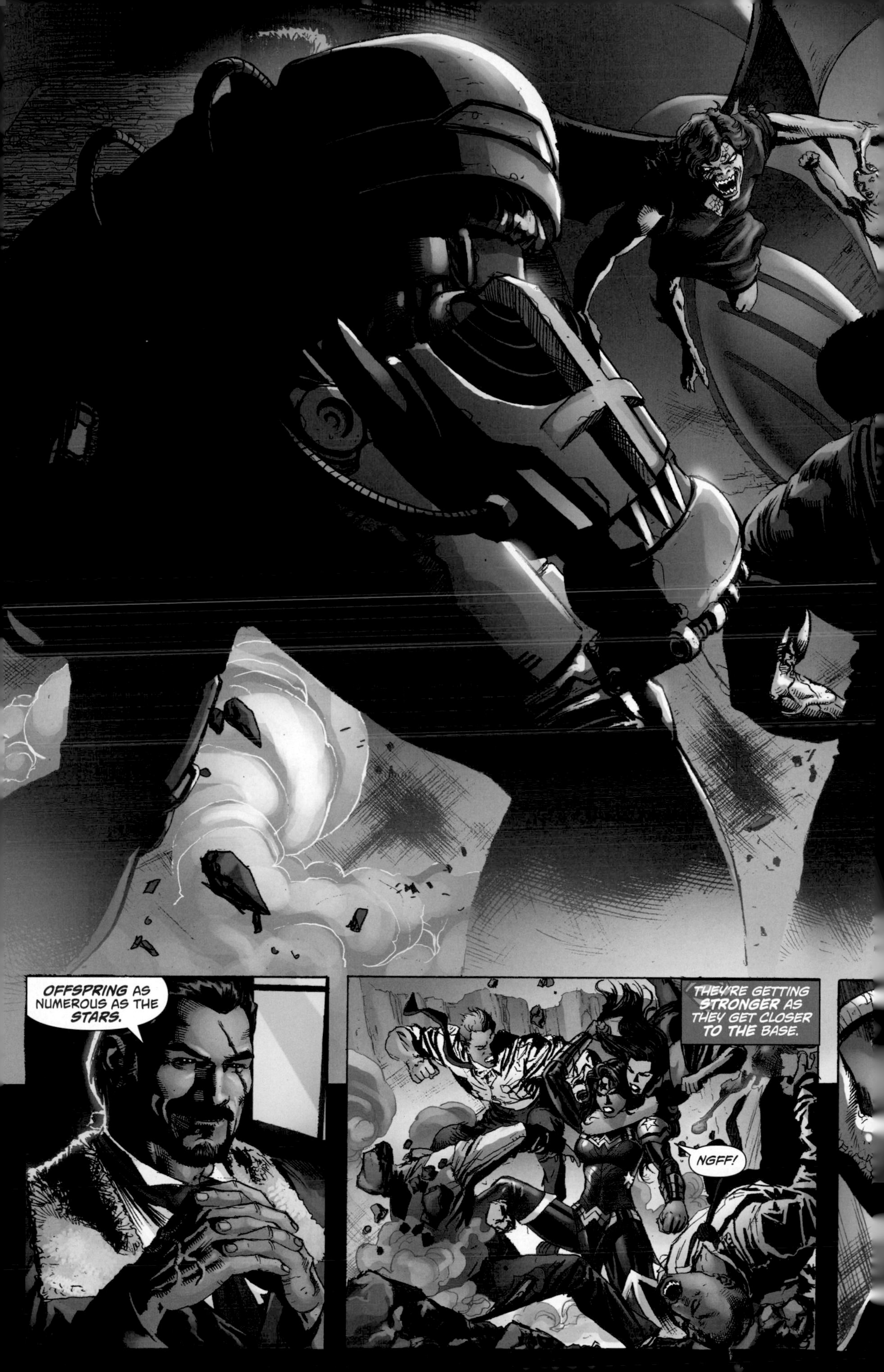
OFFSPRING AS NUMEROUS AS THE STARS.
THEY'RE GETTING STRONGER AS THEY GET CLOSER TO THE BASE.
NGFF!

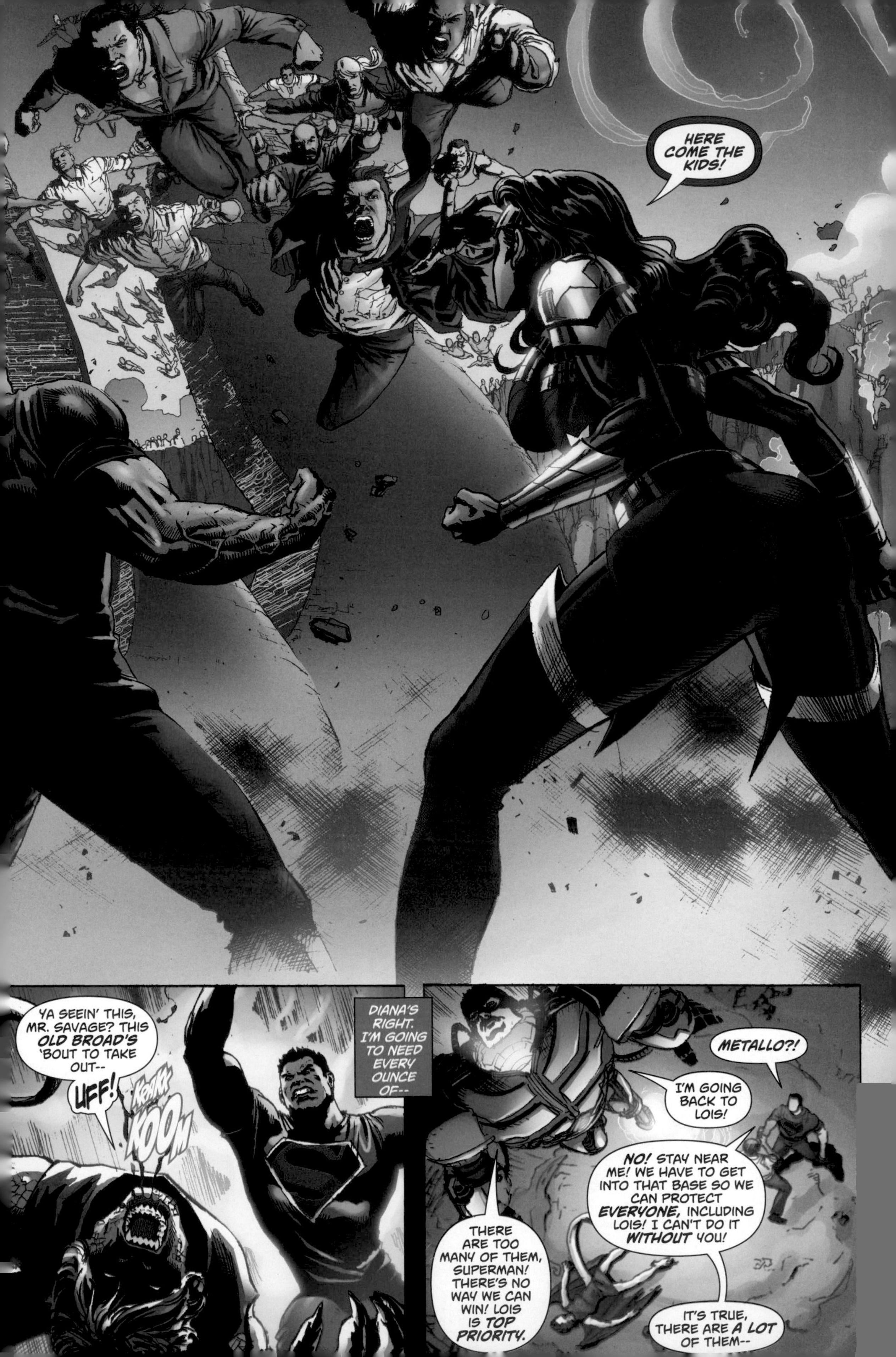
HERE COME THE KIDS!
YA SEEIN' THIS, MR. SAVAGE? THIS OLD BROAD'S 'BOUT TO TAKE OUT--
UFF!
KRAKK KOOM
DIANA'S RIGHT. I'M GOING TO NEED EVERY OUNCE OF--
METALLO?!
I'M GOING BACK TO LOIS!
NO! STAY NEAR ME! WE HAVE TO GET INTO THAT BASE SO WE CAN PROTECT EVERYONE, INCLUDING LOIS! I CAN'T DO IT WITHOUT YOU!
THERE ARE TOO MANY OF THEM, SUPERMAN! THERE'S NO WAY WE CAN WIN! LOIS IS TOP PRIORITY.
IT'S TRUE, THERE ARE A LOT OF THEM--

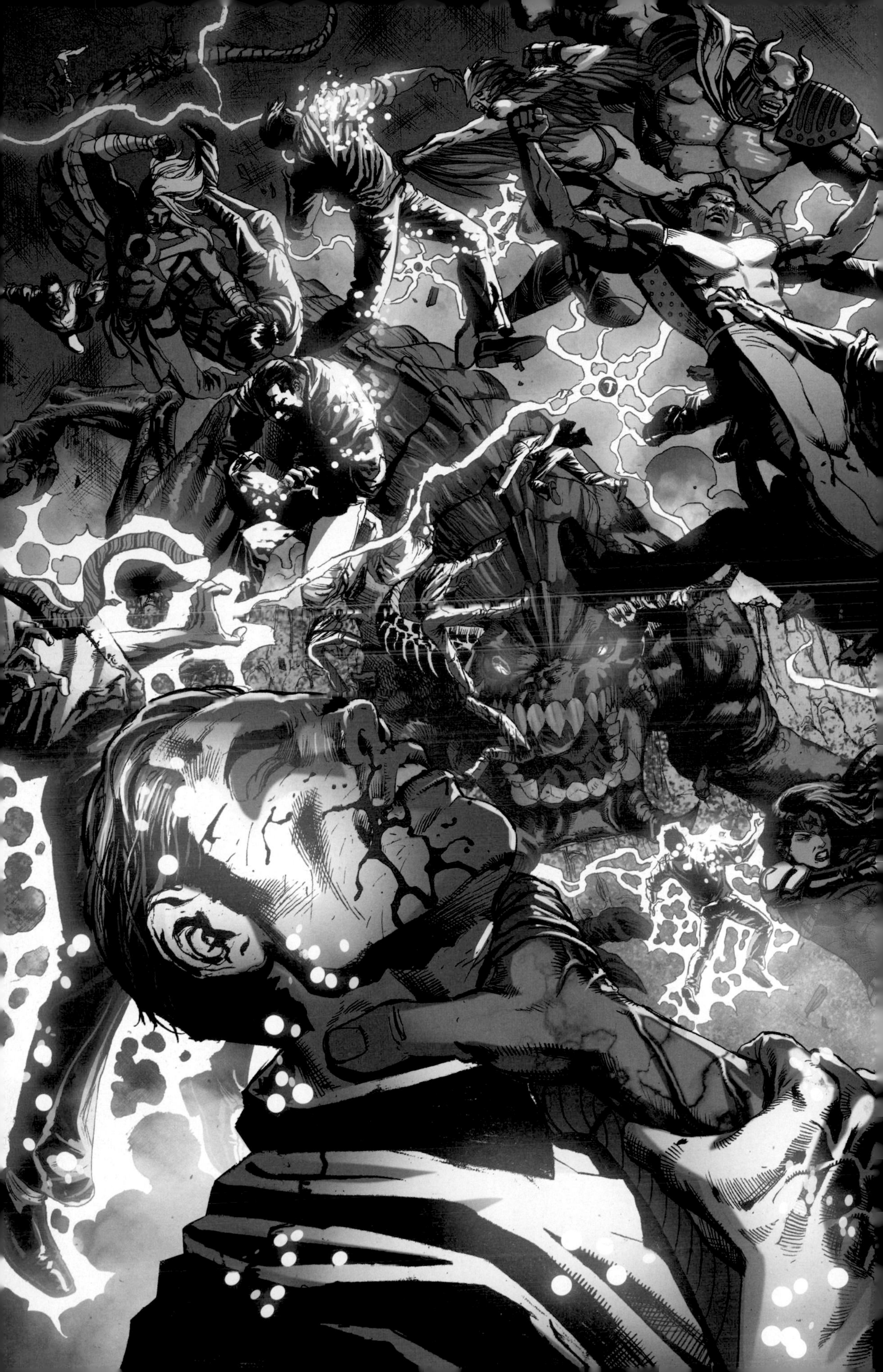

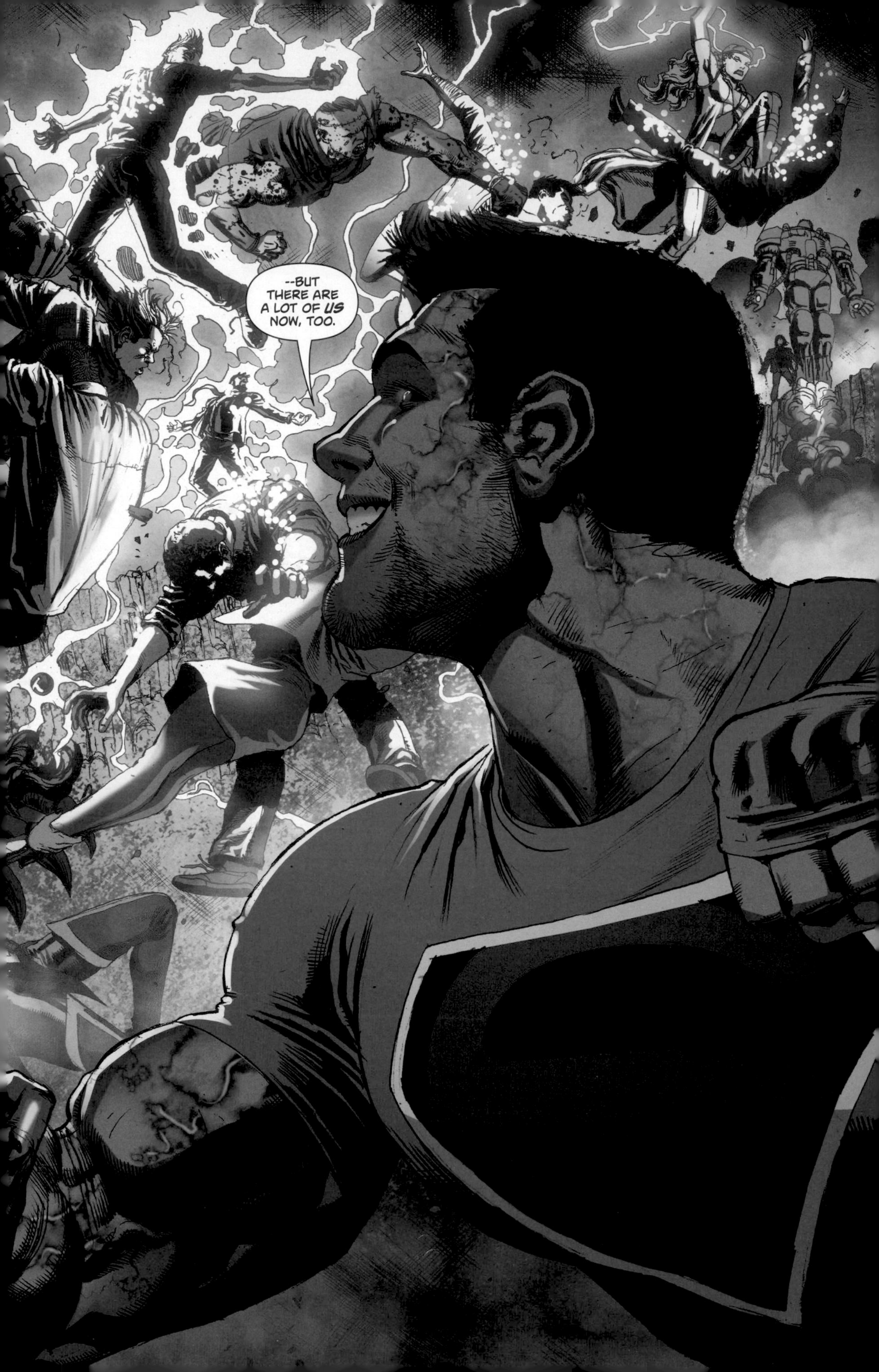
--BUT THERE ARE A LOT OF US NOW, TOO.

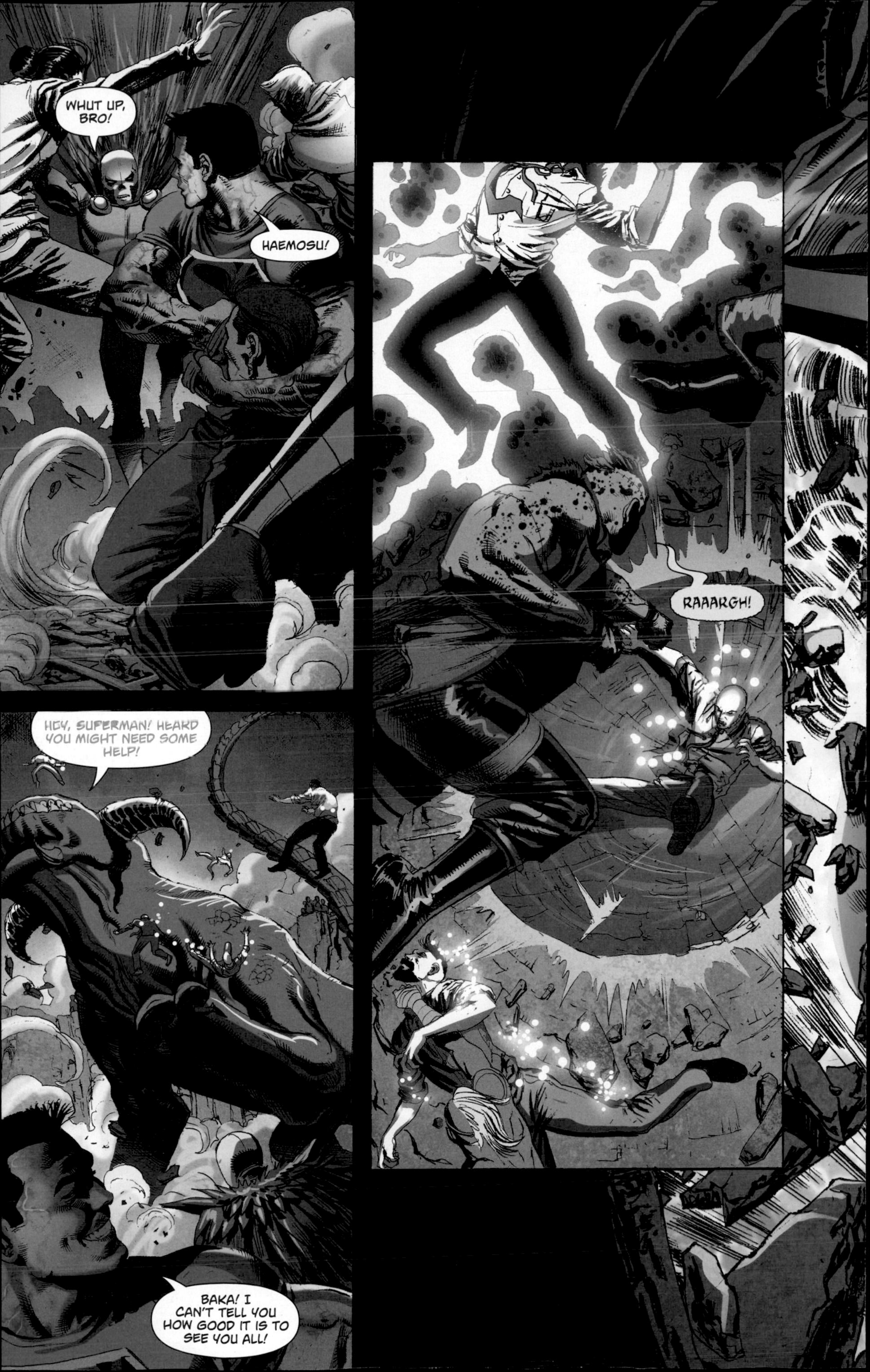
WHUT UP, BRO!
HAEMOSU!
RAAARGH!
HEY, SUPERMAN! HEARD YOU MIGHT NEED SOME HELP!
BAKA! I CAN'T TELL YOU HOW GOOD IT IS TO SEE YOU ALL!

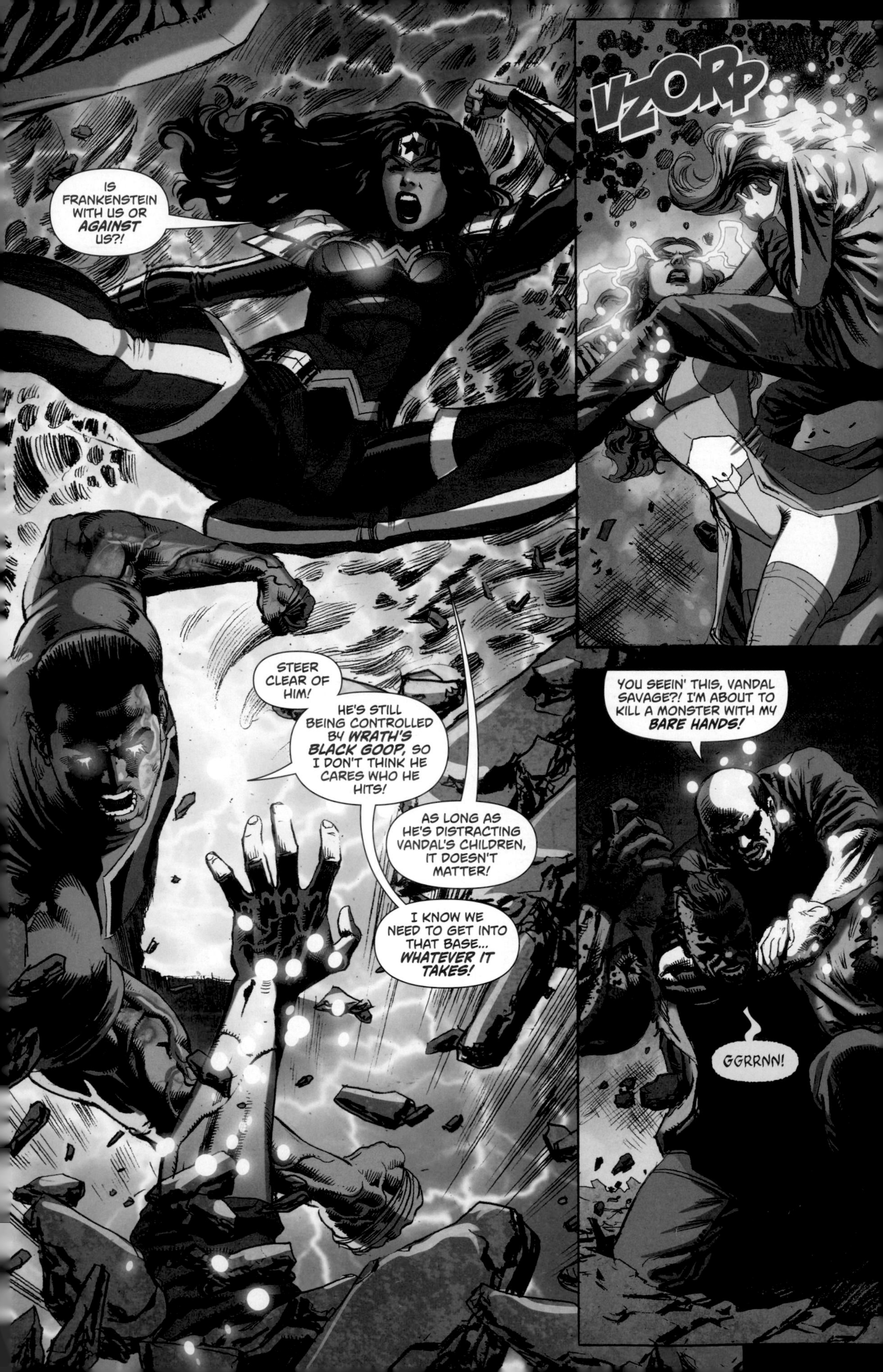
IS FRANKENSTEIN WITH US OR AGAINST US?!
VZORP
STEER CLEAR OF HIM!
HE'S STILL BEING CONTROLLED BY WRATH'S BLACK GOOP, SO I DON'T THINK HE CARES WHO HE HITS!
AS LONG AS HE'S DISTRACTING VANDAL'S CHILDREN, IT DOESN'T MATTER!
I KNOW WE NEED TO GET INTO THAT BASE... WHATEVER IT TAKES!
YOU SEEIN' THIS, VANDAL SAVAGE?! I'M ABOUT TO KILL A MONSTER WITH MY BARE HANDS!
GGRRNN!

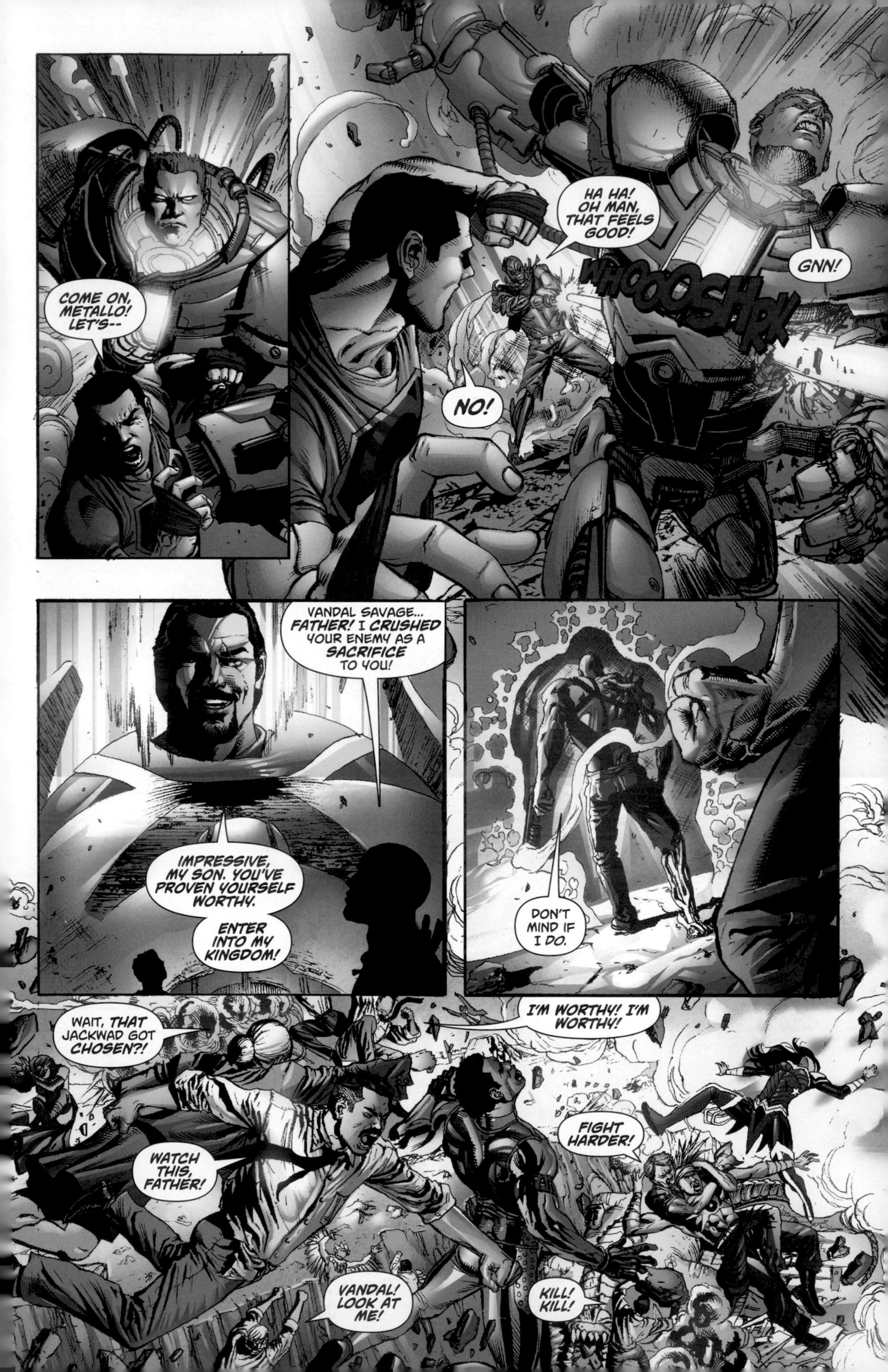
COME ON, METALLO! LET'S--
NO!
HA HA! OH MAN, THAT FEELS GOOD!
WHOOOOSHRK
GNN!
VANDAL SAVAGE... FATHER! I CRUSHED YOUR ENEMY AS A SACRIFICE TO YOU!
IMPRESSIVE, MY SON. YOU'VE PROVEN YOURSELF WORTHY.
ENTER INTO MY KINGDOM!
DON'T MIND IF I DO.
WAIT, THAT JACKWAD GOT CHOSEN?!
I'M WORTHY! I'M WORTHY!
WATCH THIS, FATHER!
FIGHT HARDER!
VANDAL! LOOK AT ME!
KILL! KILL!

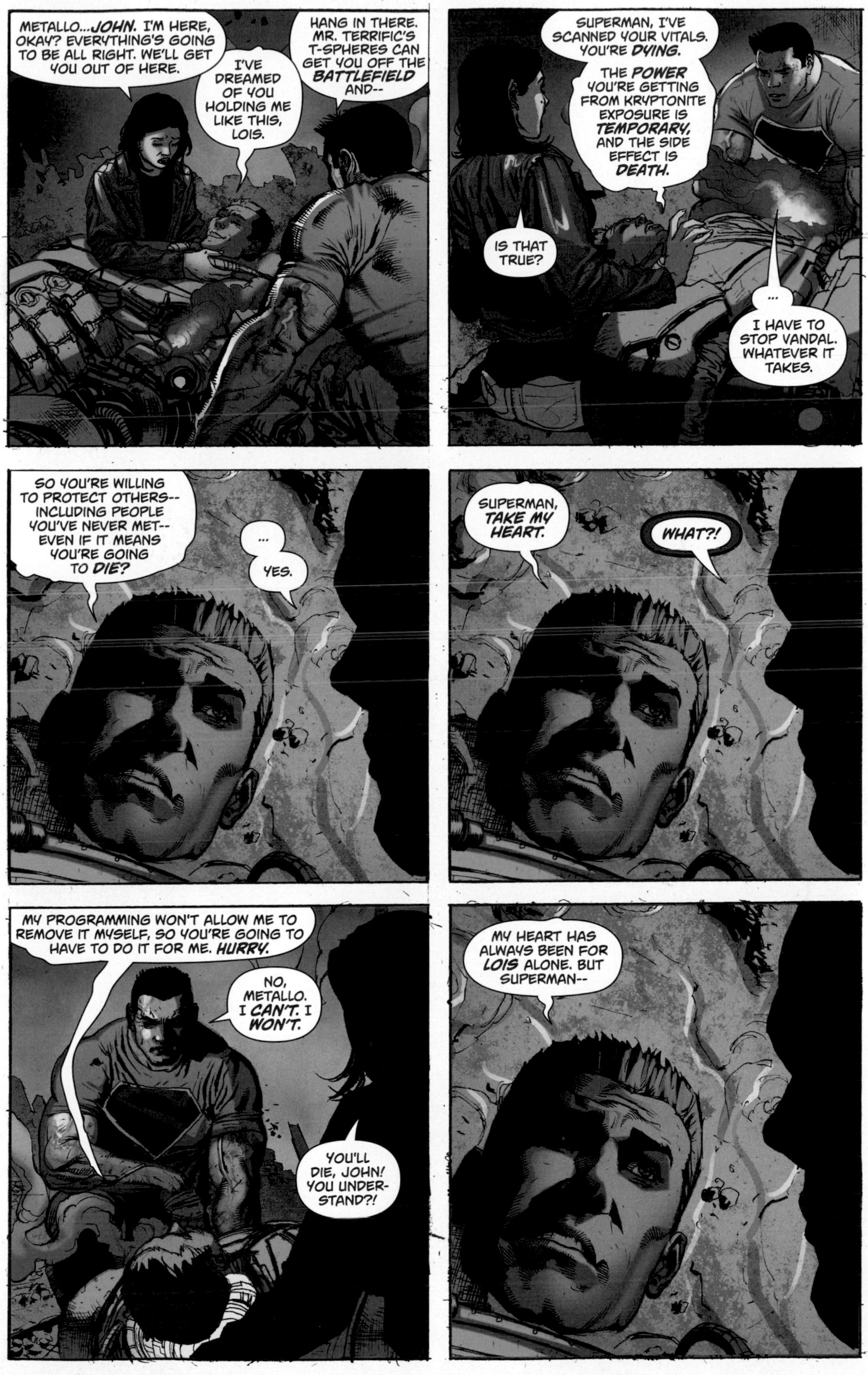
METALLO...JOHN. I'M HERE, OKAY? EVERYTHING'S GOING TO BE ALL RIGHT. WE'LL GET YOU OUT OF HERE.
I'VE DREAMED OF YOU HOLDING ME LIKE THIS, LOIS.
HANG IN THERE. MR. TERRIFIC'S T-SPHERES CAN GET YOU OFF THE BATTLEFIELD AND--
SUPERMAN, I'VE SCANNED YOUR VITALS. YOU'RE DYING.
THE POWER YOU'RE GETTING FROM KRYPTONITE EXPOSURE IS TEMPORARY, AND THE SIDE EFFECT IS DEATH.
IS THAT TRUE?
...
I HAVE TO STOP VANDAL. WHATEVER IT TAKES.
SO YOU'RE WILLING TO PROTECT OTHERS--INCLUDING PEOPLE YOU'VE NEVER MET--EVEN IF IT MEANS YOU'RE GOING TO DIE?
...
YES.
SUPERMAN, TAKE MY HEART.
WHAT?!
MY PROGRAMMING WON'T ALLOW ME TO REMOVE IT MYSELF, SO YOU'RE GOING TO HAVE TO DO IT FOR ME. HURRY.
NO, METALLO. I CAN'T. I WON'T.
YOU'LL DIE, JOHN! YOU UNDERSTAND?!
MY HEART HAS ALWAYS BEEN FOR LOIS ALONE. BUT SUPERMAN--

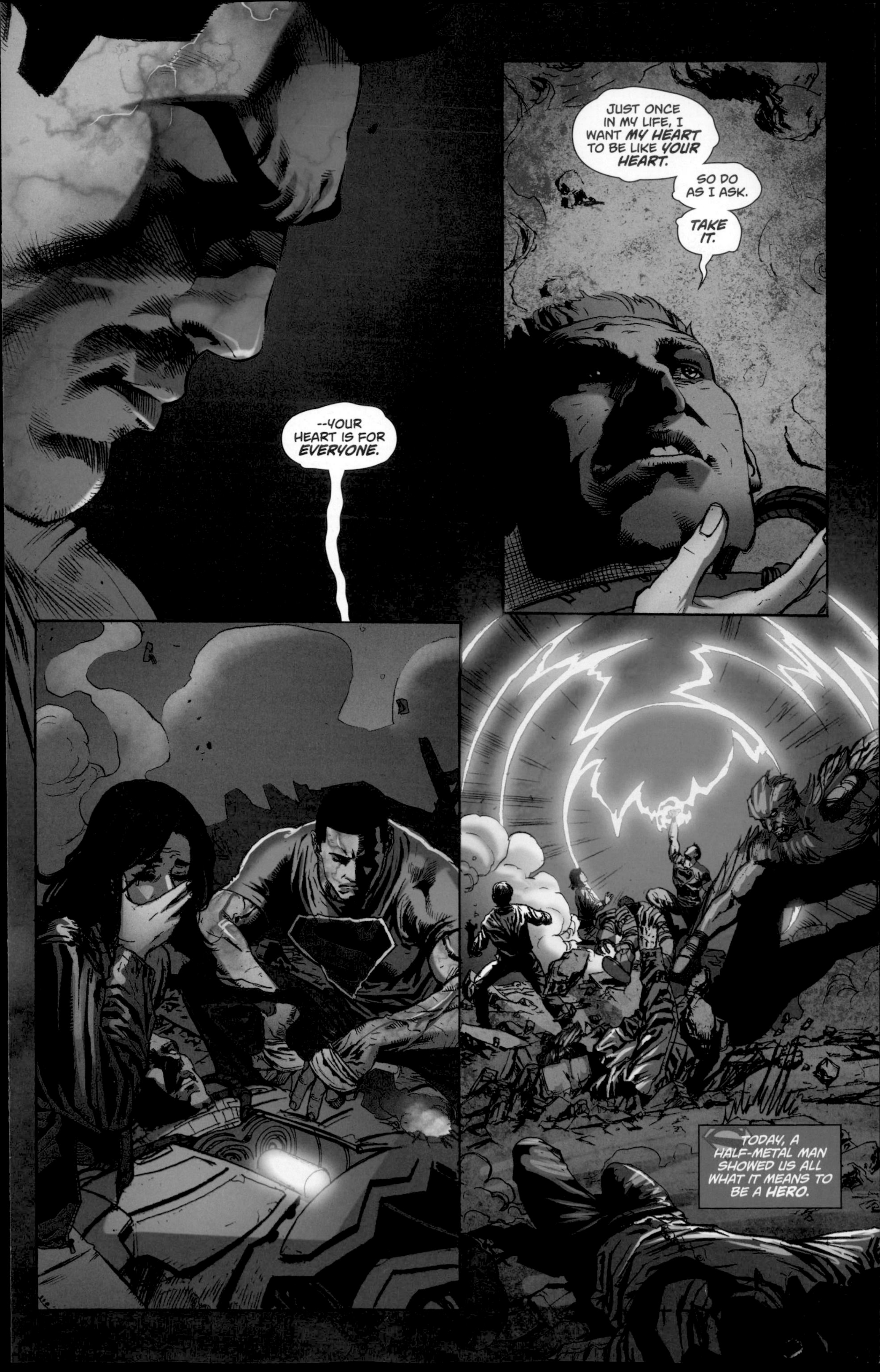
JUST ONCE IN MY LIFE, I WANT MY HEART TO BE LIKE YOUR HEART.
SO DO AS I ASK.
TAKE IT.
--YOUR HEART IS FOR EVERYONE.
TODAY, A HALF-METAL MAN SHOWED US ALL WHAT IT MEANS TO BE A HERO.

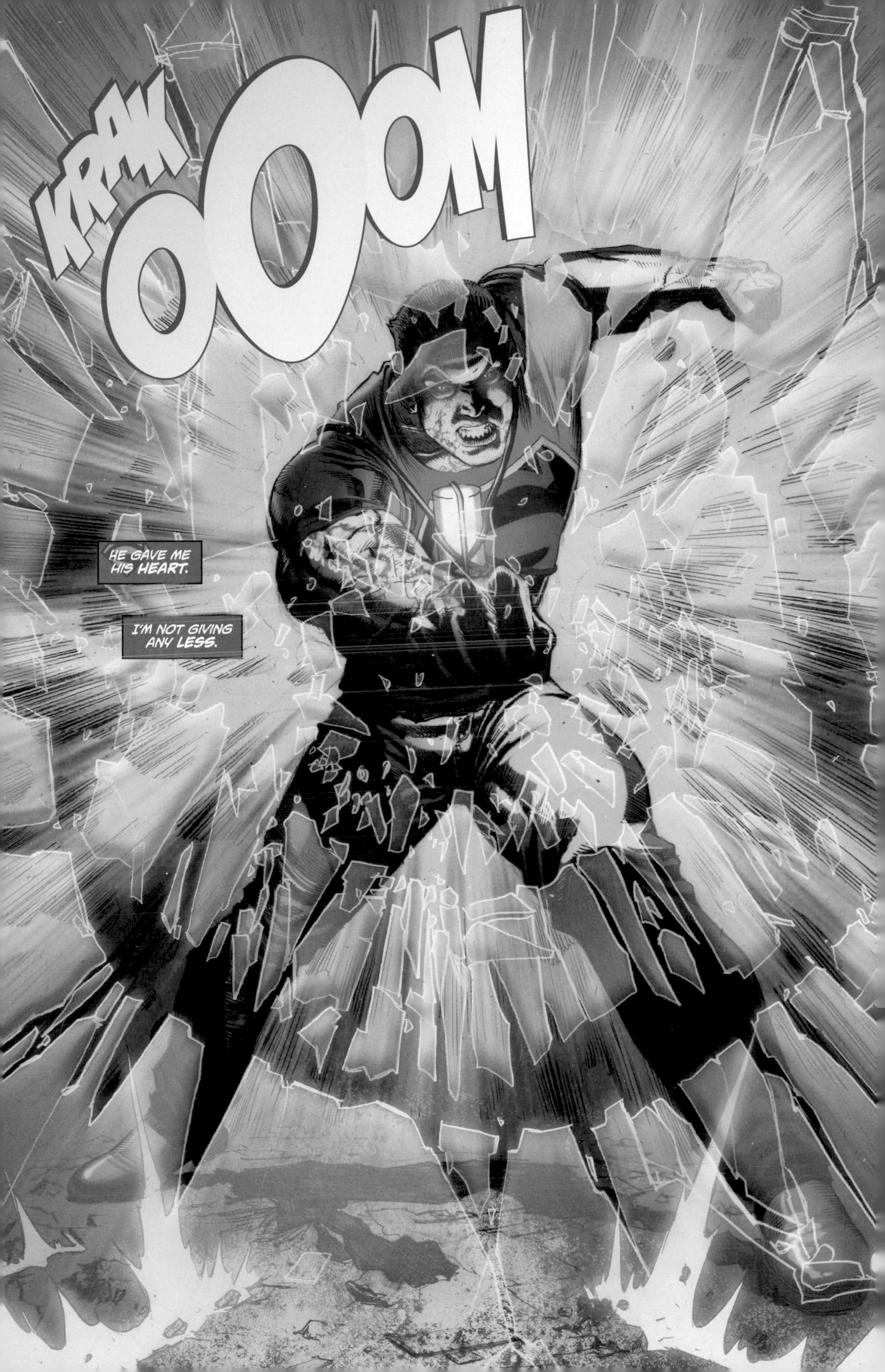

KRAKOOOM
HE GAVE ME HIS HEART.
I'M NOT GIVING ANY LESS.

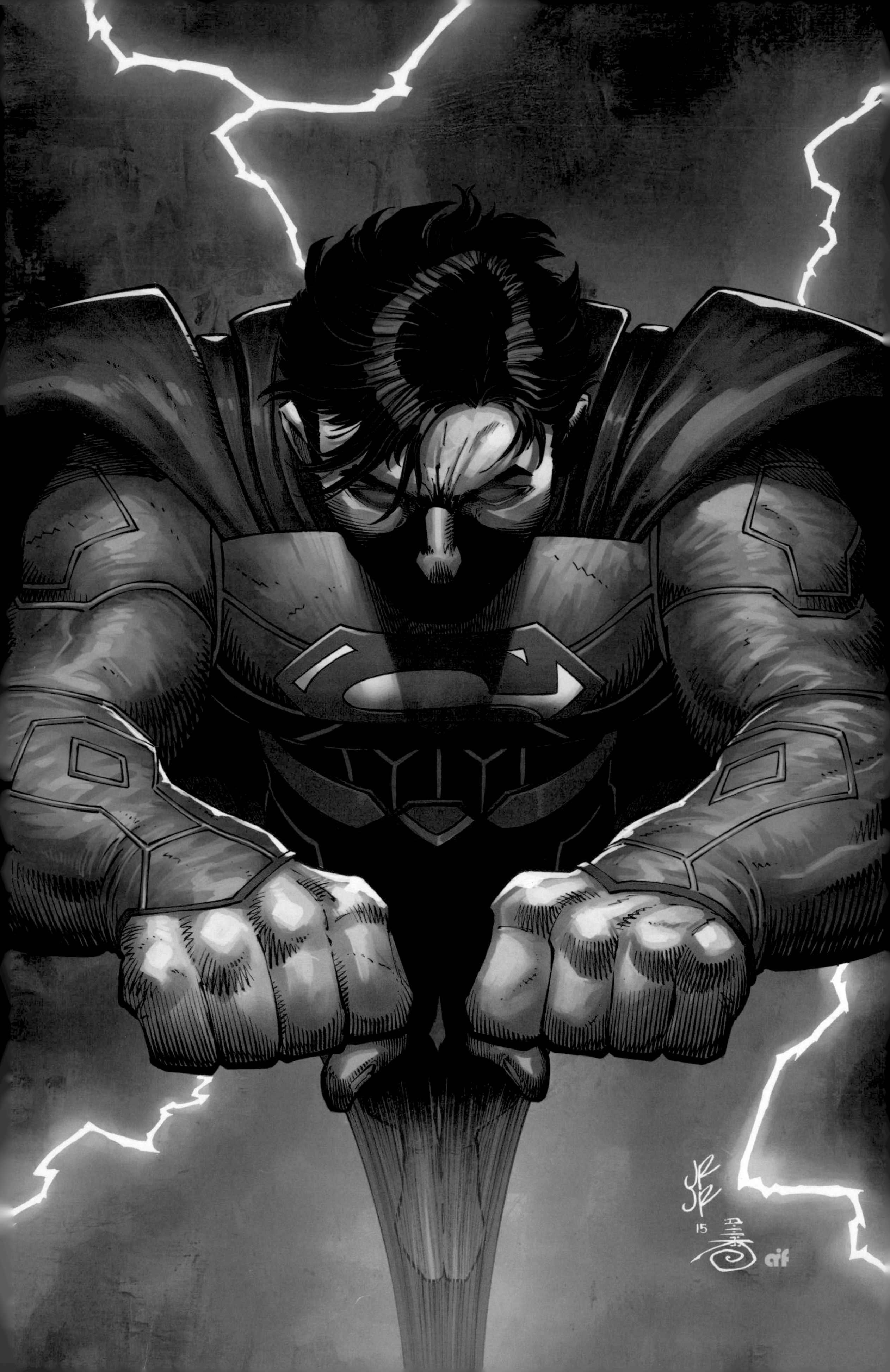

WHAT COULD HAVE BEEN, WHAT CAN STILL BE, AND WHAT IS

GENE LUEN YANG writer **HOWARD PORTER, ARDIAN SYAF, PATRICK ZIRCHER, JON BOGDANOVE** artists **HI-FI** colorist **ROB LEIGH** letterer **HOWARD PORTER, HI-FI** cover

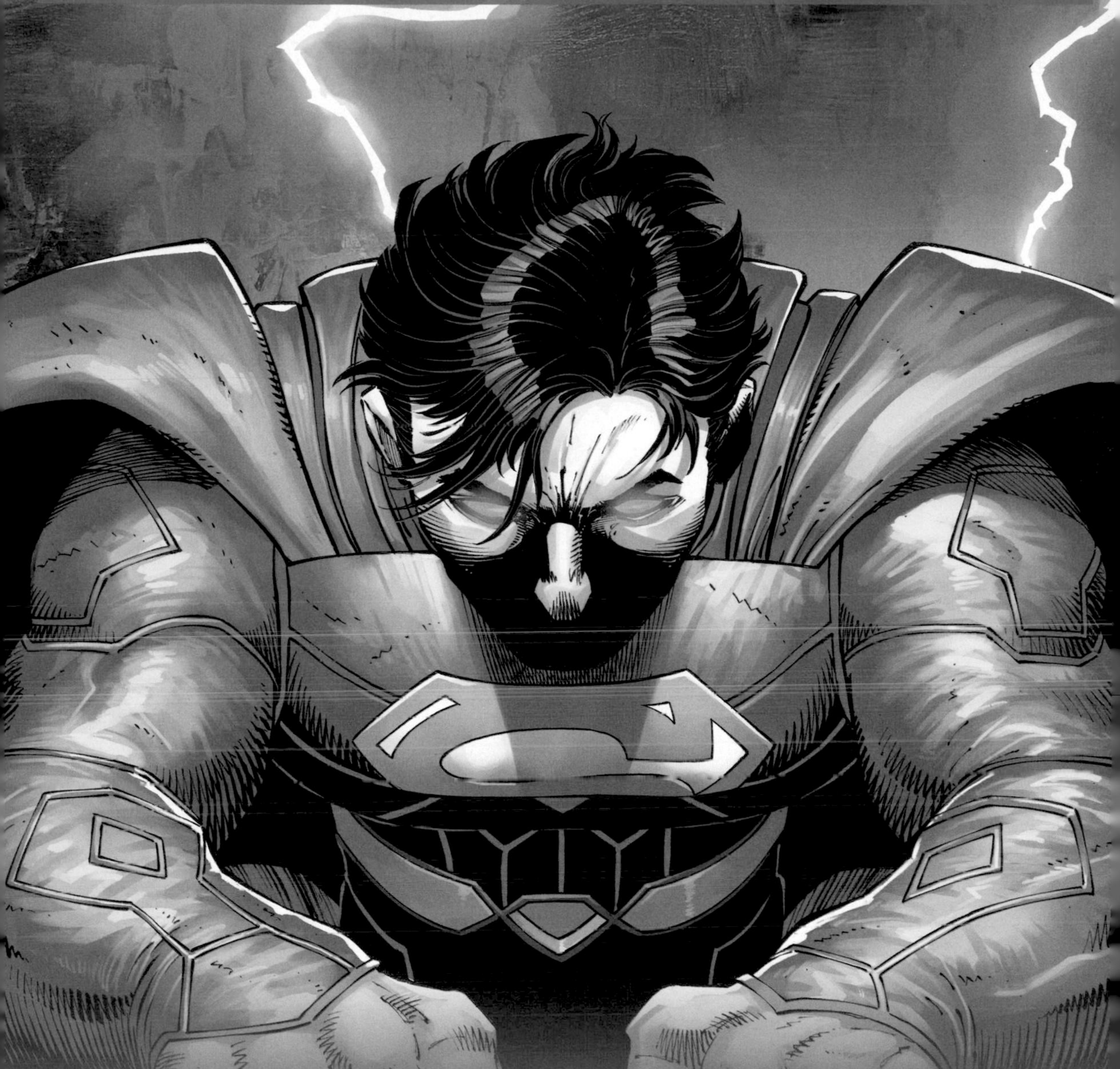

Previously, in SUPERMAN: SAVAGE DAWN ...

As the comet draws closer to Earth, the rise of the House of Savage appears inevitable. Yet Superman keeps fighting, strengthened by the Kryptonite heart given to him by Metallo in his final moments, plus the rallying support of his friends and heroic allies. After rescuing the Justice League from their imprisonment in the Watchtower, he tries to stop Vandal Savage from shuttling his children toward the approaching comet. But the immortal tyrant fires off a kill shot of toxins that sends Superman plummeting from the sky, toward his Fortress and what looks like certain demise.

Miraculously, the Fortress recognizes Superman's recharged DNA and regenerates his cells, bringing the Man of Steel back to full power. And just in time – further motivated by seeing his spawn ablaze with energy from the comet, Savage propels himself closer to the astronomical object to claim his eternal power. His progeny's bodies, however, can't contain the massive energy for long, and they literally burn themselves up while battling Wonder Woman and the Justice League. Superman, meanwhile, gives chase to the architect that's destroyed nearly every aspect of his life – and is now dangerously close to achieving unspeakable might...

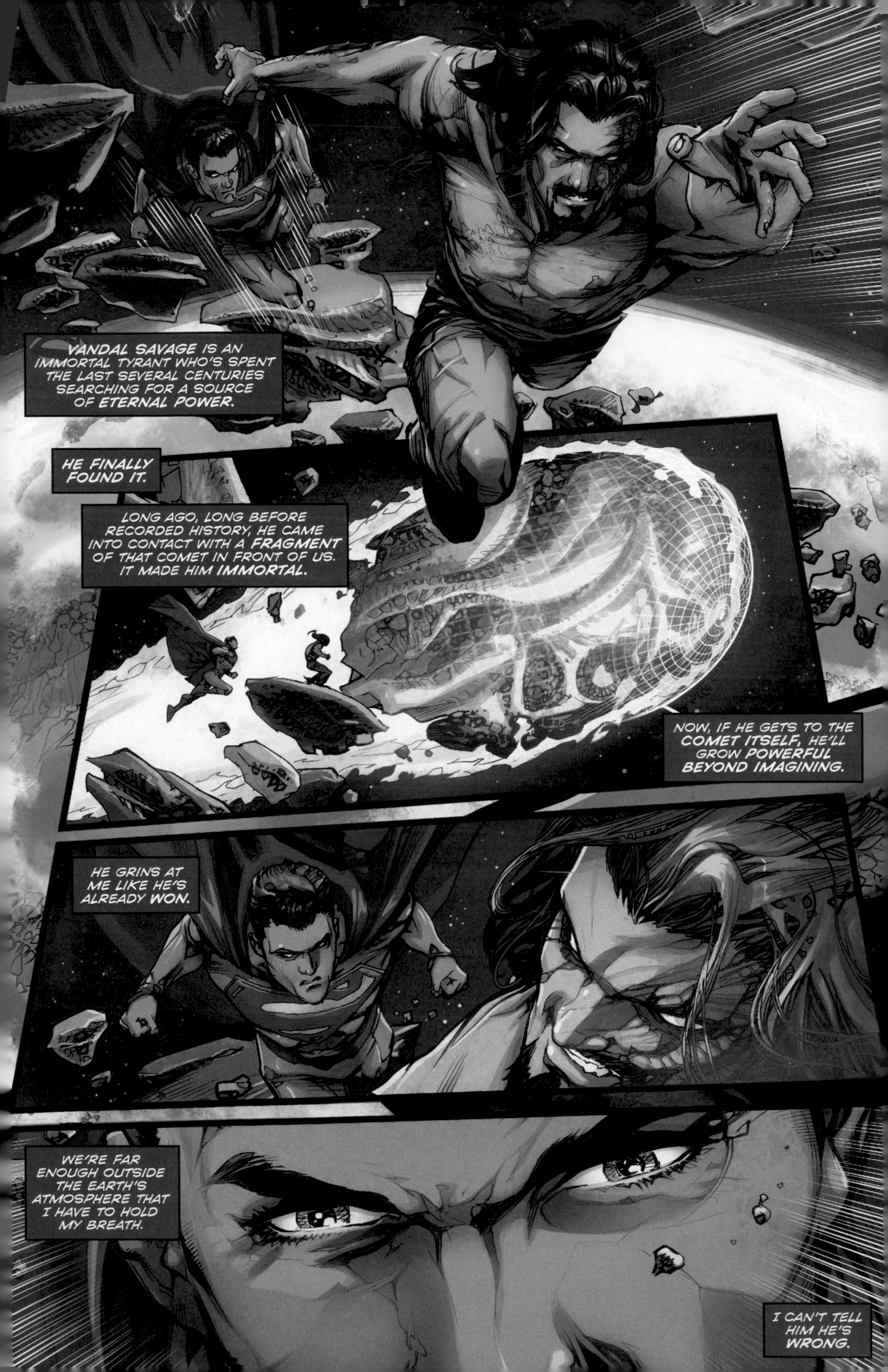
VANDAL SAVAGE IS AN IMMORTAL TYRANT WHO'S SPENT THE LAST SEVERAL CENTURIES SEARCHING FOR A SOURCE OF ETERNAL POWER.
HE FINALLY FOUND IT.
LONG AGO, LONG BEFORE RECORDED HISTORY, HE CAME INTO CONTACT WITH A FRAGMENT OF THAT COMET IN FRONT OF US. IT MADE HIM IMMORTAL.
NOW, IF HE GETS TO THE COMET ITSELF, HE'LL GROW POWERFUL BEYOND IMAGINING.
HE GRINS AT ME LIKE HE'S ALREADY WON.
WE'RE FAR ENOUGH OUTSIDE THE EARTH'S ATMOSPHERE THAT I HAVE TO HOLD MY BREATH.
I CAN'T TELL HIM HE'S WRONG.

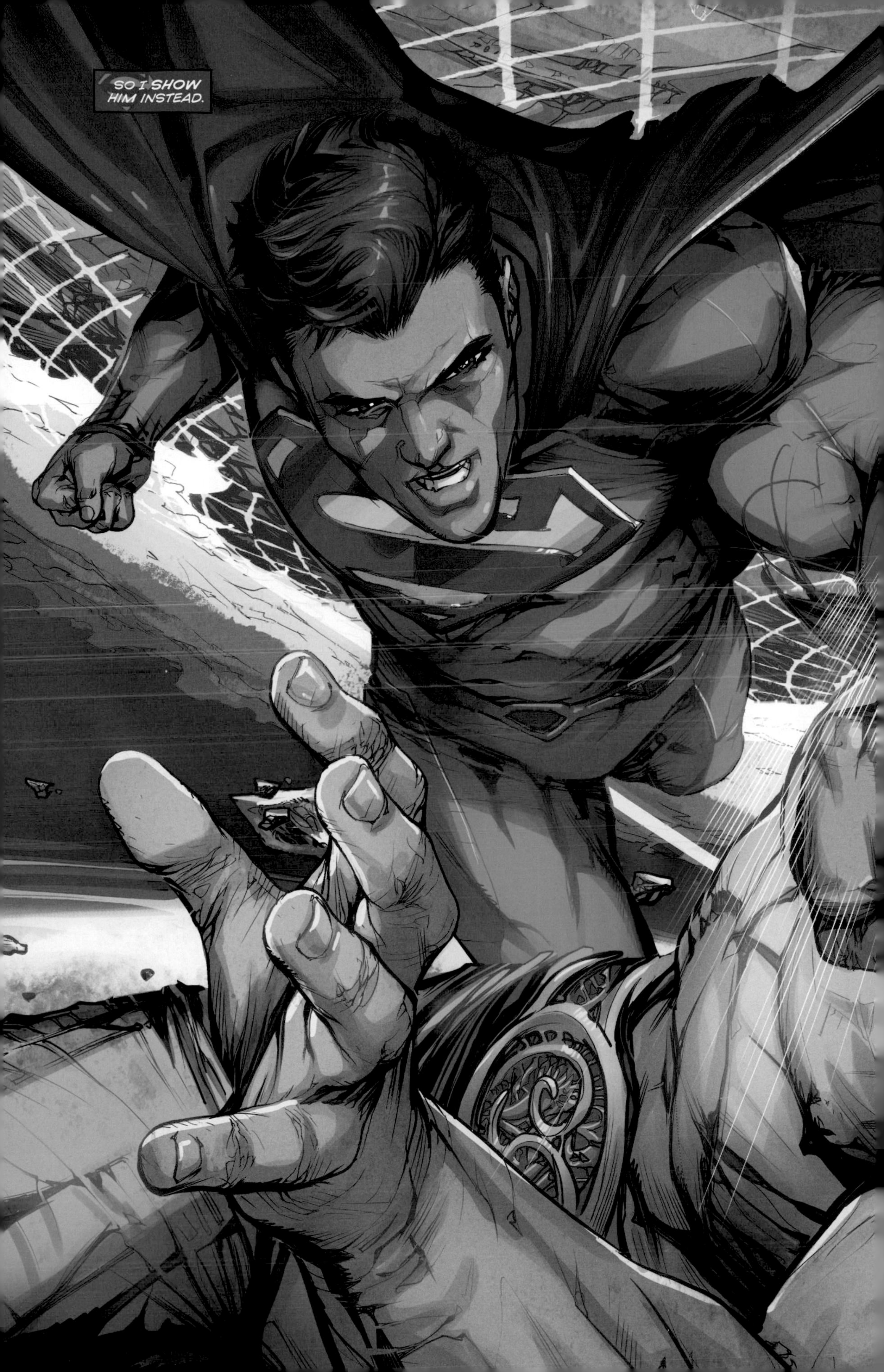
SO I SHOW HIM INSTEAD.

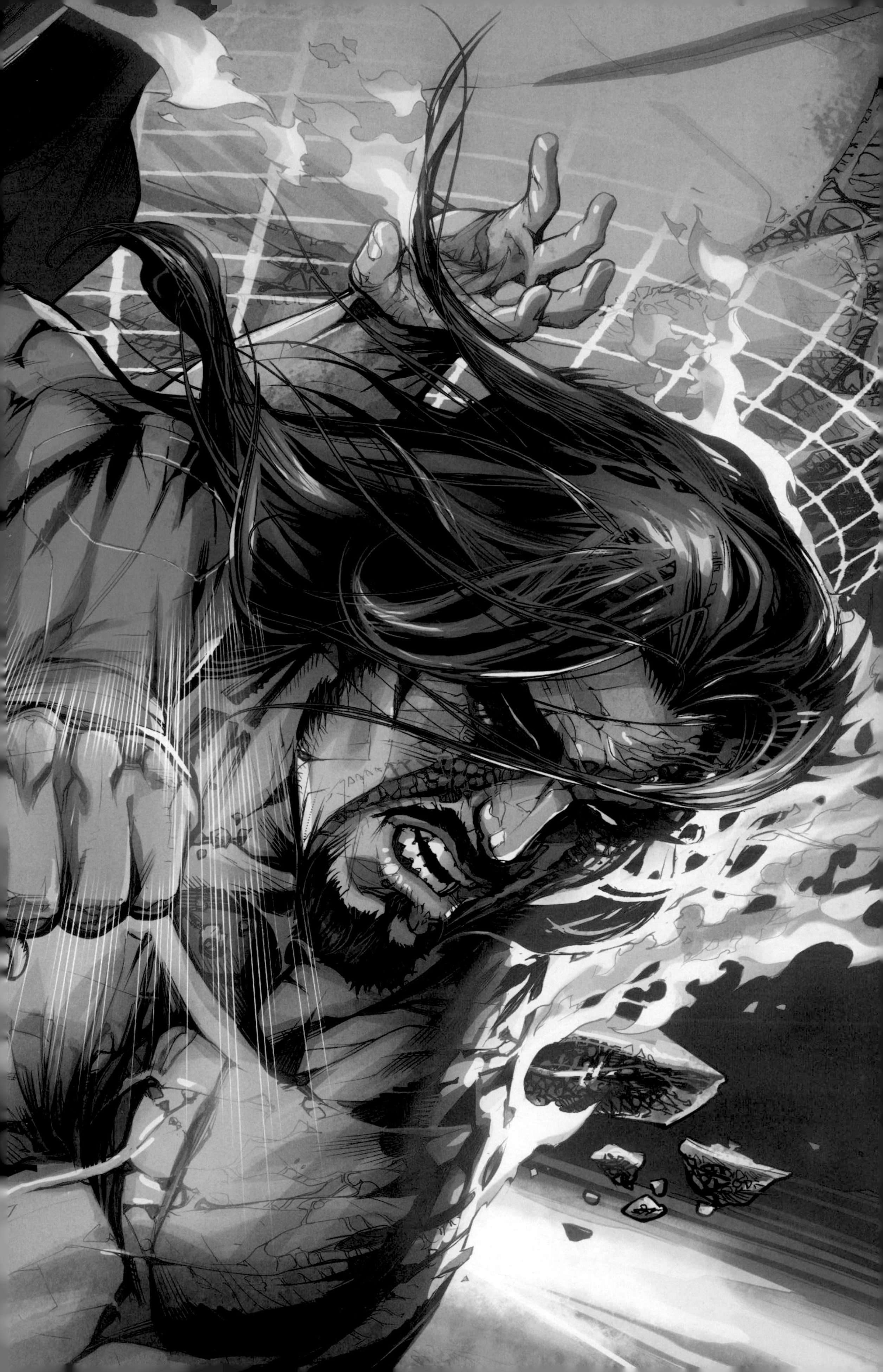

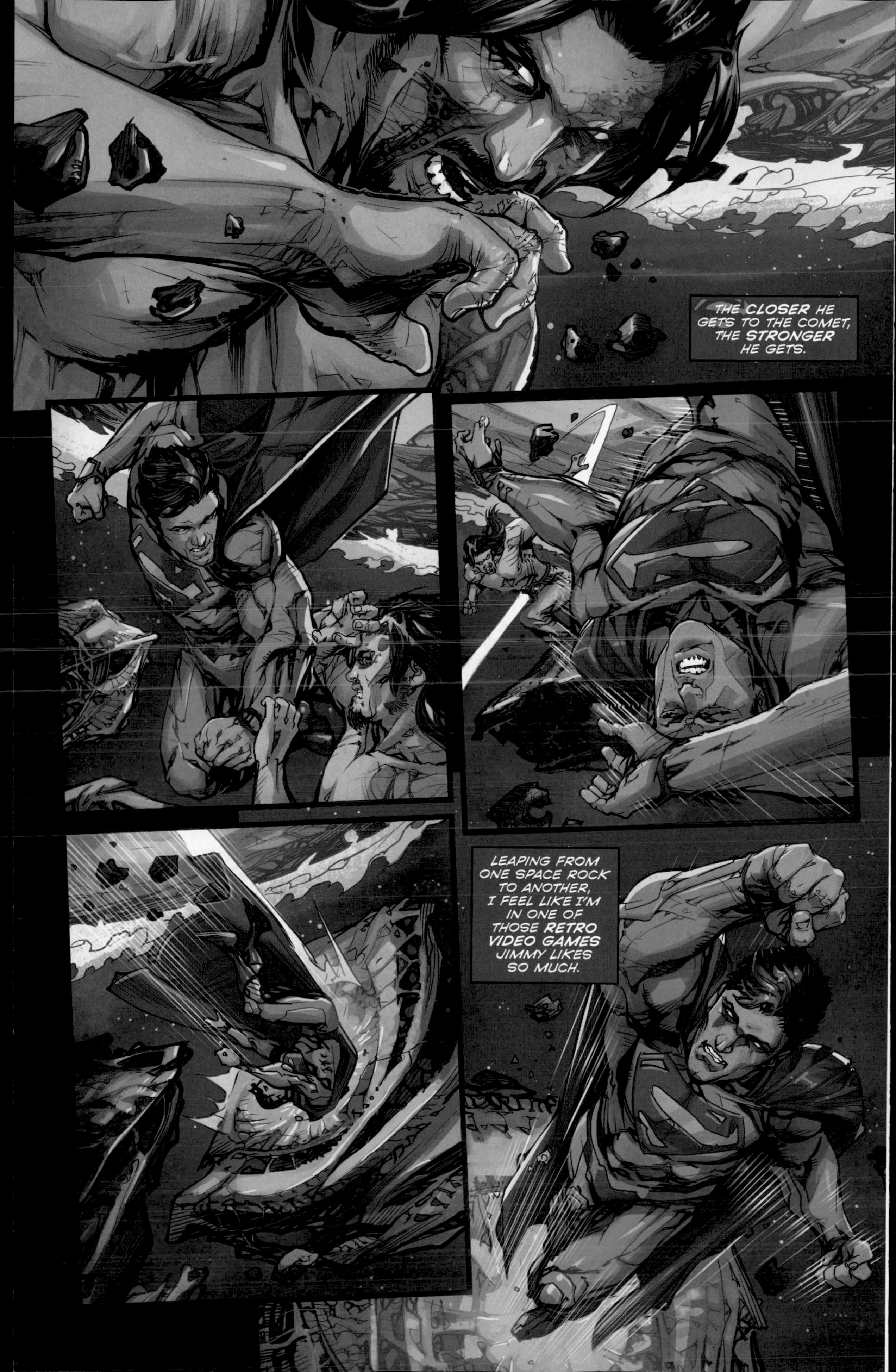
THE CLOSER HE GETS TO THE COMET, THE STRONGER HE GETS.
LEAPING FROM ONE SPACE ROCK TO ANOTHER, I FEEL LIKE I'M IN ONE OF THOSE RETRO VIDEO GAMES JIMMY LIKES SO MUCH.

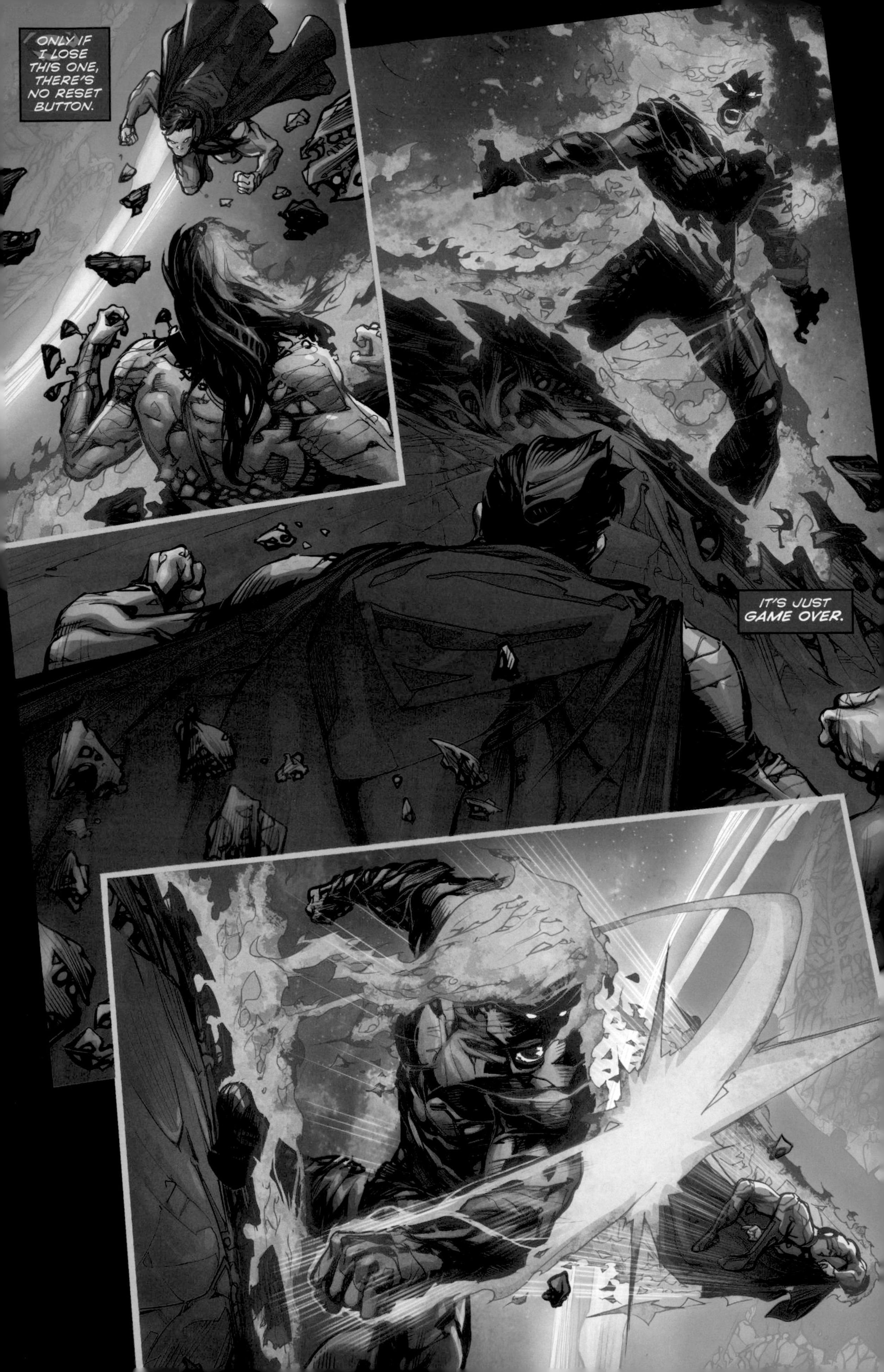
ONLY IF I LOSE THIS ONE, THERE'S NO RESET BUTTON.
IT'S JUST GAME OVER.

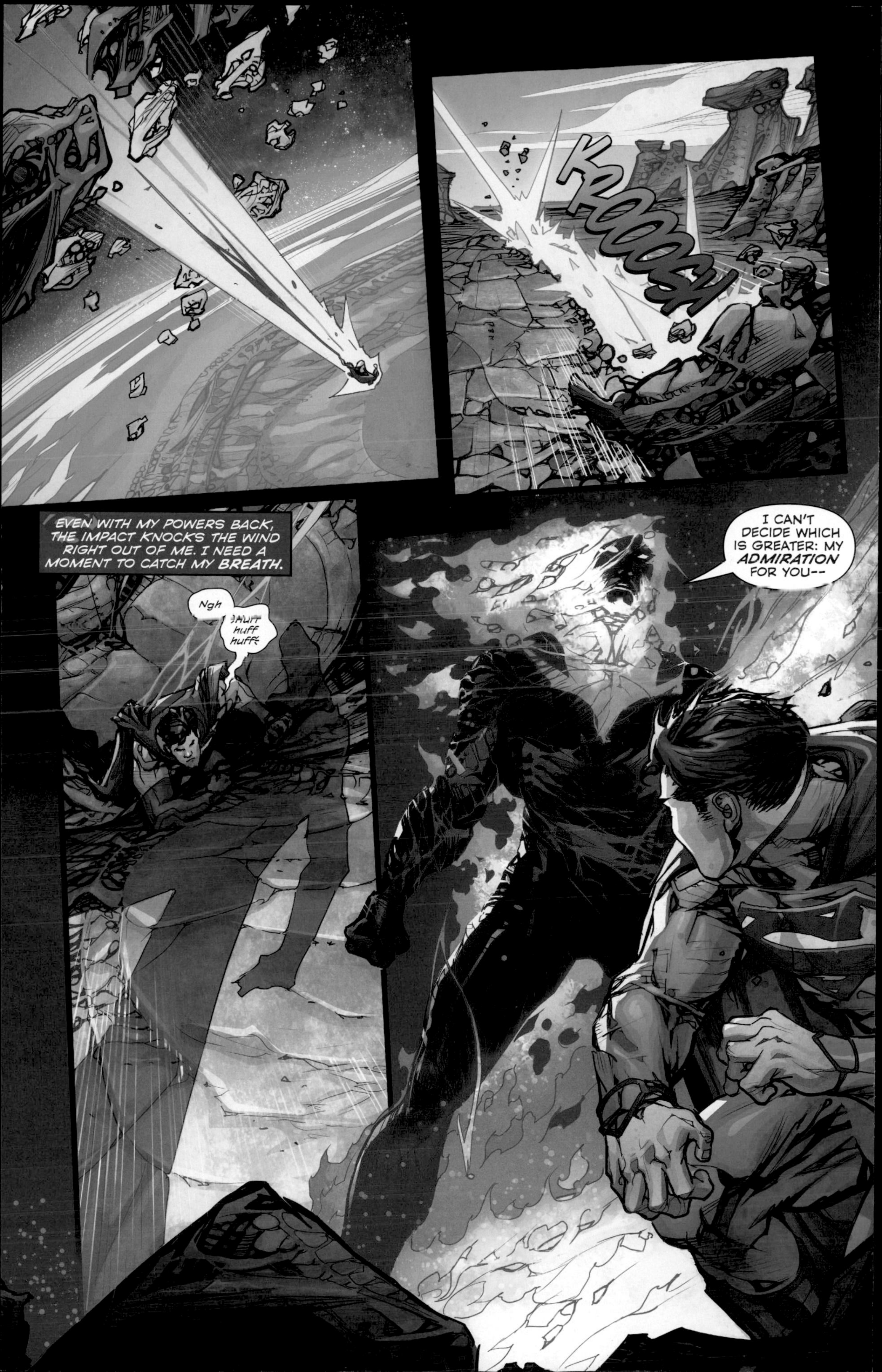
KROOOSH
EVEN WITH MY POWERS BACK, THE IMPACT KNOCKS THE WIND RIGHT OUT OF ME. I NEED A MOMENT TO CATCH MY BREATH.
Ngh
huff huff huff
I CAN'T DECIDE WHICH IS GREATER: MY ADMIRATION FOR YOU--

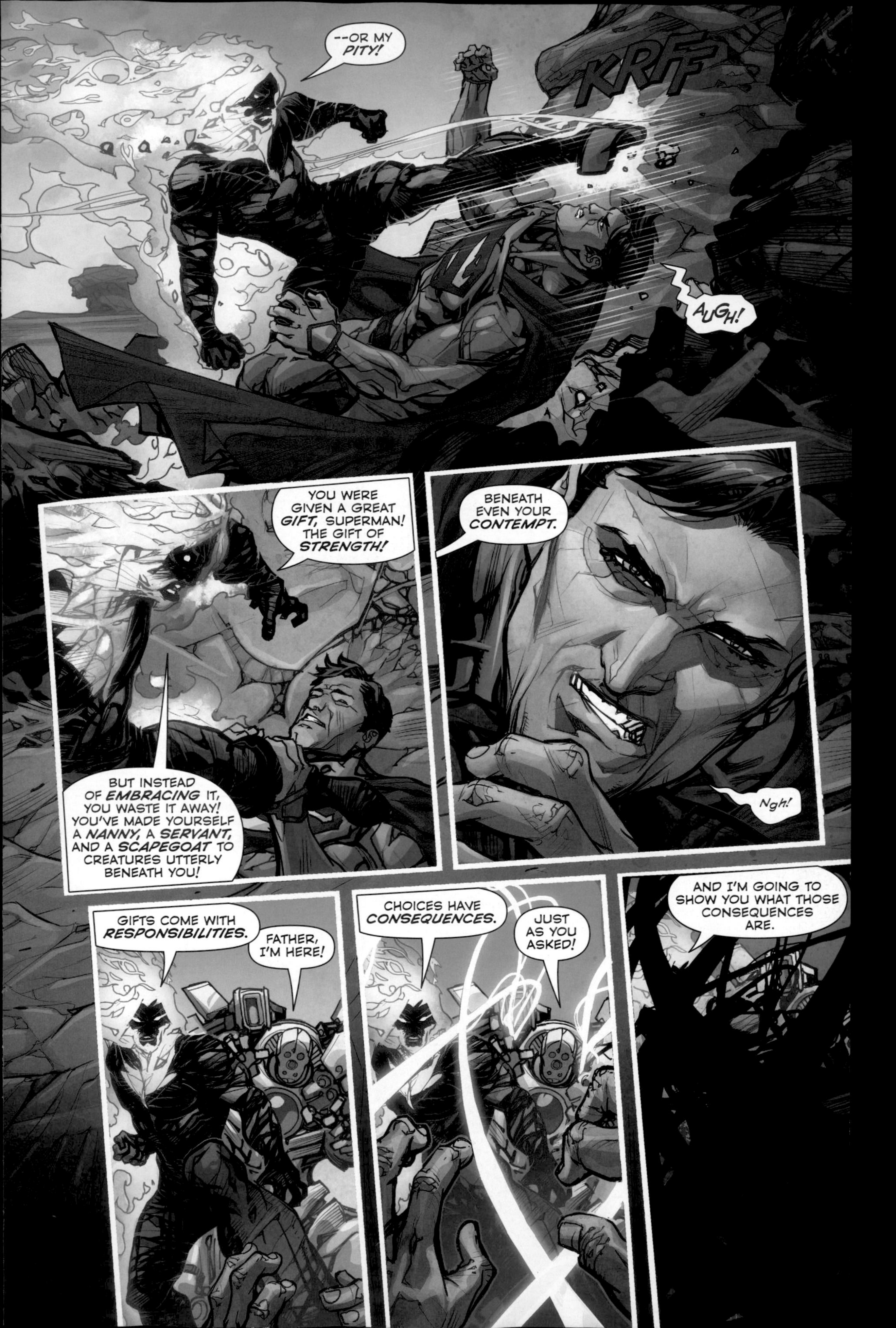
--OR MY PITY!
KRFF
AUGH!
YOU WERE GIVEN A GREAT GIFT, SUPERMAN! THE GIFT OF STRENGTH!
BUT INSTEAD OF EMBRACING IT, YOU WASTE IT AWAY! YOU'VE MADE YOURSELF A NANNY, A SERVANT, AND A SCAPEGOAT TO CREATURES UTTERLY BENEATH YOU!
BENEATH EVEN YOUR CONTEMPT.
Ngh!
GIFTS COME WITH RESPONSIBILITIES.
FATHER, I'M HERE!
CHOICES HAVE CONSEQUENCES.
JUST AS YOU ASKED!
AND I'M GOING TO SHOW YOU WHAT THOSE CONSEQUENCES ARE.

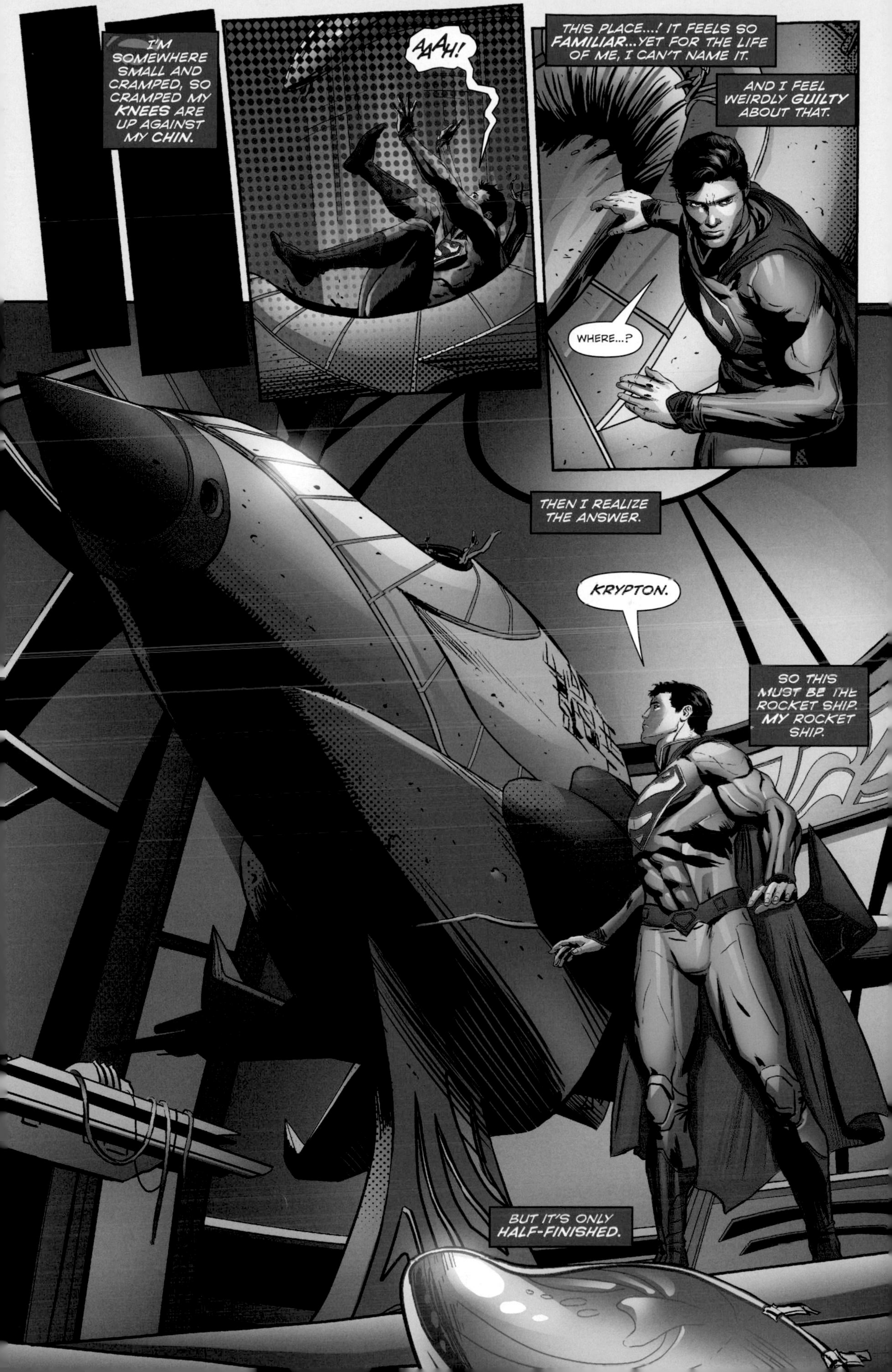
I'M SOMEWHERE SMALL AND CRAMPED, SO CRAMPED MY KNEES ARE UP AGAINST MY CHIN.
AAAH!
THIS PLACE...! IT FEELS SO FAMILIAR...YET FOR THE LIFE OF ME, I CAN'T NAME IT.
AND I FEEL WEIRDLY GUILTY ABOUT THAT.
WHERE...?
THEN I REALIZE THE ANSWER.
KRYPTON.
SO THIS MUST BE THE ROCKET SHIP. MY ROCKET SHIP.
BUT IT'S ONLY HALF-FINISHED.

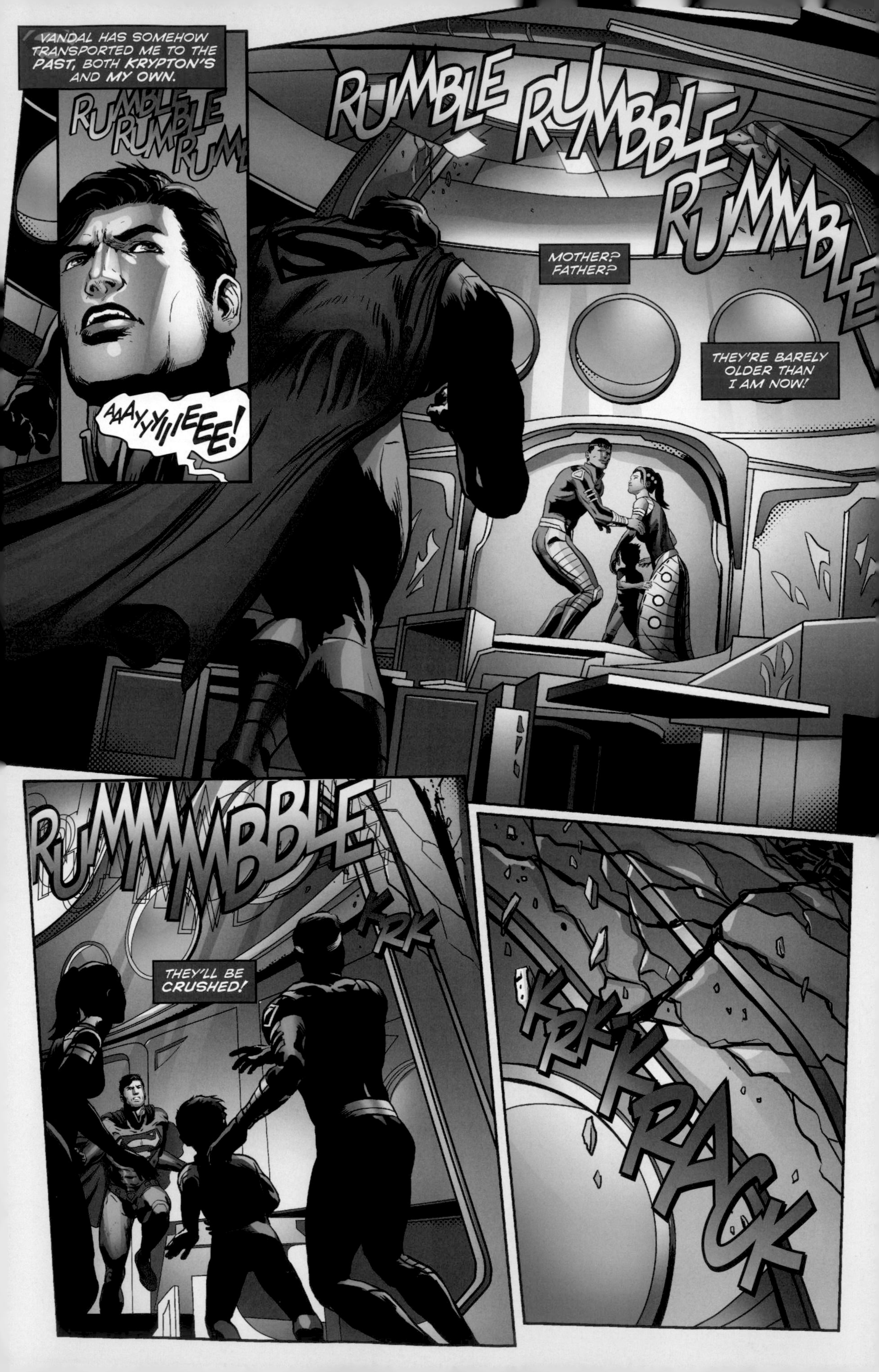

VANDAL HAS SOMEHOW TRANSPORTED ME TO THE PAST, BOTH KRYPTON'S AND MY OWN.
RUMBLE RUMBLE RUMBLE
AAAYYIIIEEE!
RUMBLE RUMBBLE RUMMBLE
MOTHER? FATHER?
THEY'RE BARELY OLDER THAN I AM NOW!
RUMMMBLE
KRK
THEY'LL BE CRUSHED!
KRK-KRACK

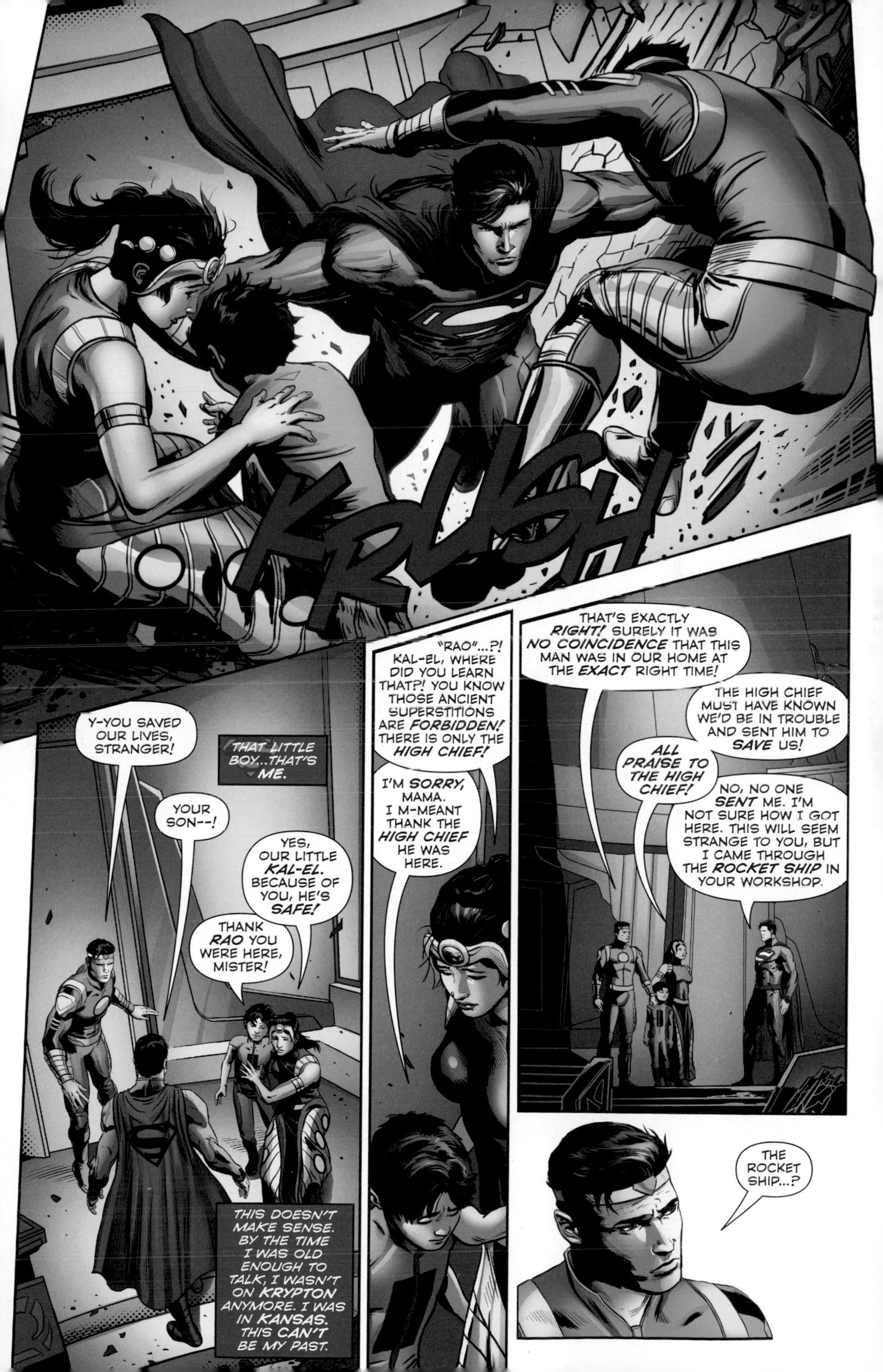
KRUSH
Y-YOU SAVED OUR LIVES, STRANGER!
YOUR SON--!
THAT LITTLE BOY...THAT'S ME.
YES, OUR LITTLE KAL-EL. BECAUSE OF YOU, HE'S SAFE!
THANK RAO YOU WERE HERE, MISTER!
THIS DOESN'T MAKE SENSE. BY THE TIME I WAS OLD ENOUGH TO TALK, I WASN'T ON KRYPTON ANYMORE. I WAS IN KANSAS. THIS CAN'T BE MY PAST.
"RAO"...?! KAL-EL, WHERE DID YOU LEARN THAT?! YOU KNOW THOSE ANCIENT SUPERSTITIONS ARE FORBIDDEN! THERE IS ONLY THE HIGH CHIEF!
I'M SORRY, MAMA. I M-MEANT THANK THE HIGH CHIEF HE WAS HERE.
THAT'S EXACTLY RIGHT! SURELY IT WAS NO COINCIDENCE THAT THIS MAN WAS IN OUR HOME AT THE EXACT RIGHT TIME!
THE HIGH CHIEF MUST HAVE KNOWN WE'D BE IN TROUBLE AND SENT HIM TO SAVE US!
ALL PRAISE TO THE HIGH CHIEF!
NO, NO ONE SENT ME. I'M NOT SURE HOW I GOT HERE. THIS WILL SEEM STRANGE TO YOU, BUT I CAME THROUGH THE ROCKET SHIP IN YOUR WORKSHOP.
THE ROCKET SHIP...?

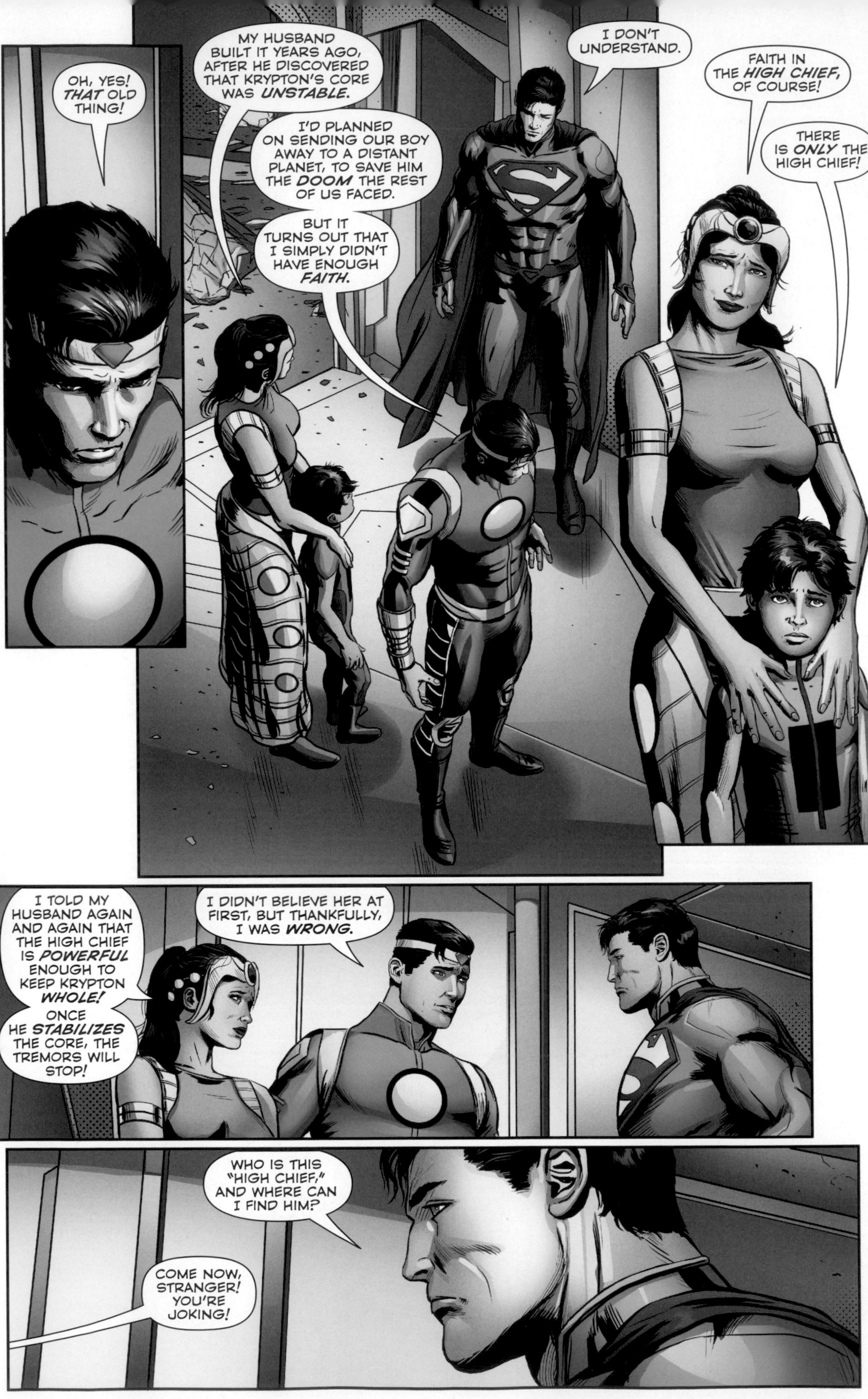
OH, YES! THAT OLD THING!
MY HUSBAND BUILT IT YEARS AGO, AFTER HE DISCOVERED THAT KRYPTON'S CORE WAS UNSTABLE.
I'D PLANNED ON SENDING OUR BOY AWAY TO A DISTANT PLANET, TO SAVE HIM THE DOOM THE REST OF US FACED.
BUT IT TURNS OUT THAT I SIMPLY DIDN'T HAVE ENOUGH FAITH.
I DON'T UNDERSTAND.
FAITH IN THE HIGH CHIEF, OF COURSE!
THERE IS ONLY THE HIGH CHIEF!
I TOLD MY HUSBAND AGAIN AND AGAIN THAT THE HIGH CHIEF IS POWERFUL ENOUGH TO KEEP KRYPTON WHOLE!
ONCE HE STABILIZES THE CORE, THE TREMORS WILL STOP!
I DIDN'T BELIEVE HER AT FIRST, BUT THANKFULLY, I WAS WRONG.
WHO IS THIS "HIGH CHIEF," AND WHERE CAN I FIND HIM?
COME NOW, STRANGER! YOU'RE JOKING!

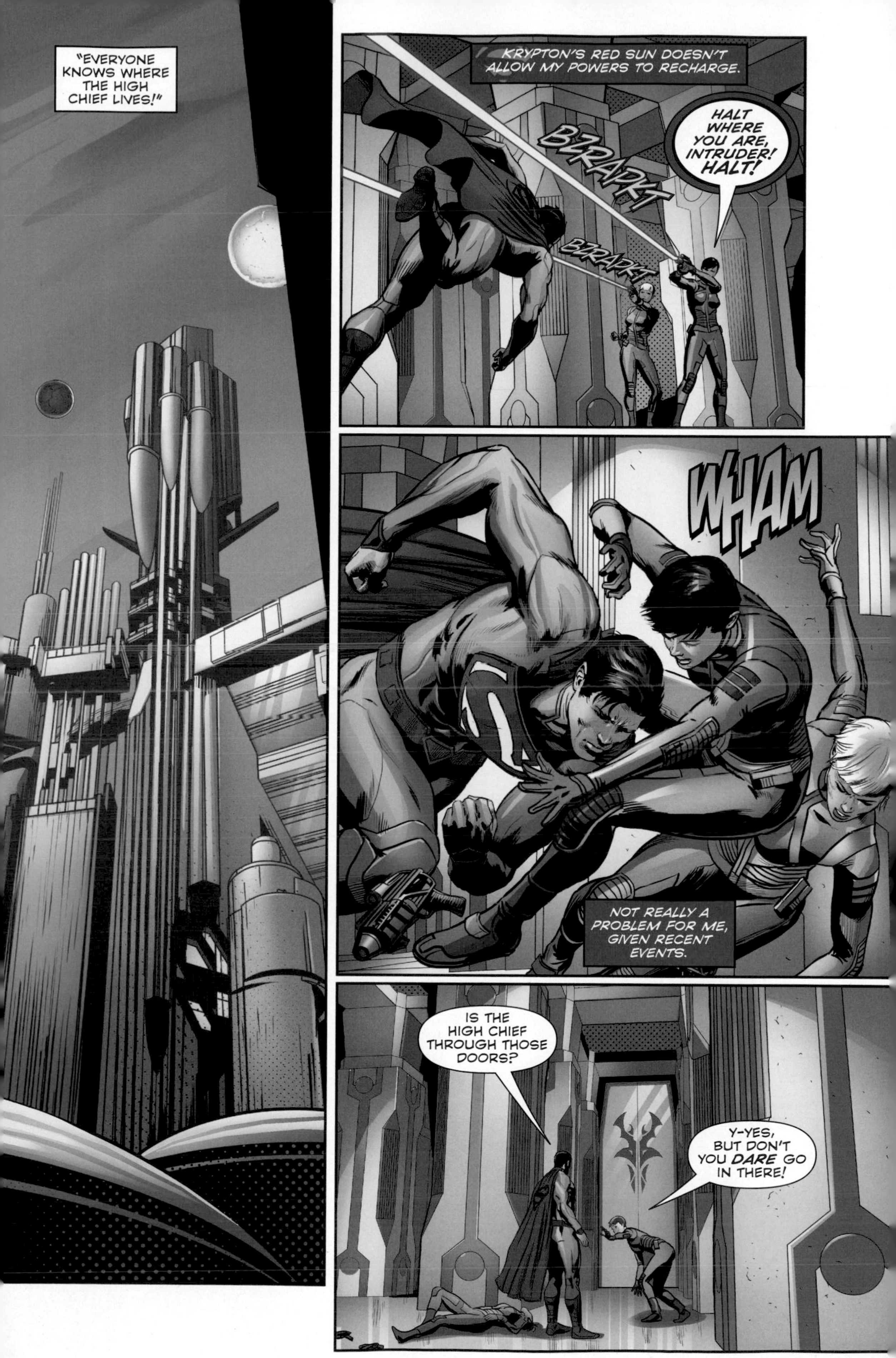
"EVERYONE KNOWS WHERE THE HIGH CHIEF LIVES!"
KRYPTON'S RED SUN DOESN'T ALLOW MY POWERS TO RECHARGE.
HALT WHERE YOU ARE, INTRUDER! HALT!
BZRAPKT
BZRAPKT
WHAM
NOT REALLY A PROBLEM FOR ME, GIVEN RECENT EVENTS.
IS THE HIGH CHIEF THROUGH THOSE DOORS?
Y-YES, BUT DON'T YOU DARE GO IN THERE!

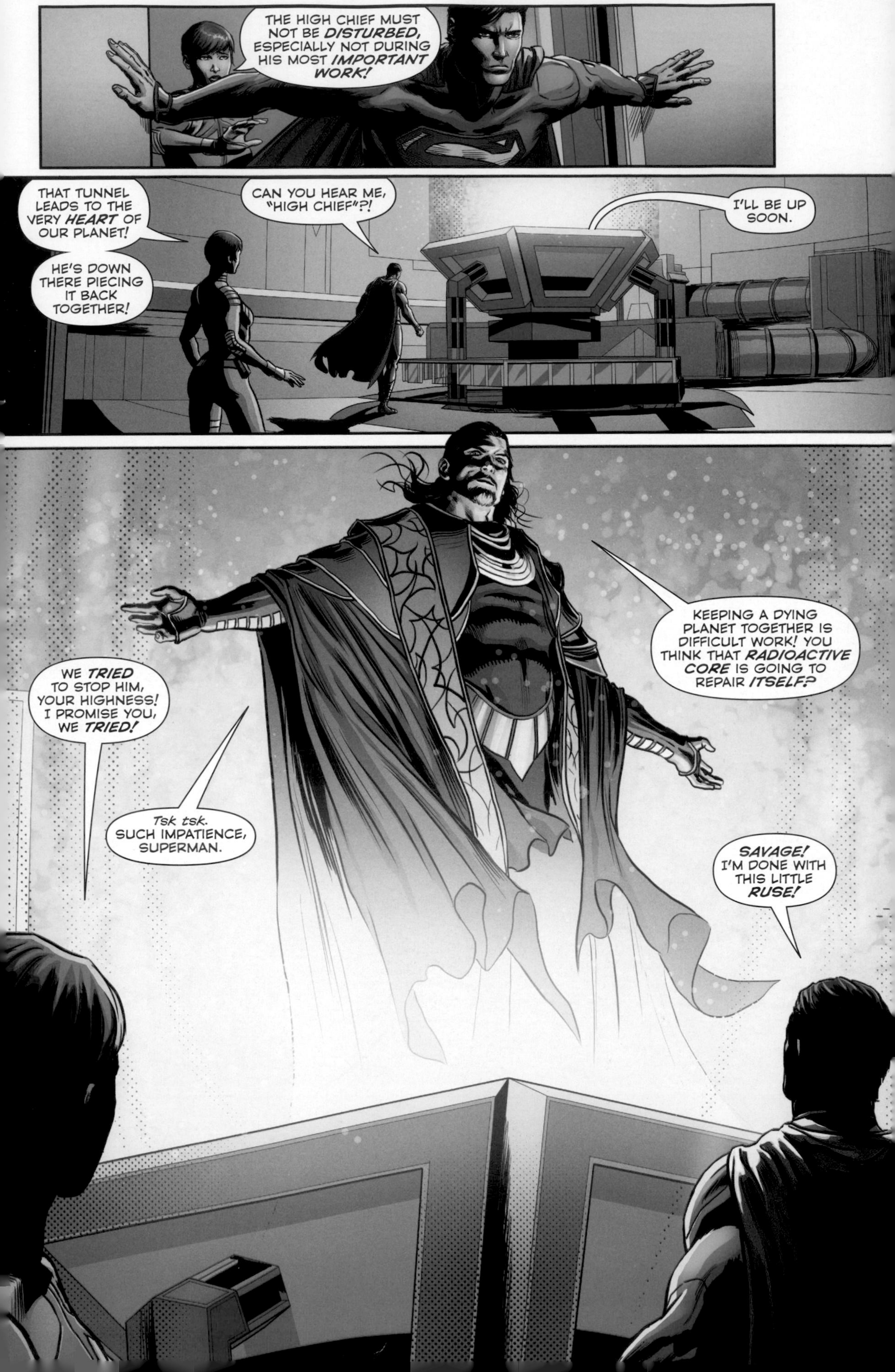
THE HIGH CHIEF MUST NOT BE *DISTURBED*, ESPECIALLY NOT DURING HIS MOST *IMPORTANT WORK!*
THAT TUNNEL LEADS TO THE VERY *HEART* OF OUR PLANET!
HE'S DOWN THERE PIECING IT BACK TOGETHER!
CAN YOU HEAR ME, "HIGH CHIEF"?!
I'LL BE UP SOON.
WE *TRIED* TO STOP HIM, YOUR HIGHNESS! I PROMISE YOU, WE *TRIED!*
Tsk tsk. SUCH IMPATIENCE, SUPERMAN.
KEEPING A DYING PLANET TOGETHER IS DIFFICULT WORK! YOU THINK THAT *RADIOACTIVE CORE* IS GOING TO REPAIR *ITSELF?*
SAVAGE! I'M DONE WITH THIS LITTLE *RUSE!*

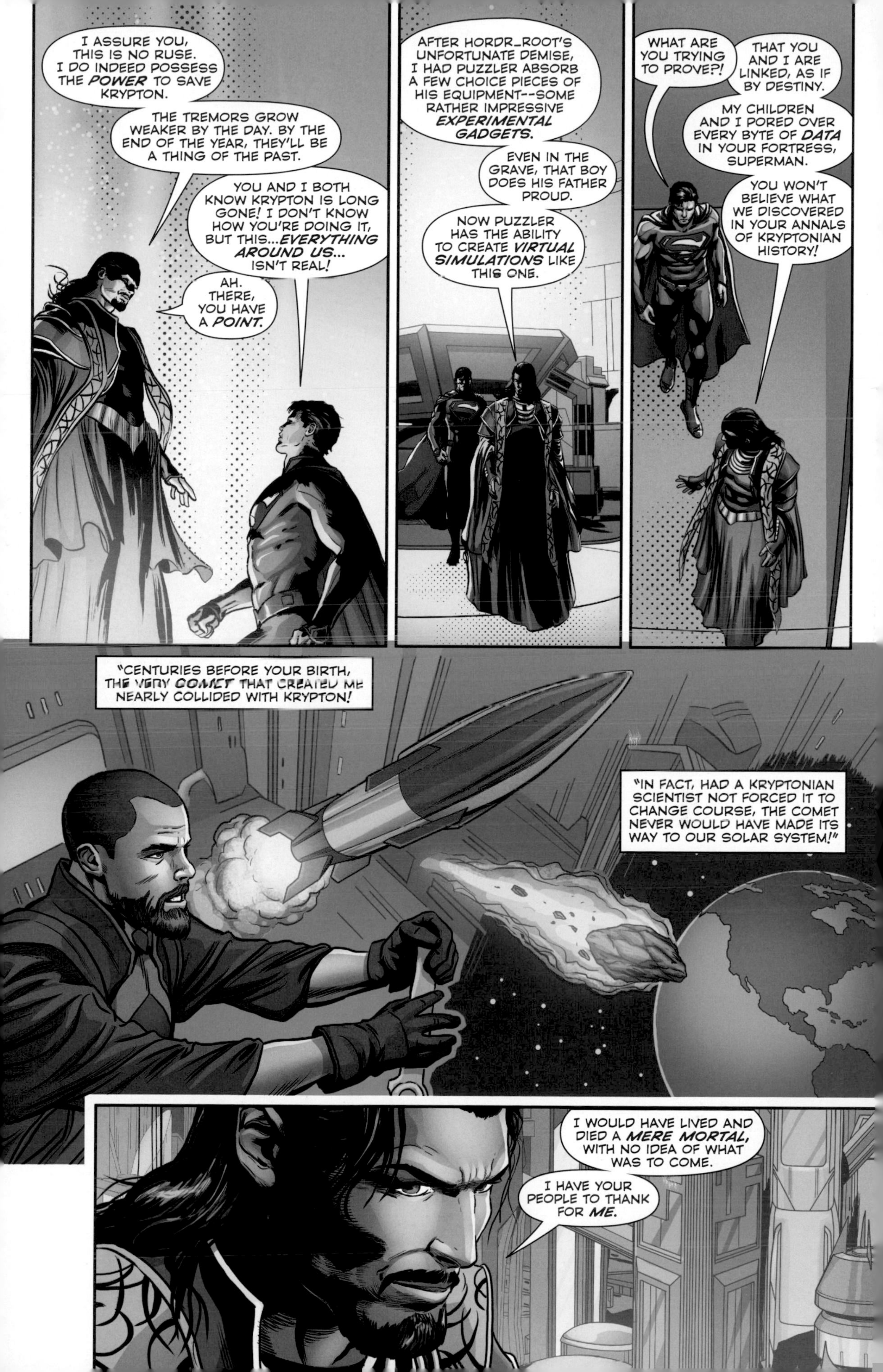
I ASSURE YOU, THIS IS NO RUSE. I DO INDEED POSSESS THE POWER TO SAVE KRYPTON.
THE TREMORS GROW WEAKER BY THE DAY. BY THE END OF THE YEAR, THEY'LL BE A THING OF THE PAST.
YOU AND I BOTH KNOW KRYPTON IS LONG GONE! I DON'T KNOW HOW YOU'RE DOING IT, BUT THIS...EVERYTHING AROUND US... ISN'T REAL!
AH. THERE, YOU HAVE A POINT.
AFTER HORDR_ROOT'S UNFORTUNATE DEMISE, I HAD PUZZLER ABSORB A FEW CHOICE PIECES OF HIS EQUIPMENT--SOME RATHER IMPRESSIVE EXPERIMENTAL GADGETS.
EVEN IN THE GRAVE, THAT BOY DOES HIS FATHER PROUD.
NOW PUZZLER HAS THE ABILITY TO CREATE VIRTUAL SIMULATIONS LIKE THIS ONE.
WHAT ARE YOU TRYING TO PROVE?!
THAT YOU AND I ARE LINKED, AS IF BY DESTINY.
MY CHILDREN AND I PORED OVER EVERY BYTE OF DATA IN YOUR FORTRESS, SUPERMAN.
YOU WON'T BELIEVE WHAT WE DISCOVERED IN YOUR ANNALS OF KRYPTONIAN HISTORY!
"CENTURIES BEFORE YOUR BIRTH, THE VERY COMET THAT CREATED ME NEARLY COLLIDED WITH KRYPTON!
"IN FACT, HAD A KRYPTONIAN SCIENTIST NOT FORCED IT TO CHANGE COURSE, THE COMET NEVER WOULD HAVE MADE ITS WAY TO OUR SOLAR SYSTEM!"
I WOULD HAVE LIVED AND DIED A MERE MORTAL, WITH NO IDEA OF WHAT WAS TO COME.
I HAVE YOUR PEOPLE TO THANK FOR ME.

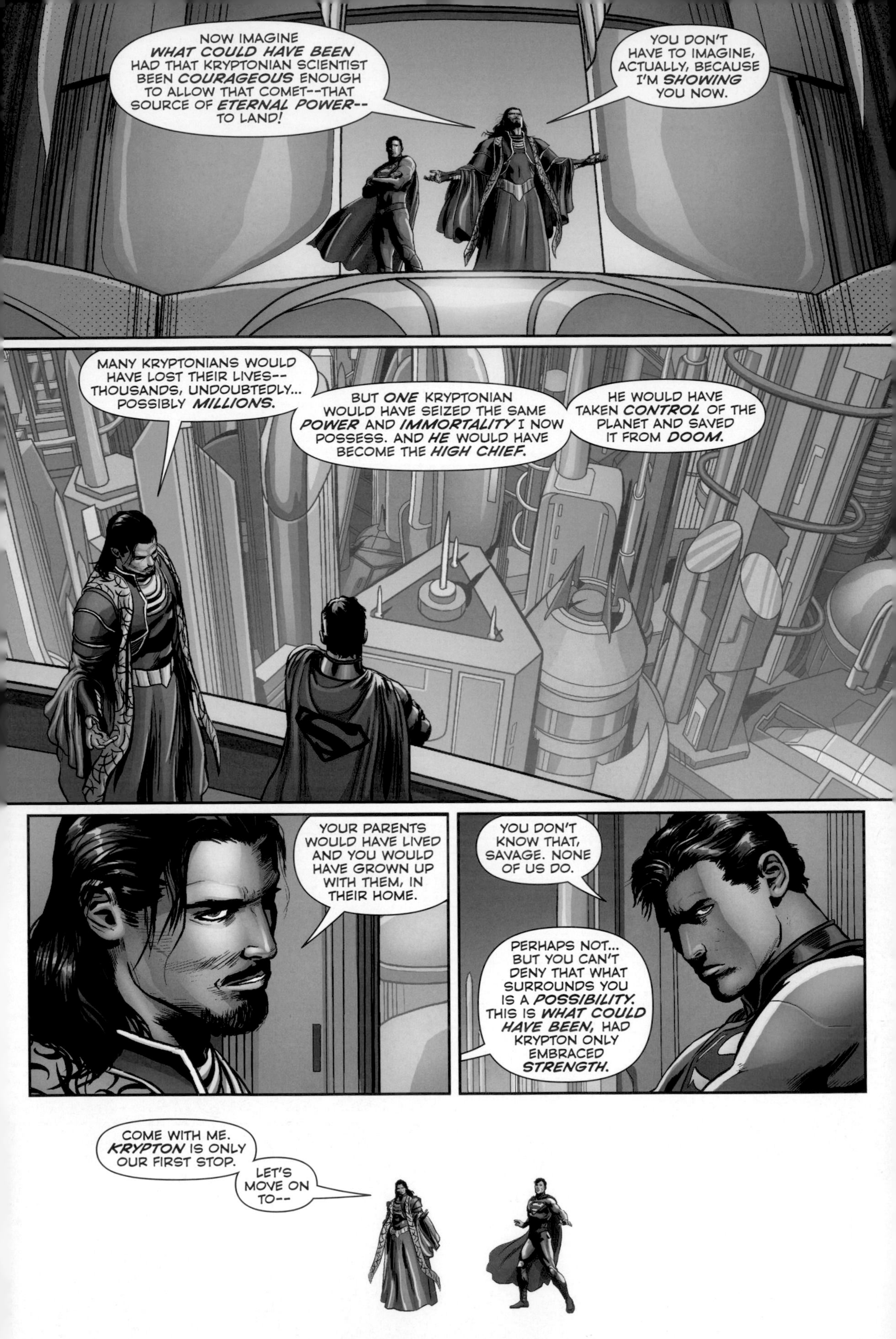
NOW IMAGINE *WHAT COULD HAVE BEEN* HAD THAT KRYPTONIAN SCIENTIST BEEN *COURAGEOUS* ENOUGH TO ALLOW THAT COMET--THAT SOURCE OF *ETERNAL POWER*-- TO LAND!
YOU DON'T HAVE TO IMAGINE, ACTUALLY, BECAUSE I'M *SHOWING* YOU NOW.
MANY KRYPTONIANS WOULD HAVE LOST THEIR LIVES-- THOUSANDS, UNDOUBTEDLY... POSSIBLY *MILLIONS*.
BUT *ONE* KRYPTONIAN WOULD HAVE SEIZED THE SAME *POWER* AND *IMMORTALITY* I NOW POSSESS. AND *HE* WOULD HAVE BECOME THE *HIGH CHIEF*.
HE WOULD HAVE TAKEN *CONTROL* OF THE PLANET AND SAVED IT FROM *DOOM*.
YOUR PARENTS WOULD HAVE LIVED AND YOU WOULD HAVE GROWN UP WITH THEM, IN THEIR HOME.
YOU DON'T KNOW THAT, SAVAGE. NONE OF US DO.
PERHAPS NOT... BUT YOU CAN'T DENY THAT WHAT SURROUNDS YOU IS A *POSSIBILITY*. THIS IS *WHAT COULD HAVE BEEN*, HAD KRYPTON ONLY EMBRACED *STRENGTH*.
COME WITH ME. *KRYPTON* IS ONLY OUR FIRST STOP.
LET'S MOVE ON TO--

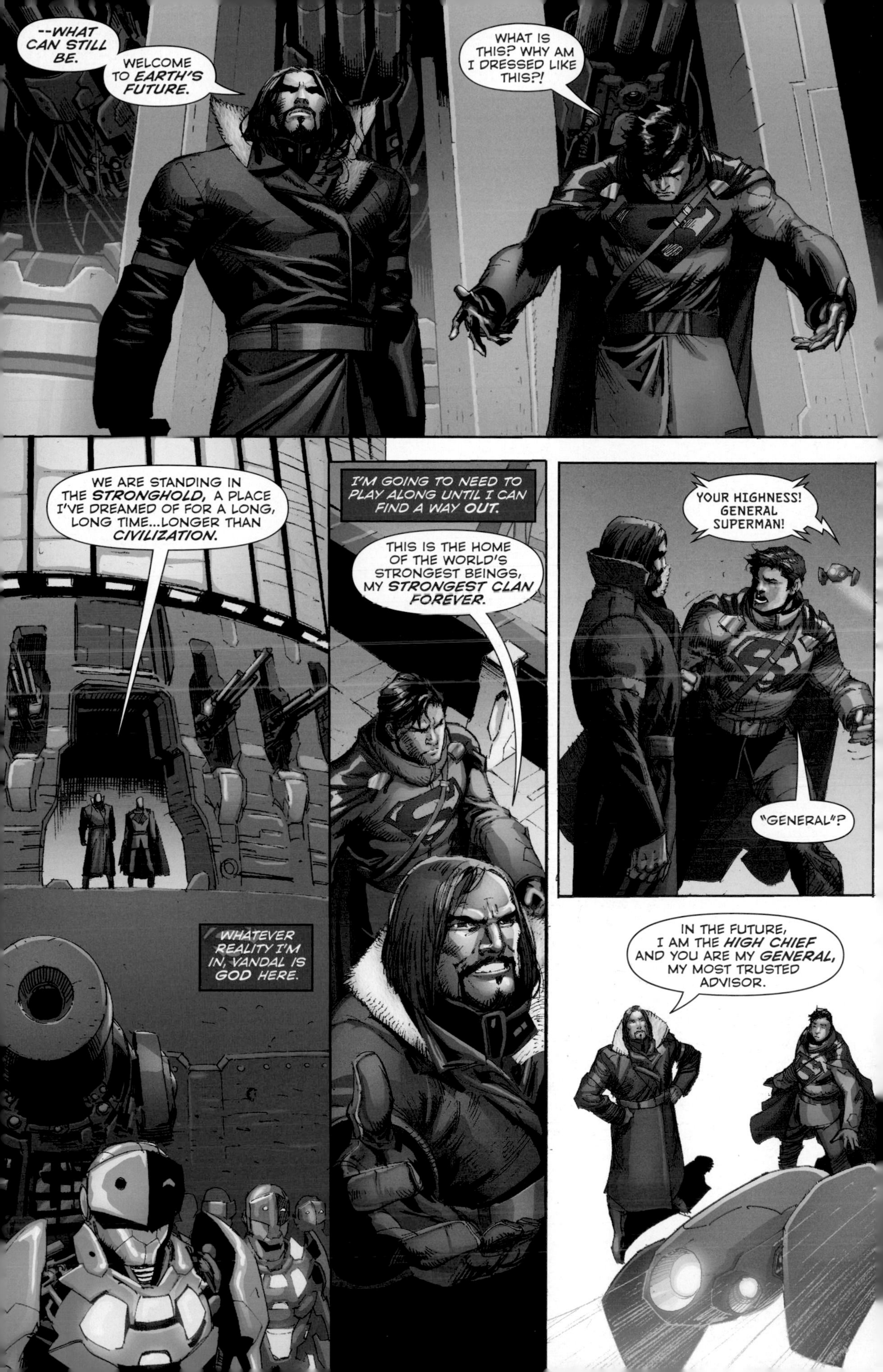

--WHAT CAN STILL BE.
WELCOME TO EARTH'S FUTURE.
WHAT IS THIS? WHY AM I DRESSED LIKE THIS?!
WE ARE STANDING IN THE STRONGHOLD, A PLACE I'VE DREAMED OF FOR A LONG, LONG TIME...LONGER THAN CIVILIZATION.
I'M GOING TO NEED TO PLAY ALONG UNTIL I CAN FIND A WAY OUT.
THIS IS THE HOME OF THE WORLD'S STRONGEST BEINGS, MY STRONGEST CLAN FOREVER.
YOUR HIGHNESS! GENERAL SUPERMAN!
"GENERAL"?
WHATEVER REALITY I'M IN, VANDAL IS GOD HERE.
IN THE FUTURE, I AM THE HIGH CHIEF AND YOU ARE MY GENERAL, MY MOST TRUSTED ADVISOR.

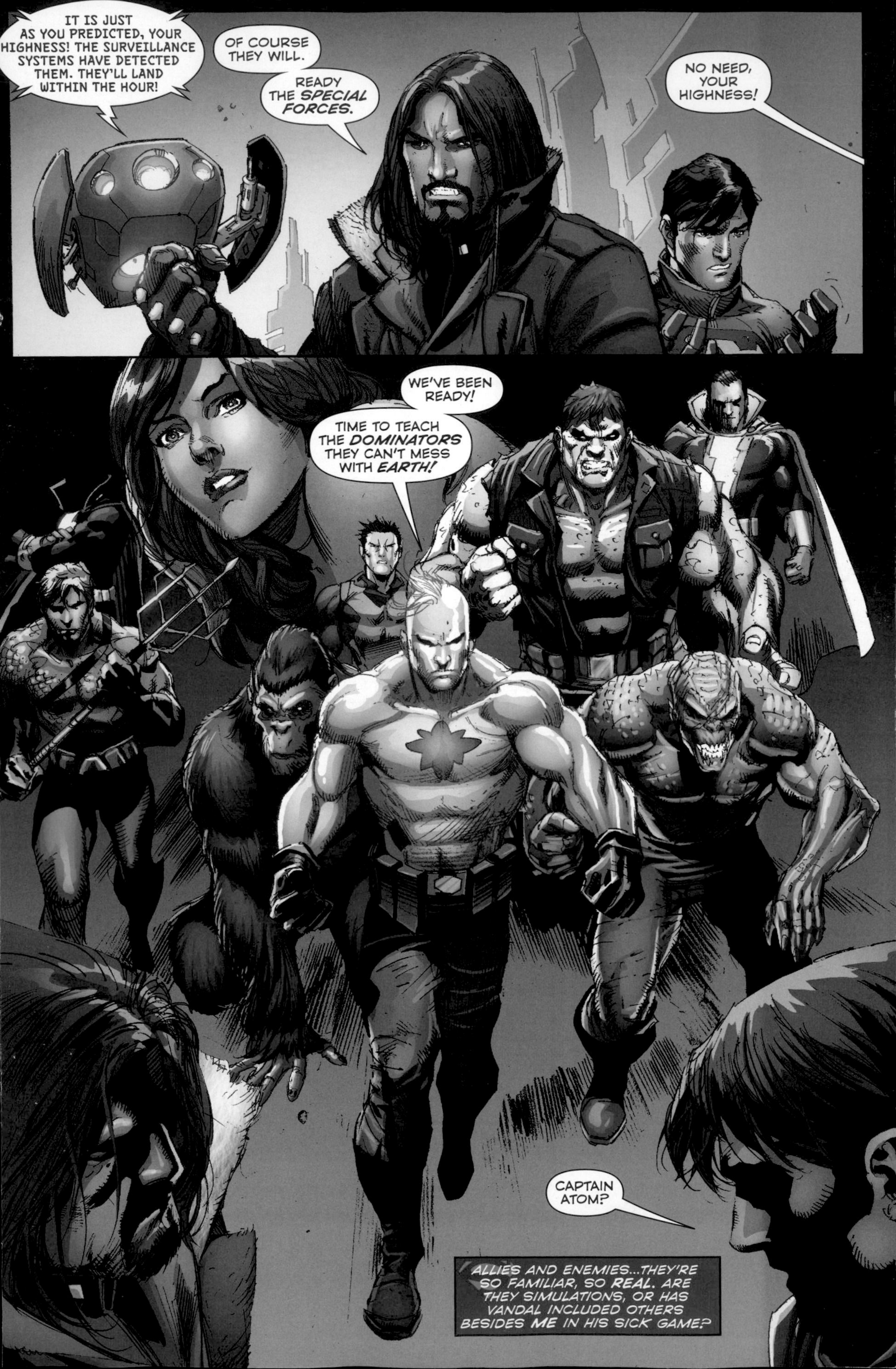
IT IS JUST AS YOU PREDICTED, YOUR HIGHNESS! THE SURVEILLANCE SYSTEMS HAVE DETECTED THEM. THEY'LL LAND WITHIN THE HOUR!
OF COURSE THEY WILL.
READY THE SPECIAL FORCES.
NO NEED, YOUR HIGHNESS!
WE'VE BEEN READY!
TIME TO TEACH THE DOMINATORS THEY CAN'T MESS WITH EARTH!
CAPTAIN ATOM?
ALLIES AND ENEMIES...THEY'RE SO FAMILIAR, SO REAL. ARE THEY SIMULATIONS, OR HAS VANDAL INCLUDED OTHERS BESIDES ME IN HIS SICK GAME?

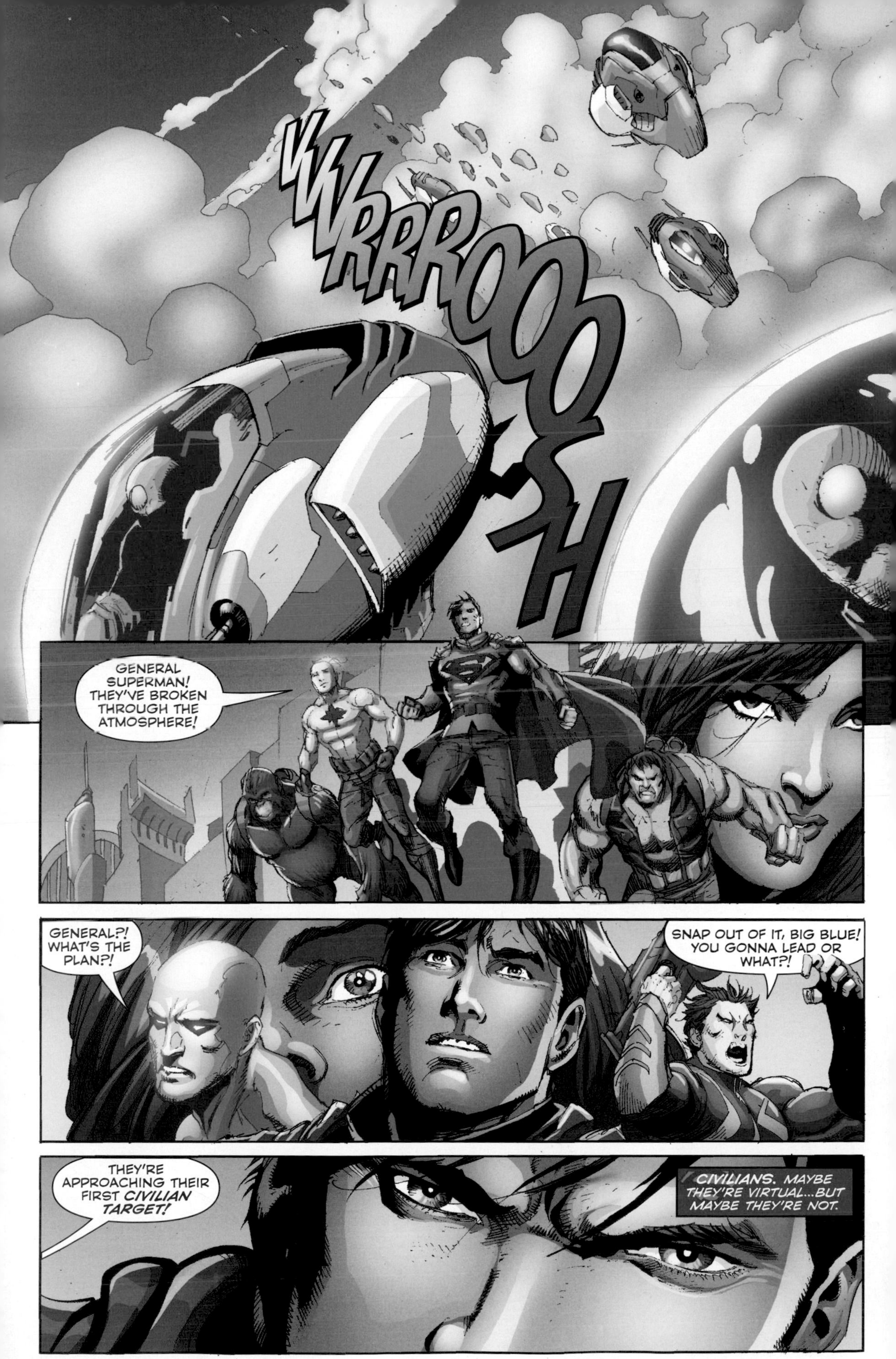
VVRRROOOOSH
GENERAL SUPERMAN! THEY'VE BROKEN THROUGH THE ATMOSPHERE!
GENERAL?! WHAT'S THE PLAN?!
SNAP OUT OF IT, BIG BLUE! YOU GONNA LEAD OR WHAT?!
THEY'RE APPROACHING THEIR FIRST CIVILIAN TARGET!
CIVILIANS. MAYBE THEY'RE VIRTUAL...BUT MAYBE THEY'RE NOT.

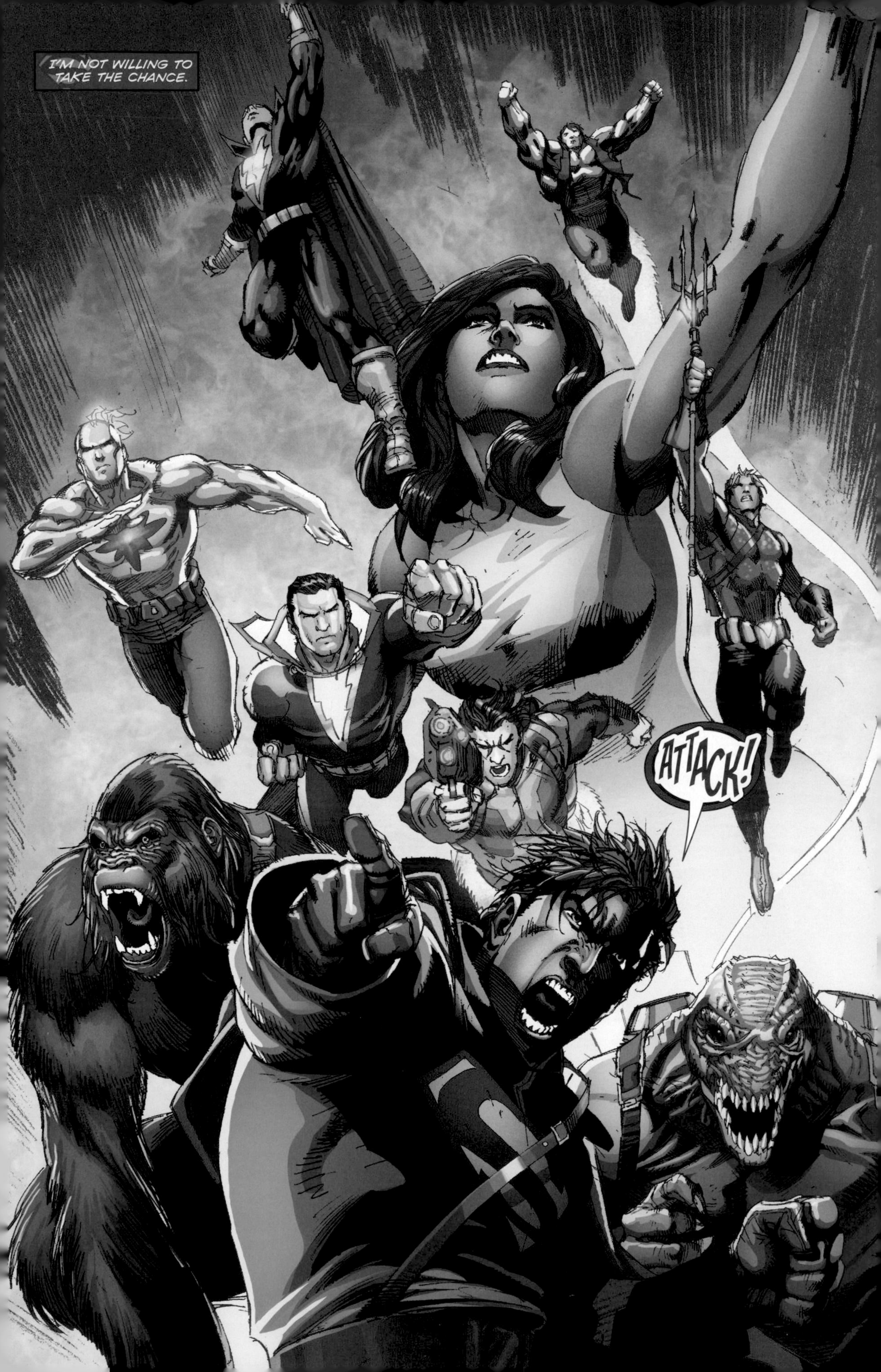
I'M NOT WILLING TO TAKE THE CHANCE.
ATTACK!

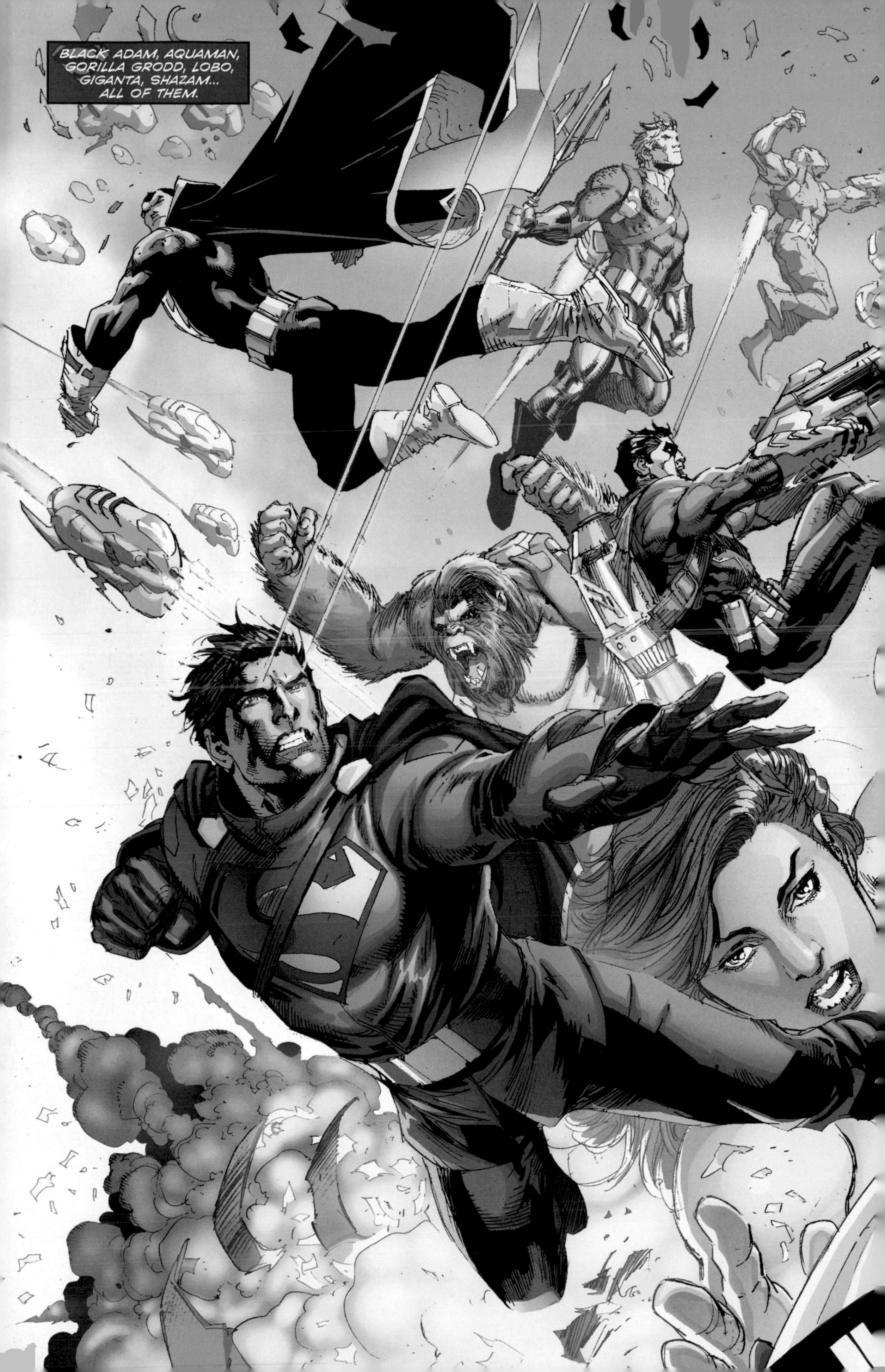
BLACK ADAM, AQUAMAN, GORILLA GRODD, LOBO, GIGANTA, SHAZAM... ALL OF THEM.

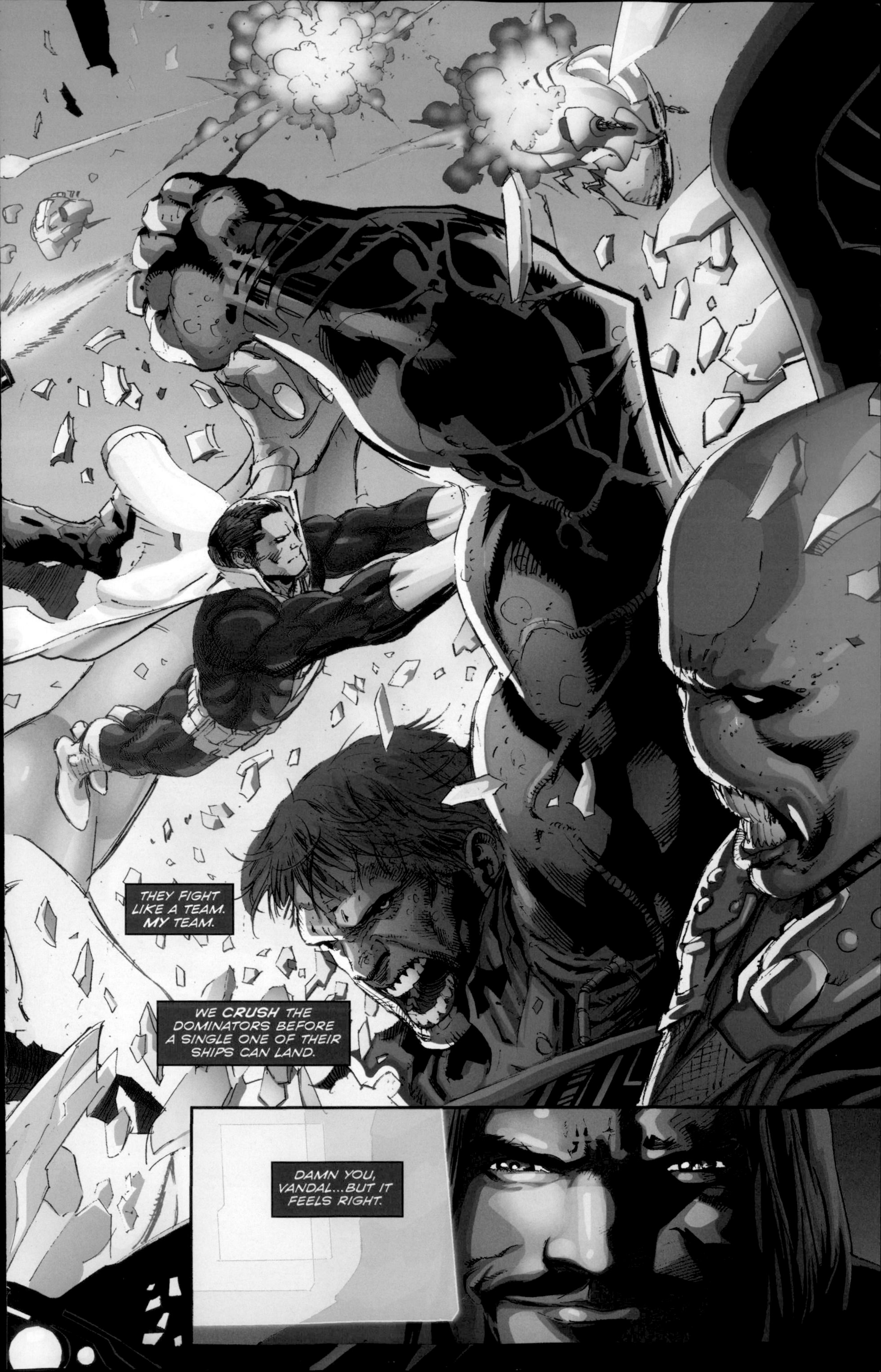
THEY FIGHT LIKE A TEAM. MY TEAM.
WE CRUSH THE DOMINATORS BEFORE A SINGLE ONE OF THEIR SHIPS CAN LAND.
DAMN YOU, VANDAL...BUT IT FEELS RIGHT.

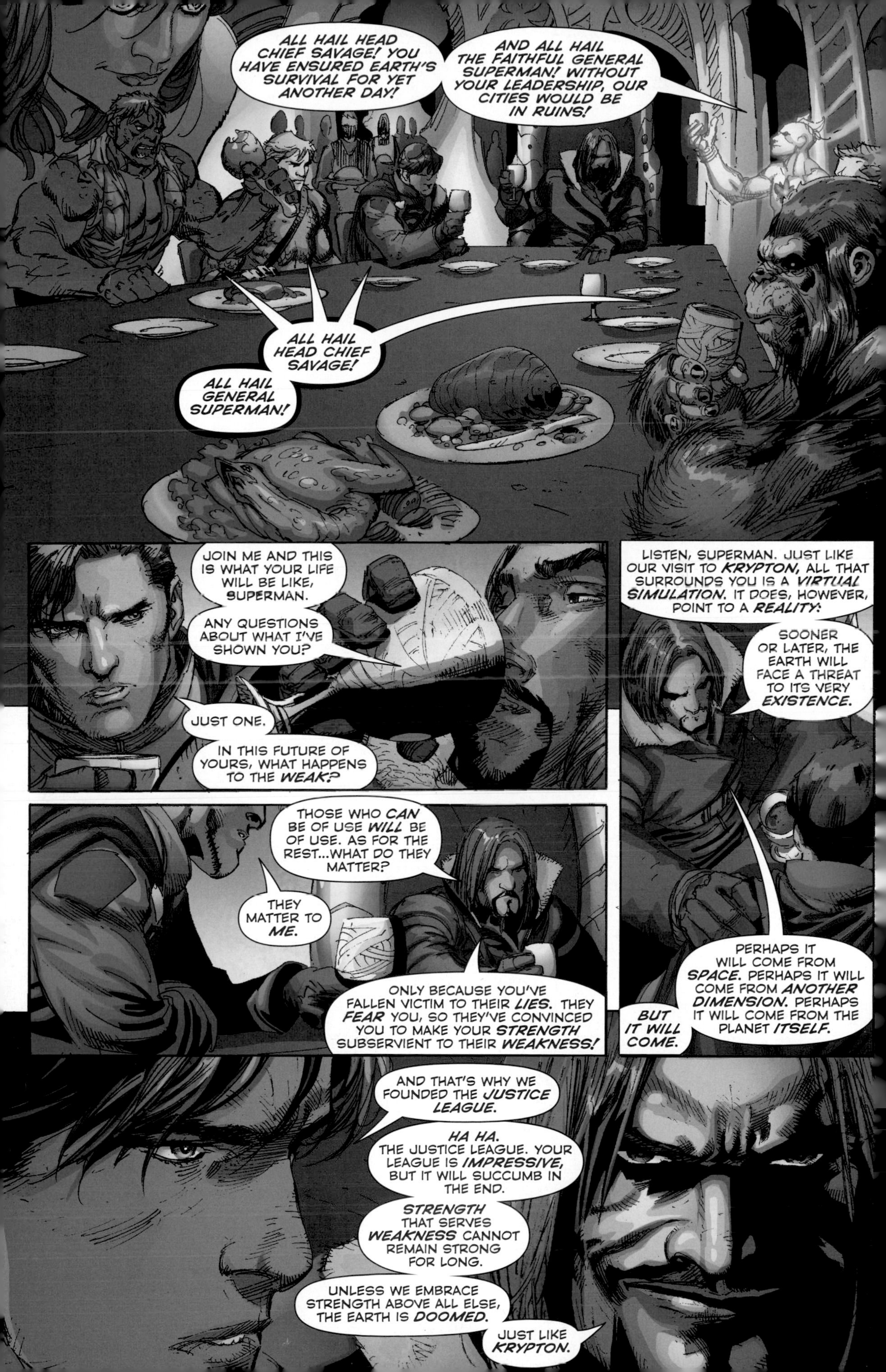
ALL HAIL HEAD CHIEF SAVAGE! YOU HAVE ENSURED EARTH'S SURVIVAL FOR YET ANOTHER DAY!
AND ALL HAIL THE FAITHFUL GENERAL SUPERMAN! WITHOUT YOUR LEADERSHIP, OUR CITIES WOULD BE IN RUINS!
ALL HAIL HEAD CHIEF SAVAGE!
ALL HAIL GENERAL SUPERMAN!
JOIN ME AND THIS IS WHAT YOUR LIFE WILL BE LIKE, SUPERMAN.
ANY QUESTIONS ABOUT WHAT I'VE SHOWN YOU?
JUST ONE.
IN THIS FUTURE OF YOURS, WHAT HAPPENS TO THE WEAK?
THOSE WHO CAN BE OF USE WILL BE OF USE. AS FOR THE REST...WHAT DO THEY MATTER?
THEY MATTER TO ME.
ONLY BECAUSE YOU'VE FALLEN VICTIM TO THEIR LIES. THEY FEAR YOU, SO THEY'VE CONVINCED YOU TO MAKE YOUR STRENGTH SUBSERVIENT TO THEIR WEAKNESS!
LISTEN, SUPERMAN. JUST LIKE OUR VISIT TO KRYPTON, ALL THAT SURROUNDS YOU IS A VIRTUAL SIMULATION. IT DOES, HOWEVER, POINT TO A REALITY:
SOONER OR LATER, THE EARTH WILL FACE A THREAT TO ITS VERY EXISTENCE.
PERHAPS IT WILL COME FROM SPACE. PERHAPS IT WILL COME FROM ANOTHER DIMENSION. PERHAPS IT WILL COME FROM THE PLANET ITSELF.
BUT IT WILL COME.
AND THAT'S WHY WE FOUNDED THE JUSTICE LEAGUE.
HA HA. THE JUSTICE LEAGUE. YOUR LEAGUE IS IMPRESSIVE, BUT IT WILL SUCCUMB IN THE END.
STRENGTH THAT SERVES WEAKNESS CANNOT REMAIN STRONG FOR LONG.
UNLESS WE EMBRACE STRENGTH ABOVE ALL ELSE, THE EARTH IS DOOMED.
JUST LIKE KRYPTON.

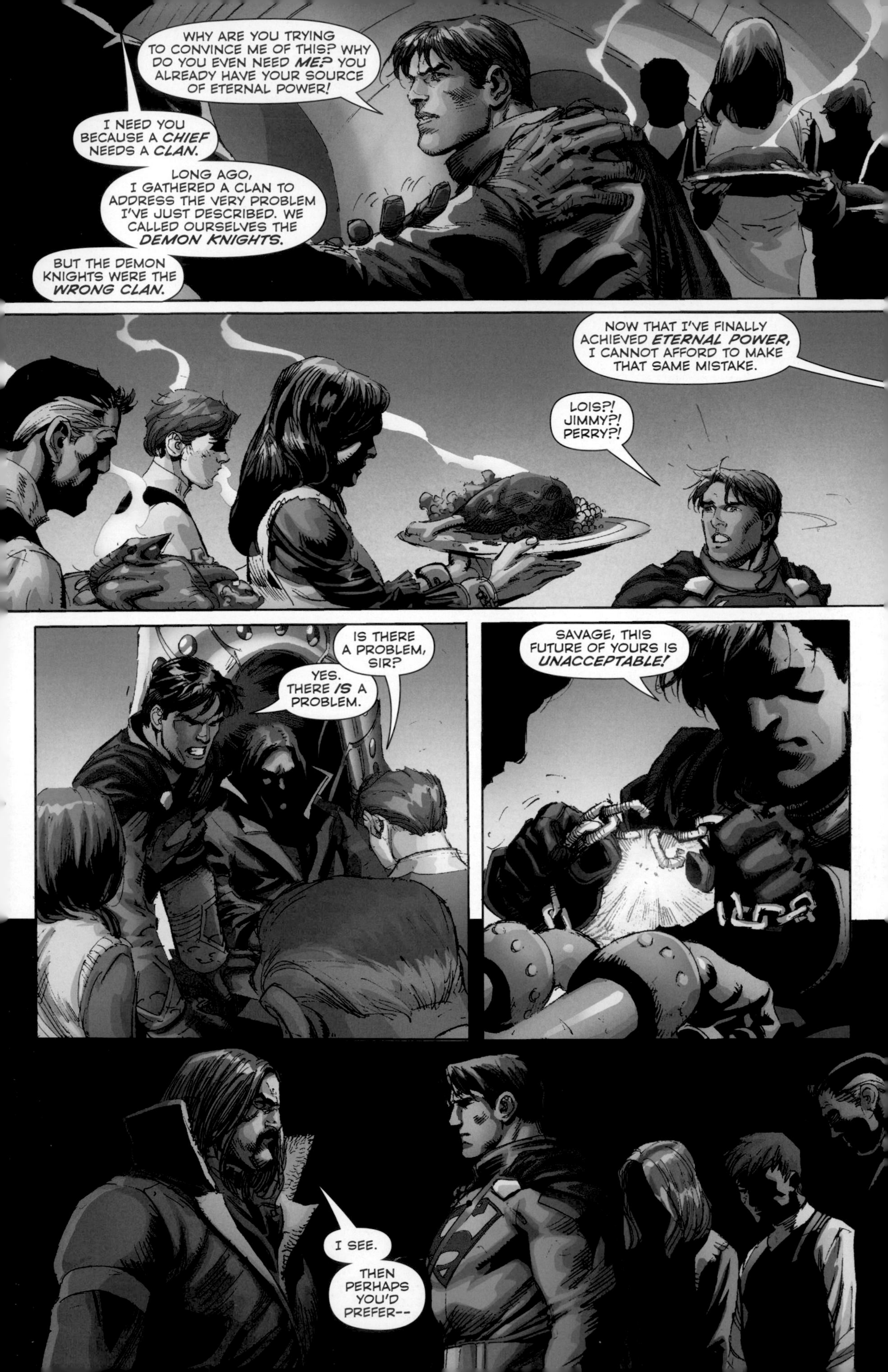
WHY ARE YOU TRYING TO CONVINCE ME OF THIS? WHY DO YOU EVEN NEED *ME?* YOU ALREADY HAVE YOUR SOURCE OF ETERNAL POWER!
I NEED YOU BECAUSE A *CHIEF* NEEDS A *CLAN.*
LONG AGO, I GATHERED A CLAN TO ADDRESS THE VERY PROBLEM I'VE JUST DESCRIBED. WE CALLED OURSELVES THE *DEMON KNIGHTS.*
BUT THE DEMON KNIGHTS WERE THE *WRONG CLAN.*
NOW THAT I'VE FINALLY ACHIEVED *ETERNAL POWER,* I CANNOT AFFORD TO MAKE THAT SAME MISTAKE.
LOIS?! JIMMY?! PERRY?!
IS THERE A PROBLEM, SIR?
YES. THERE *IS* A PROBLEM.
SAVAGE, THIS FUTURE OF YOURS IS *UNACCEPTABLE!*
I SEE.
THEN PERHAPS YOU'D PREFER--

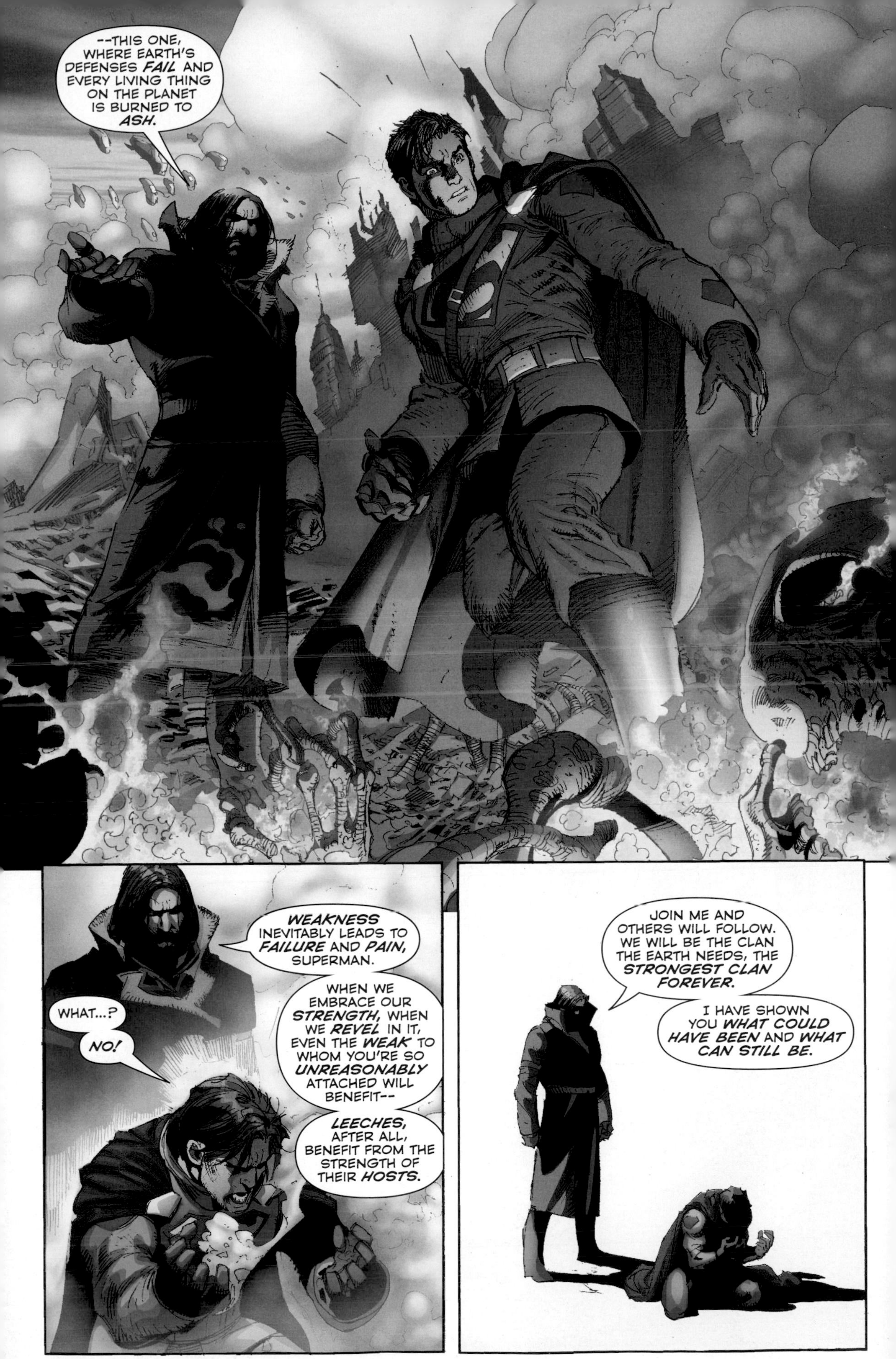
--THIS ONE, WHERE EARTH'S DEFENSES *FAIL* AND EVERY LIVING THING ON THE PLANET IS BURNED TO *ASH*.
WEAKNESS INEVITABLY LEADS TO *FAILURE* AND *PAIN,* SUPERMAN.
WHAT...?
NO!
WHEN WE EMBRACE OUR *STRENGTH,* WHEN WE *REVEL* IN IT, EVEN THE *WEAK* TO WHOM YOU'RE SO *UNREASONABLY* ATTACHED WILL BENEFIT--
LEECHES, AFTER ALL, BENEFIT FROM THE STRENGTH OF THEIR *HOSTS*.
JOIN ME AND OTHERS WILL FOLLOW. WE WILL BE THE CLAN THE EARTH NEEDS, THE *STRONGEST CLAN FOREVER*.
I HAVE SHOWN YOU *WHAT COULD HAVE BEEN* AND *WHAT CAN STILL BE*.

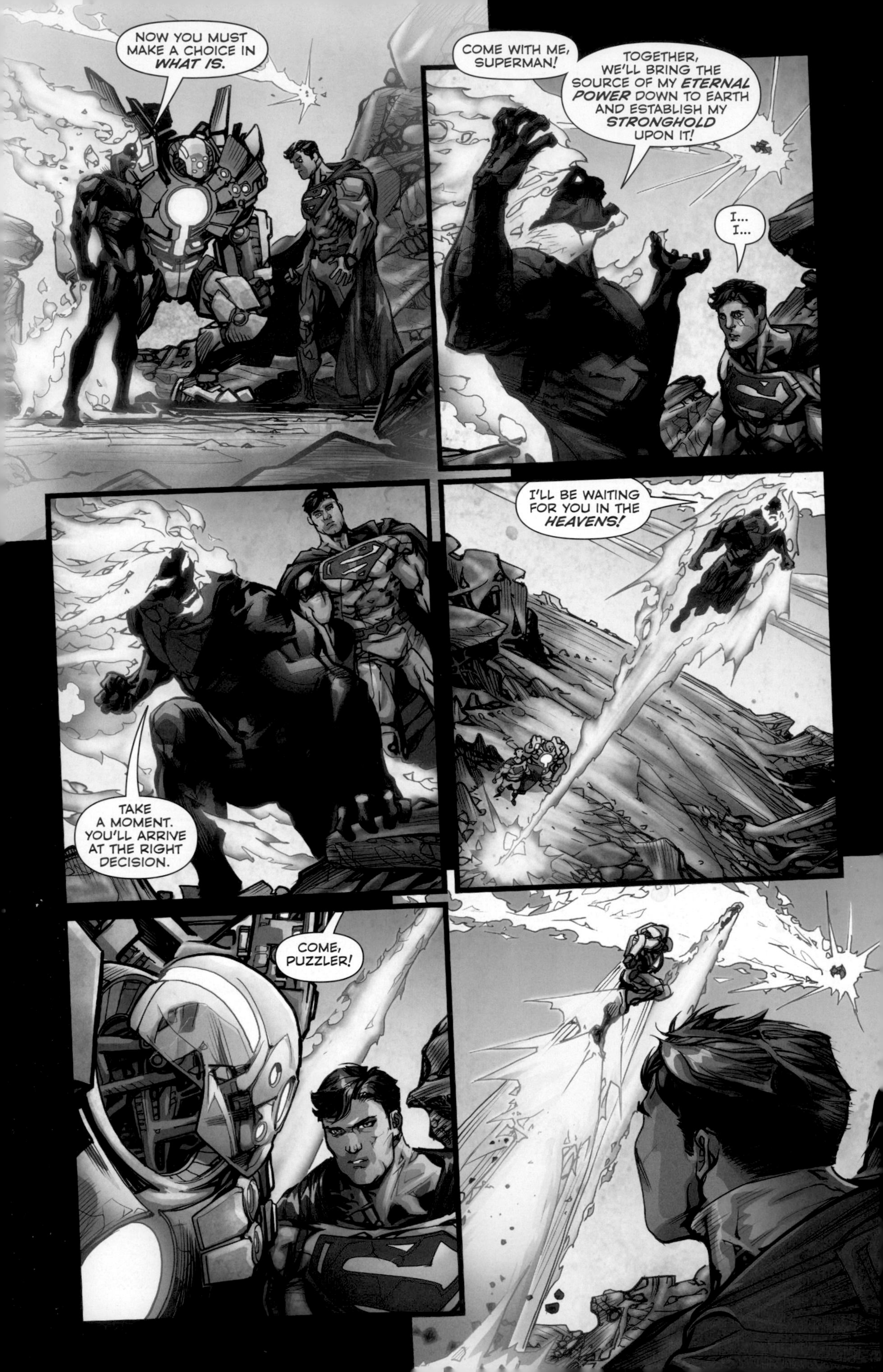
NOW YOU MUST MAKE A CHOICE IN ***WHAT IS.***
COME WITH ME, SUPERMAN!
TOGETHER, WE'LL BRING THE SOURCE OF MY ***ETERNAL POWER*** DOWN TO EARTH AND ESTABLISH MY ***STRONGHOLD*** UPON IT!
I... I...
TAKE A MOMENT. YOU'LL ARRIVE AT THE RIGHT DECISION.
I'LL BE WAITING FOR YOU IN THE ***HEAVENS!***
COME, PUZZLER!

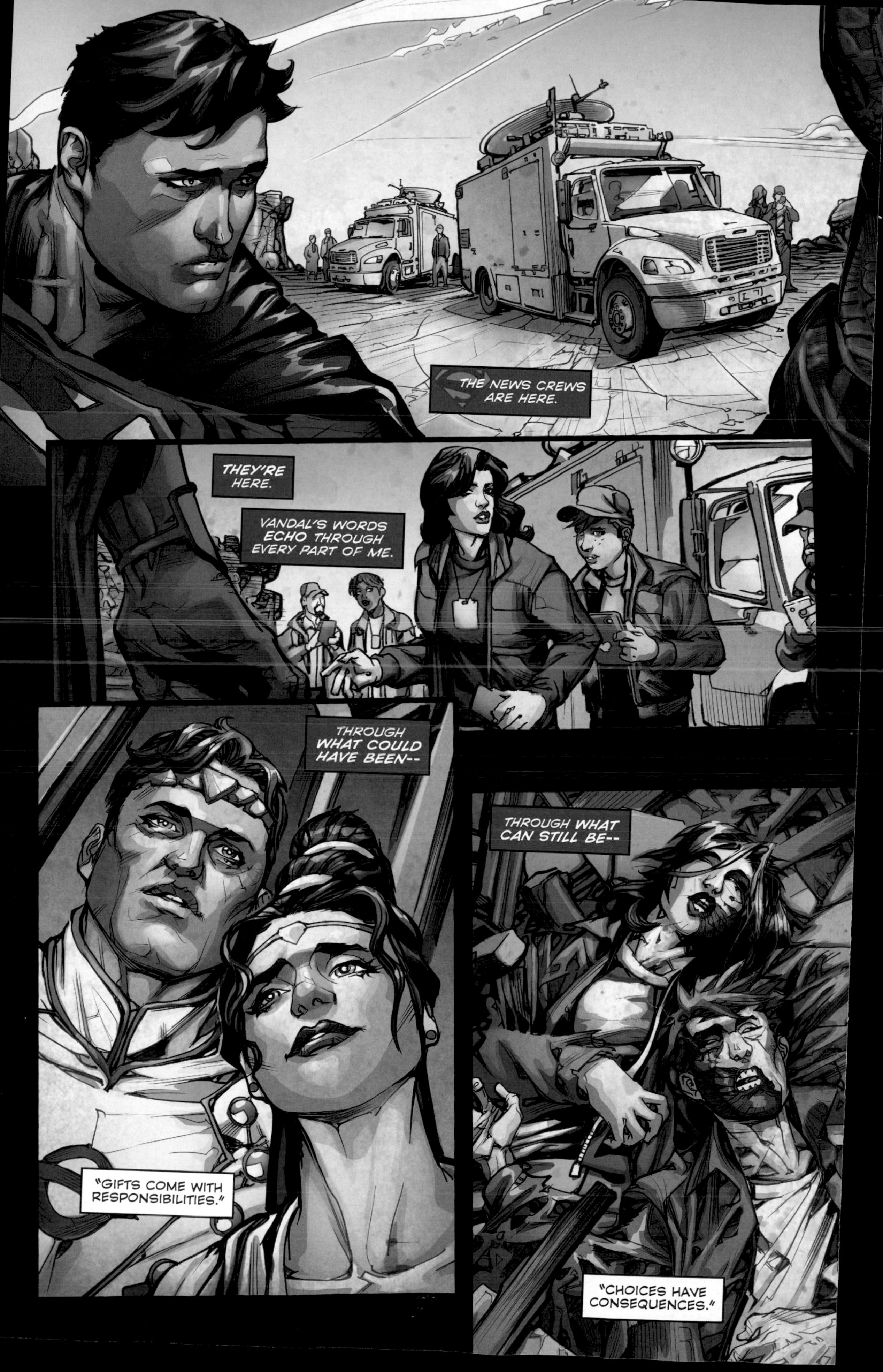
THE NEWS CREWS ARE HERE.
THEY'RE HERE.
VANDAL'S WORDS ECHO THROUGH EVERY PART OF ME.
THROUGH WHAT COULD HAVE BEEN--
"GIFTS COME WITH RESPONSIBILITIES."
THROUGH WHAT CAN STILL BE--
"CHOICES HAVE CONSEQUENCES."

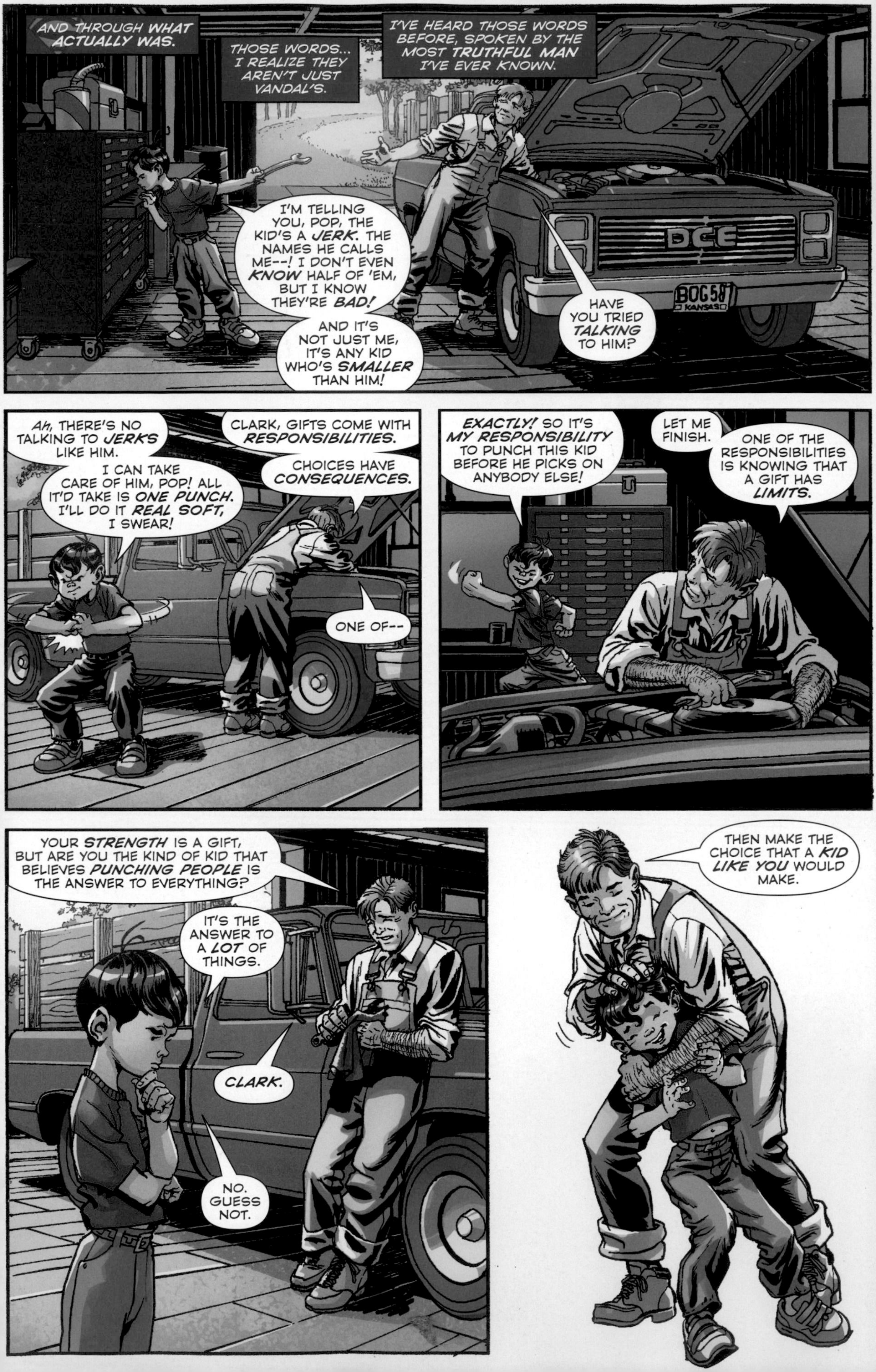
AND THROUGH WHAT ACTUALLY WAS.
THOSE WORDS... I REALIZE THEY AREN'T JUST VANDAL'S.
I'VE HEARD THOSE WORDS BEFORE, SPOKEN BY THE MOST TRUTHFUL MAN I'VE EVER KNOWN.
I'M TELLING YOU, POP, THE KID'S A JERK. THE NAMES HE CALLS ME--! I DON'T EVEN KNOW HALF OF 'EM, BUT I KNOW THEY'RE BAD!
AND IT'S NOT JUST ME, IT'S ANY KID WHO'S SMALLER THAN HIM!
DCE
BOC 58
KANSAS
HAVE YOU TRIED TALKING TO HIM?
Ah, THERE'S NO TALKING TO JERKS LIKE HIM.
I CAN TAKE CARE OF HIM, POP! ALL IT'D TAKE IS ONE PUNCH. I'LL DO IT REAL SOFT, I SWEAR!
CLARK, GIFTS COME WITH RESPONSIBILITIES.
CHOICES HAVE CONSEQUENCES.
ONE OF--
EXACTLY! SO IT'S MY RESPONSIBILITY TO PUNCH THIS KID BEFORE HE PICKS ON ANYBODY ELSE!
LET ME FINISH.
ONE OF THE RESPONSIBILITIES IS KNOWING THAT A GIFT HAS LIMITS.
YOUR STRENGTH IS A GIFT, BUT ARE YOU THE KIND OF KID THAT BELIEVES PUNCHING PEOPLE IS THE ANSWER TO EVERYTHING?
IT'S THE ANSWER TO A LOT OF THINGS.
CLARK.
NO. GUESS NOT.
THEN MAKE THE CHOICE THAT A KID LIKE YOU WOULD MAKE.

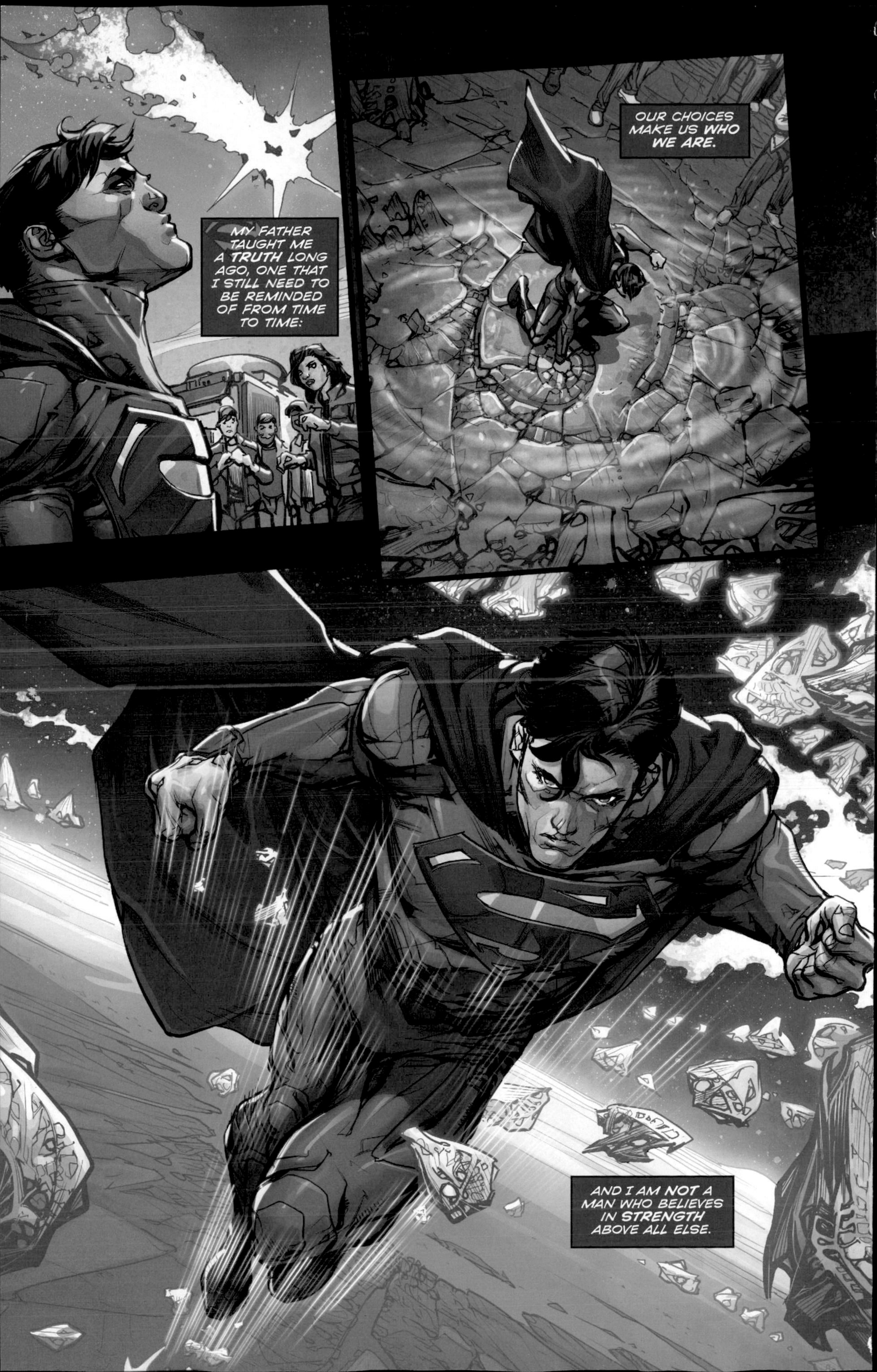
MY FATHER TAUGHT ME A TRUTH LONG AGO, ONE THAT I STILL NEED TO BE REMINDED OF FROM TIME TO TIME:
OUR CHOICES MAKE US WHO WE ARE.
AND I AM NOT A MAN WHO BELIEVES IN STRENGTH ABOVE ALL ELSE.

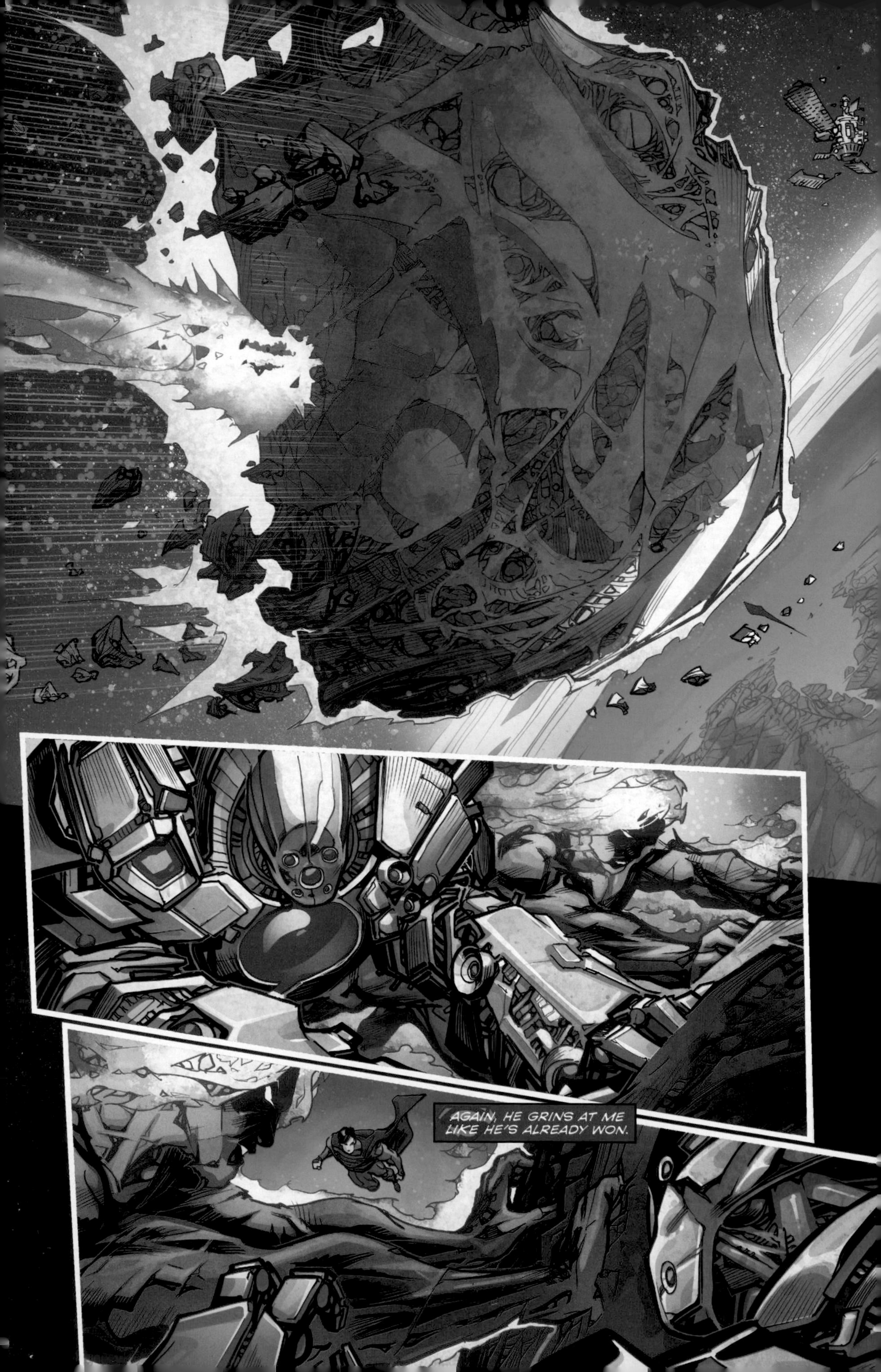
AGAIN, HE GRINS AT ME LIKE HE'S ALREADY WON.

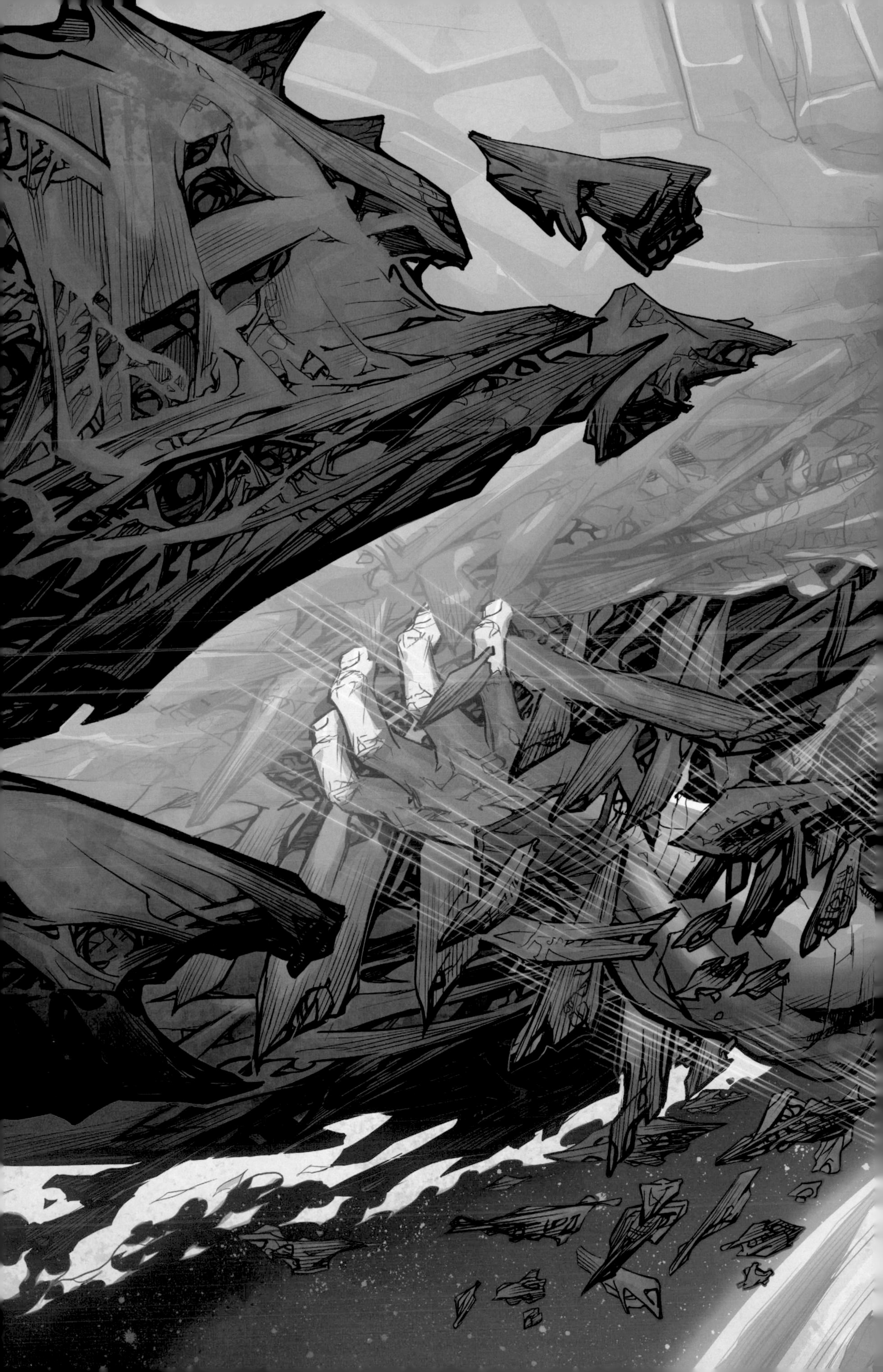

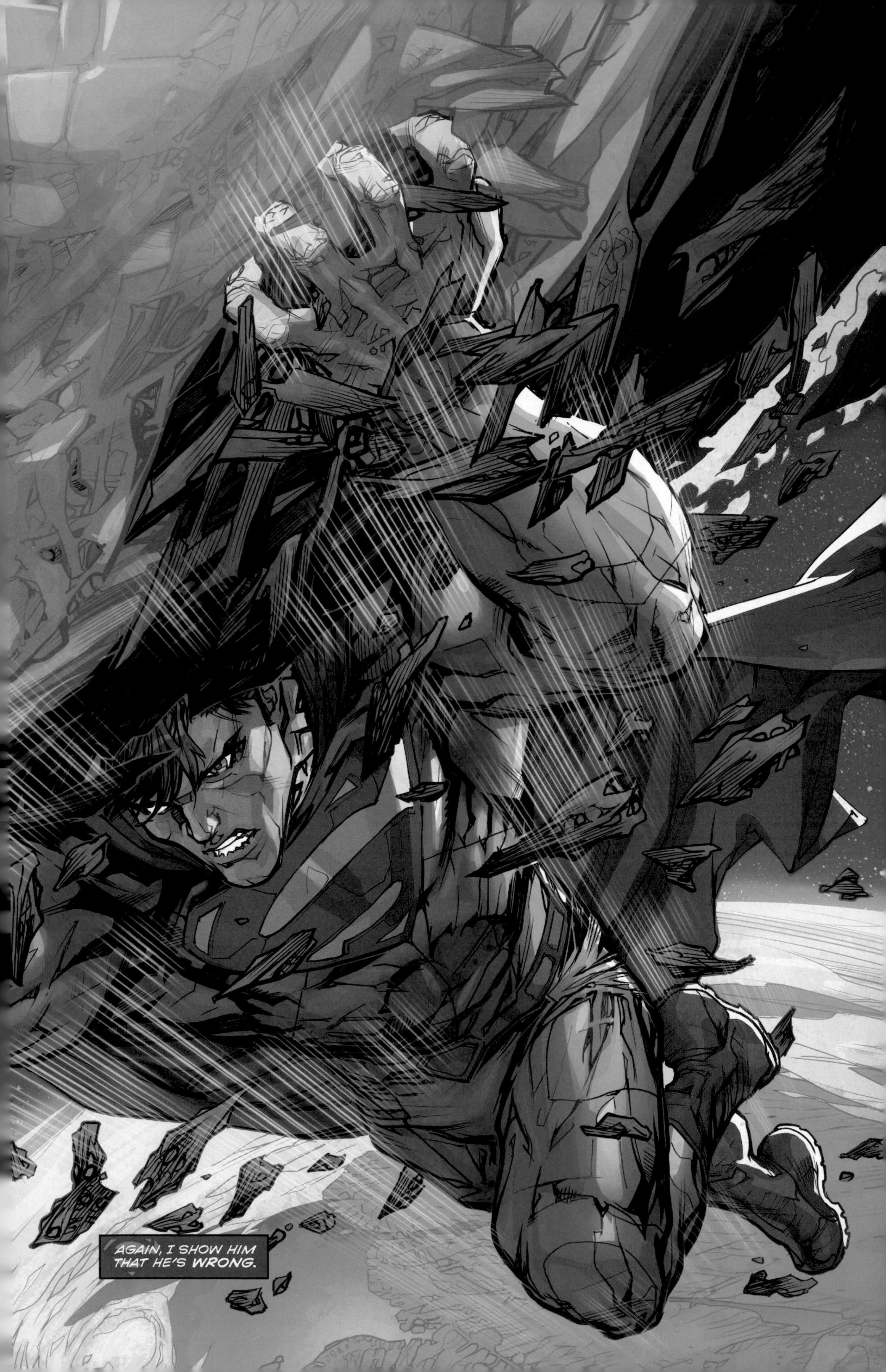
AGAIN, I SHOW HIM THAT HE'S WRONG.

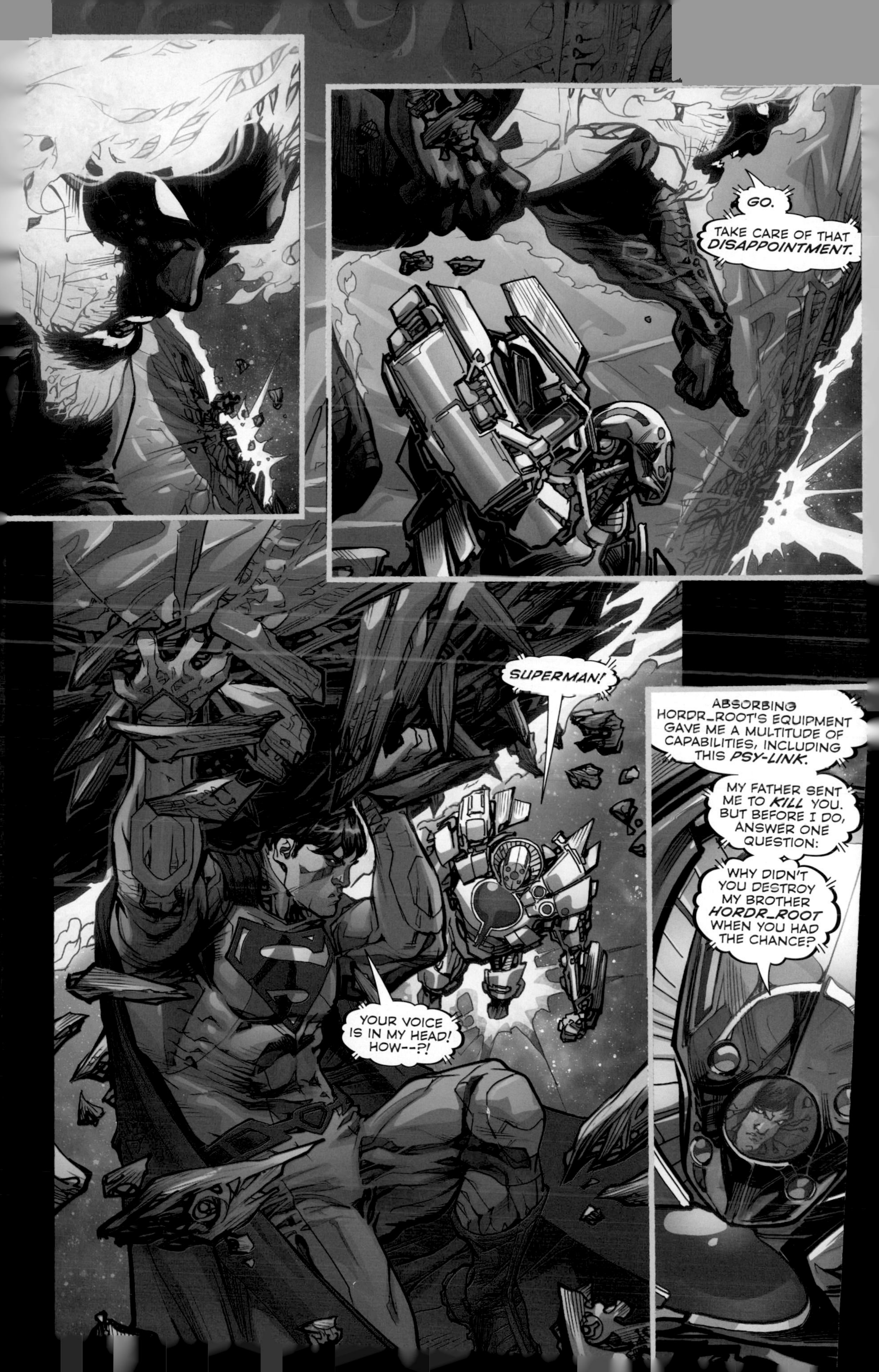
GO.
TAKE CARE OF THAT DISAPPOINTMENT.
SUPERMAN!
ABSORBING HORDR_ROOT'S EQUIPMENT GAVE ME A MULTITUDE OF CAPABILITIES, INCLUDING THIS PSY-LINK.
MY FATHER SENT ME TO KILL YOU. BUT BEFORE I DO, ANSWER ONE QUESTION:
WHY DIDN'T YOU DESTROY MY BROTHER HORDR_ROOT WHEN YOU HAD THE CHANCE?
YOUR VOICE IS IN MY HEAD! HOW--?!

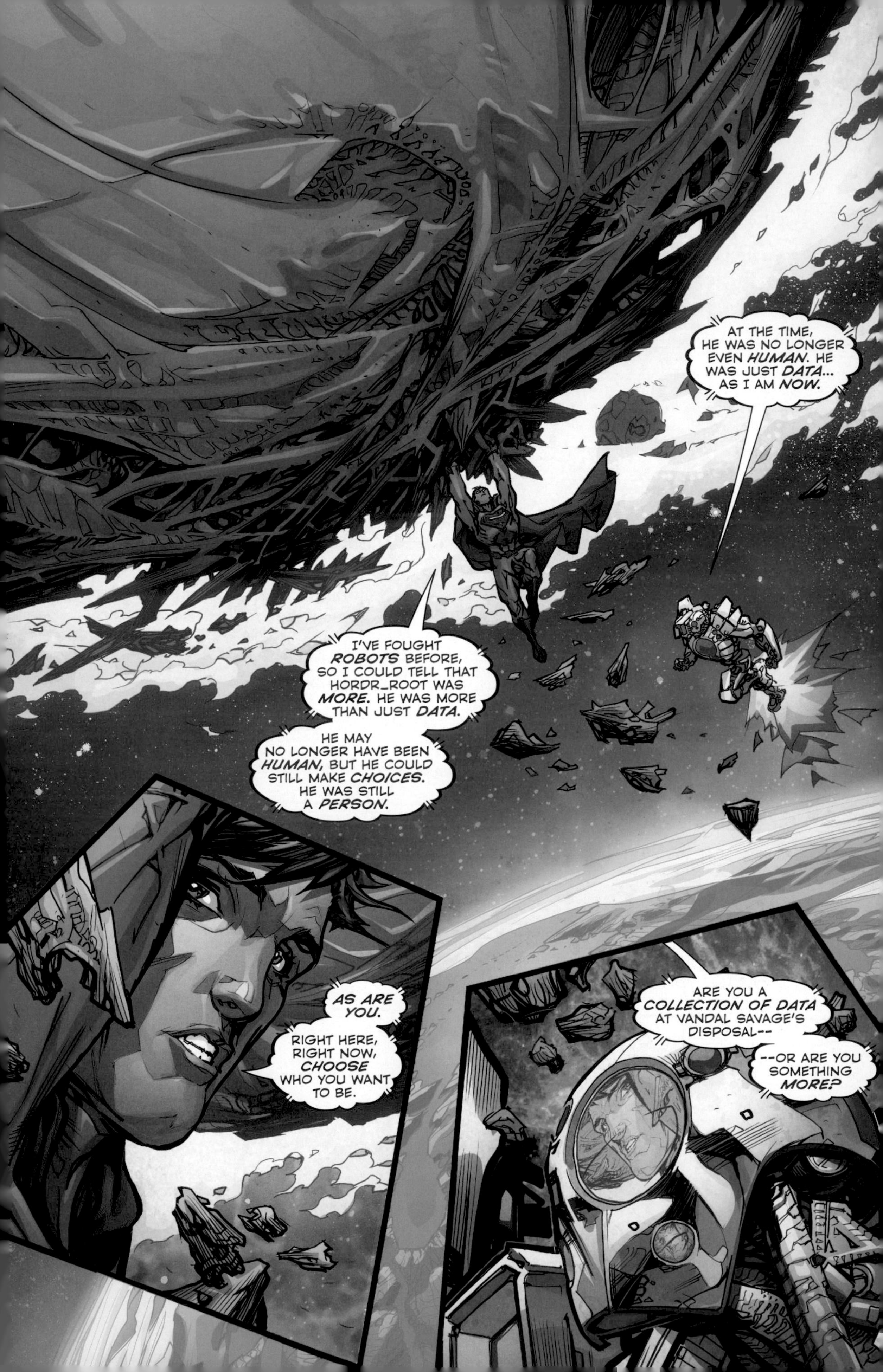
AT THE TIME, HE WAS NO LONGER EVEN HUMAN. HE WAS JUST DATA... AS I AM NOW.
I'VE FOUGHT ROBOTS BEFORE, SO I COULD TELL THAT HORDR_ROOT WAS MORE. HE WAS MORE THAN JUST DATA.
HE MAY NO LONGER HAVE BEEN HUMAN, BUT HE COULD STILL MAKE CHOICES. HE WAS STILL A PERSON.
AS ARE YOU.
RIGHT HERE, RIGHT NOW, CHOOSE WHO YOU WANT TO BE.
ARE YOU A COLLECTION OF DATA AT VANDAL SAVAGE'S DISPOSAL--
--OR ARE YOU SOMETHING MORE?

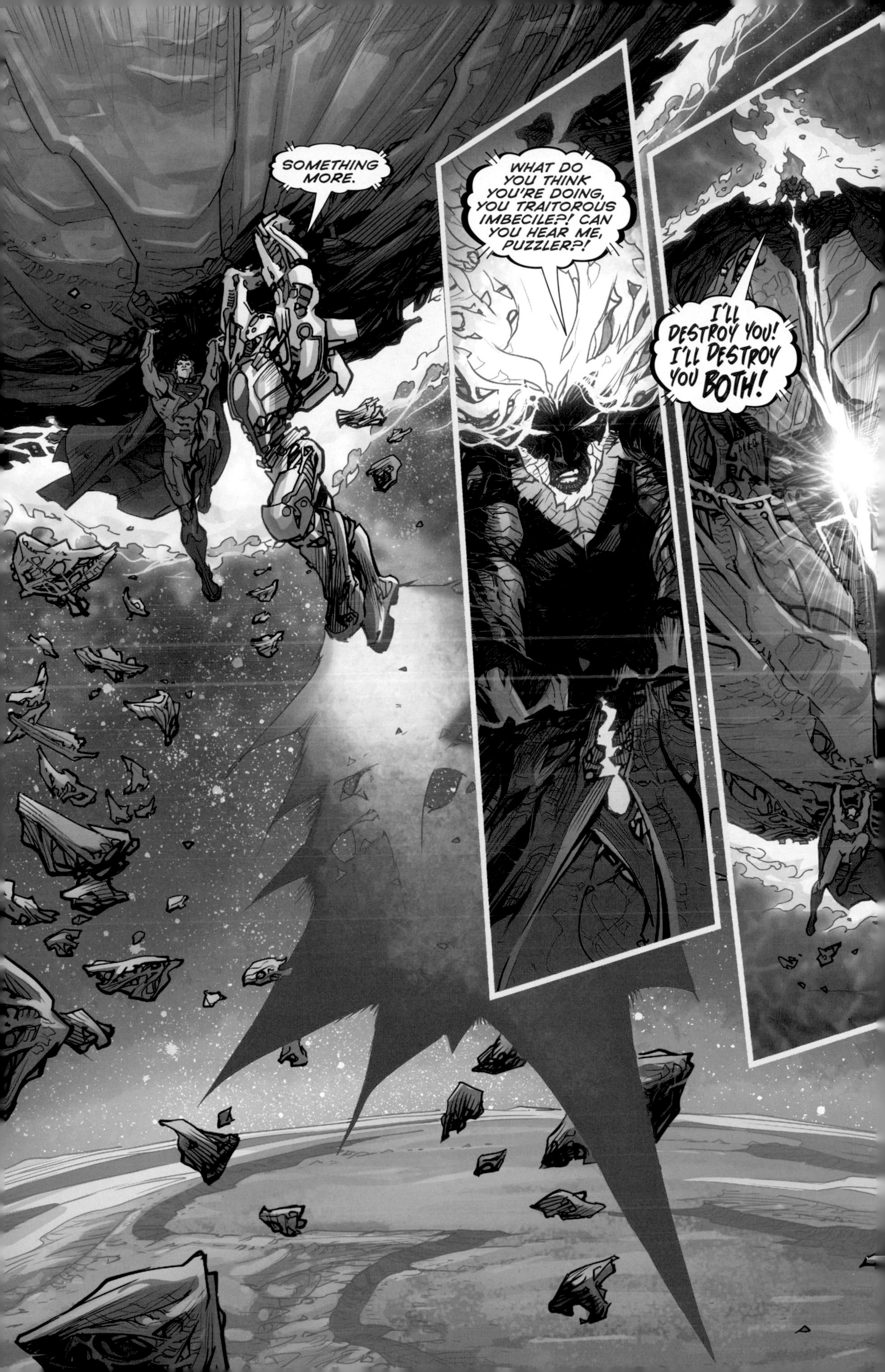
SOMETHING MORE.
WHAT DO YOU THINK YOU'RE DOING, YOU TRAITOROUS IMBECILE?! CAN YOU HEAR ME, PUZZLER?!
I'LL DESTROY YOU! I'LL DESTROY YOU BOTH!

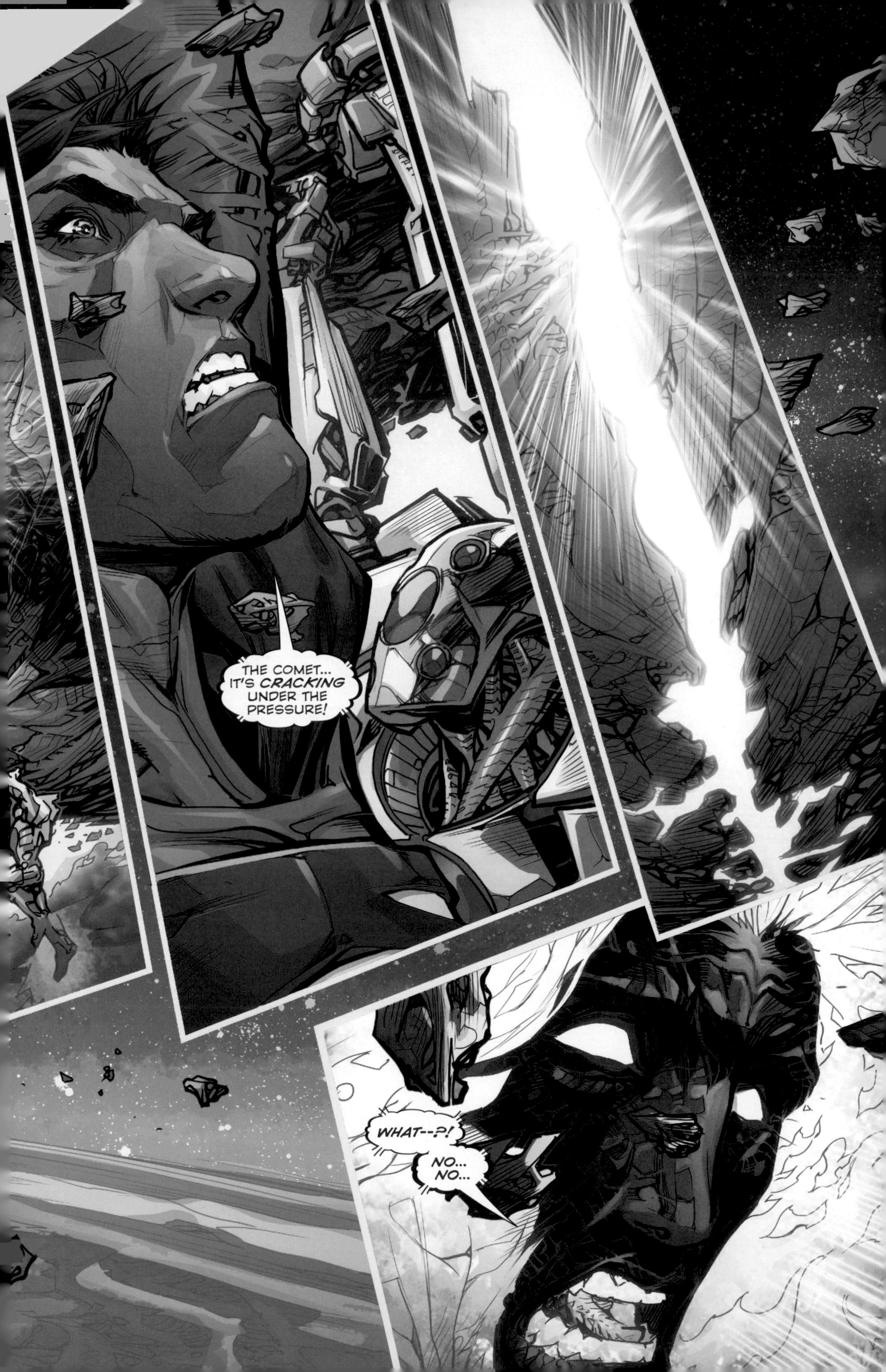
THE COMET... IT'S CRACKING UNDER THE PRESSURE!
WHAT--?!
NO... NO...

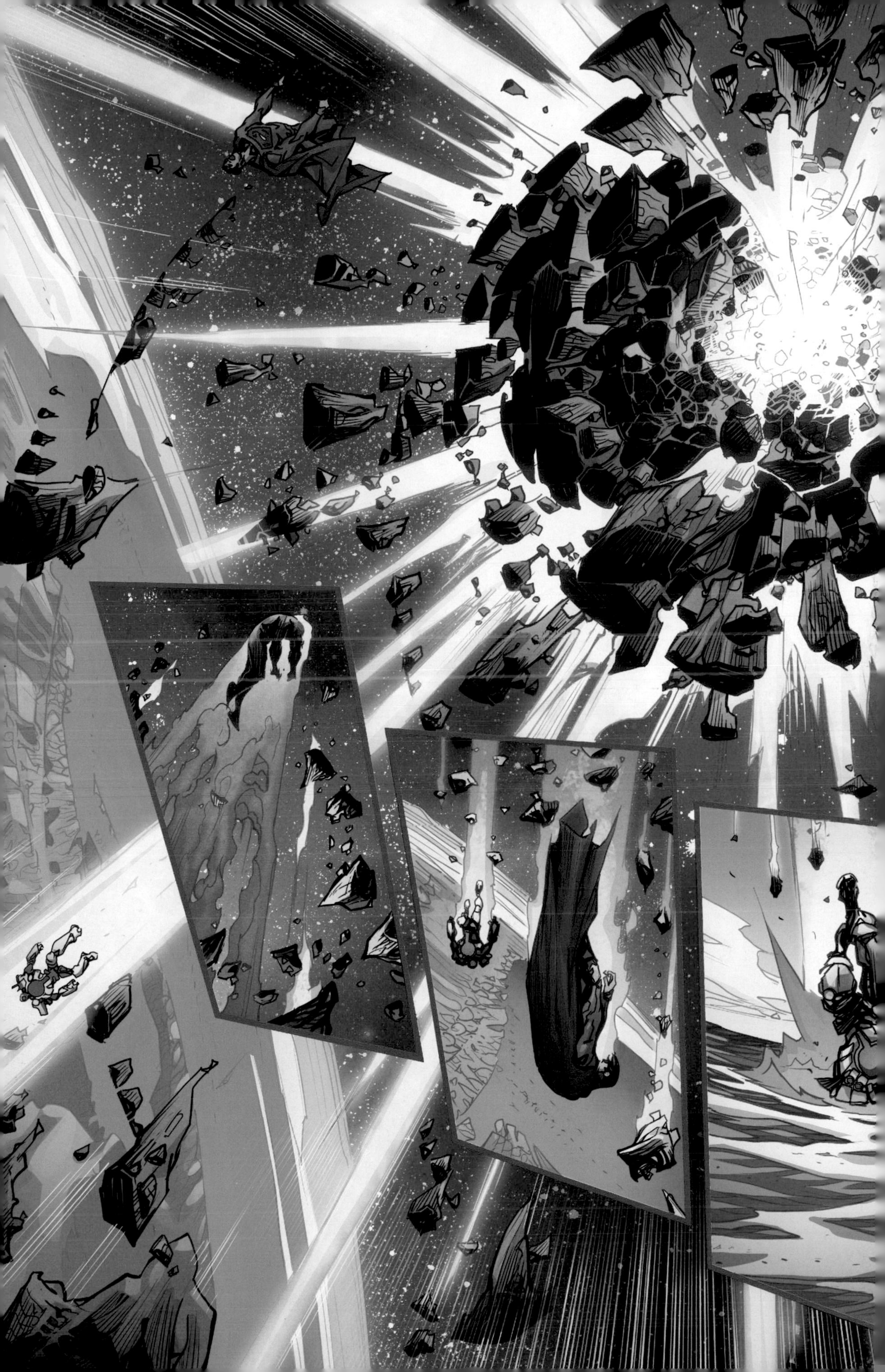

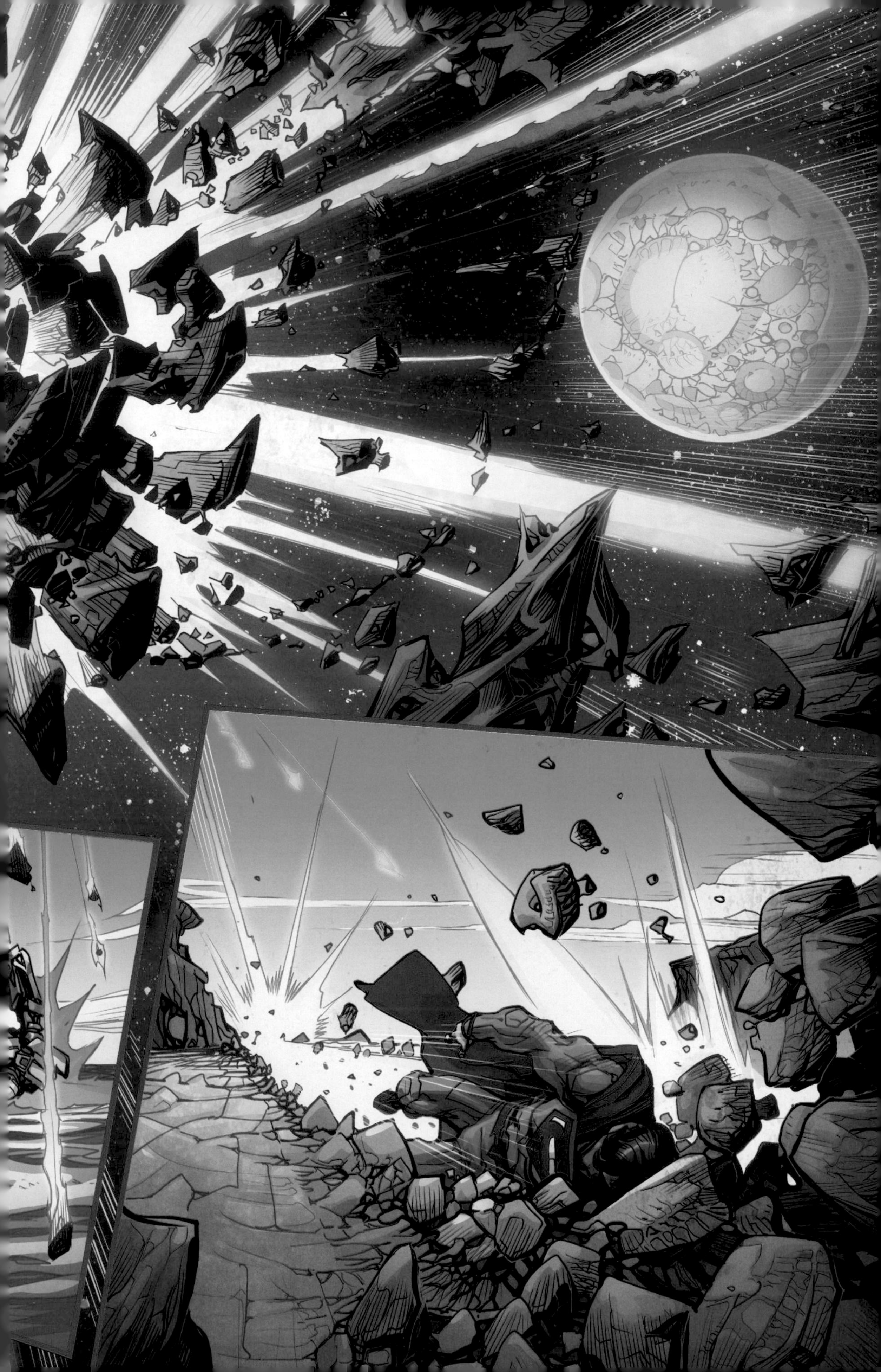

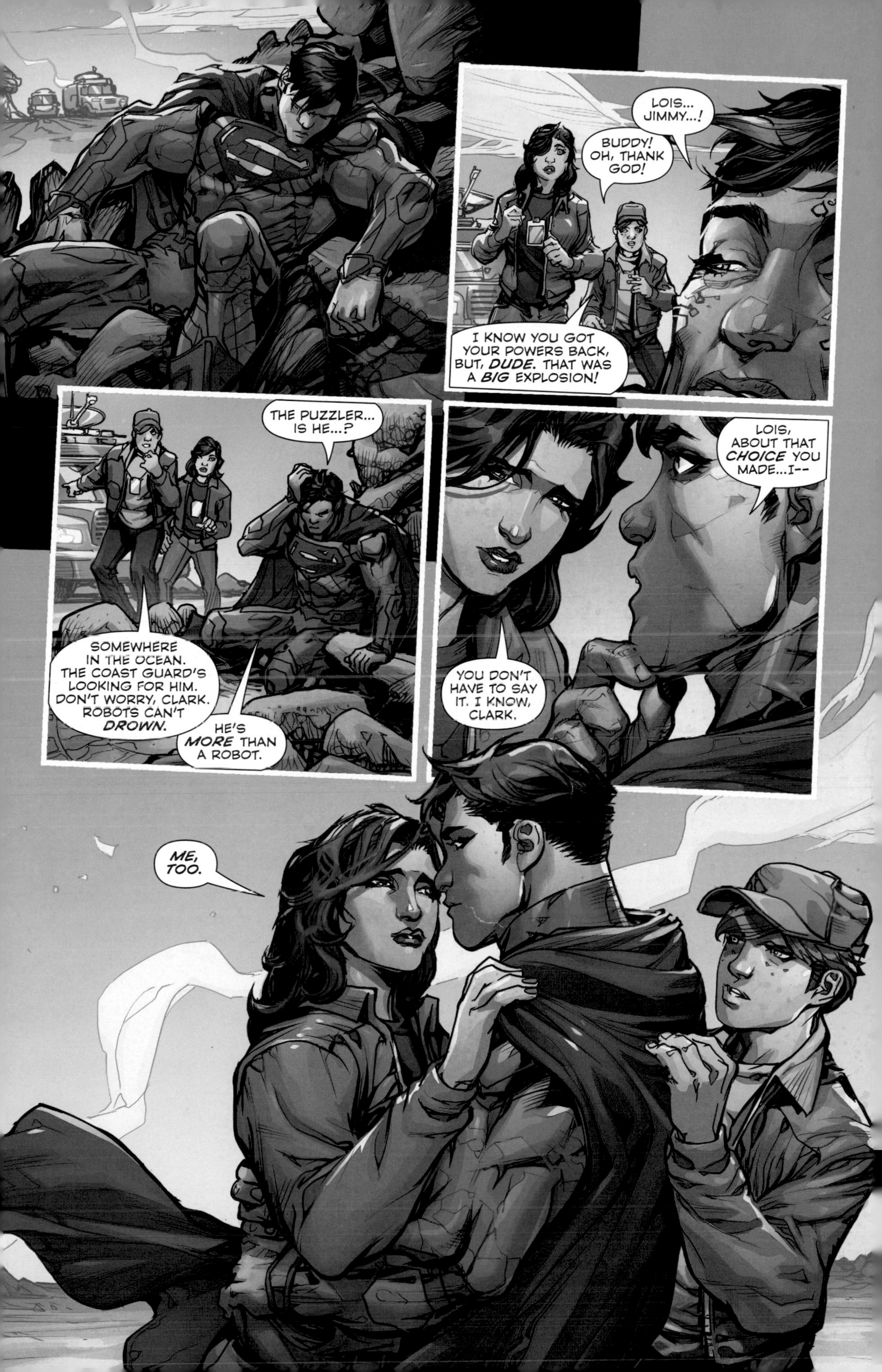

LOIS... JIMMY...!
BUDDY! OH, THANK GOD!
I KNOW YOU GOT YOUR POWERS BACK, BUT, DUDE. THAT WAS A BIG EXPLOSION!
THE PUZZLER... IS HE...?
SOMEWHERE IN THE OCEAN. THE COAST GUARD'S LOOKING FOR HIM. DON'T WORRY, CLARK. ROBOTS CAN'T DROWN.
HE'S MORE THAN A ROBOT.
LOIS, ABOUT THAT CHOICE YOU MADE...I--
YOU DON'T HAVE TO SAY IT. I KNOW, CLARK.
ME, TOO.

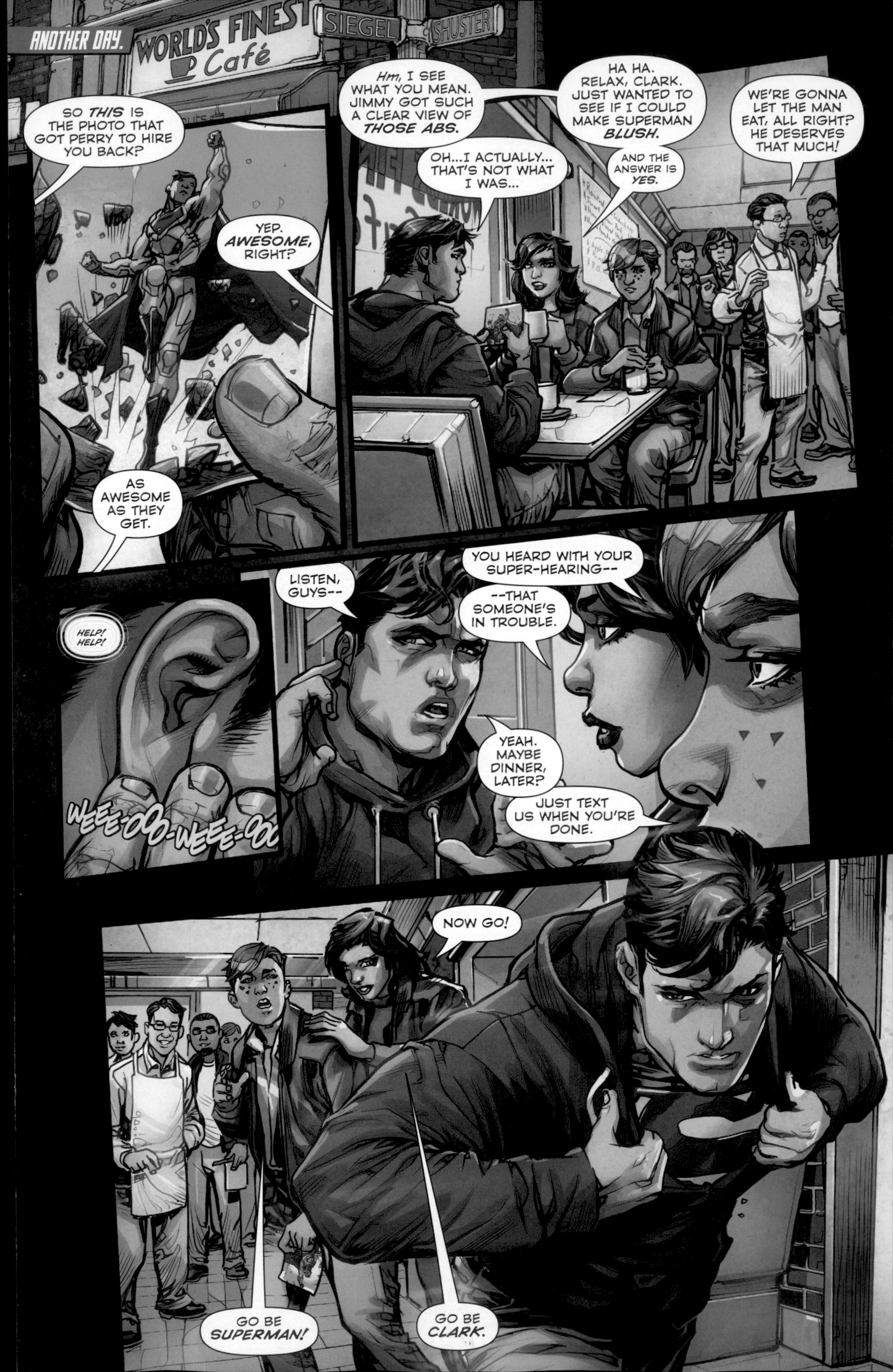

ANOTHER DAY.
WORLD'S FINEST Café
SIEGEL
SHUSTER
SO THIS IS THE PHOTO THAT GOT PERRY TO HIRE YOU BACK?
YEP. AWESOME, RIGHT?
AS AWESOME AS THEY GET.
Hm, I SEE WHAT YOU MEAN. JIMMY GOT SUCH A CLEAR VIEW OF THOSE ABS.
OH...I ACTUALLY... THAT'S NOT WHAT I WAS...
HA HA. RELAX, CLARK. JUST WANTED TO SEE IF I COULD MAKE SUPERMAN BLUSH.
AND THE ANSWER IS YES.
WE'RE GONNA LET THE MAN EAT, ALL RIGHT? HE DESERVES THAT MUCH!
HELP! HELP!
WEEE-OOO-WEEE-OOO
LISTEN, GUYS--
YOU HEARD WITH YOUR SUPER-HEARING--
--THAT SOMEONE'S IN TROUBLE.
YEAH. MAYBE DINNER, LATER?
JUST TEXT US WHEN YOU'RE DONE.
NOW GO!
GO BE SUPERMAN!
GO BE CLARK.

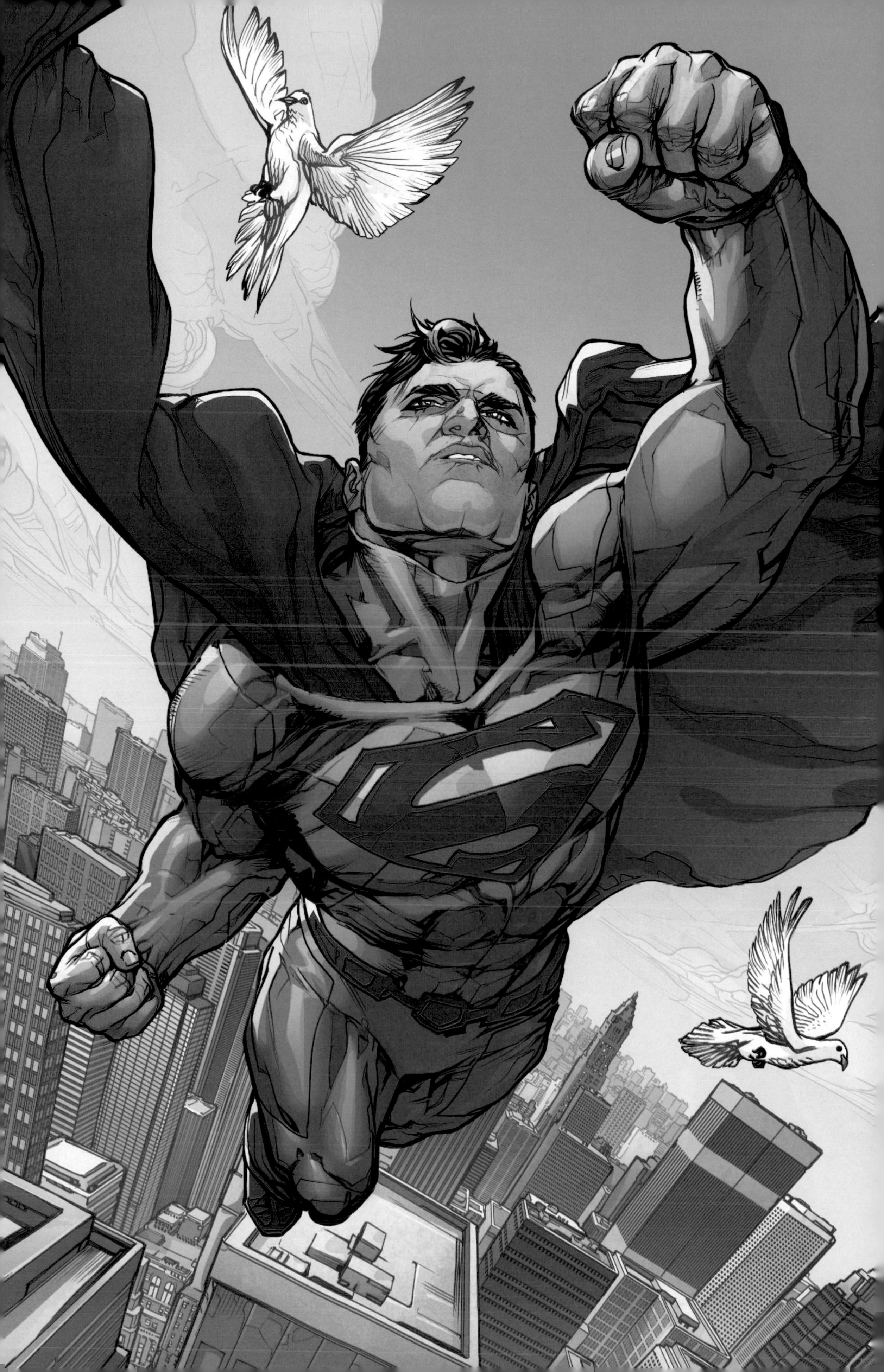

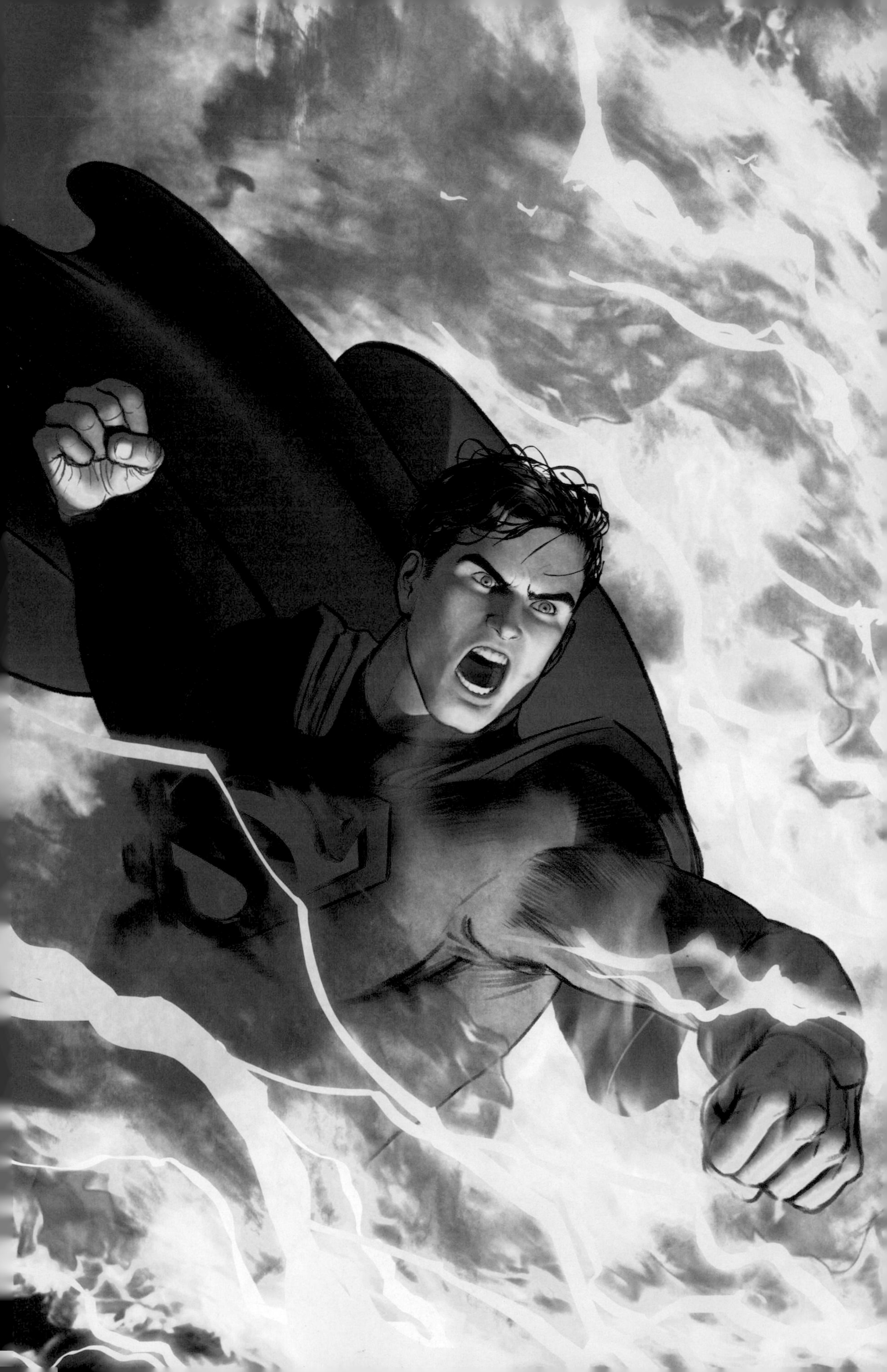

THE FINAL DAYS OF SUPERMAN PART 1: THIS MORTAL COIL

PETER J. TOMASI writer **MIKEL JANÍN** artist **MIKEL JANÍN** colorist **ROB LEIGH** letterer **MIKEL JANÍN** cover

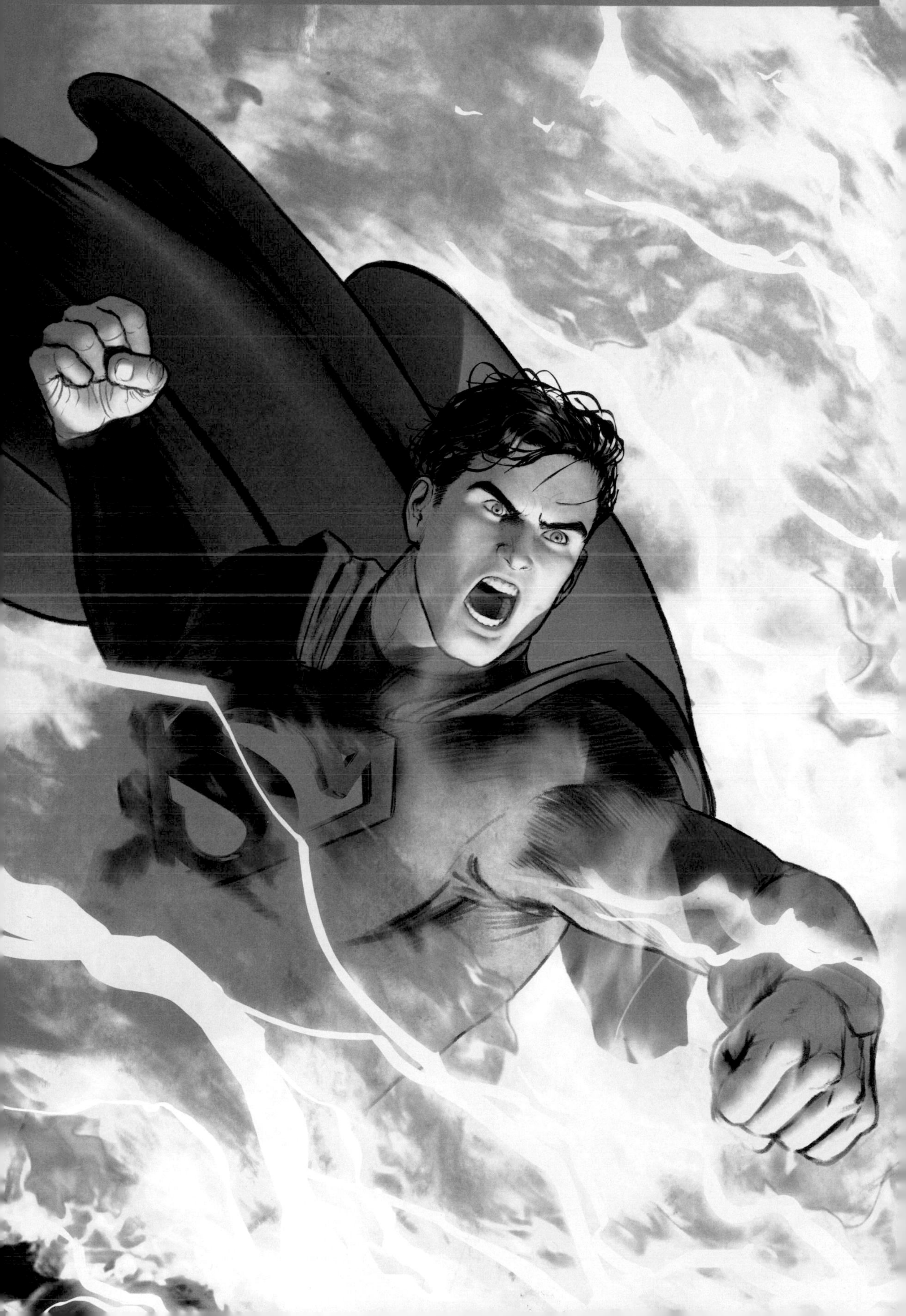

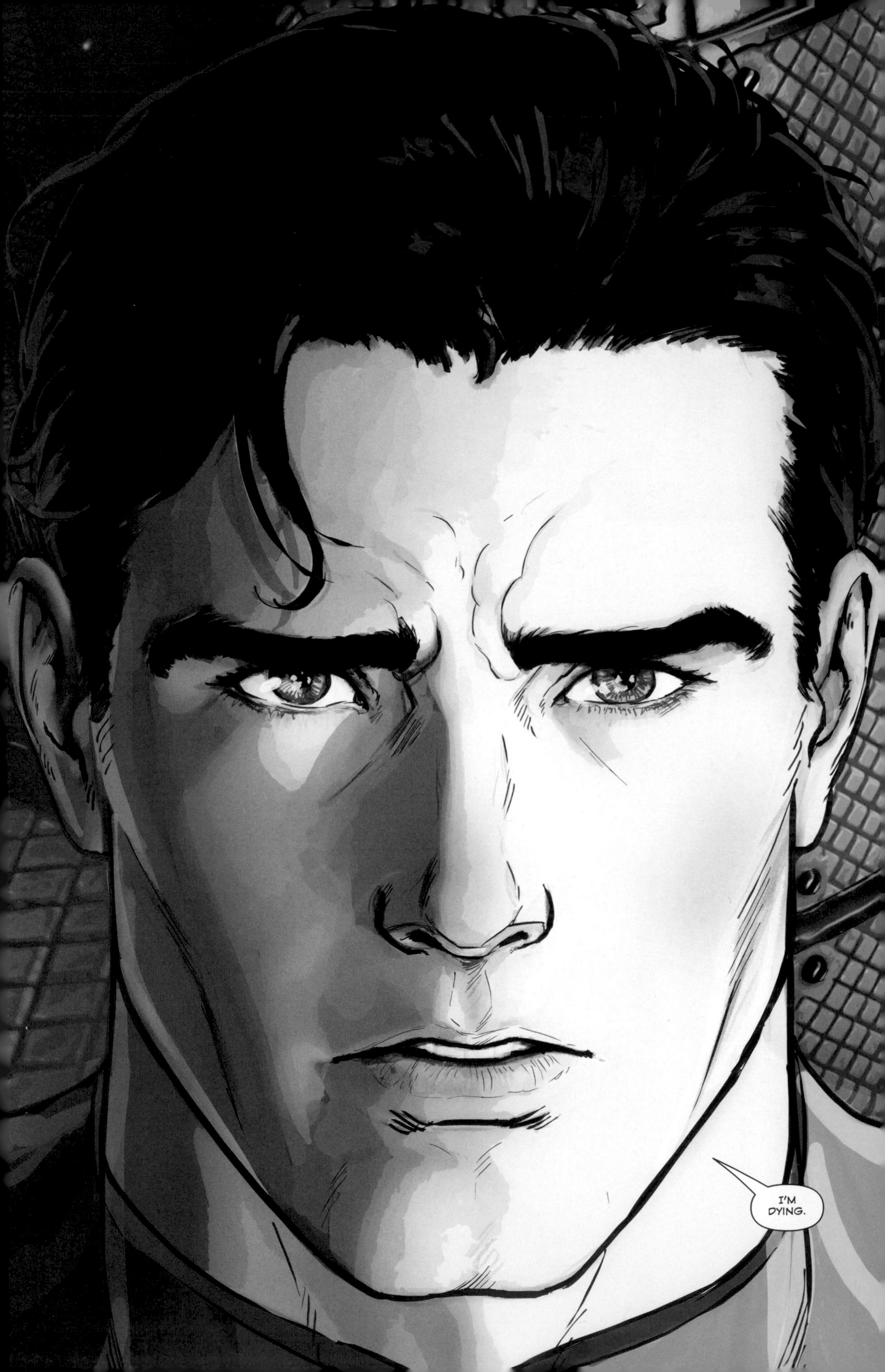
I'M DYING.

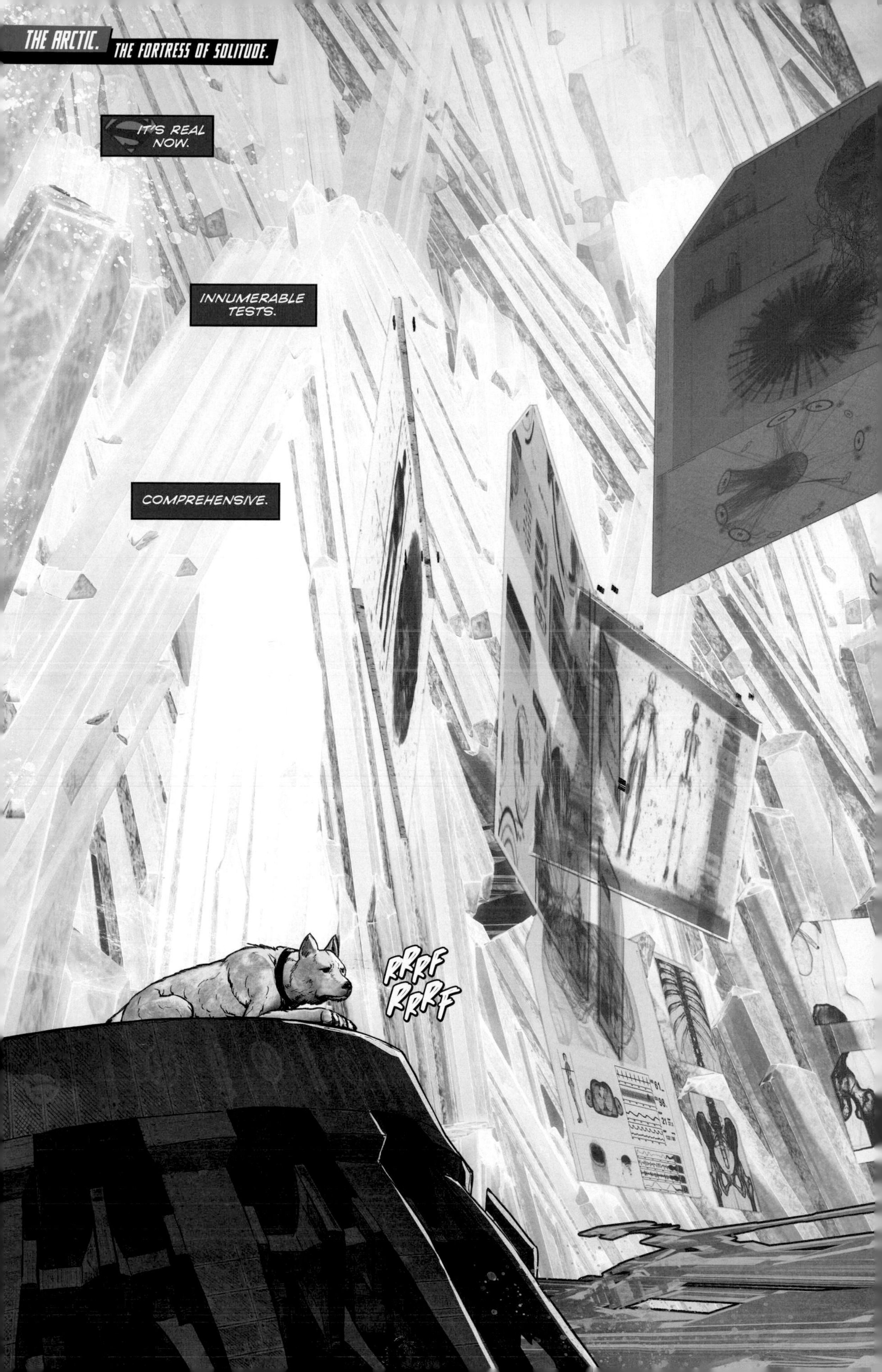
THE ARCTIC.
THE FORTRESS OF SOLITUDE.
IT'S REAL NOW.
INNUMERABLE TESTS.
COMPREHENSIVE.
RRRF RRRF

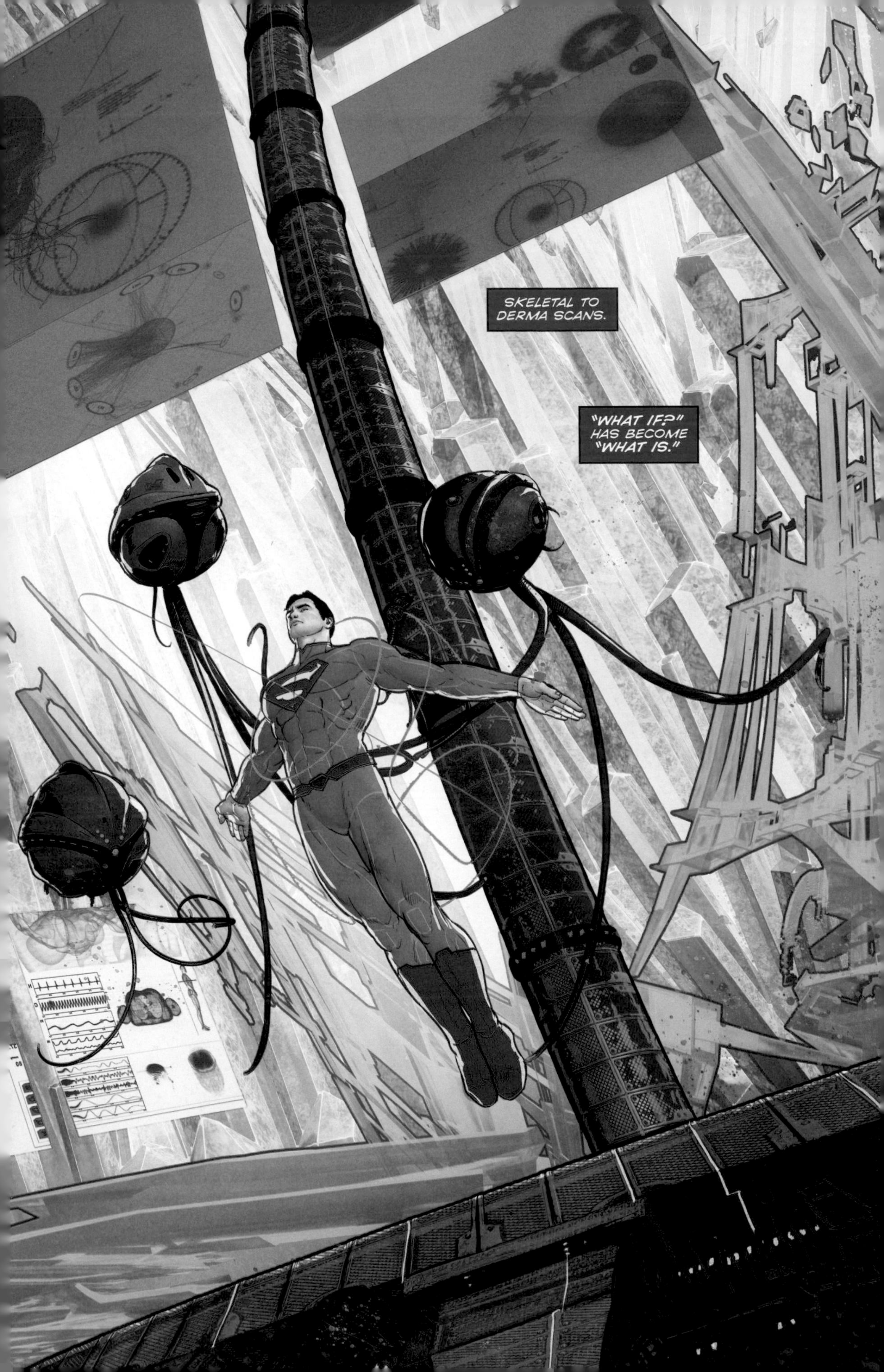
SKELETAL TO DERMA SCANS.
"WHAT IF?" HAS BECOME "WHAT IS."

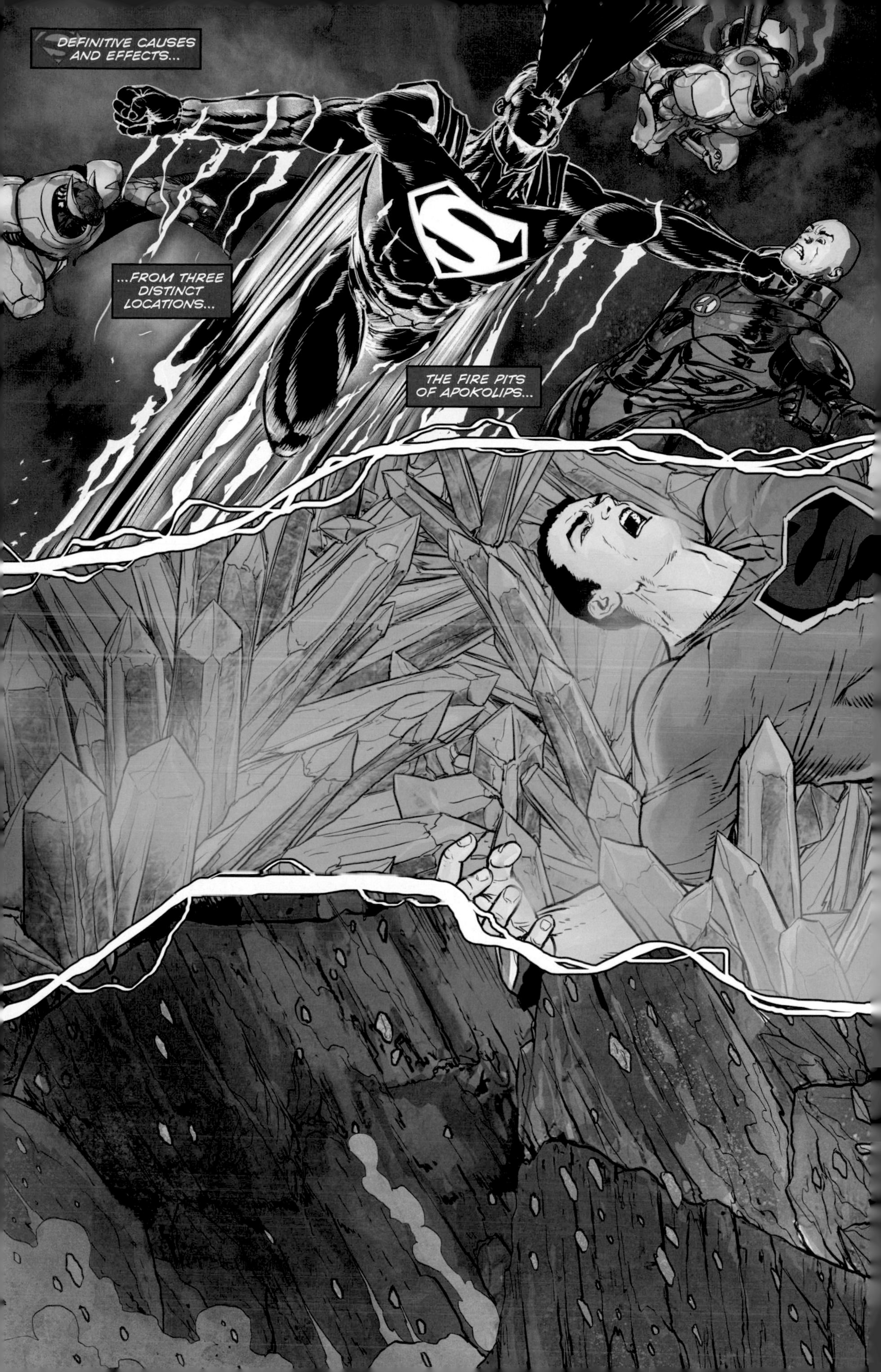
DEFINITIVE CAUSES AND EFFECTS...
...FROM THREE DISTINCT LOCATIONS...
THE FIRE PITS OF APOKOLIPS...

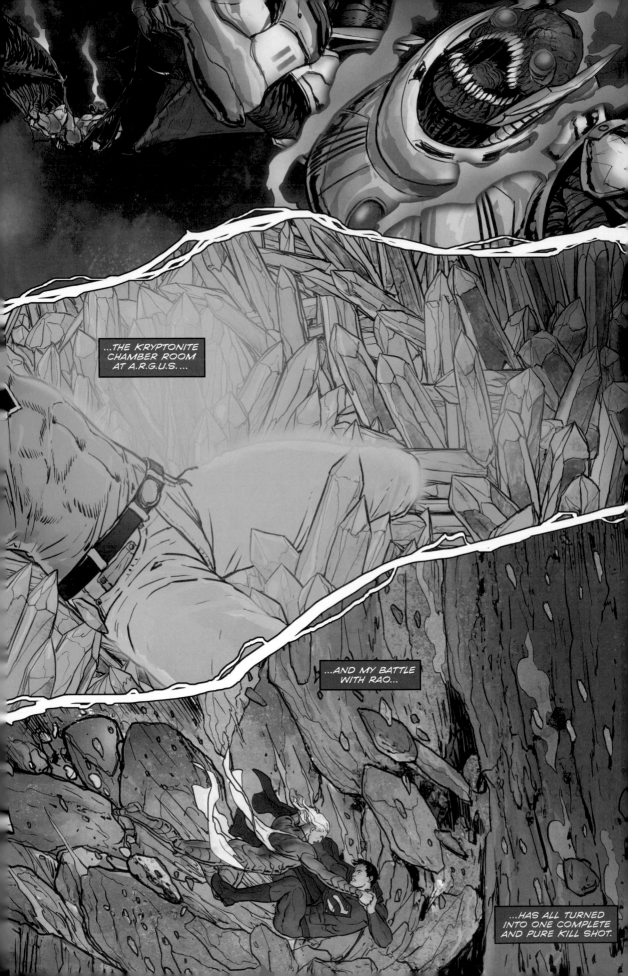

...THE KRYPTONITE CHAMBER ROOM AT A.R.G.U.S....

...AND MY BATTLE WITH RAO...

...HAS ALL TURNED INTO ONE COMPLETE AND PURE KILL SHOT.

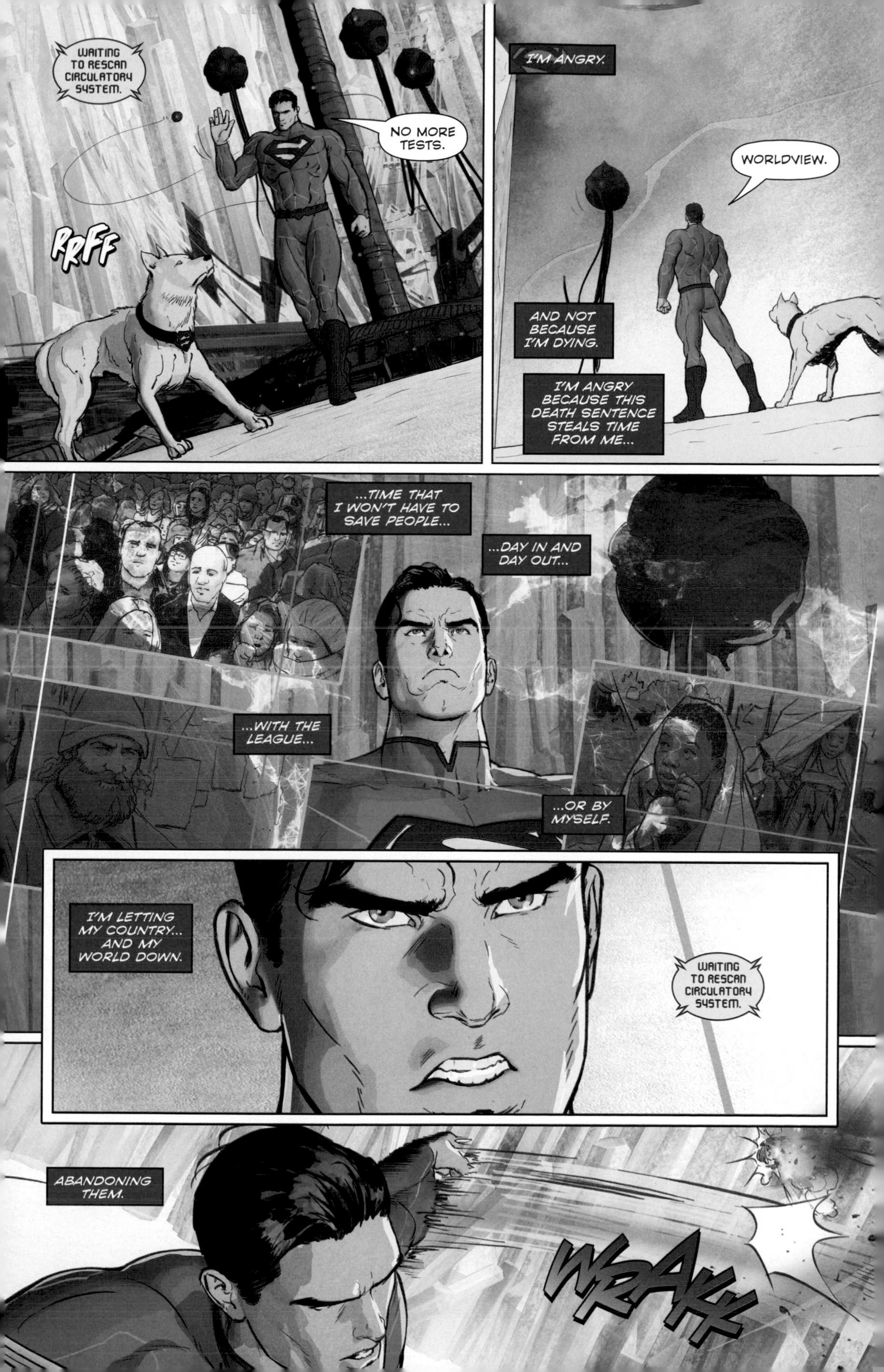
WAITING TO RESCAN CIRCULATORY SYSTEM.
NO MORE TESTS.
RRFF
I'M ANGRY.
WORLDVIEW.
AND NOT BECAUSE I'M DYING.
I'M ANGRY BECAUSE THIS DEATH SENTENCE STEALS TIME FROM ME...
...TIME THAT I WON'T HAVE TO SAVE PEOPLE...
...DAY IN AND DAY OUT...
...WITH THE LEAGUE...
...OR BY MYSELF.
I'M LETTING MY COUNTRY... AND MY WORLD DOWN.
WAITING TO RESCAN CIRCULATORY SYSTEM.
ABANDONING THEM.
WRAKK

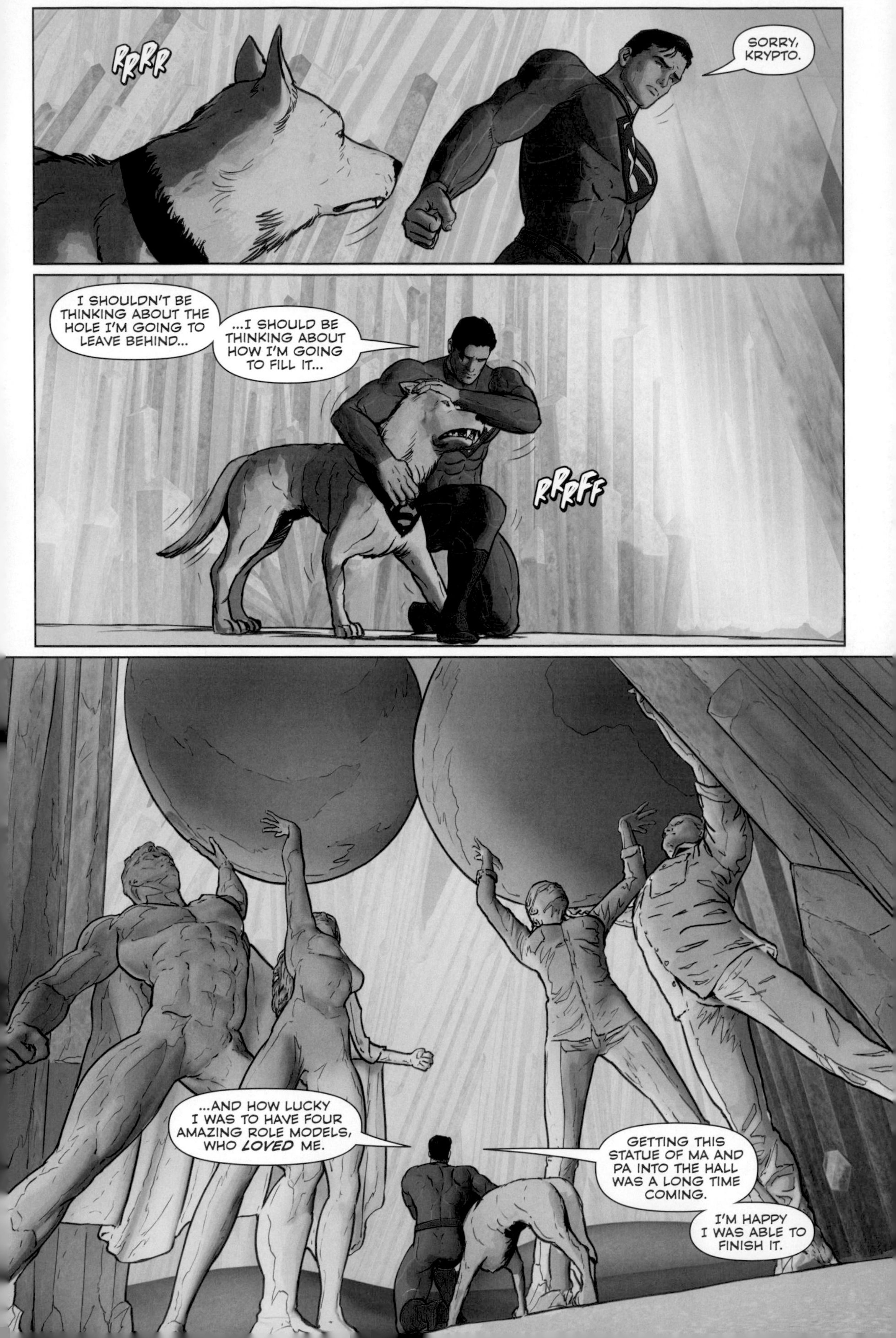
RRRR
SORRY, KRYPTO.
I SHOULDN'T BE THINKING ABOUT THE HOLE I'M GOING TO LEAVE BEHIND...
...I SHOULD BE THINKING ABOUT HOW I'M GOING TO FILL IT...
RRRFF
...AND HOW LUCKY I WAS TO HAVE FOUR AMAZING ROLE MODELS, WHO LOVED ME.
GETTING THIS STATUE OF MA AND PA INTO THE HALL WAS A LONG TIME COMING.
I'M HAPPY I WAS ABLE TO FINISH IT.

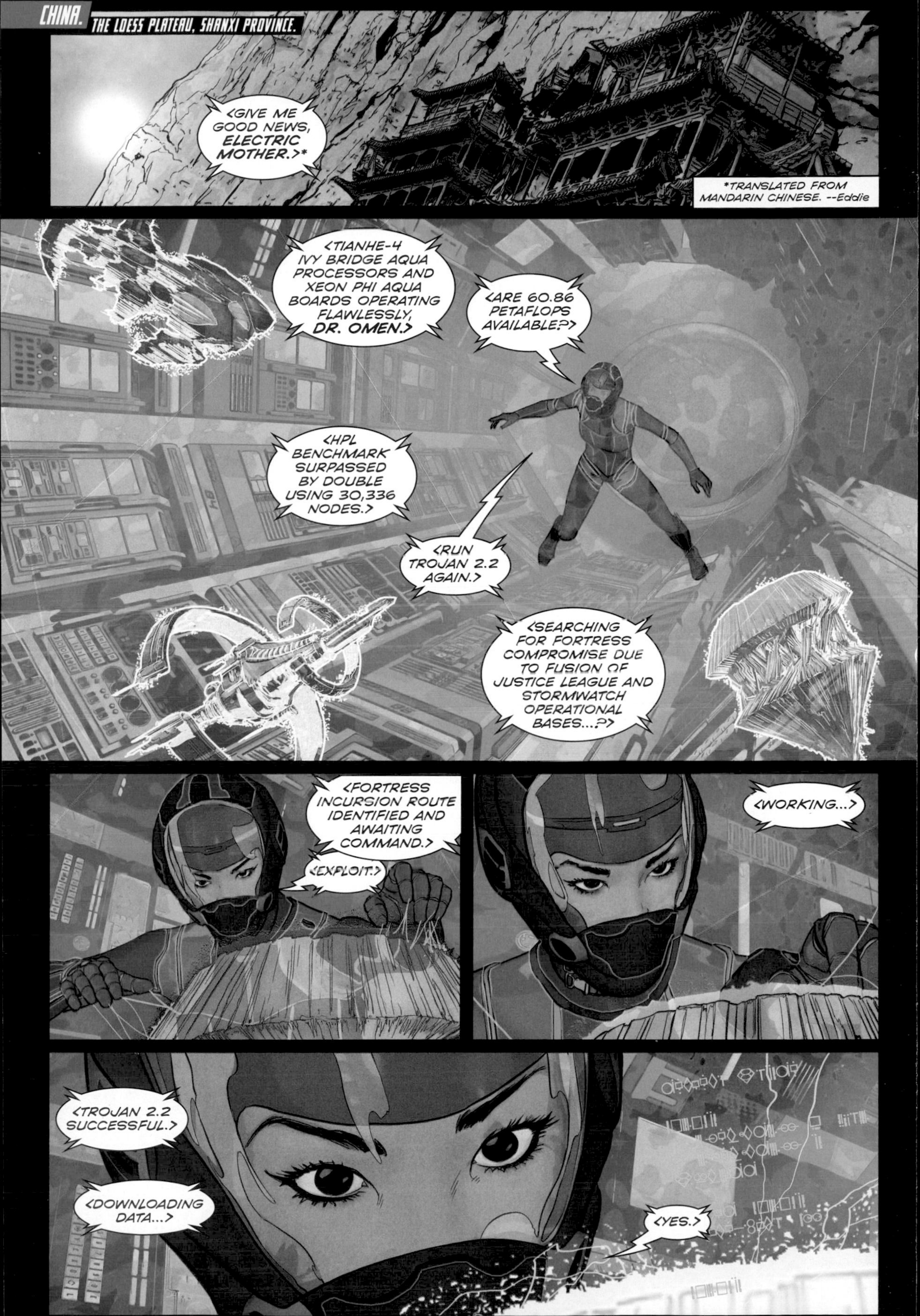
CHINA.
THE LOESS PLATEAU, SHANXI PROVINCE.
<GIVE ME GOOD NEWS, ELECTRIC MOTHER.>*
*TRANSLATED FROM MANDARIN CHINESE. --Eddie
<TIANHE-4 IVY BRIDGE AQUA PROCESSORS AND XEON PHI AQUA BOARDS OPERATING FLAWLESSLY, DR. OMEN.>
<ARE 60.86 PETAFLOPS AVAILABLE?>
<HPL BENCHMARK SURPASSED BY DOUBLE USING 30,336 NODES.>
<RUN TROJAN 2.2 AGAIN.>
<SEARCHING FOR FORTRESS COMPROMISE DUE TO FUSION OF JUSTICE LEAGUE AND STORMWATCH OPERATIONAL BASES...?>
<FORTRESS INCURSION ROUTE IDENTIFIED AND AWAITING COMMAND.>
<EXPLOIT.>
<WORKING...>
<TROJAN 2.2 SUCCESSFUL.>
<DOWNLOADING DATA...>
<YES.>

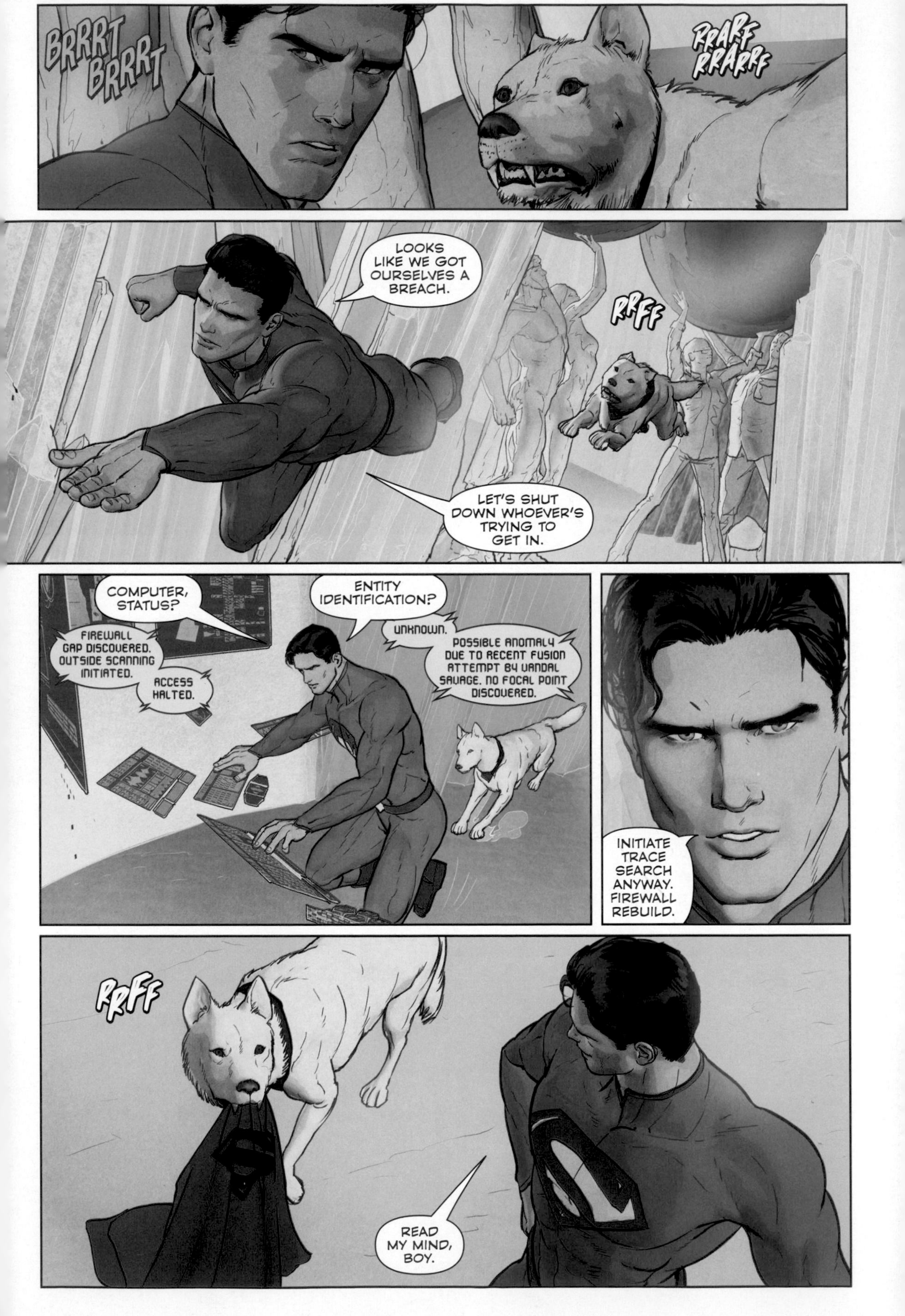
BRRRT BRRRT
RRARF RRARRF
LOOKS LIKE WE GOT OURSELVES A BREACH.
RRFF
LET'S SHUT DOWN WHOEVER'S TRYING TO GET IN.
COMPUTER, STATUS?
FIREWALL GAP DISCOVERED. OUTSIDE SCANNING INITIATED.
ACCESS HALTED.
ENTITY IDENTIFICATION?
UNKNOWN.
POSSIBLE ANOMALY DUE TO RECENT FUSION ATTEMPT BY VANDAL SAVAGE. NO FOCAL POINT DISCOVERED.
INITIATE TRACE SEARCH ANYWAY. FIREWALL REBUILD.
RRFF
READ MY MIND, BOY.

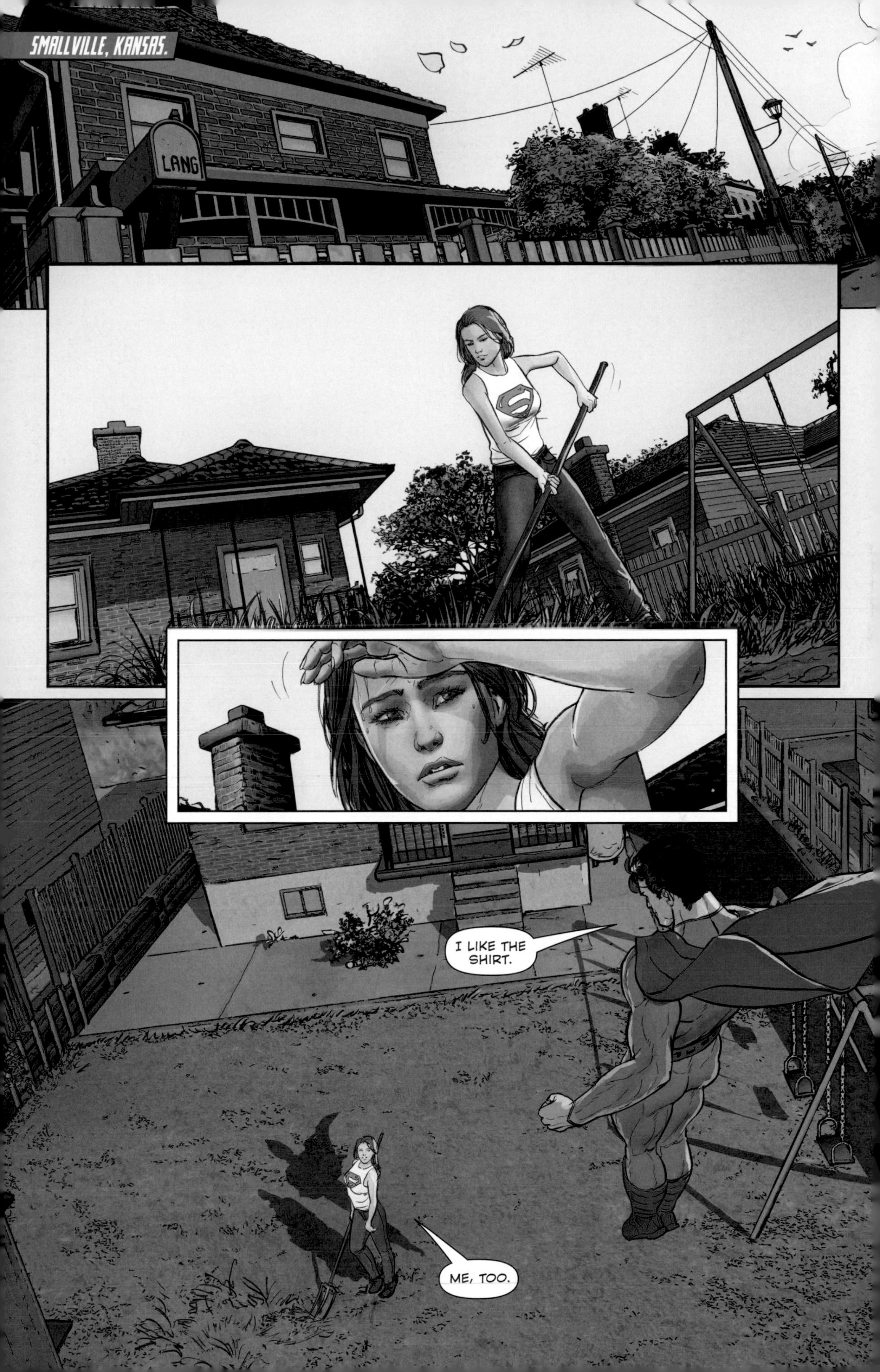
SMALLVILLE, KANSAS.
LANG
I LIKE THE SHIRT.
ME, TOO.

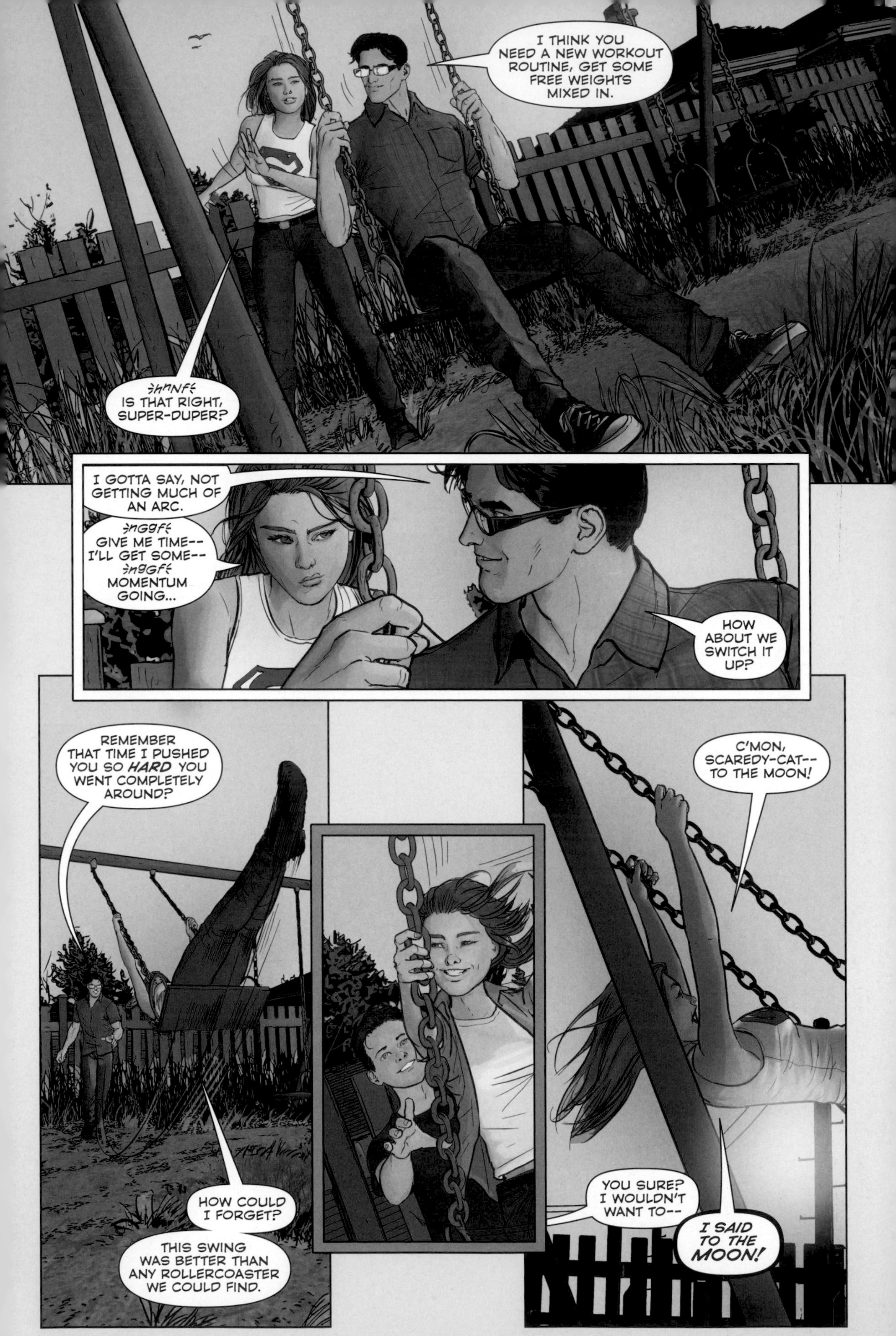
I THINK YOU NEED A NEW WORKOUT ROUTINE, GET SOME FREE WEIGHTS MIXED IN.
HNNF IS THAT RIGHT, SUPER-DUPER?
I GOTTA SAY, NOT GETTING MUCH OF AN ARC.
NGGF GIVE ME TIME-- I'LL GET SOME-- NGGF MOMENTUM GOING...
HOW ABOUT WE SWITCH IT UP?
REMEMBER THAT TIME I PUSHED YOU SO HARD YOU WENT COMPLETELY AROUND?
HOW COULD I FORGET?
THIS SWING WAS BETTER THAN ANY ROLLERCOASTER WE COULD FIND.
C'MON, SCAREDY-CAT-- TO THE MOON!
YOU SURE? I WOULDN'T WANT TO--
I SAID TO THE MOON!

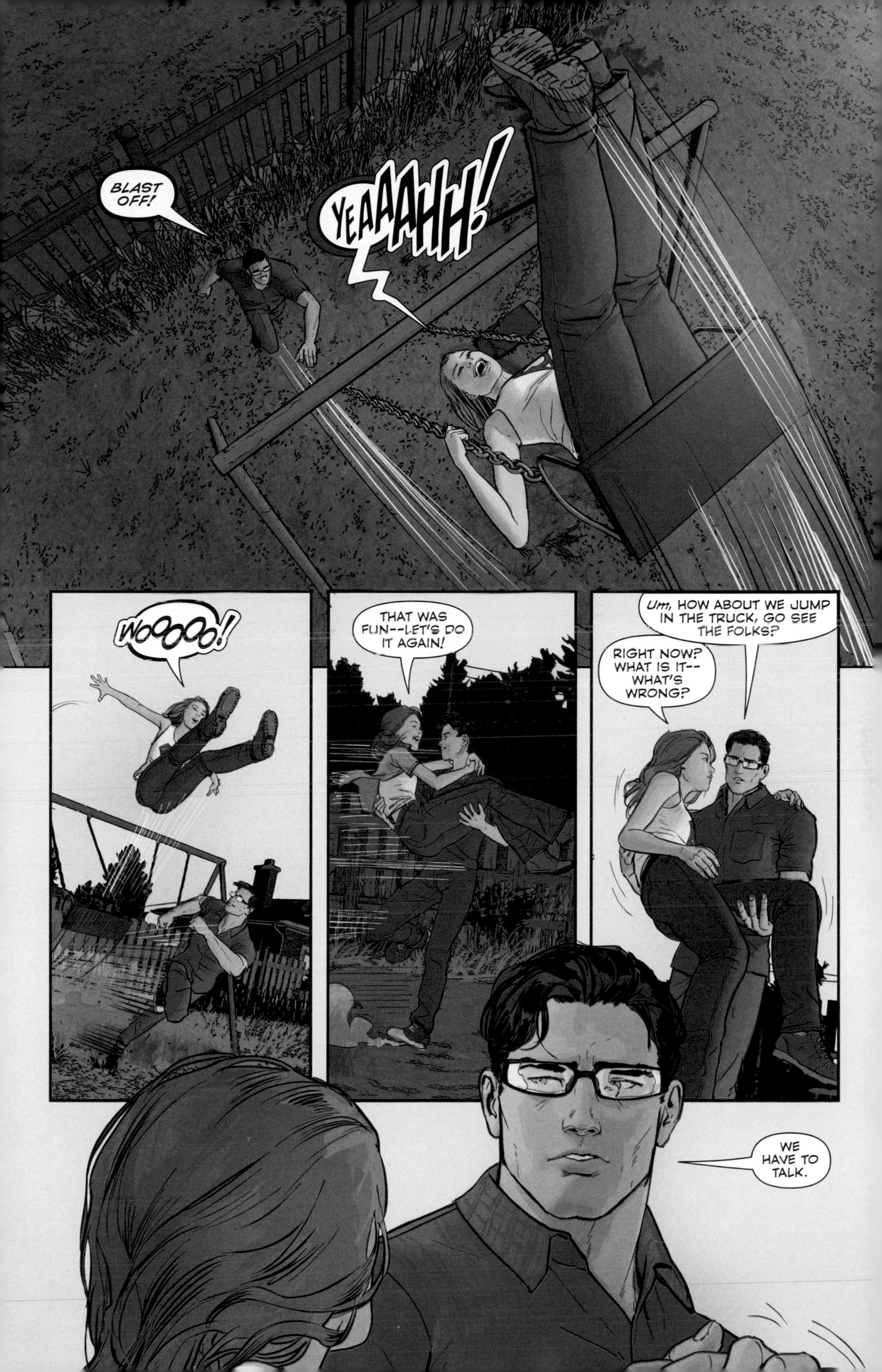
BLAST OFF!
YEAAAHH!
WOOOOO!
THAT WAS FUN--LET'S DO IT AGAIN!
Um, HOW ABOUT WE JUMP IN THE TRUCK, GO SEE THE FOLKS?
RIGHT NOW? WHAT IS IT--WHAT'S WRONG?
WE HAVE TO TALK.

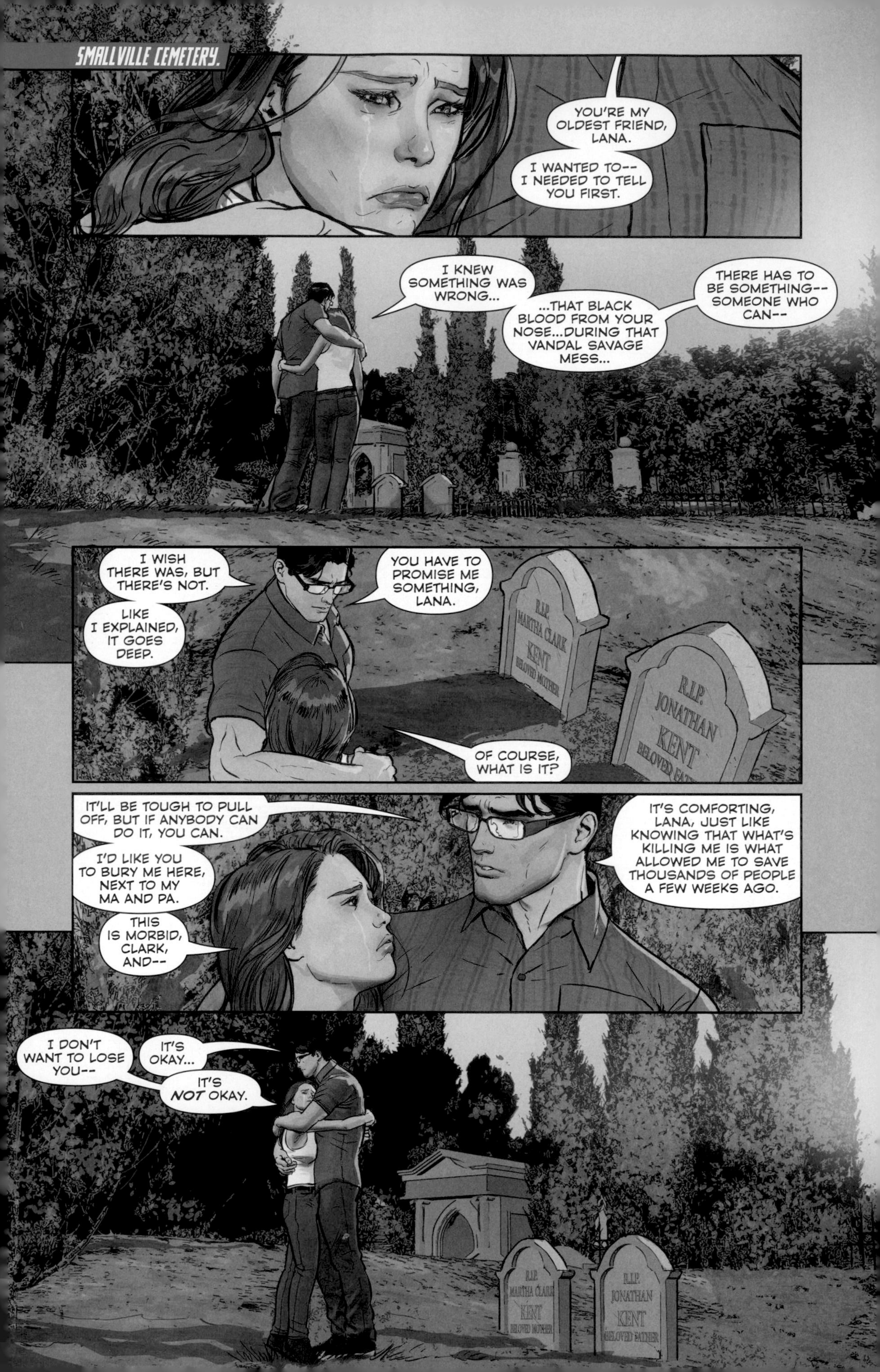
SMALLVILLE CEMETERY.
YOU'RE MY OLDEST FRIEND, LANA.
I WANTED TO-- I NEEDED TO TELL YOU FIRST.
I KNEW SOMETHING WAS WRONG...
...THAT BLACK BLOOD FROM YOUR NOSE...DURING THAT VANDAL SAVAGE MESS...
THERE HAS TO BE SOMETHING-- SOMEONE WHO CAN--
I WISH THERE WAS, BUT THERE'S NOT.
LIKE I EXPLAINED, IT GOES DEEP.
YOU HAVE TO PROMISE ME SOMETHING, LANA.
R.I.P. MARTHA CLARK KENT BELOVED MOTHER
R.I.P. JONATHAN KENT
OF COURSE, WHAT IS IT?
IT'LL BE TOUGH TO PULL OFF, BUT IF ANYBODY CAN DO IT, YOU CAN.
I'D LIKE YOU TO BURY ME HERE, NEXT TO MY MA AND PA.
THIS IS MORBID, CLARK, AND--
IT'S COMFORTING, LANA, JUST LIKE KNOWING THAT WHAT'S KILLING ME IS WHAT ALLOWED ME TO SAVE THOUSANDS OF PEOPLE A FEW WEEKS AGO.
I DON'T WANT TO LOSE YOU--
IT'S OKAY...
IT'S *NOT* OKAY.
R.I.P. MARTHA CLARK KENT BELOVED MOTHER
R.I.P. JONATHAN KENT BELOVED FATHER

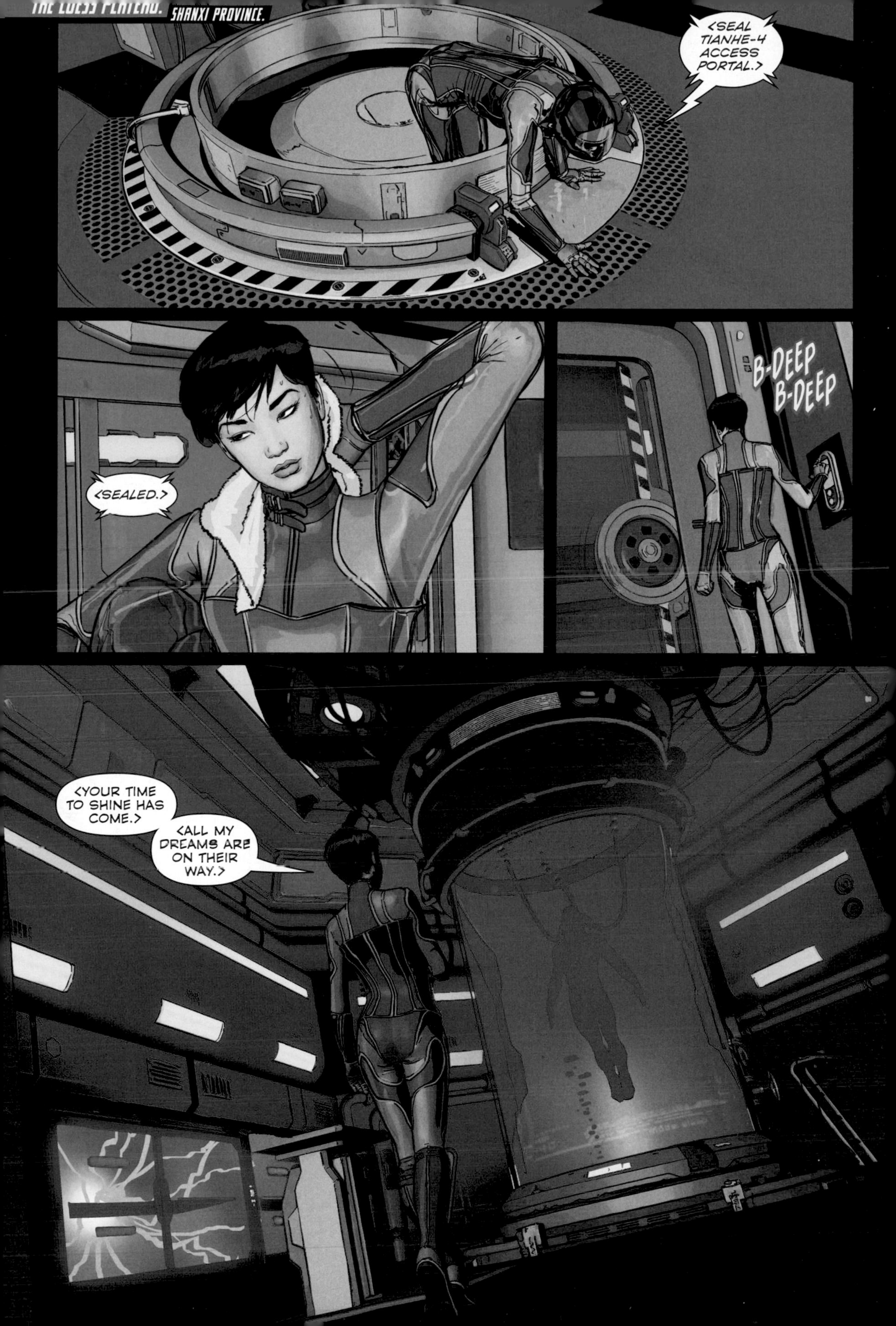
SHANXI PROVINCE.
<SEAL TIANHE-4 ACCESS PORTAL.>
<SEALED.>
B-DEEP B-DEEP
<YOUR TIME TO SHINE HAS COME.>
<ALL MY DREAMS ARE ON THEIR WAY.>

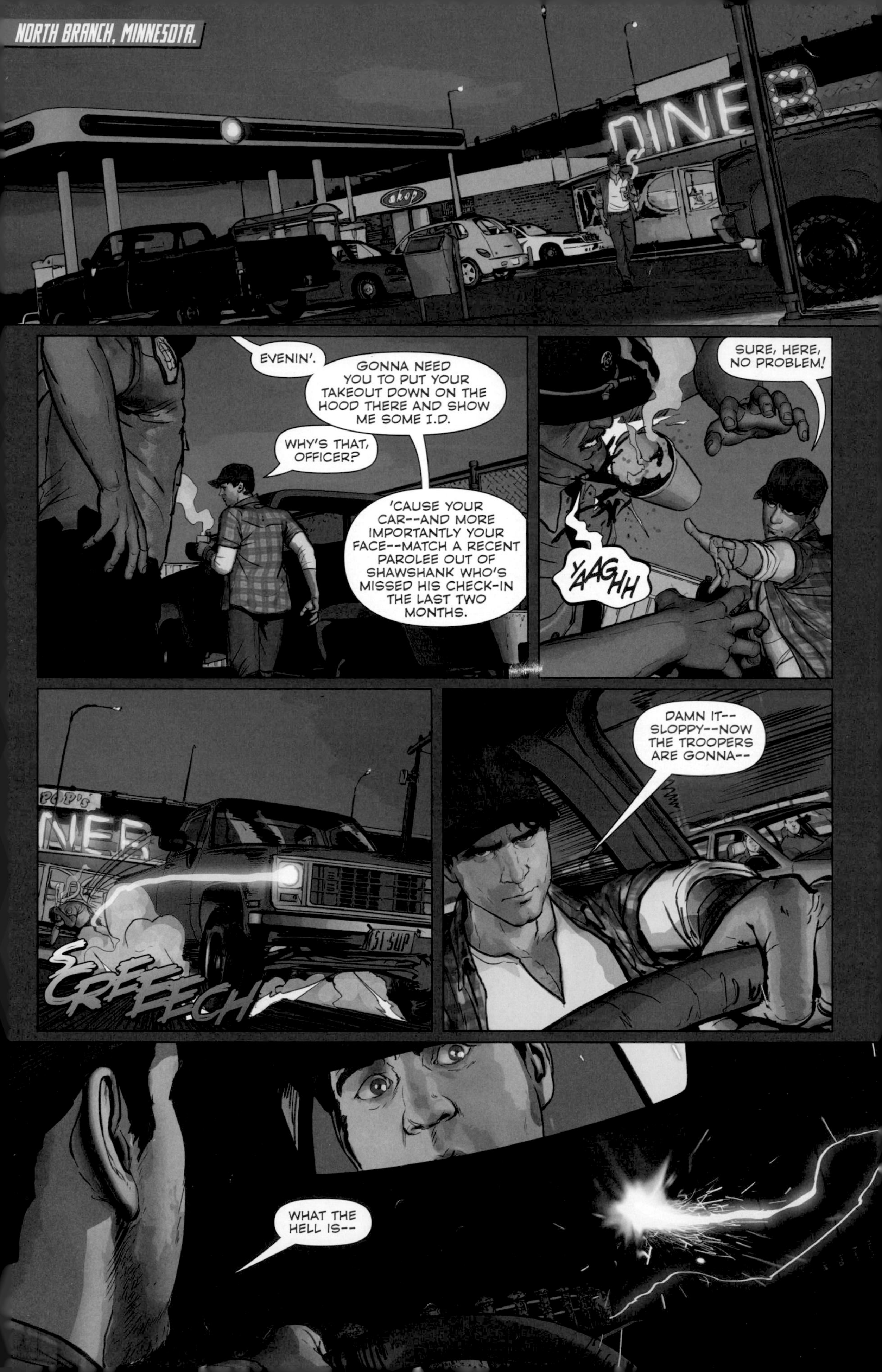
NORTH BRANCH, MINNESOTA.
DINER
EVENIN'.
GONNA NEED YOU TO PUT YOUR TAKEOUT DOWN ON THE HOOD THERE AND SHOW ME SOME I.D.
WHY'S THAT, OFFICER?
'CAUSE YOUR CAR--AND MORE IMPORTANTLY YOUR FACE--MATCH A RECENT PAROLEE OUT OF SHAWSHANK WHO'S MISSED HIS CHECK-IN THE LAST TWO MONTHS.
SURE, HERE, NO PROBLEM!
YAAGHH
POP'S
NER
K51 SUP
CREEEECH
DAMN IT--SLOPPY--NOW THE TROOPERS ARE GONNA--
WHAT THE HELL IS--

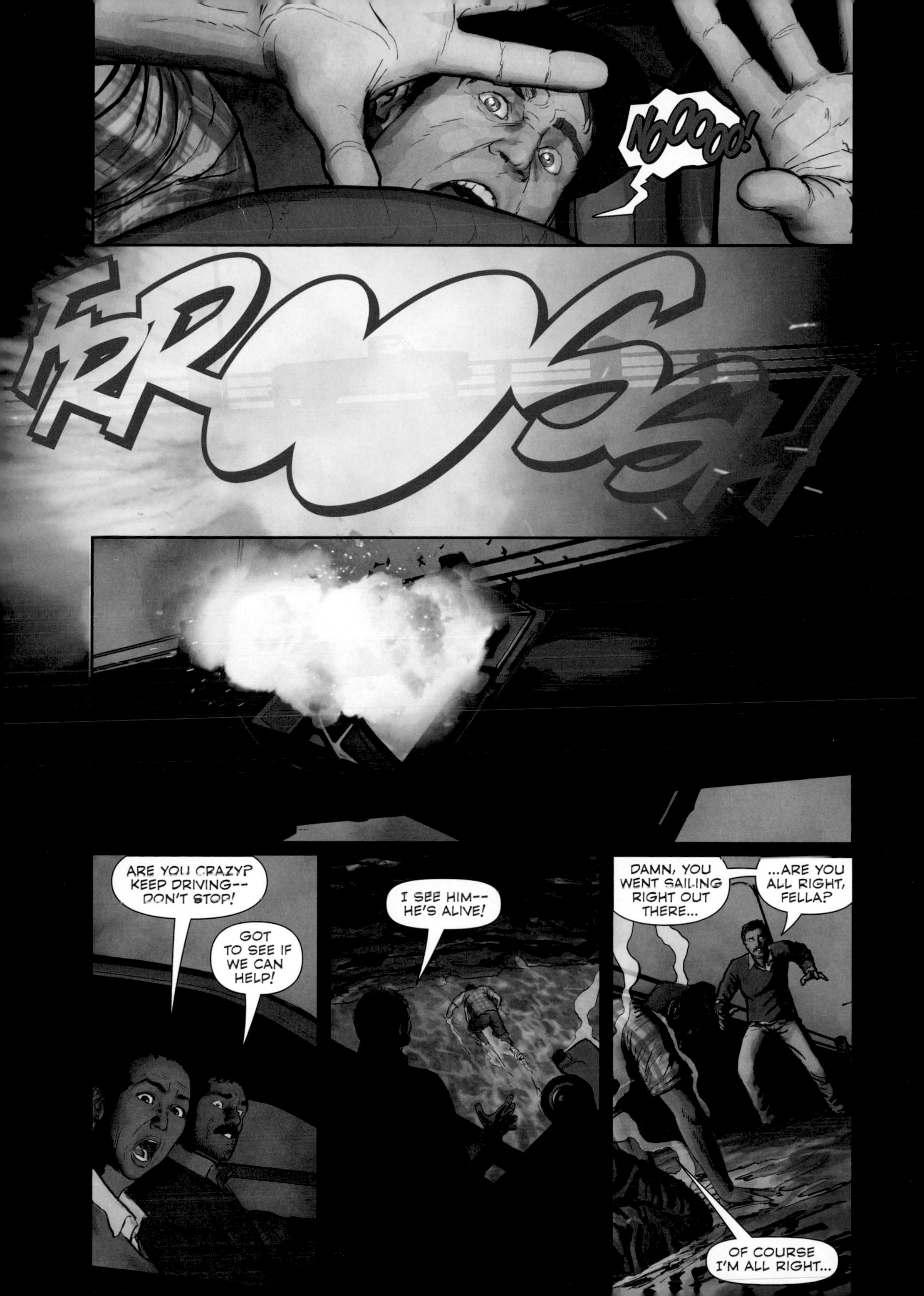
NOOOOOO!
FRROOSSH
ARE YOU CRAZY? KEEP DRIVING-- DON'T STOP!
GOT TO SEE IF WE CAN HELP!
I SEE HIM-- HE'S ALIVE!
DAMN, YOU WENT SAILING RIGHT OUT THERE...
...ARE YOU ALL RIGHT, FELLA?
OF COURSE I'M ALL RIGHT...

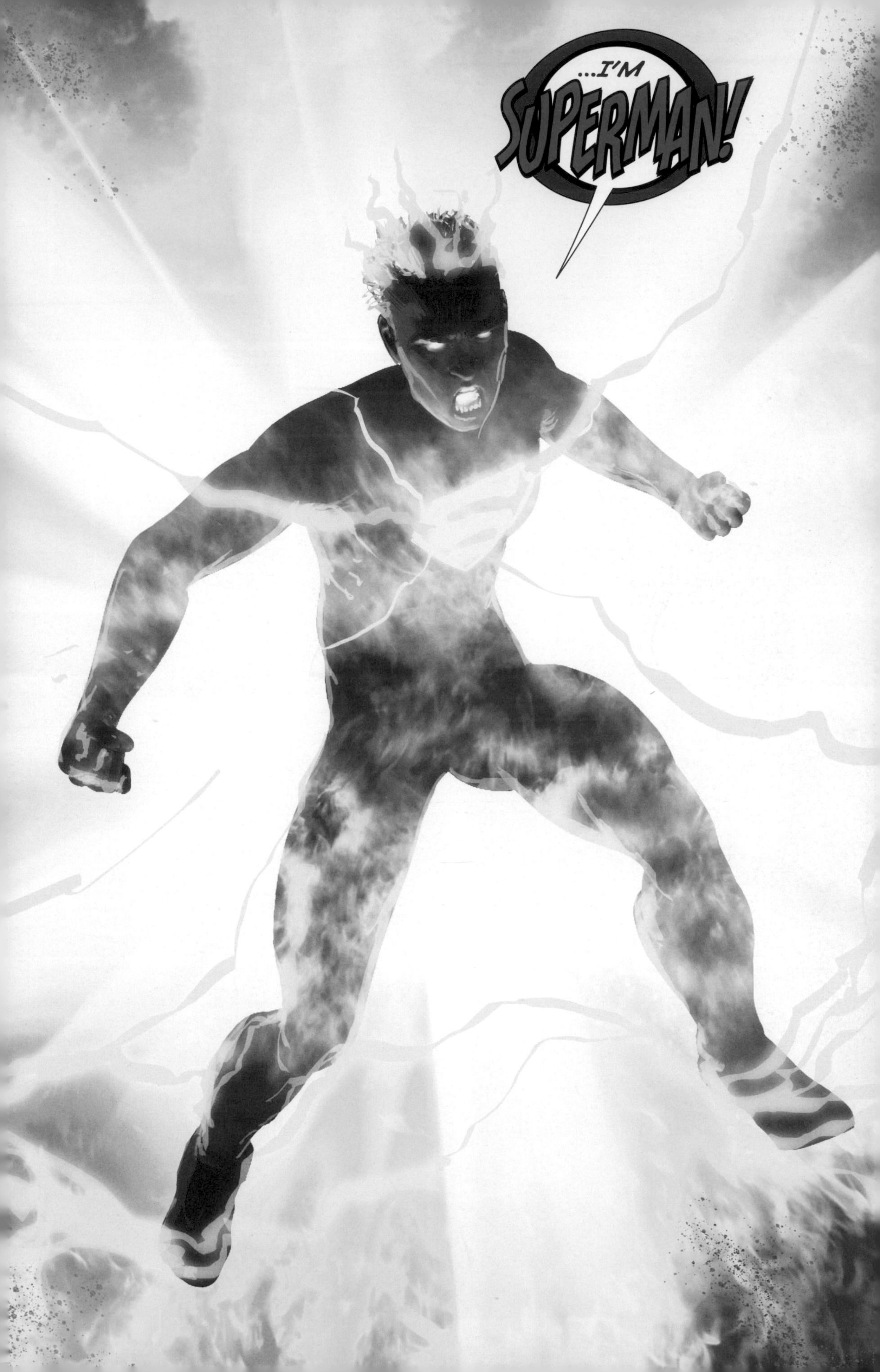
...I'M SUPERMAN!

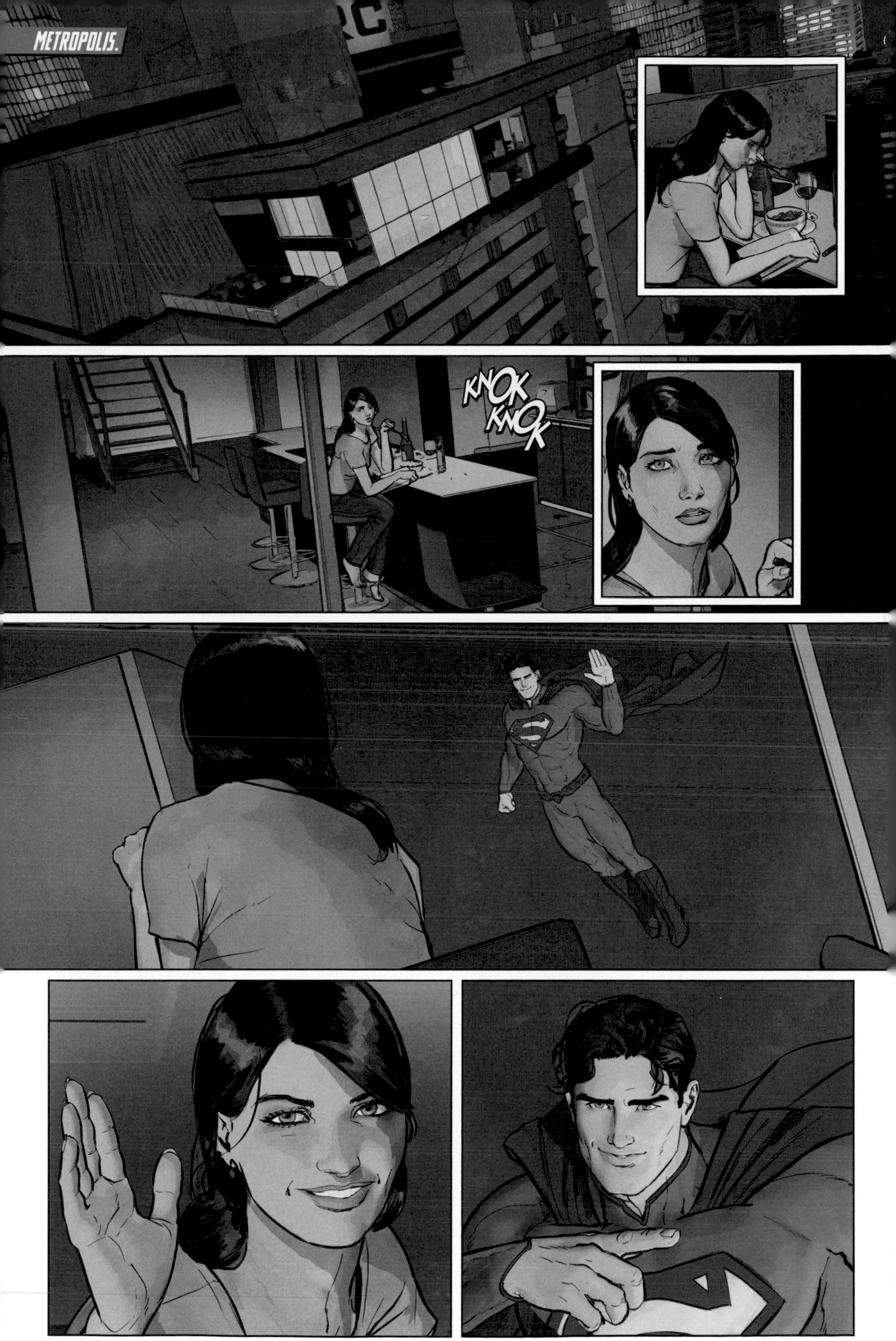
METROPOLIS.
KNOK KNOK KNOK

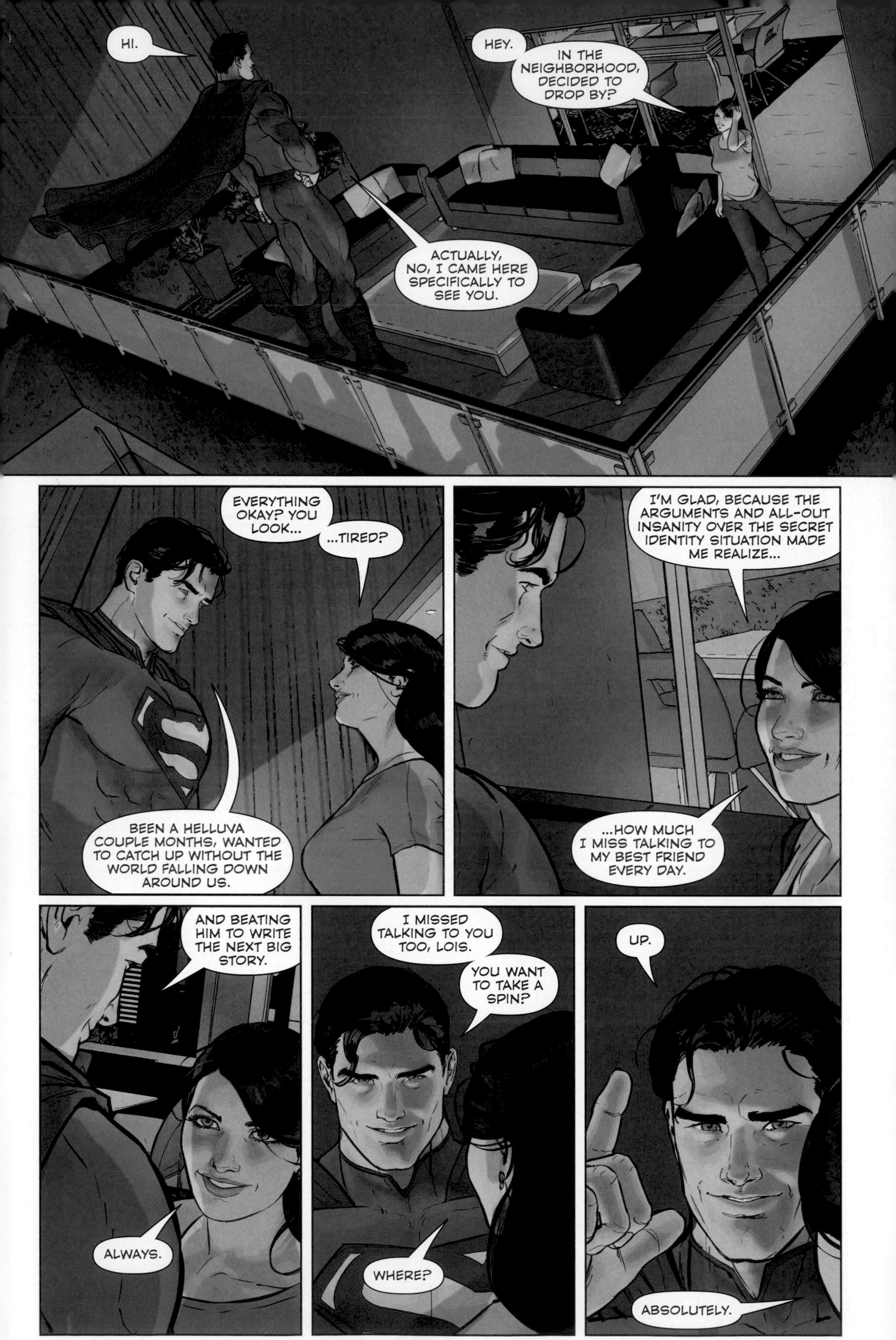
HI.
HEY.
IN THE NEIGHBORHOOD, DECIDED TO DROP BY?
ACTUALLY, NO, I CAME HERE SPECIFICALLY TO SEE YOU.
EVERYTHING OKAY? YOU LOOK...
...TIRED?
BEEN A HELLUVA COUPLE MONTHS, WANTED TO CATCH UP WITHOUT THE WORLD FALLING DOWN AROUND US.
I'M GLAD, BECAUSE THE ARGUMENTS AND ALL-OUT INSANITY OVER THE SECRET IDENTITY SITUATION MADE ME REALIZE...
...HOW MUCH I MISS TALKING TO MY BEST FRIEND EVERY DAY.
AND BEATING HIM TO WRITE THE NEXT BIG STORY.
ALWAYS.
I MISSED TALKING TO YOU TOO, LOIS.
YOU WANT TO TAKE A SPIN?
WHERE?
UP.
ABSOLUTELY.

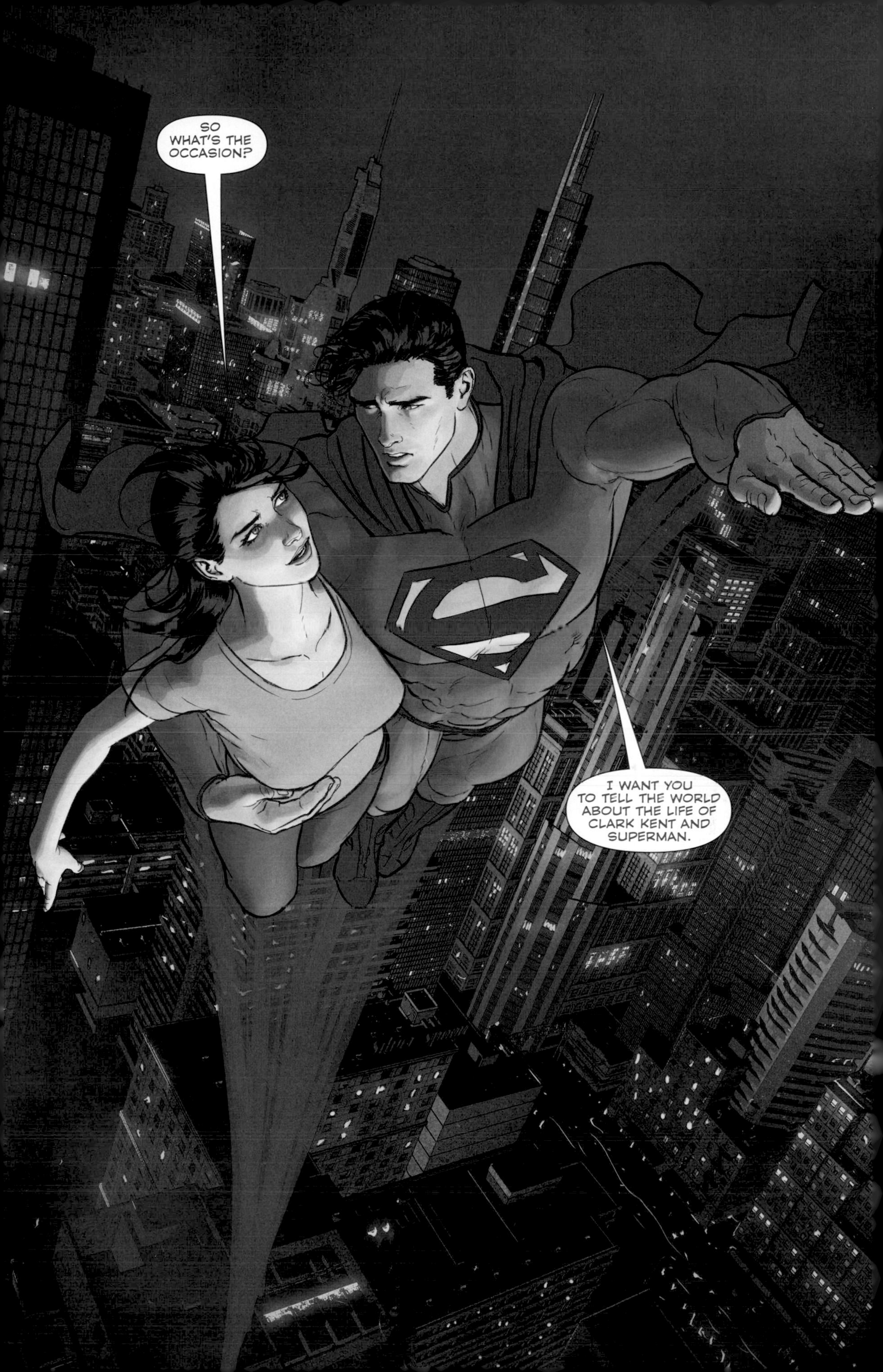
SO WHAT'S THE OCCASION?
I WANT YOU TO TELL THE WORLD ABOUT THE LIFE OF CLARK KENT AND SUPERMAN.

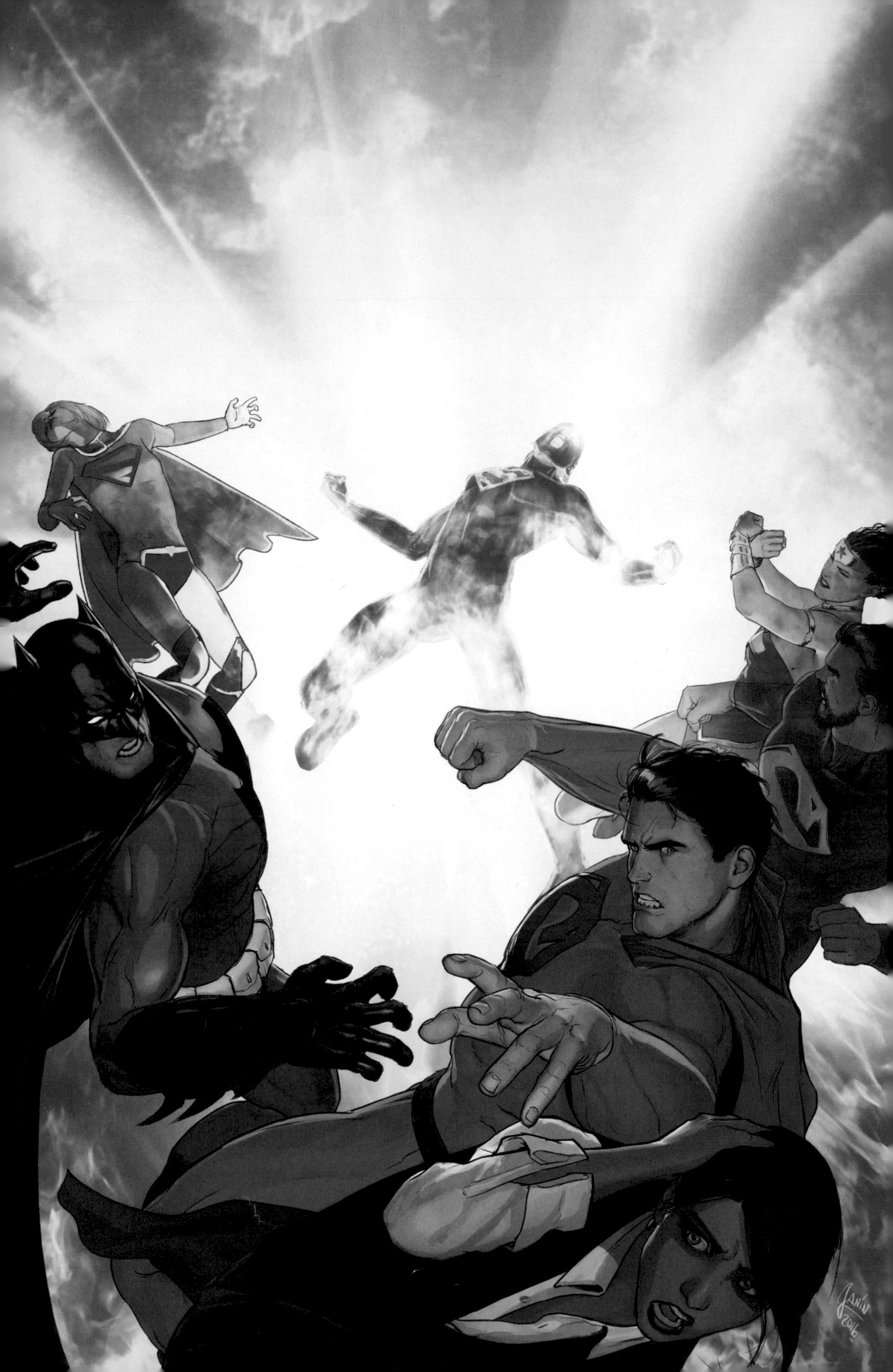

THE FINAL DAYS OF SUPERMAN PART 8: DO OR DIE

PETER J. TOMASI writer MIKEL JANIN, MIGUEL SEPULVEDA artist MIKEL JANIN, JEROMY COX colorist ROB LEIGH letterer MIKEL JANIN cover

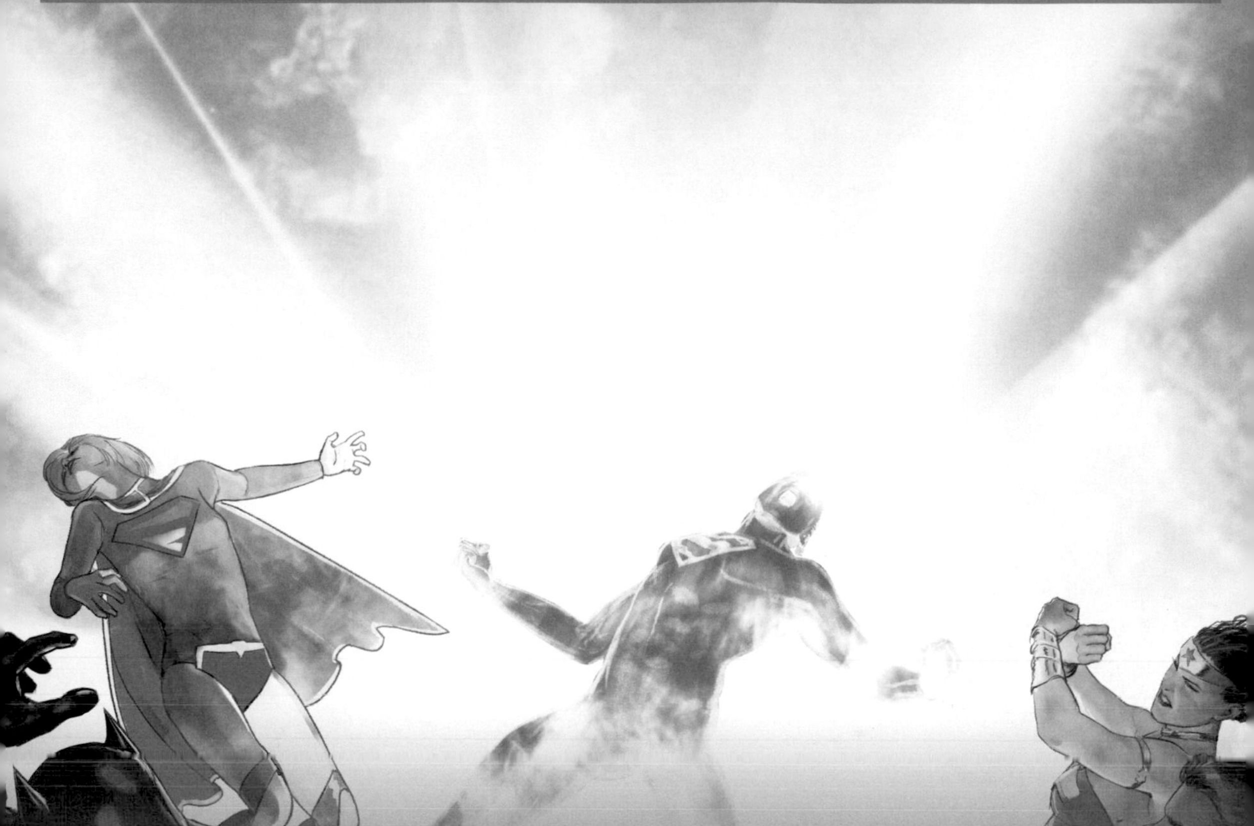

Previously, in SUPERMAN: THE FINAL DAYS OF SUPERMAN...

Superman spends the last of his days revealing his fate to those closest to him, including Batman, Supergirl – who's working with the D.E.O. to regain the powers leeched from her by Vandal Savage – and Wonder Woman. But not before he and the Dark Knight are first attacked by monstrous embodiments from the Chinese Zodiac, one of which manages to draw blood from Superman before being turned away.

Meanwhile, Denny Swan, the escaped convict transformed by the Man of Steel's residual solar energy flares into a "Solar-Superman," believes he's not only Krypton's last son, but Clark Kent as well. After an attempt to resume his duties at the Daily Planet results in casualties, "Clark" is stopped by Lois Lane and confined by A.R.G.U.S. That is, until the rage of seeing Diana "betray" him with another Kal-El ignites an explosive escape.

Rejoined by Batman, Superman and Wonder Woman think they've located the energy signature of the Man of Steel's solar doppelgänger in China. Following a misunderstanding with the heroic Great Ten, the trio learns the signature is actually emanating from Dr. Omen's genetic "Super-Functionary," created from Superman's blood sample and powered by his residual solar energy flares. Just as she's incarcerated, Dr. Omen sets her creation free, and the heroes, leaving the Great Ten to track down the Super-Functionary, return home.

"Solar-Superman," meanwhile, thinks his place is now with Lois. After surprising her outside her apartment and trying to explain his actions, he brings her to a secluded home in California that he's inexplicably drawn to – a safe house where another Superman and Lois Lane live with their son, Jon. Outraged, the solar creature attacks the supposed "imposter," only to be interrupted by the arrival of the dying Superman, Wonder Woman and Batman. While the Dark Knight gets one Lois to safety and the "Superman family" finds sanctuary in Colorado, the solar creature fells Wonder Woman, and is about to prove to the dying Man of Steel why he's the one true Superman ...

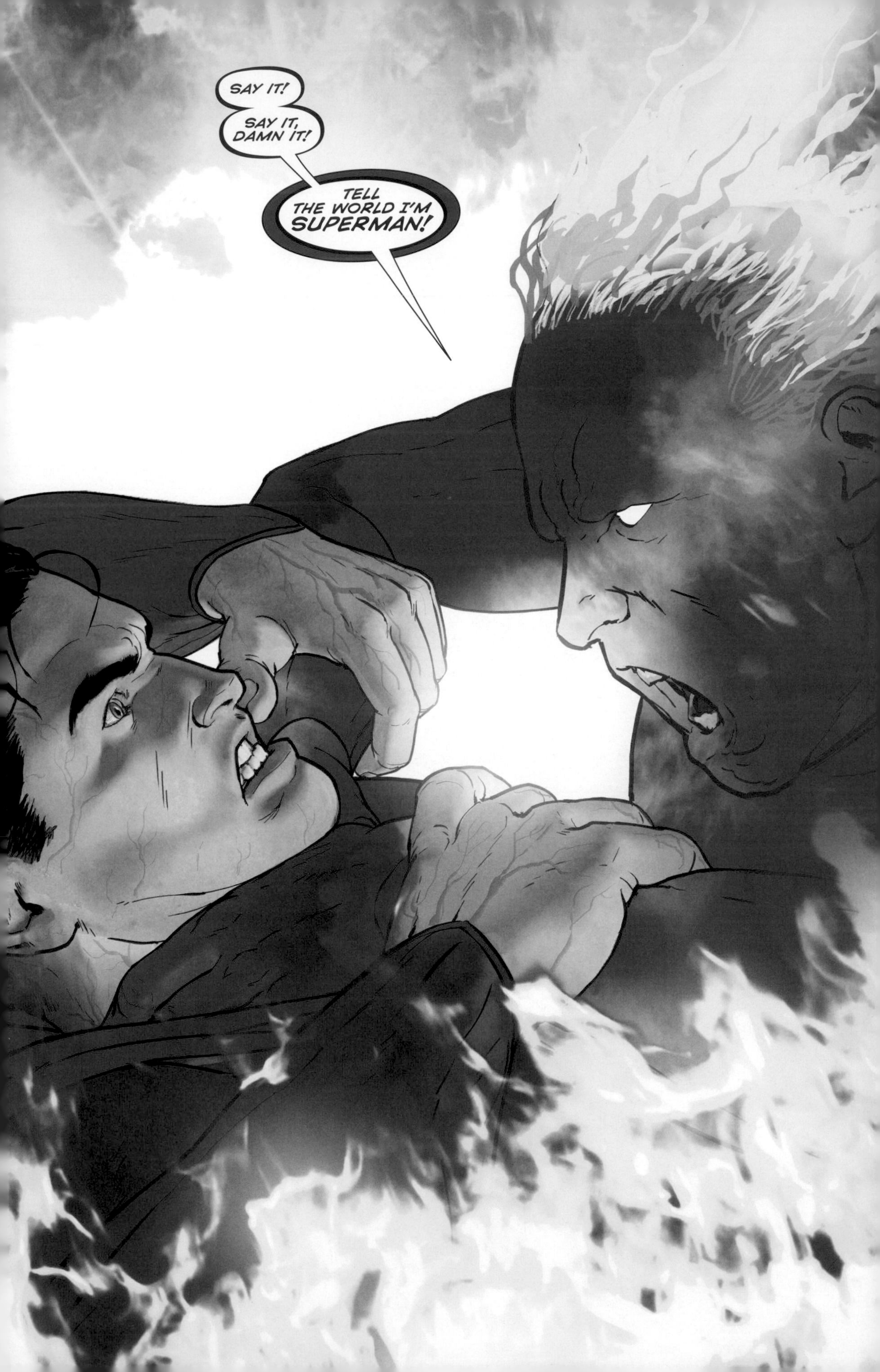
SAY IT!
SAY IT, DAMN IT!
TELL THE WORLD I'M SUPERMAN!

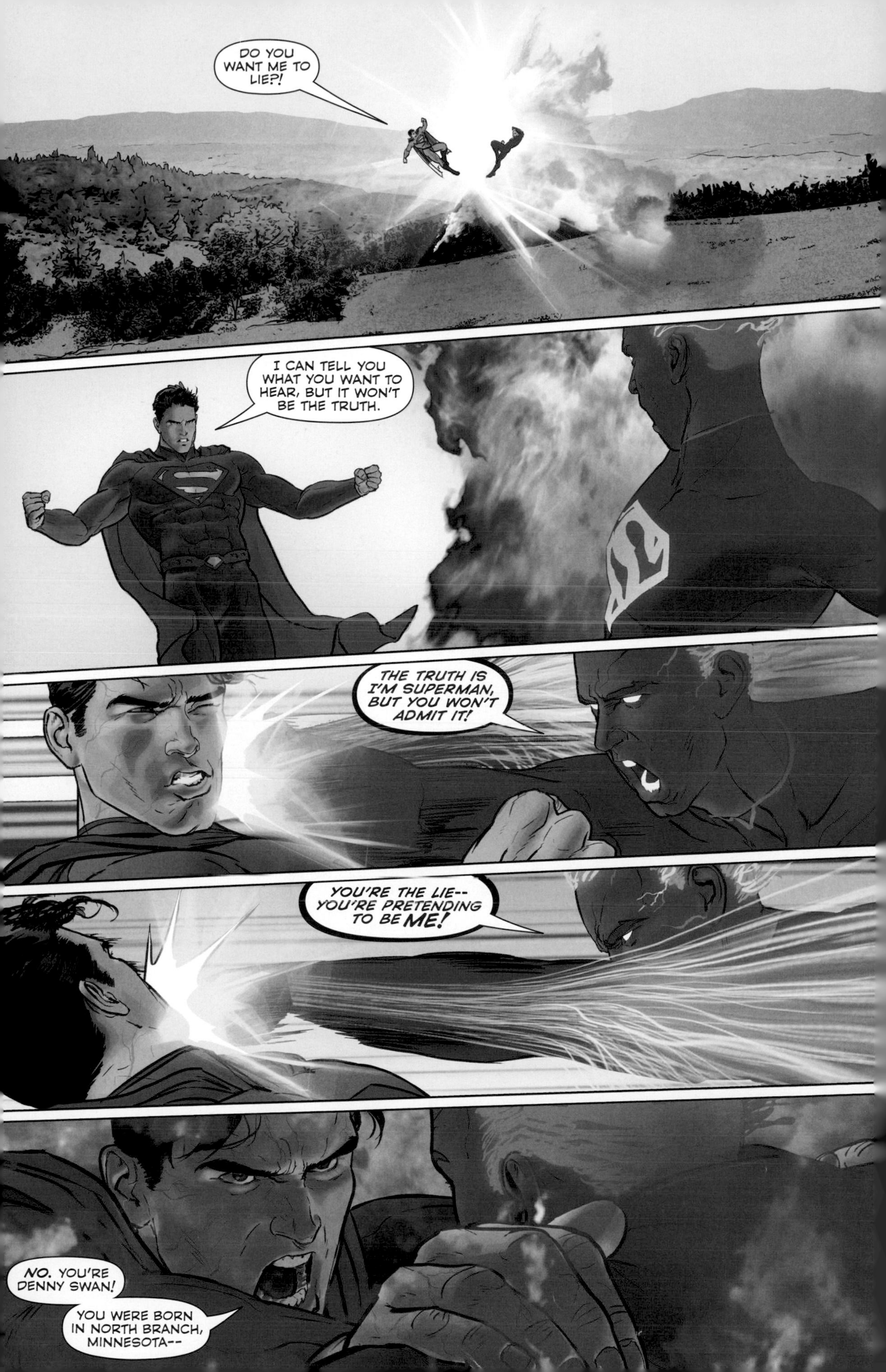
DO YOU WANT ME TO LIE?!
I CAN TELL YOU WHAT YOU WANT TO HEAR, BUT IT WON'T BE THE TRUTH.
THE TRUTH IS I'M SUPERMAN, BUT YOU WON'T ADMIT IT!
YOU'RE THE LIE-- YOU'RE PRETENDING TO BE ME!
NO. YOU'RE DENNY SWAN!
YOU WERE BORN IN NORTH BRANCH, MINNESOTA--

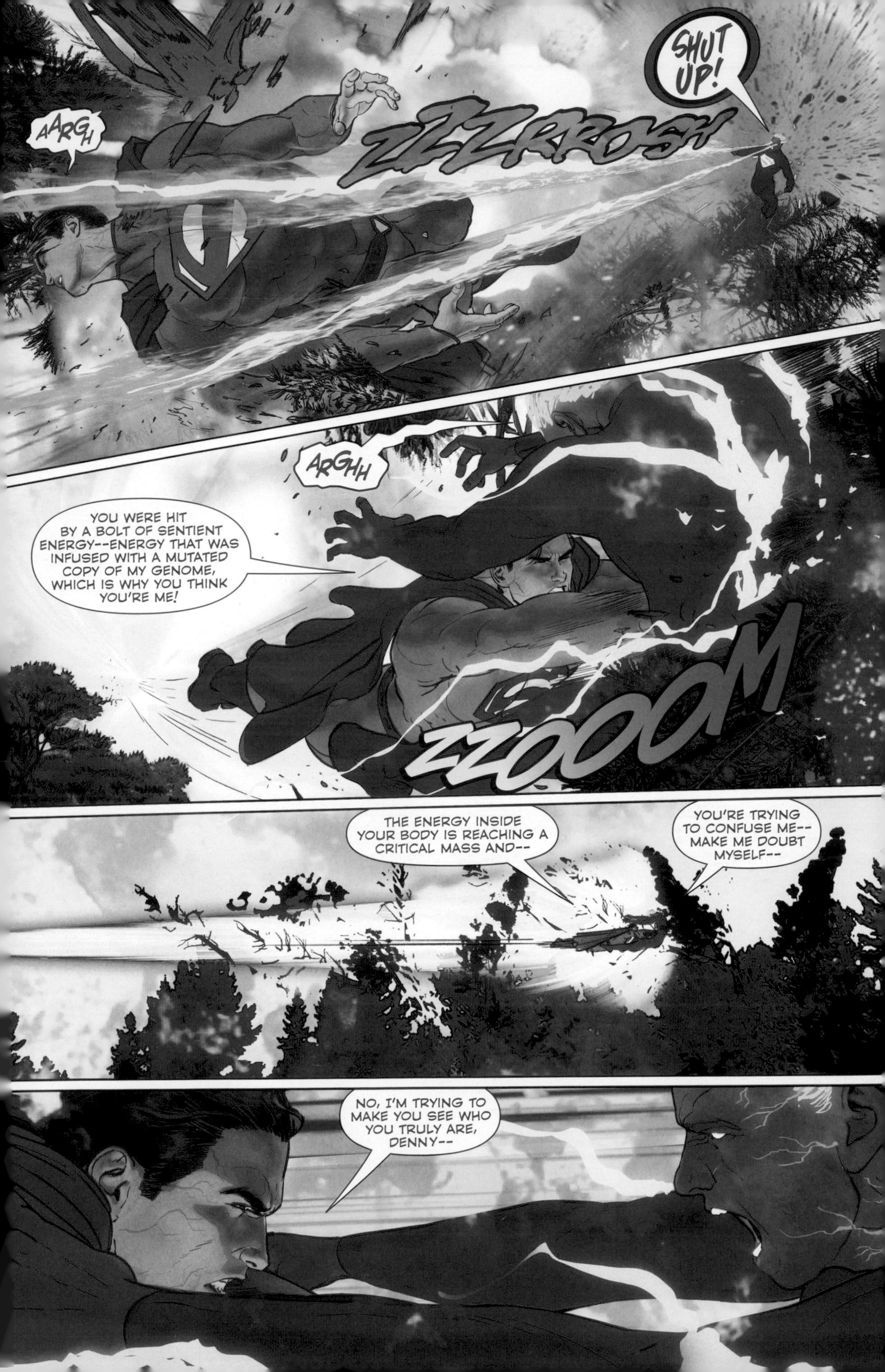

SHUT UP!
AARGH
ZZZRRRSH
ARGHH
YOU WERE HIT BY A BOLT OF SENTIENT ENERGY--ENERGY THAT WAS INFUSED WITH A MUTATED COPY OF MY GENOME, WHICH IS WHY YOU THINK YOU'RE ME!
ZZOOOM
THE ENERGY INSIDE YOUR BODY IS REACHING A CRITICAL MASS AND--
YOU'RE TRYING TO CONFUSE ME-- MAKE ME DOUBT MYSELF--
NO, I'M TRYING TO MAKE YOU SEE WHO YOU TRULY ARE, DENNY--

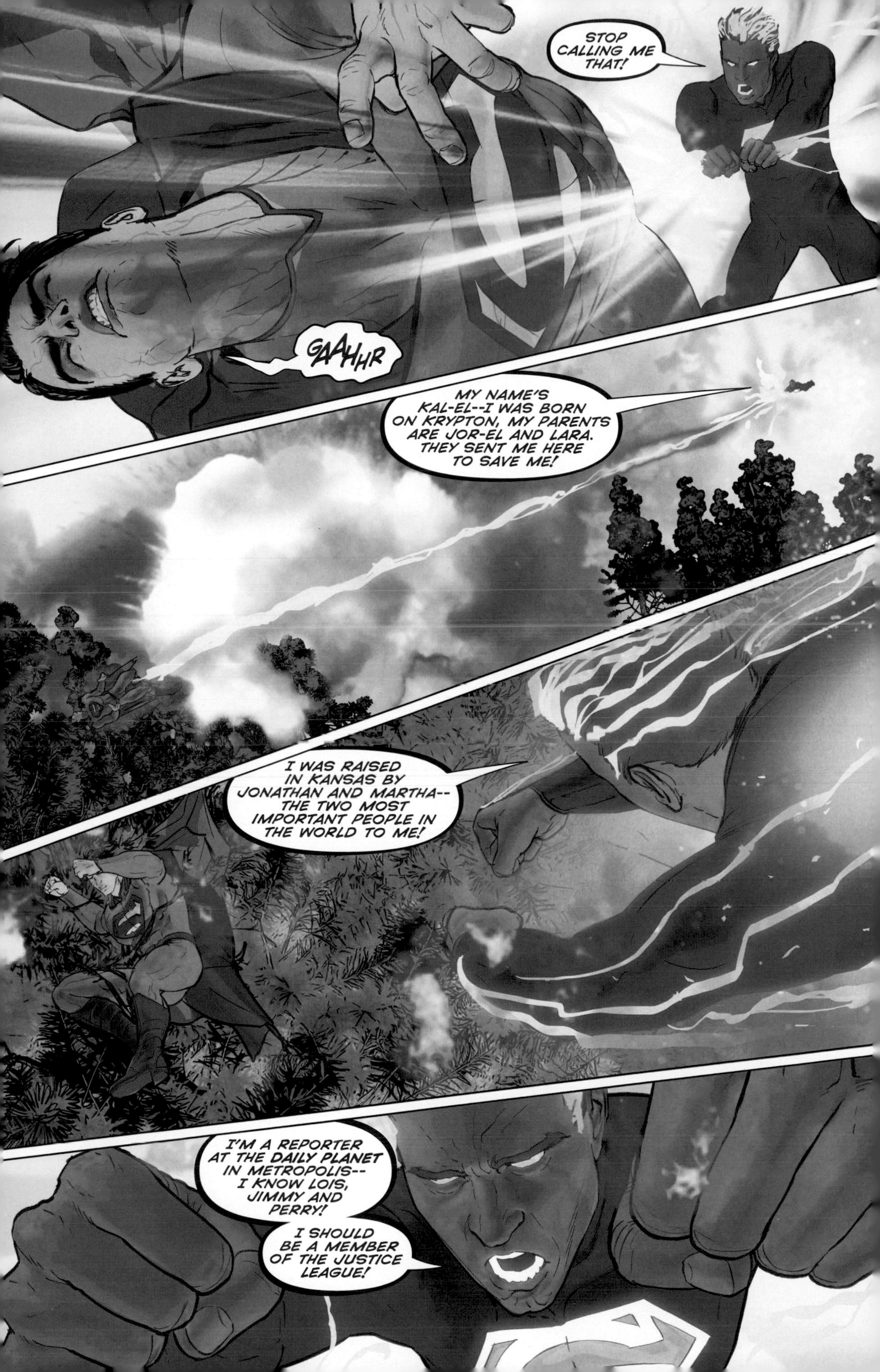
STOP CALLING ME THAT!
GAAHHR
MY NAME'S KAL-EL--I WAS BORN ON KRYPTON, MY PARENTS ARE JOR-EL AND LARA. THEY SENT ME HERE TO SAVE ME!
I WAS RAISED IN KANSAS BY JONATHAN AND MARTHA-- THE TWO MOST IMPORTANT PEOPLE IN THE WORLD TO ME!
I'M A REPORTER AT THE DAILY PLANET IN METROPOLIS-- I KNOW LOIS, JIMMY AND PERRY!
I SHOULD BE A MEMBER OF THE JUSTICE LEAGUE!

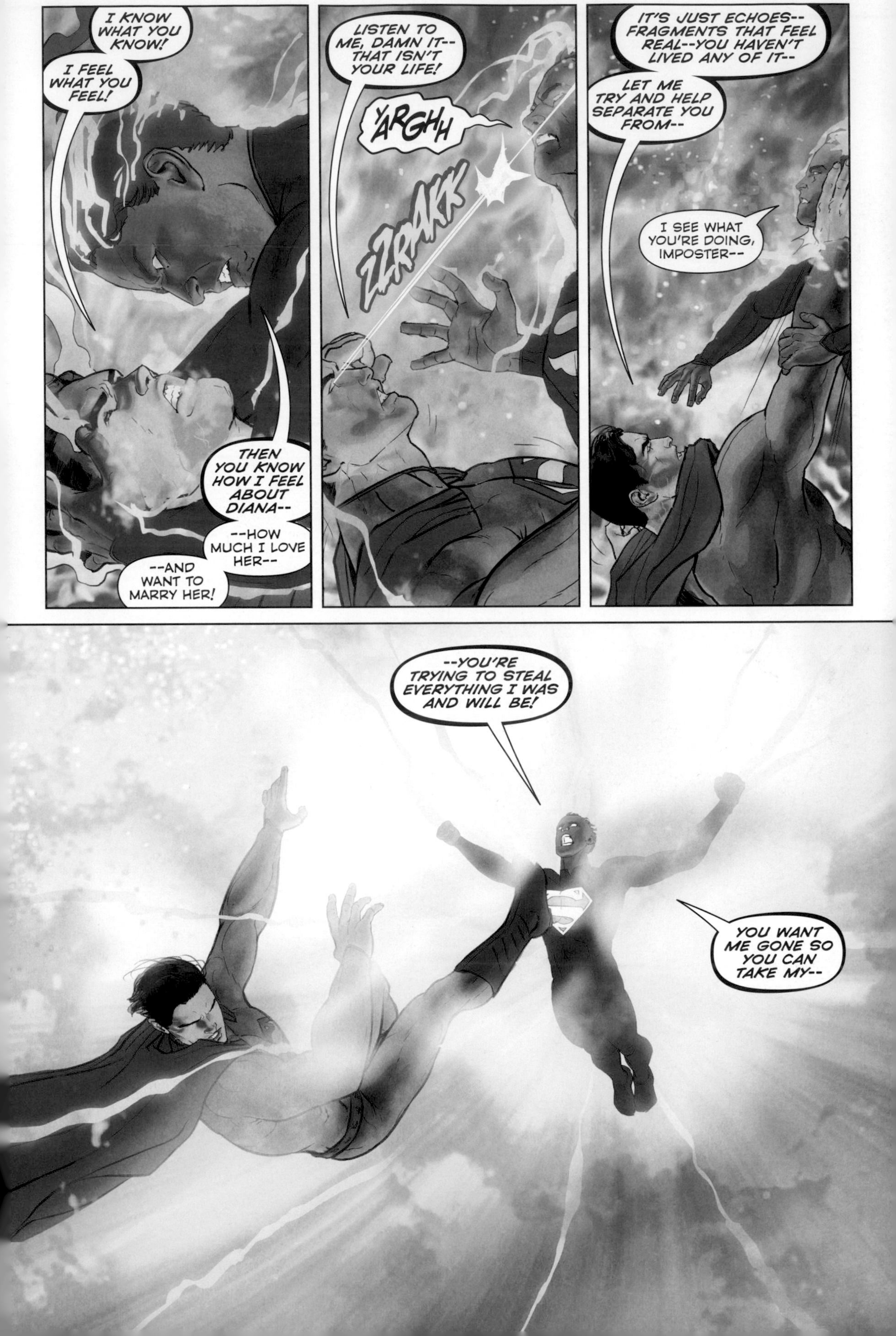
I KNOW WHAT YOU KNOW!
I FEEL WHAT YOU FEEL!
THEN YOU KNOW HOW I FEEL ABOUT DIANA--
--HOW MUCH I LOVE HER--
--AND WANT TO MARRY HER!
LISTEN TO ME, DAMN IT-- THAT ISN'T YOUR LIFE!
YARGHH
ZZRAKK
IT'S JUST ECHOES-- FRAGMENTS THAT FEEL REAL--YOU HAVEN'T LIVED ANY OF IT--
LET ME TRY AND HELP SEPARATE YOU FROM--
I SEE WHAT YOU'RE DOING, IMPOSTER--
--YOU'RE TRYING TO STEAL EVERYTHING I WAS AND WILL BE!
YOU WANT ME GONE SO YOU CAN TAKE MY--

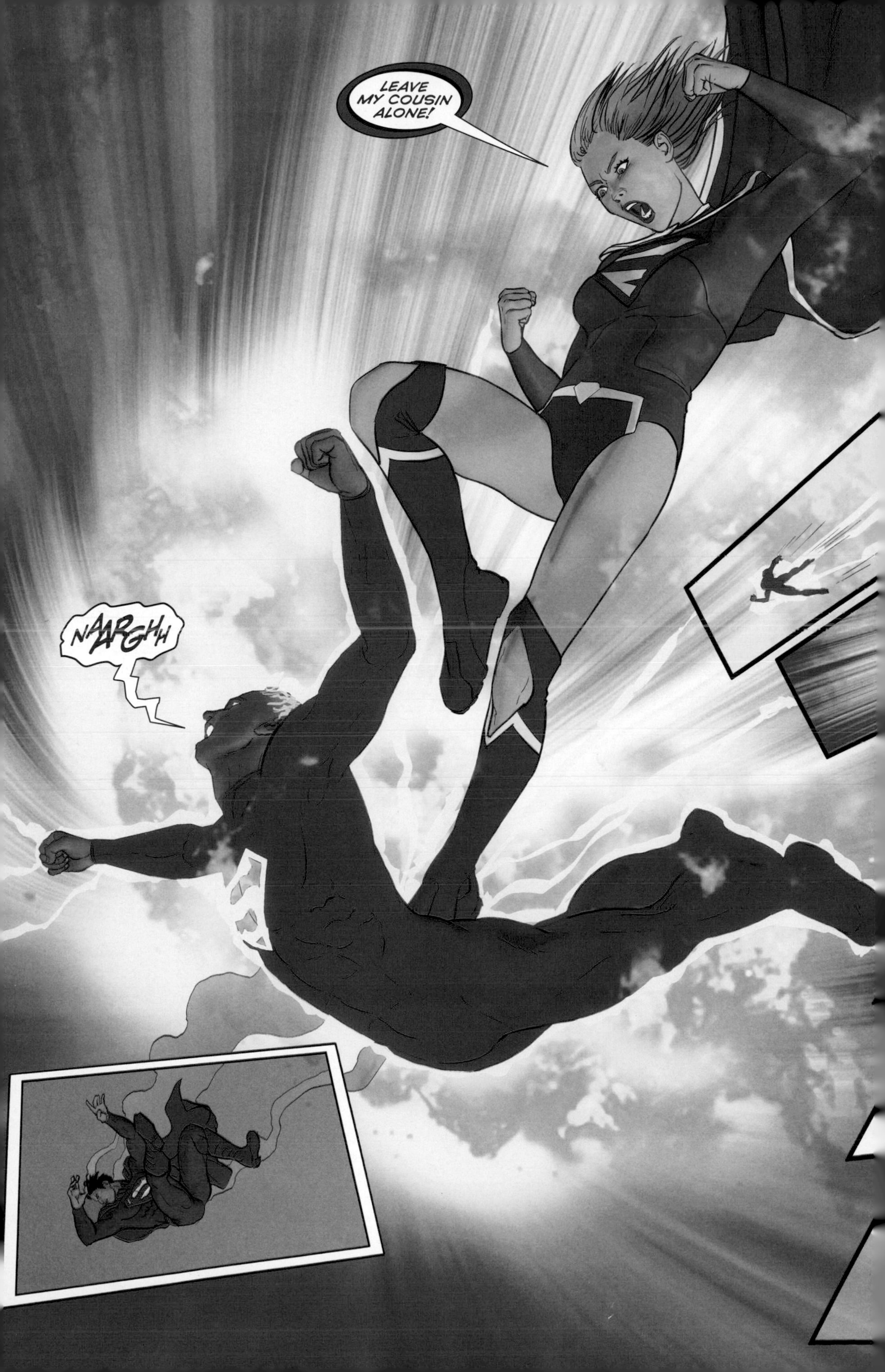
LEAVE MY COUSIN ALONE!
NAARGHH

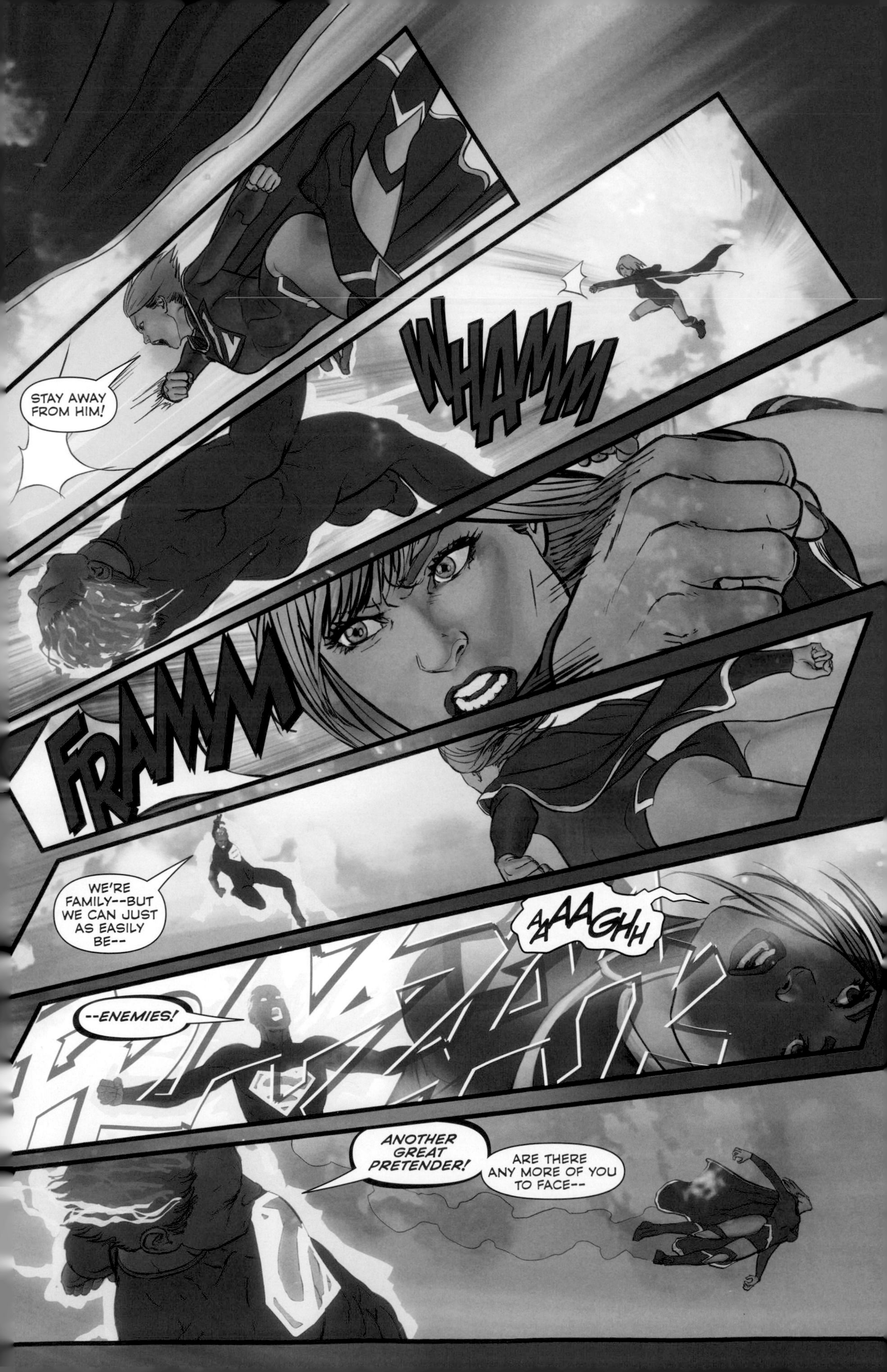
STAY AWAY FROM HIM!
WHAMM
FRAMM
WE'RE FAMILY--BUT WE CAN JUST AS EASILY BE--
AAAAGHH
--ENEMIES!
ANOTHER GREAT PRETENDER!
ARE THERE ANY MORE OF YOU TO FACE--

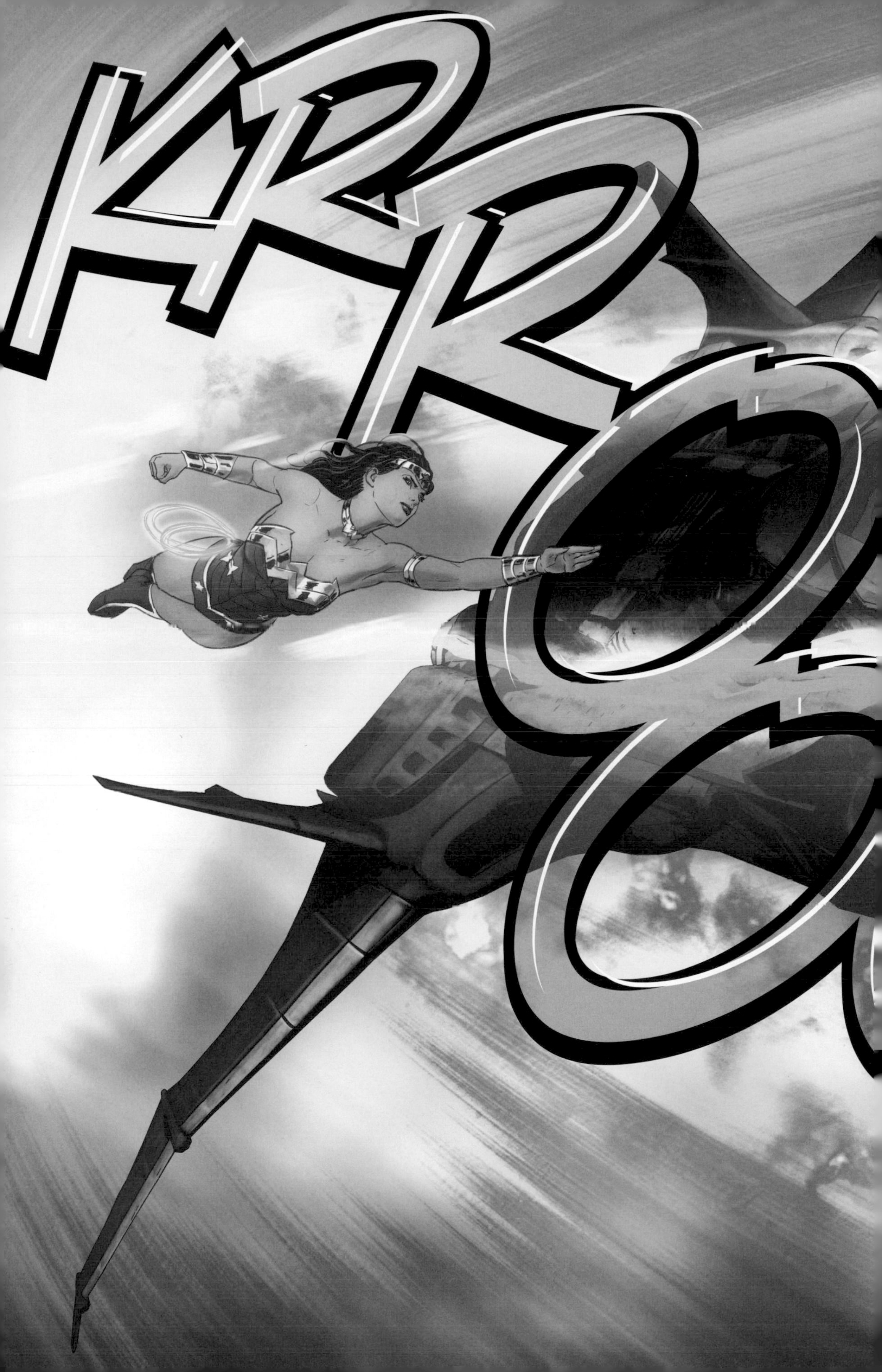
KRROO

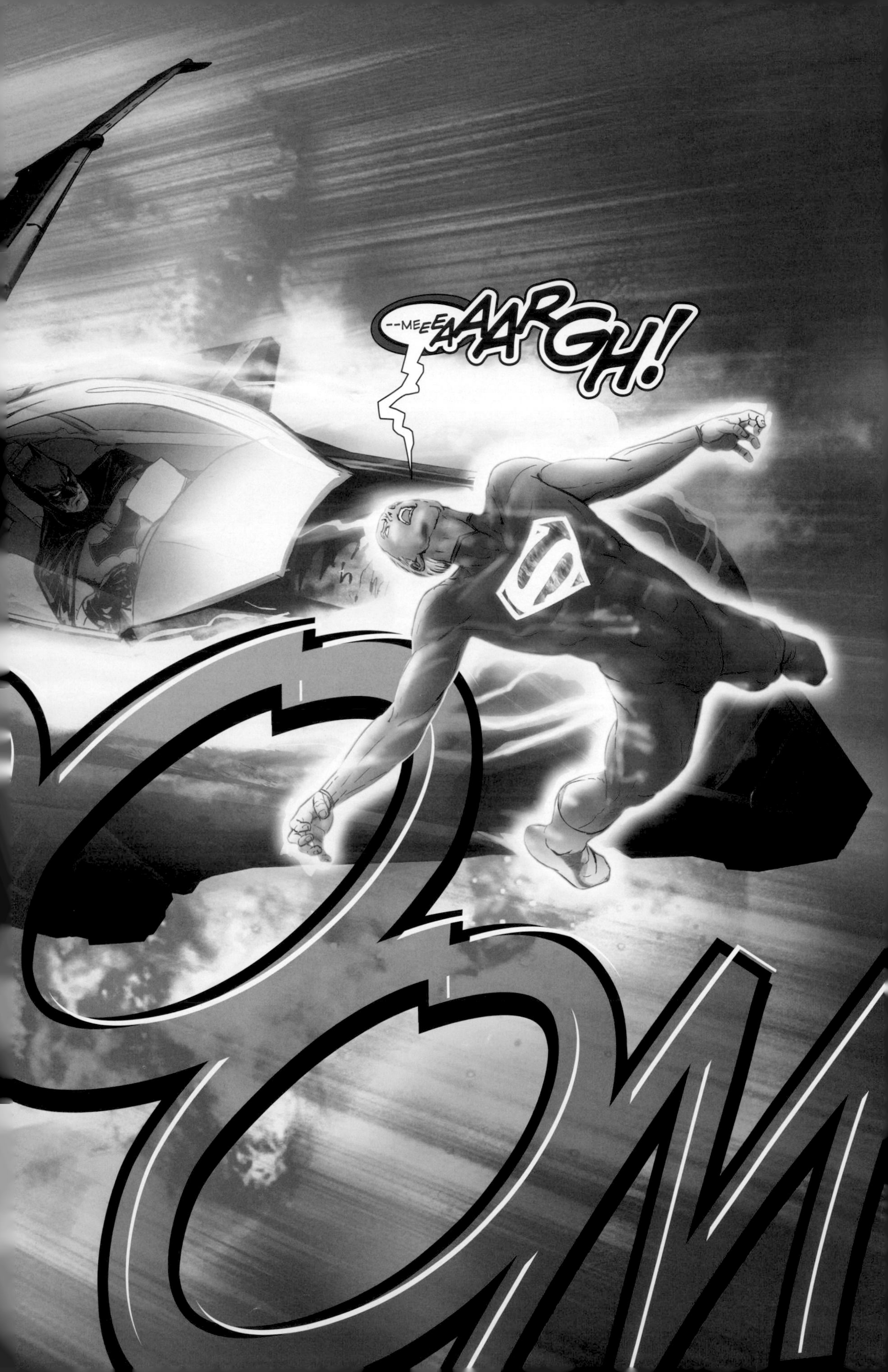
--MEEEAAARGH!
OOM

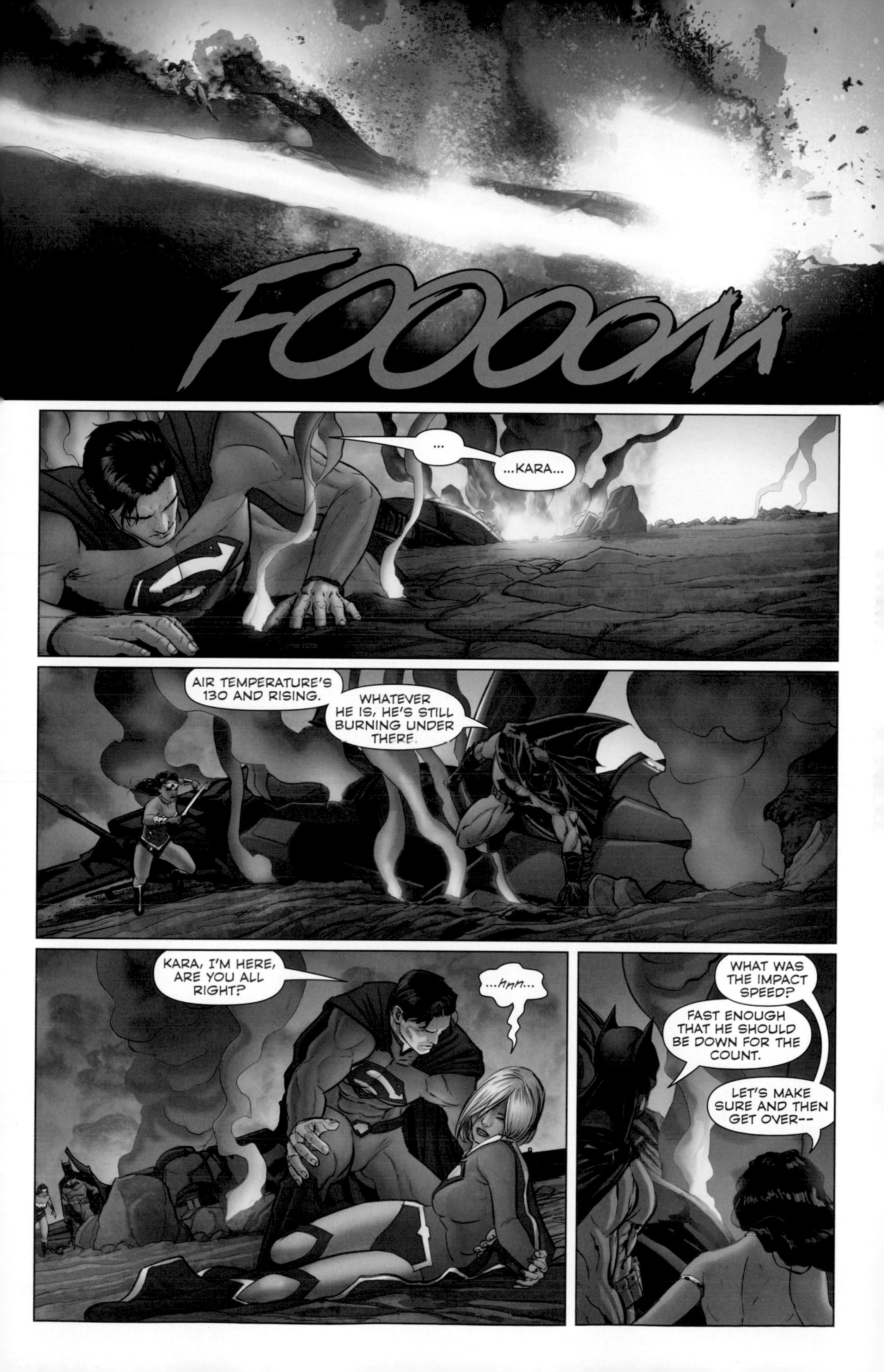
FOOOOM
...
...KARA...
AIR TEMPERATURE'S 130 AND RISING.
WHATEVER HE IS, HE'S STILL BURNING UNDER THERE.
KARA, I'M HERE, ARE YOU ALL RIGHT?
...hnn...
WHAT WAS THE IMPACT SPEED?
FAST ENOUGH THAT HE SHOULD BE DOWN FOR THE COUNT.
LET'S MAKE SURE AND THEN GET OVER--

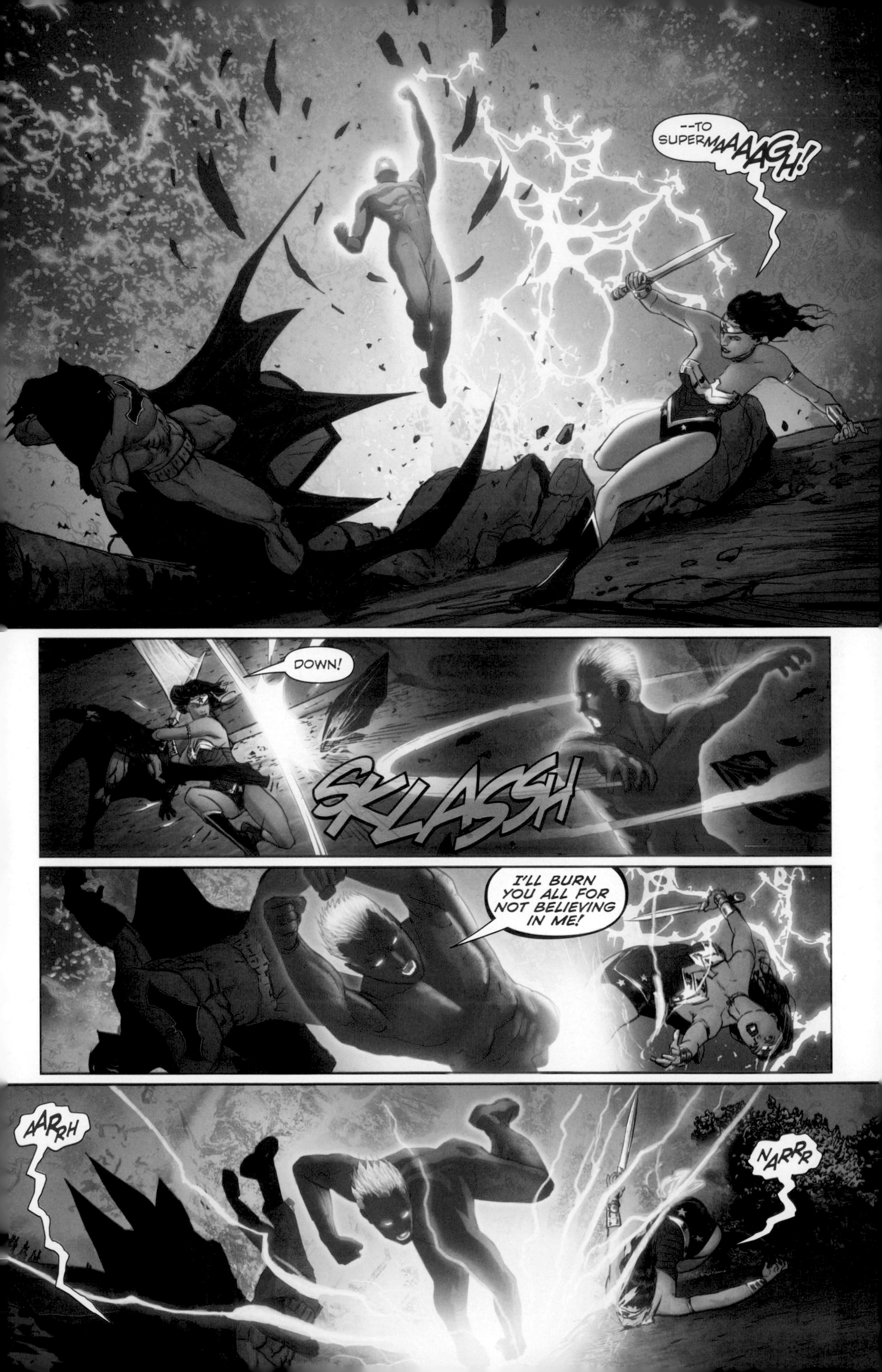
--TO SUPERMAAAAGH!
DOWN!
SKLASSH
I'LL BURN YOU ALL FOR NOT BELIEVING IN ME!
AARRH
NARRR

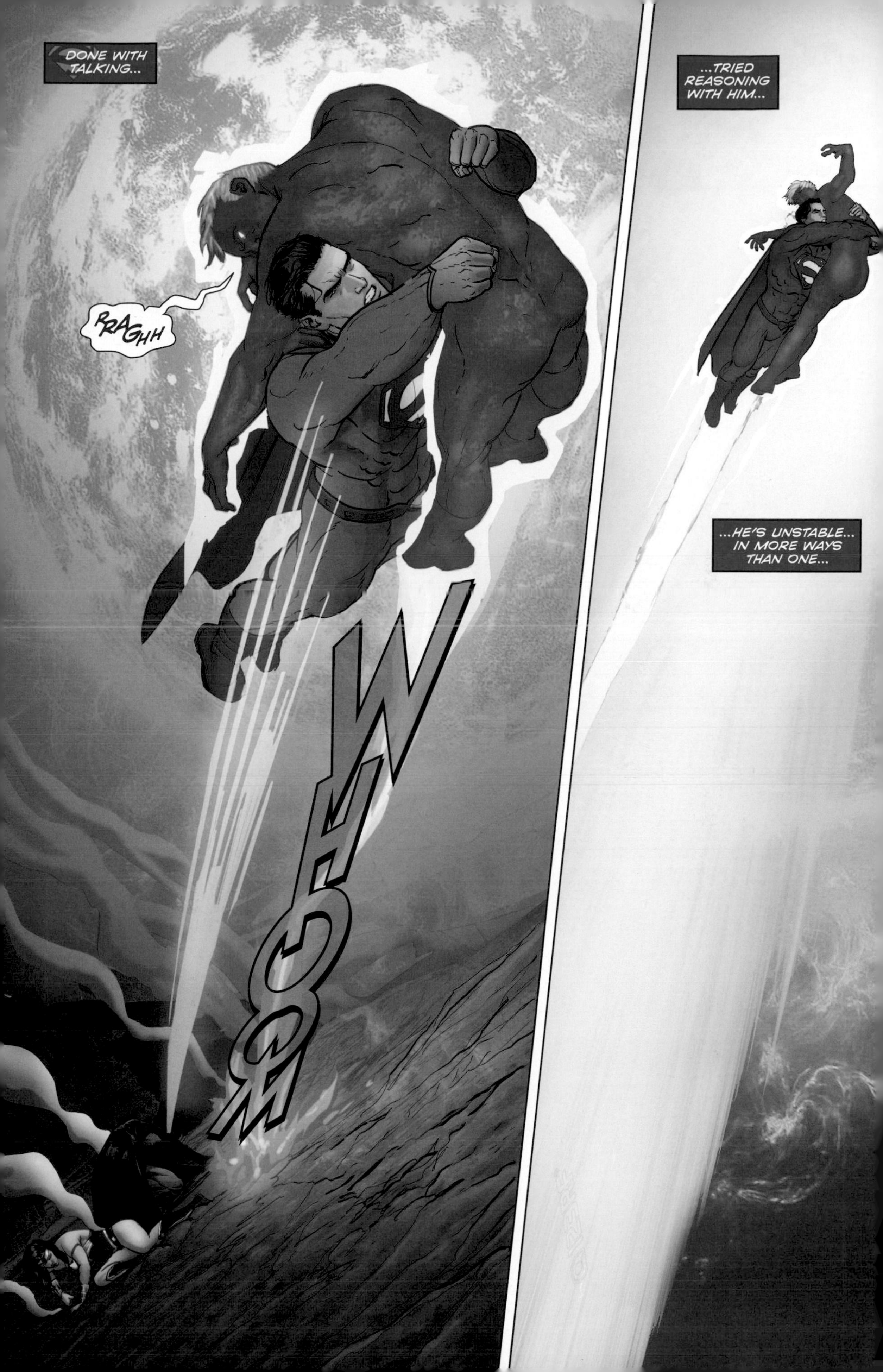
DONE WITH TALKING...
RRAGHH
WHOOM
...TRIED REASONING WITH HIM...
...HE'S UNSTABLE... IN MORE WAYS THAN ONE...

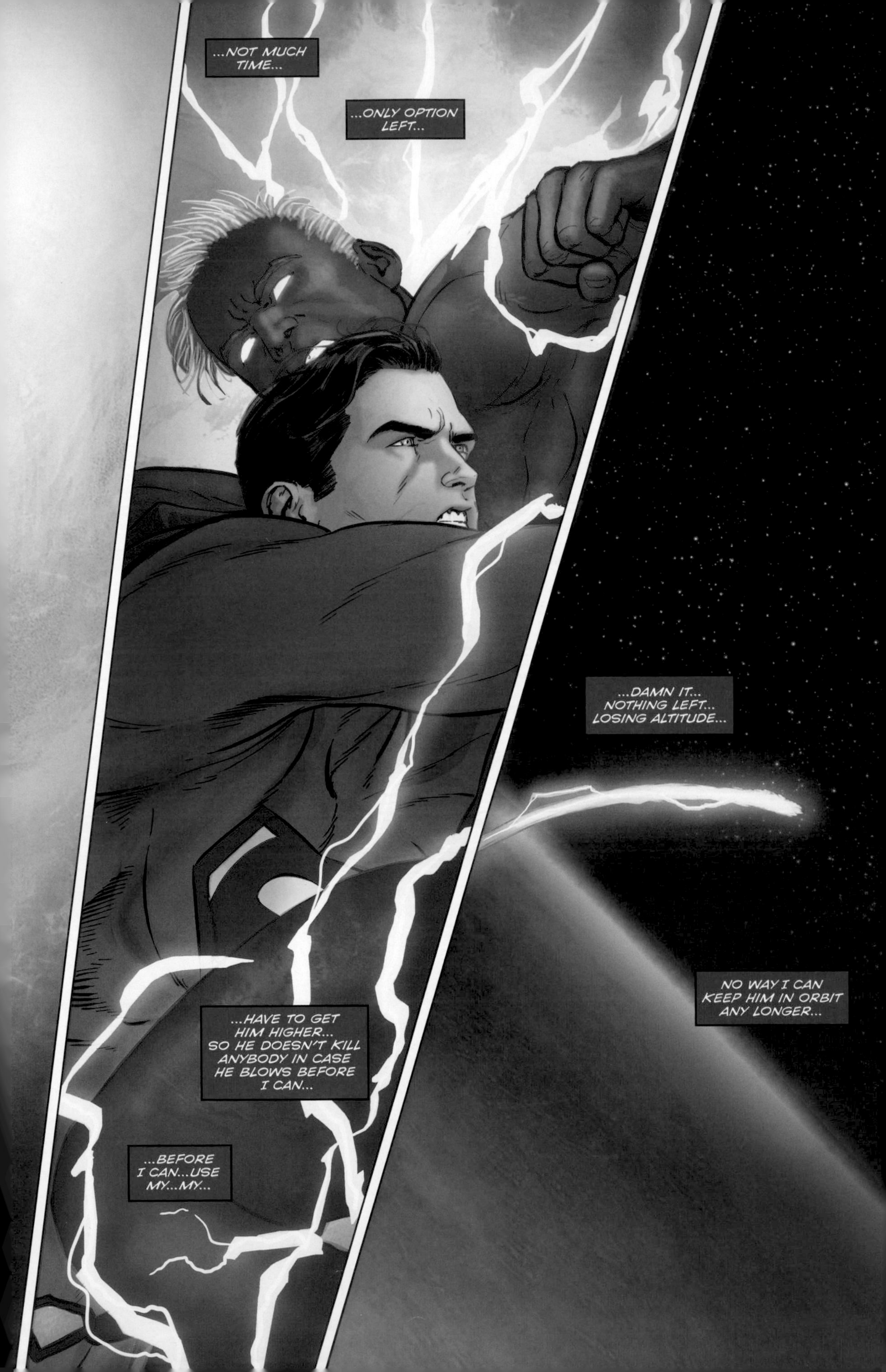
...NOT MUCH TIME...
...ONLY OPTION LEFT...
...HAVE TO GET HIM HIGHER... SO HE DOESN'T KILL ANYBODY IN CASE HE BLOWS BEFORE I CAN...
...BEFORE I CAN...USE MY...MY...
...DAMN IT... NOTHING LEFT... LOSING ALTITUDE...
NO WAY I CAN KEEP HIM IN ORBIT ANY LONGER...

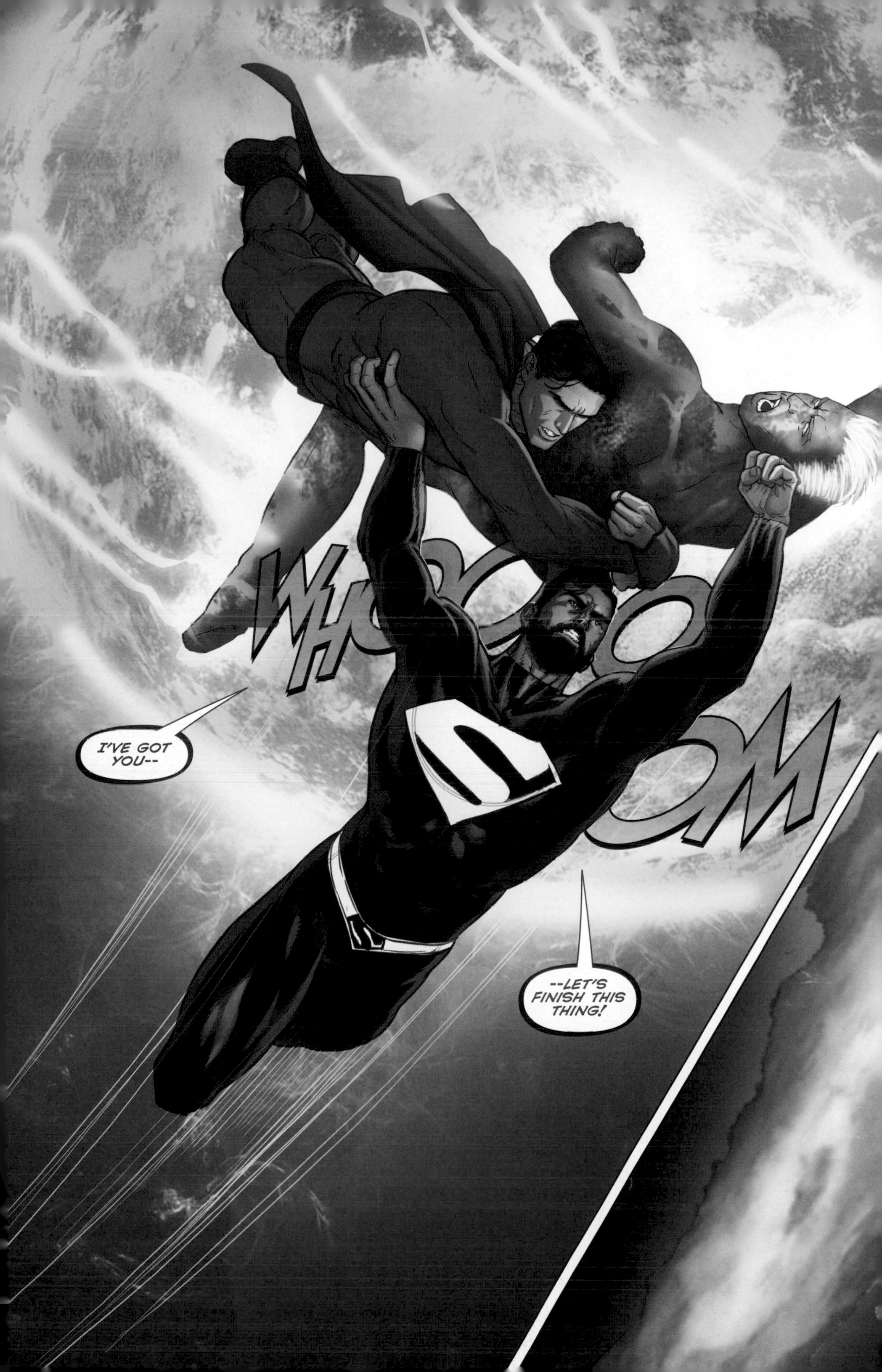

WHOOOOM
I'VE GOT YOU--
--LET'S FINISH THIS THING!

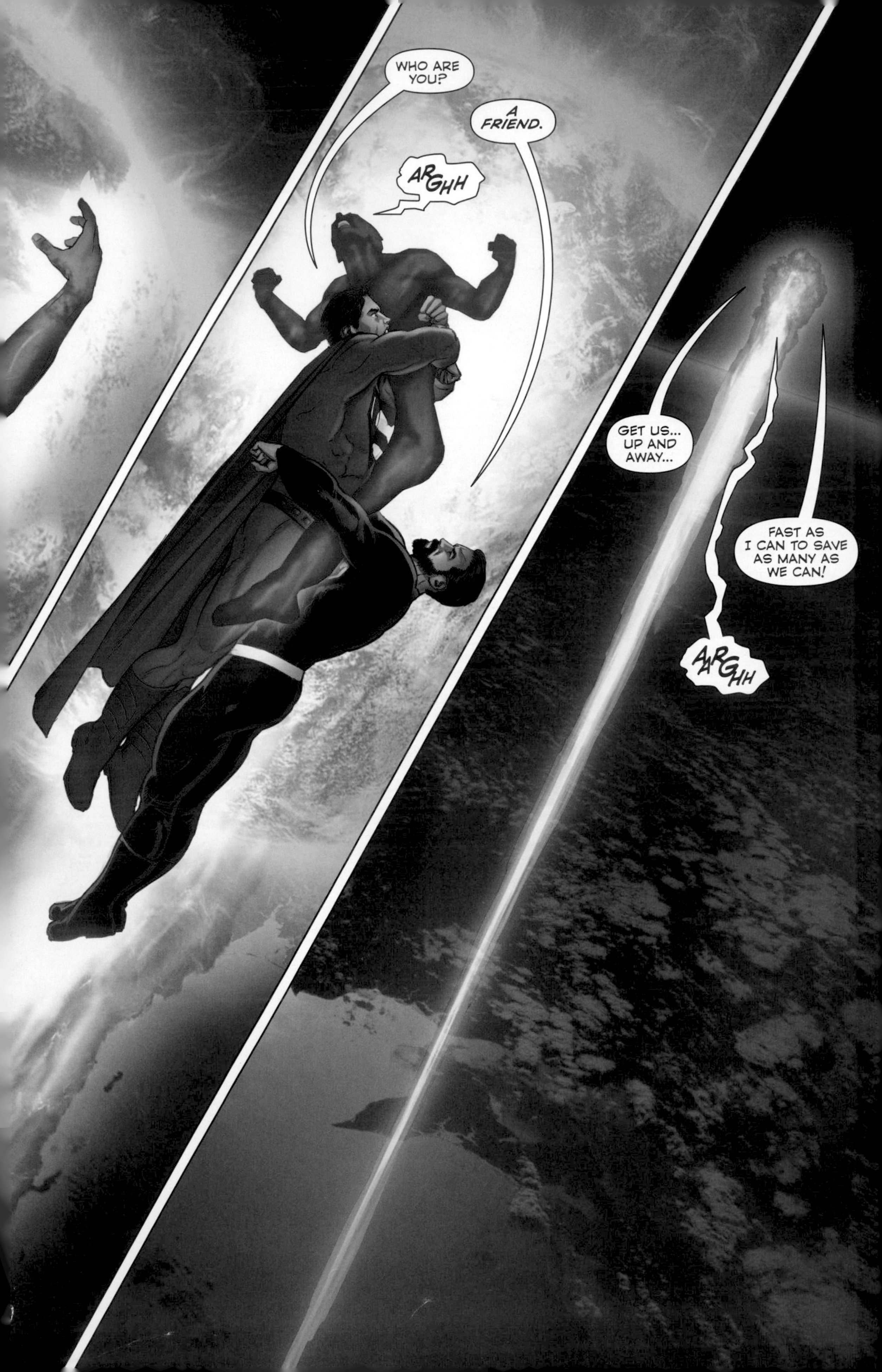
WHO ARE YOU?
A FRIEND.
ARGHH
GET US... UP AND AWAY...
FAST AS I CAN TO SAVE AS MANY AS WE CAN!
AARGHH

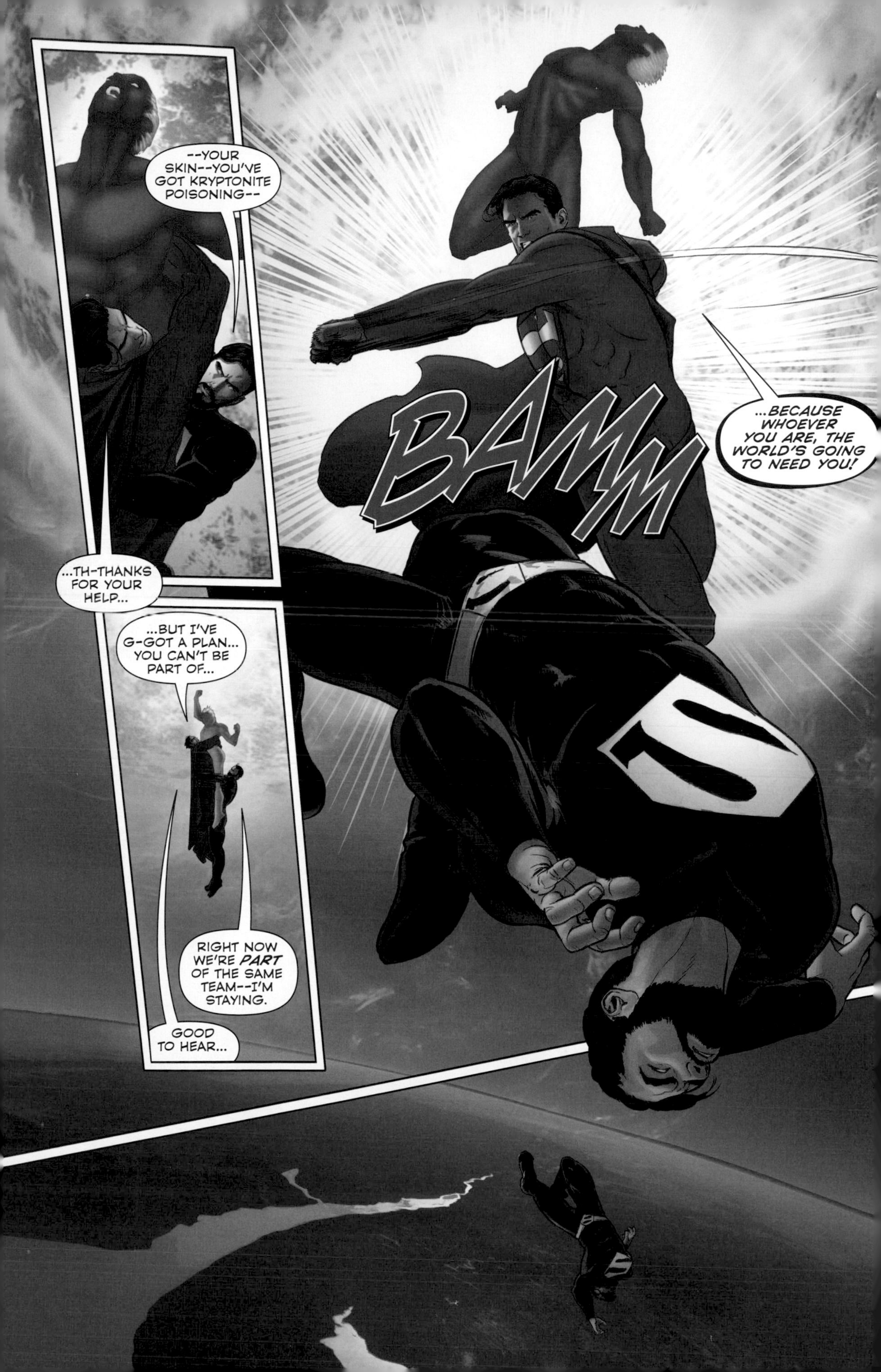
--YOUR SKIN--YOU'VE GOT KRYPTONITE POISONING--
...BECAUSE WHOEVER YOU ARE, THE WORLD'S GOING TO NEED YOU!
BAMM
...TH-THANKS FOR YOUR HELP...
...BUT I'VE G-GOT A PLAN... YOU CAN'T BE PART OF...
RIGHT NOW WE'RE *PART* OF THE SAME TEAM--I'M STAYING.
GOOD TO HEAR...

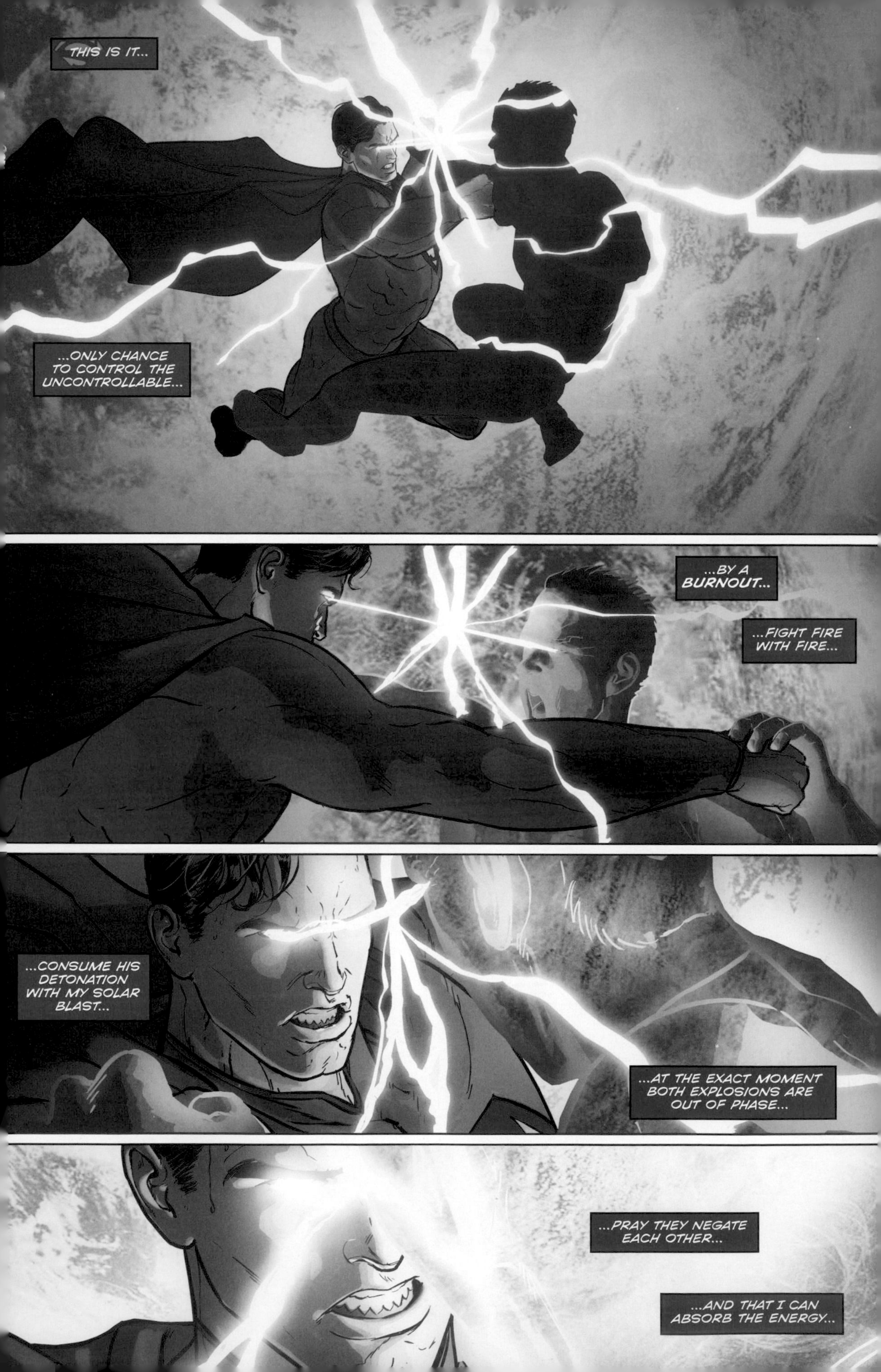
THIS IS IT...
...ONLY CHANCE TO CONTROL THE UNCONTROLLABLE...
...BY A BURNOUT...
...FIGHT FIRE WITH FIRE...
...CONSUME HIS DETONATION WITH MY SOLAR BLAST...
...AT THE EXACT MOMENT BOTH EXPLOSIONS ARE OUT OF PHASE...
...PRAY THEY NEGATE EACH OTHER...
...AND THAT I CAN ABSORB THE ENERGY...

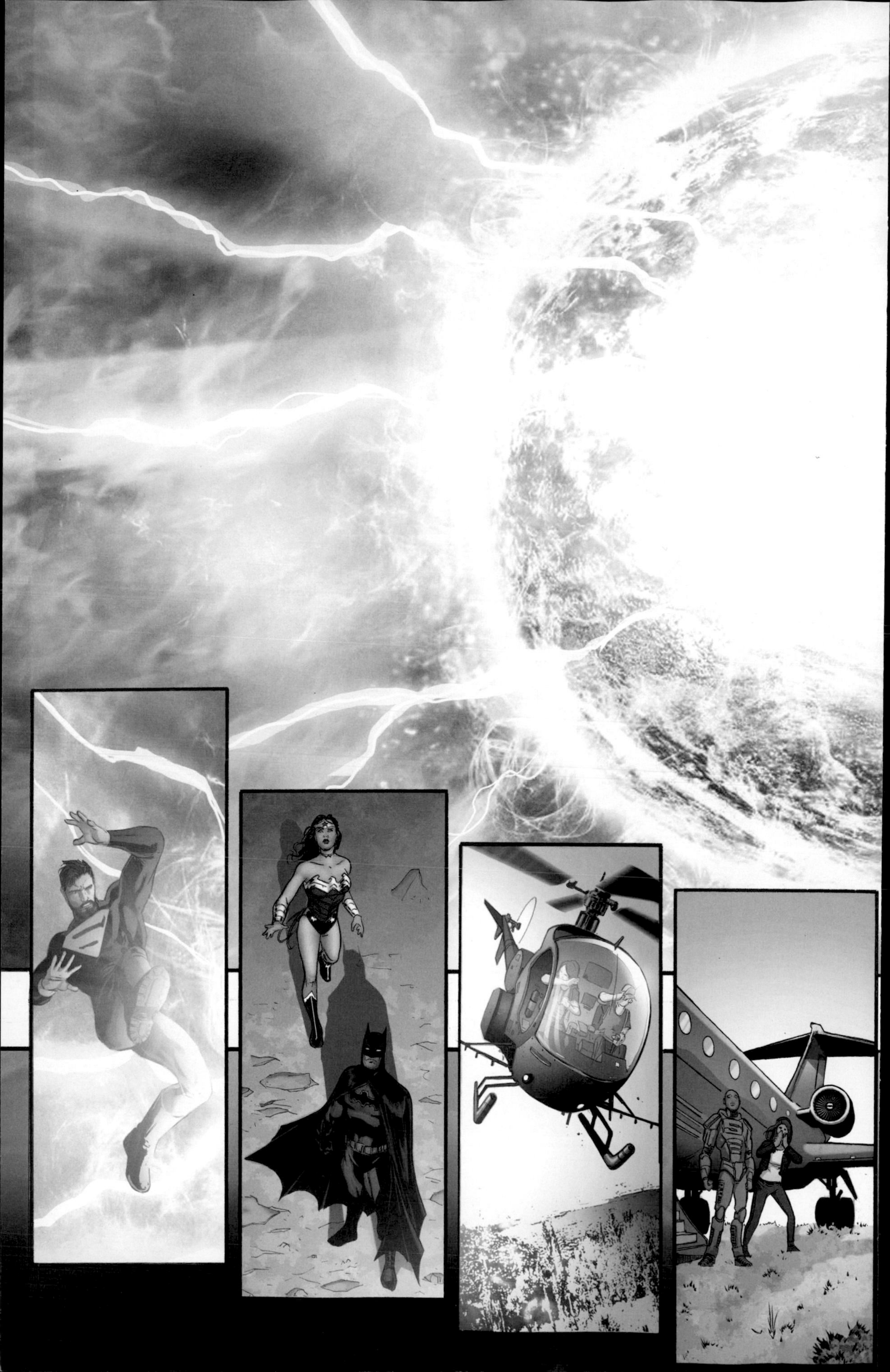

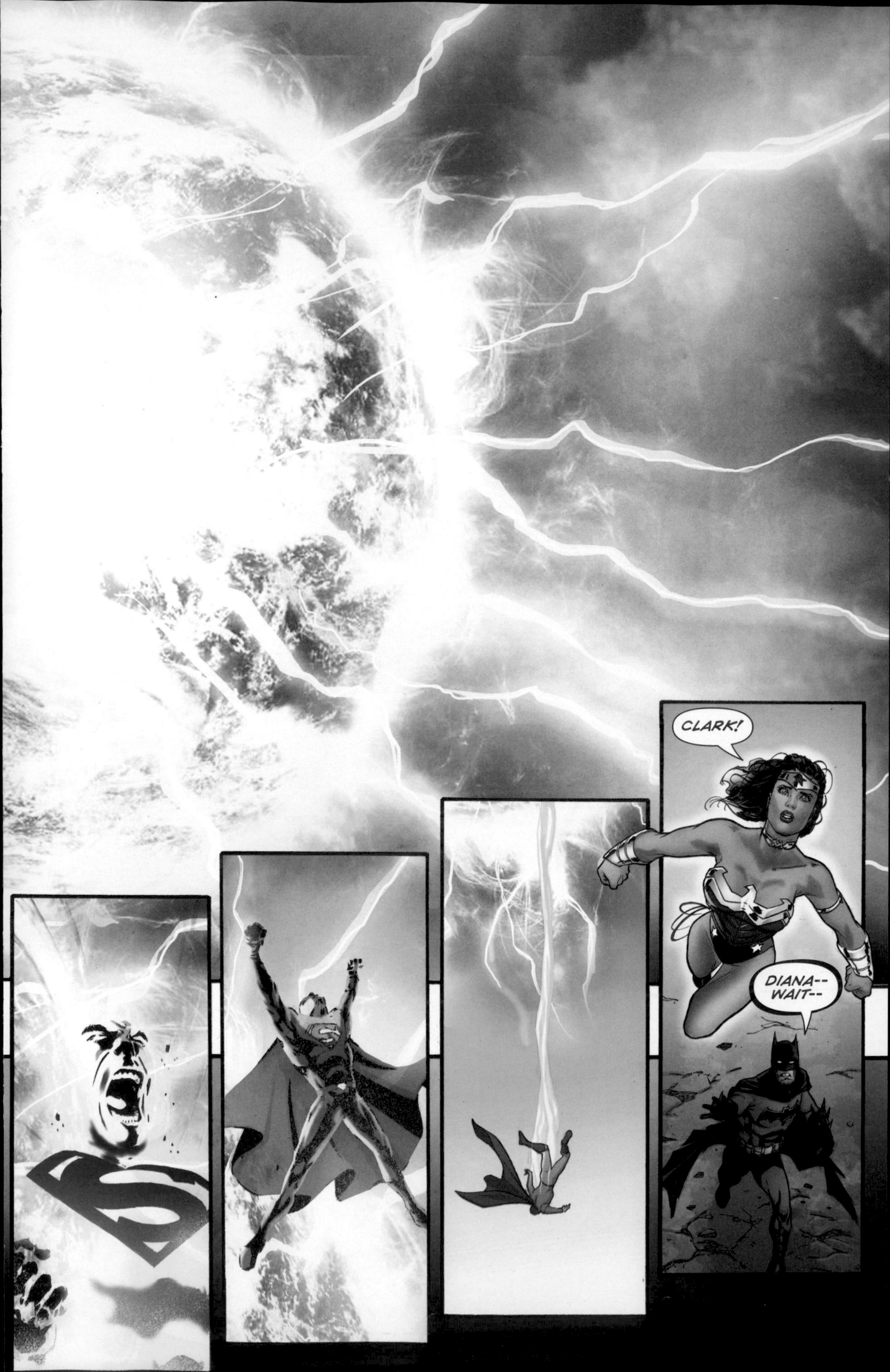
CLARK!
DIANA--
WAIT--

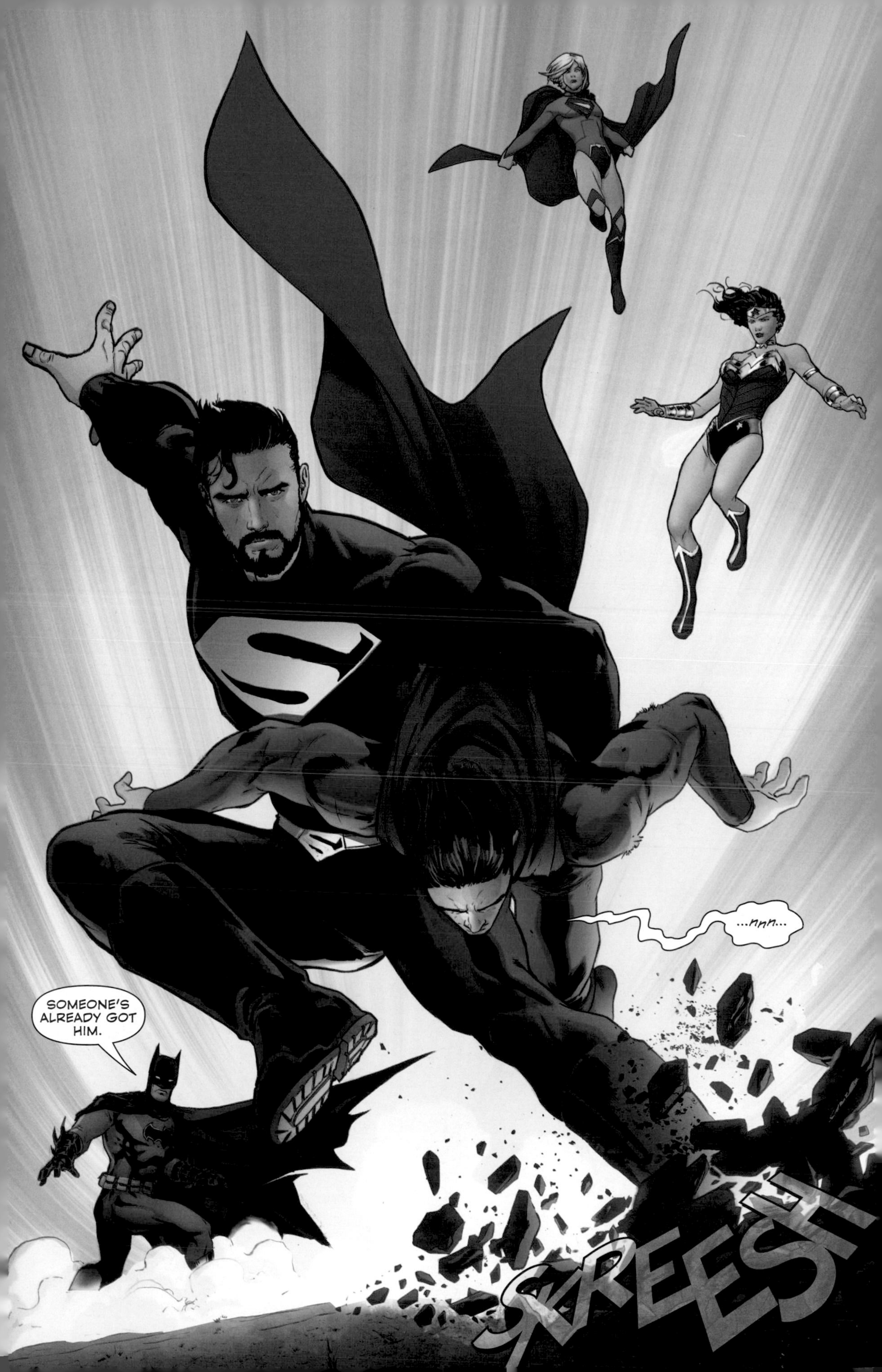
...nnn...
SOMEONE'S ALREADY GOT HIM.
SKREEEST

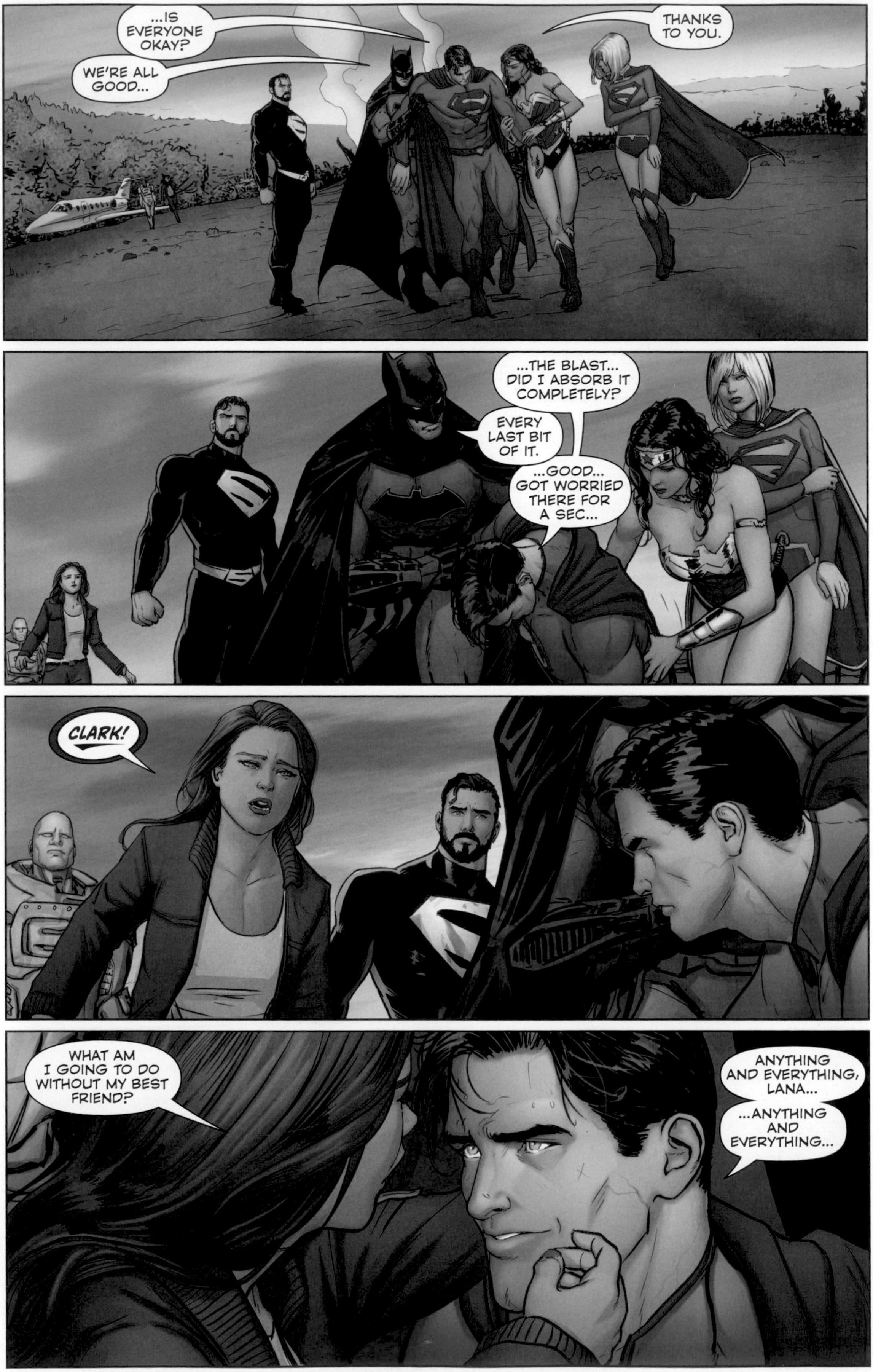
...IS EVERYONE OKAY?
WE'RE ALL GOOD...
THANKS TO YOU.
...THE BLAST... DID I ABSORB IT COMPLETELY?
EVERY LAST BIT OF IT.
...GOOD... GOT WORRIED THERE FOR A SEC...
CLARK!
WHAT AM I GOING TO DO WITHOUT MY BEST FRIEND?
ANYTHING AND EVERYTHING, LANA...
...ANYTHING AND EVERYTHING...

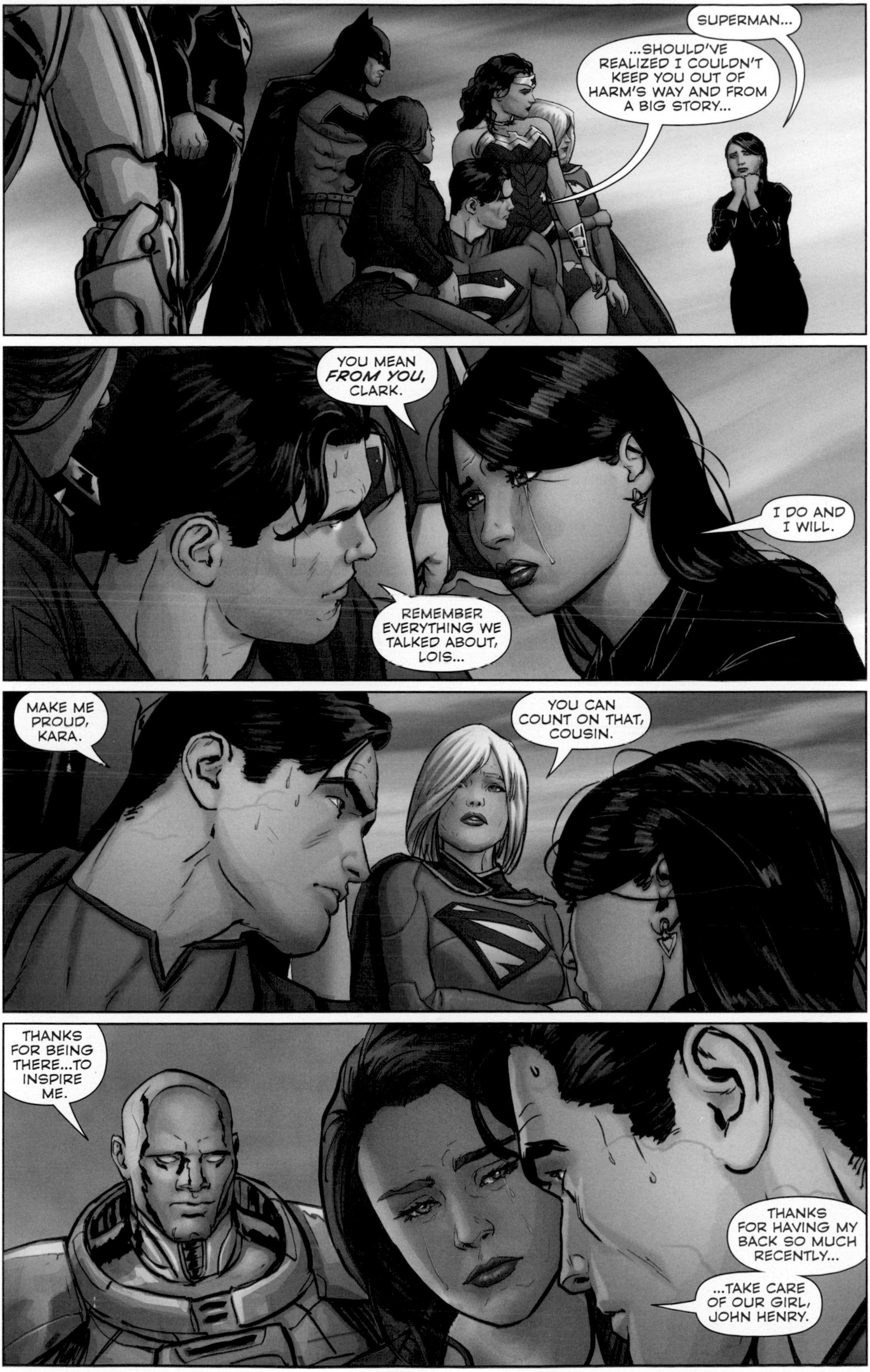
SUPERMAN...
...SHOULD'VE REALIZED I COULDN'T KEEP YOU OUT OF HARM'S WAY AND FROM A BIG STORY...
YOU MEAN *FROM YOU,* CLARK.
I DO AND I WILL.
REMEMBER EVERYTHING WE TALKED ABOUT, LOIS...
MAKE ME PROUD, KARA.
YOU CAN COUNT ON THAT, COUSIN.
THANKS FOR BEING THERE...TO INSPIRE ME.
THANKS FOR HAVING MY BACK SO MUCH RECENTLY...
...TAKE CARE OF OUR GIRL, JOHN HENRY.

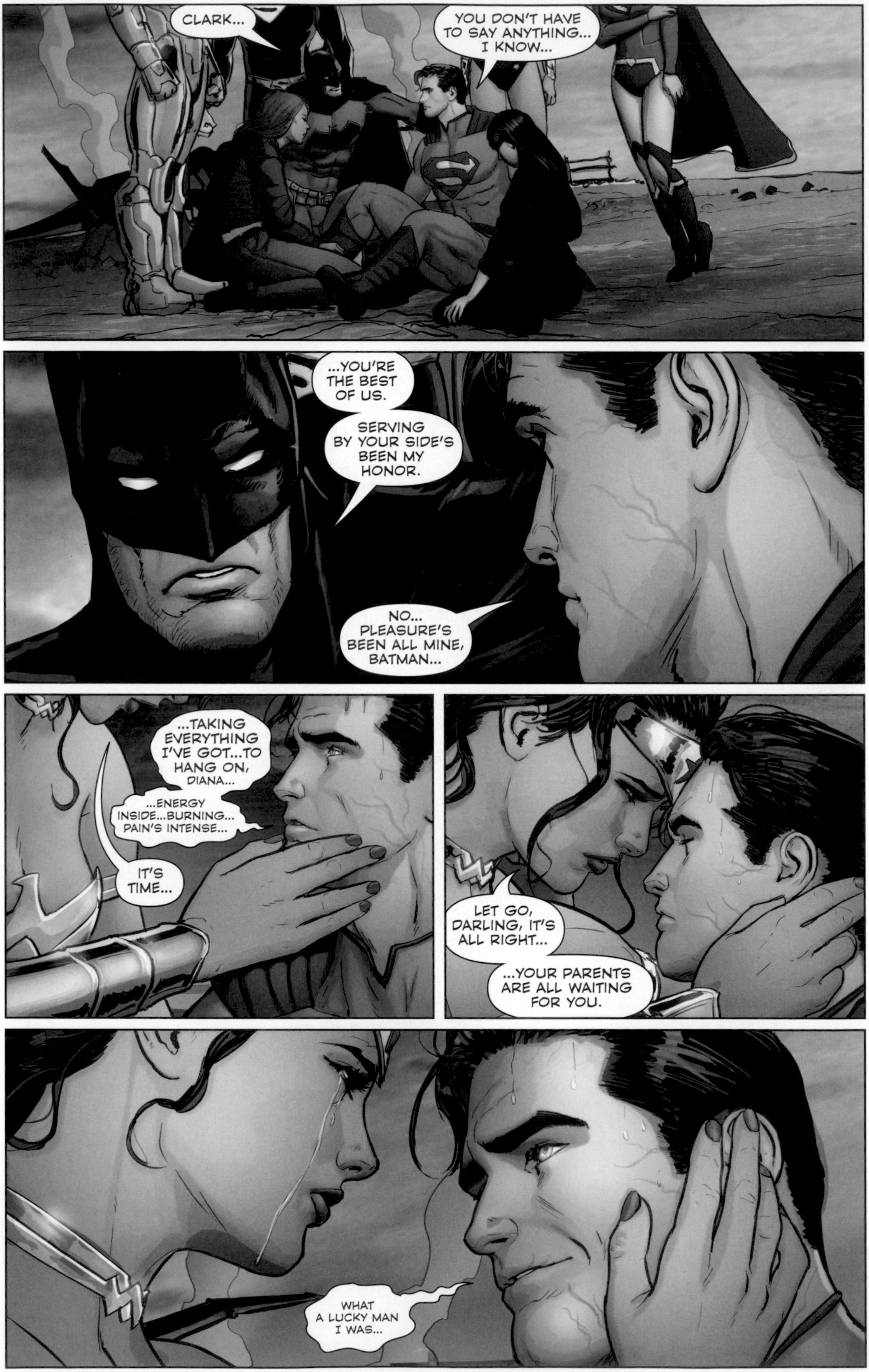
CLARK...
YOU DON'T HAVE TO SAY ANYTHING... I KNOW...
...YOU'RE THE BEST OF US.
SERVING BY YOUR SIDE'S BEEN MY HONOR.
NO... PLEASURE'S BEEN ALL MINE, BATMAN...
...TAKING EVERYTHING I'VE GOT...TO HANG ON, DIANA...
...ENERGY INSIDE...BURNING... PAIN'S INTENSE...
IT'S TIME...
LET GO, DARLING, IT'S ALL RIGHT...
...YOUR PARENTS ARE ALL WAITING FOR YOU.
WHAT A LUCKY MAN I WAS...

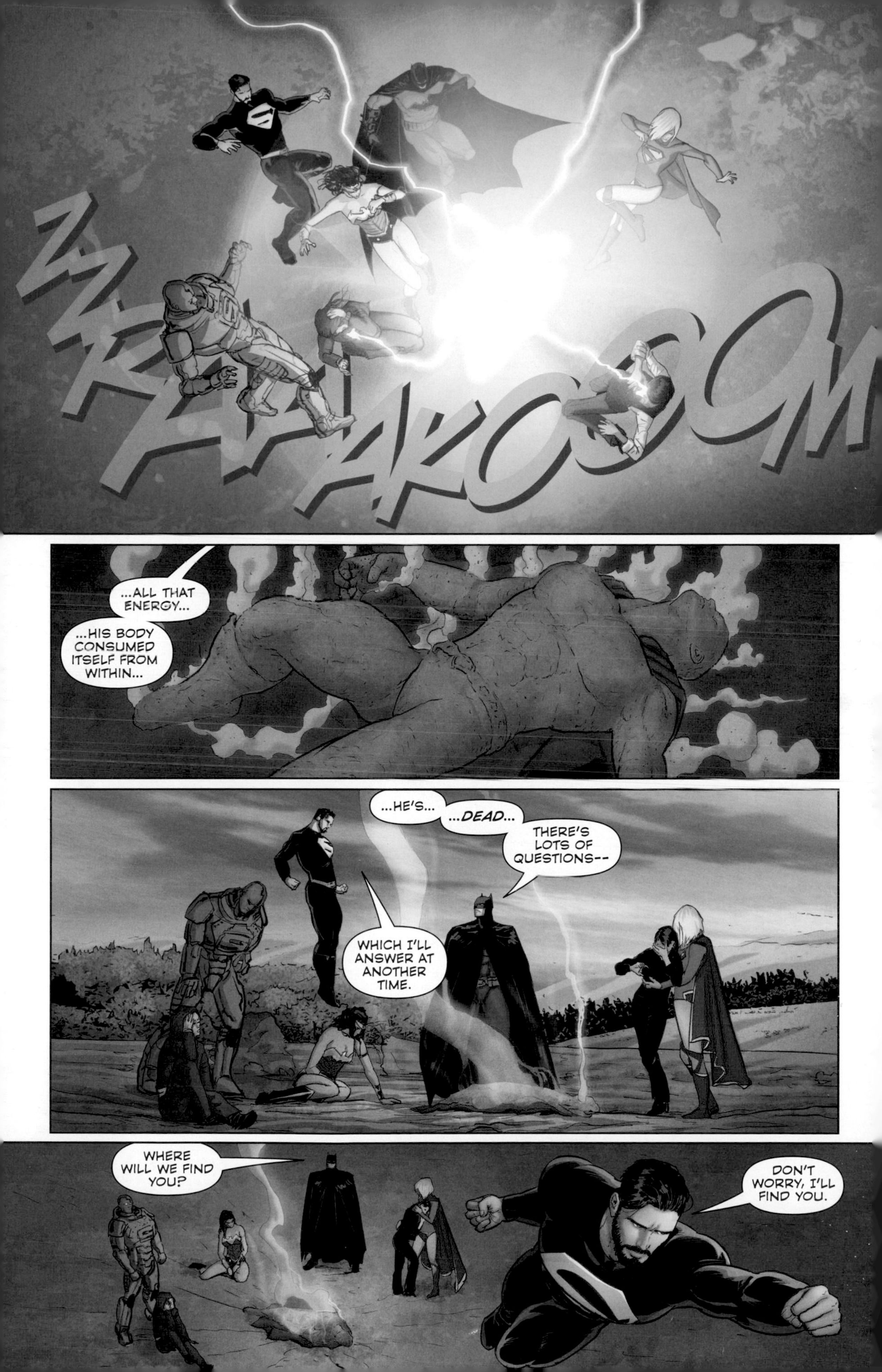
KRAKOOOM
...ALL THAT ENERGY...
...HIS BODY CONSUMED ITSELF FROM WITHIN...
...HE'S...
...*DEAD*...
THERE'S LOTS OF QUESTIONS--
WHICH I'LL ANSWER AT ANOTHER TIME.
WHERE WILL WE FIND YOU?
DON'T WORRY, I'LL FIND YOU.

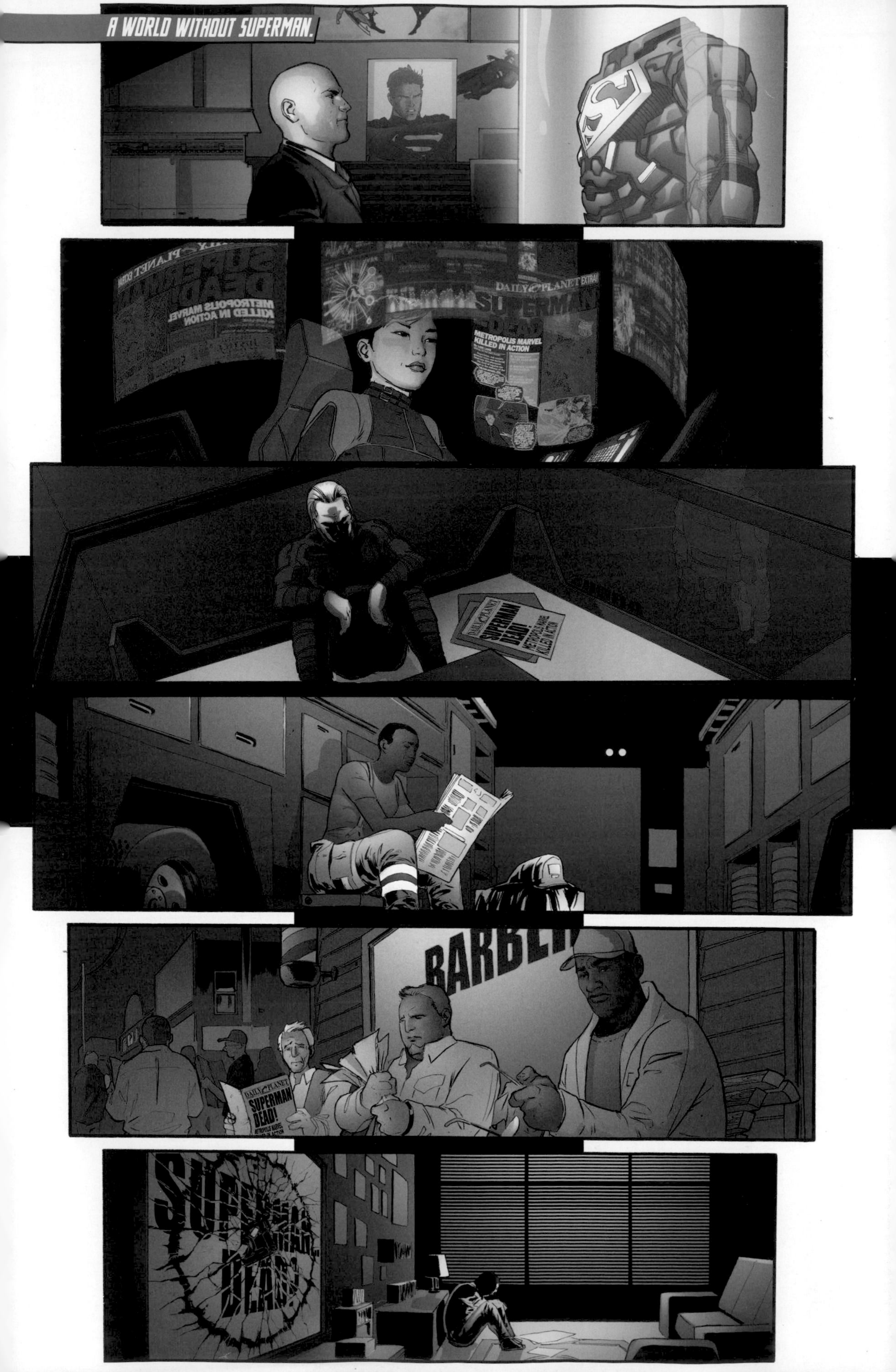
A WORLD WITHOUT SUPERMAN.
DAILY PLANET EXTRA!
SUPERMAN DEAD!
METROPOLIS MARVEL KILLED IN ACTION
DAILY PLANET
SUPERMAN DEAD!
METROPOLIS MARVEL KILLED IN ACTION
DAILY PLANET
SUPERMAN DEAD!
METROPOLIS MARVEL KILLED IN ACTION

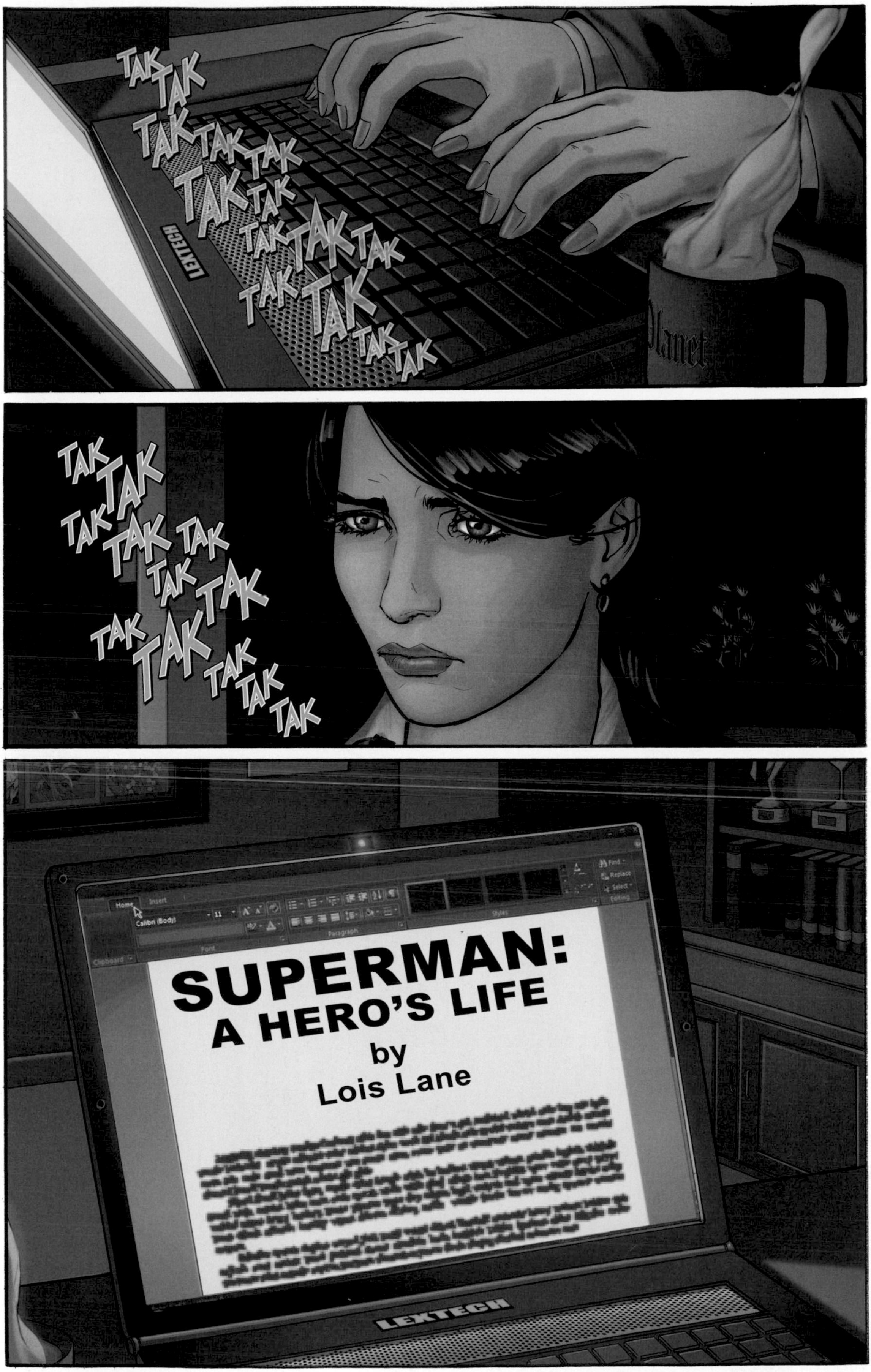
TAK TAK TAK TAK TAK TAK TAK TAK TAK TAK TAK TAK TAK TAK TAK
LEXTECH
Planet
TAK TAK TAK TAK TAK TAK TAK TAK TAK TAK TAK TAK
SUPERMAN:
A HERO'S LIFE
by
Lois Lane
LEXTECH

VARIANT COVER GALLERY

SUPERMAN #45
MONSTER MONTH VARIANT BY
CULLY HAMNER

SUPERMAN #46
LOONEY TUNES VARIANT BY
RYAN SOOK, SPIKE BRANDT

SUPERMAN #47
HARLEY'S LITTLE BLACK BOOK VARIANT BY
LEE BERMEJO

SUPERMAN #48
ADULT COLORING BOOK VARIANT BY
ANDY SMITH

SUPERMAN #49
NEAL ADAMS VARIANT BY
NEAL ADAMS, SIMON BISLEY, TERRY DODSON

SUPERMAN #50
VARIANT BY KAARE ANDREWS,
DAVE JOHNSON, DAVE McCRAIG

SUPERMAN #50/BATMAN #50
DCBS VARIANT BY NEAL ADAMS, JEROMY COX

SUPERMAN #50/BATMAN #50
COMIXPOSURE VARIANT BY GUILLEM MARCH

SUPERMAN #50/BATMAN #50
VARIANT BY DAVE JOHNSON

SUPERMAN #50/BATMAN #50
PULP'S COMICS AND PARIS COMICS EXPO VARIANT
BY LEE BERMEJO

SUPERMAN #50/BATMAN #50
FRIED PIE VARIANT BY RAFAEL ALBUQUERQUE

SUPERMAN #50/BATMAN #50
BULLETPROOF COMICS VARIANT BY
GABRIELE DELL'OTTO

SUPERMAN #50/BATMAN #50
MIDTOWN COMICS VARIANT BY
TERRY DODSON, RACHEL DODSON

SUPERMAN #50/BATMAN #50
DYNAMIC FORCES VARIANT BY AMANDA CONNER

SUPERMAN #50/BATMAN #50
NEWBURY COMICS VARIANT BY
TIM SALE, BRENNAN WAGNER

SUPERMAN #50/BATMAN #50
BEYOND COMICS VARIANT BY
ED BENES, TOMEU MOREY

SUPERMAN #50/BATMAN #50
COMIC CON BOX VARIANT BY
PAT GLEASON, MICK GRAY, JOHN KALISZ

SUPERMAN #50/BATMAN #50
MADNESS GAMES & COMICS VARIANT BY
JOSHUA MIDDLETON

SUPERMAN #50/BATMAN #50
FORBIDDEN PLANET LIMITED VARIANT BY
SEAN GORDON MURPHY, DAVE McCAIG

SUPERMAN #50/BATMAN #50
HASTINGS VARIANT BY
TYLER KIRKHAM, TOMEU MOREY

SUPERMAN #51
JOHN ROMITA JR. VARIANT BY
JOHN ROMITA JR., DANNY MIKI & LAURA MARTIN

SUPERMAN #52
NEW 52 VARIANT BY MIKEL JANÍN

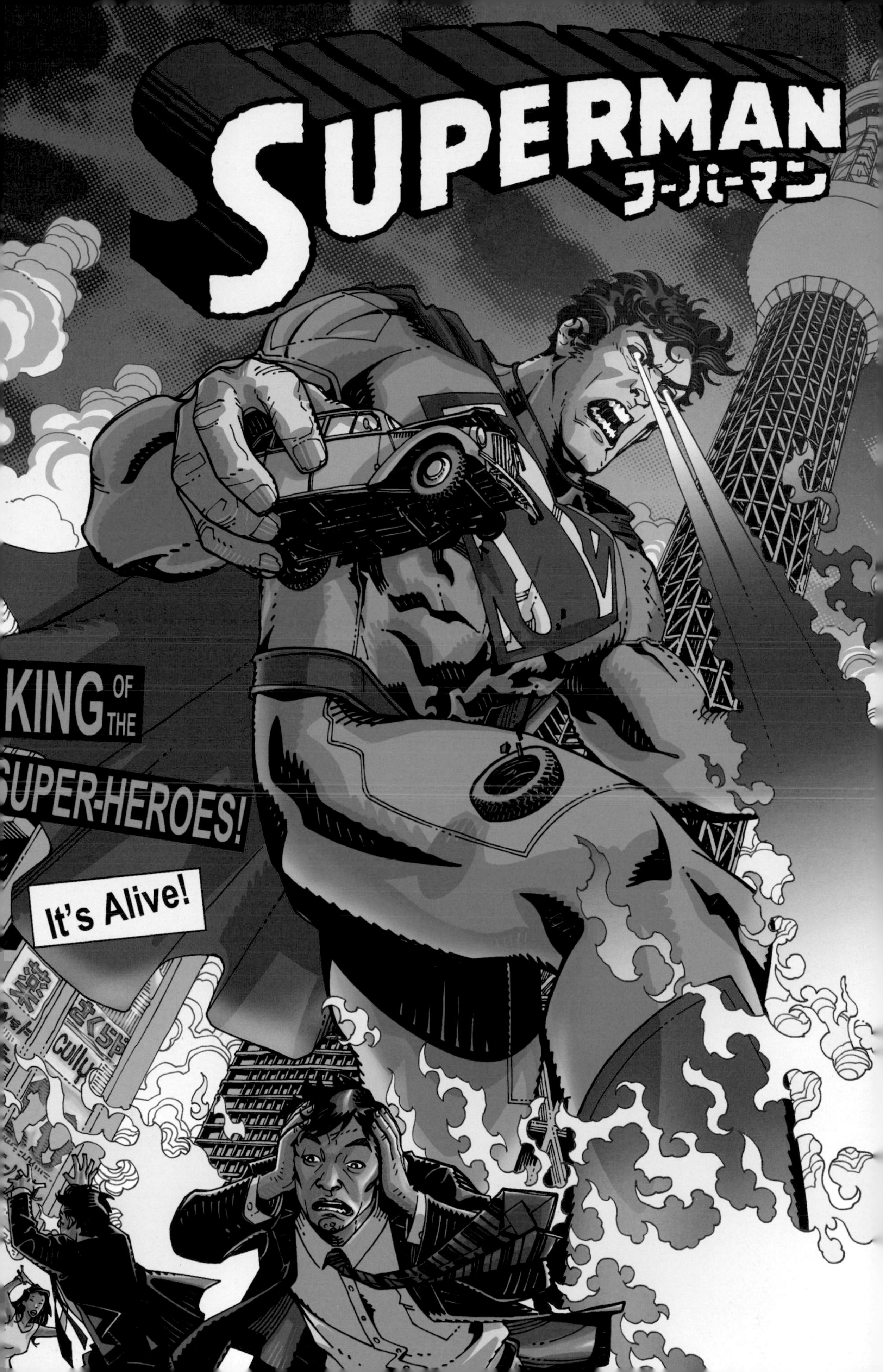
SUPERMAN
スーパーマン
KING OF THE
SUPER-HEROES!
It's Alive!

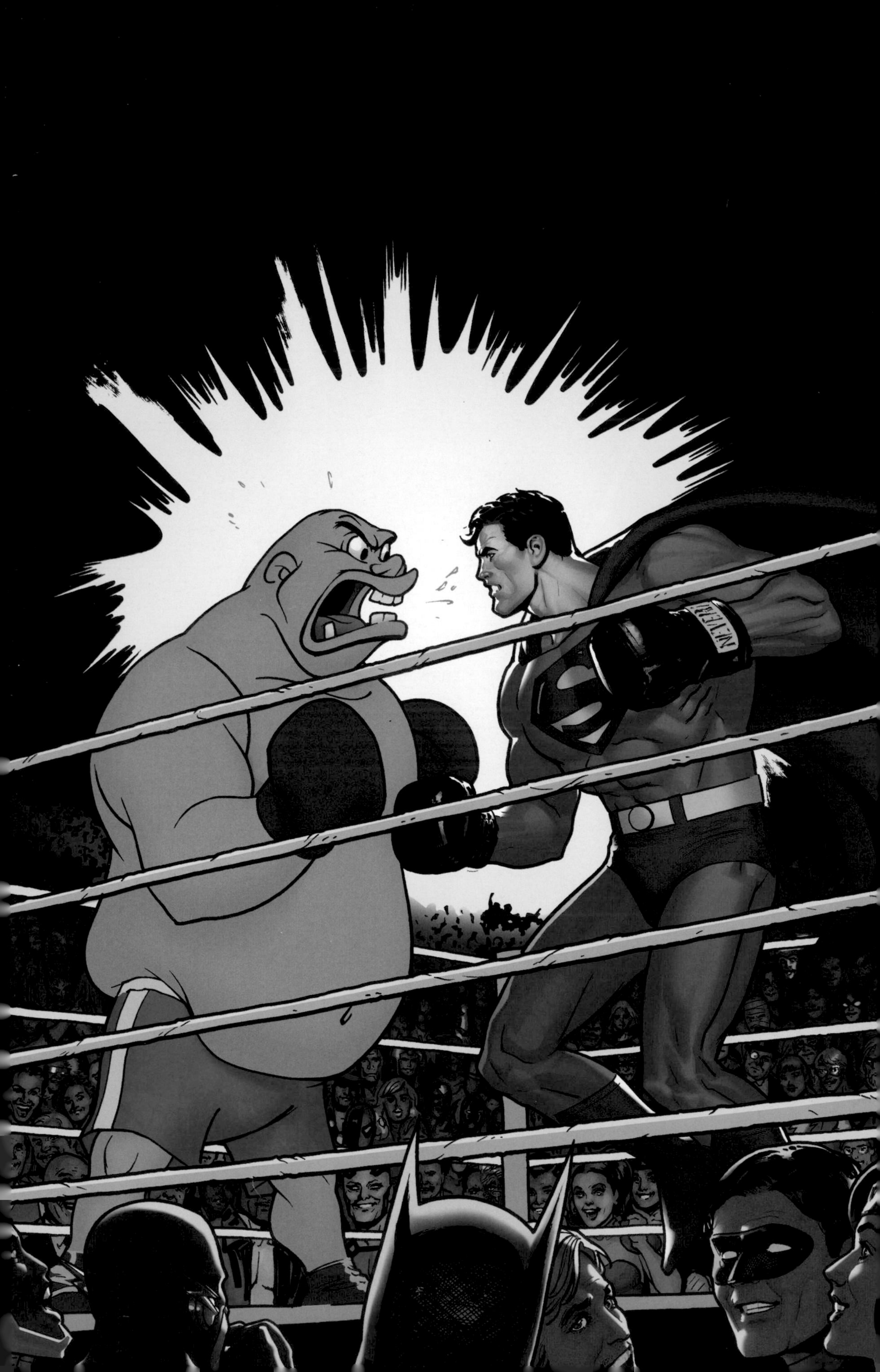

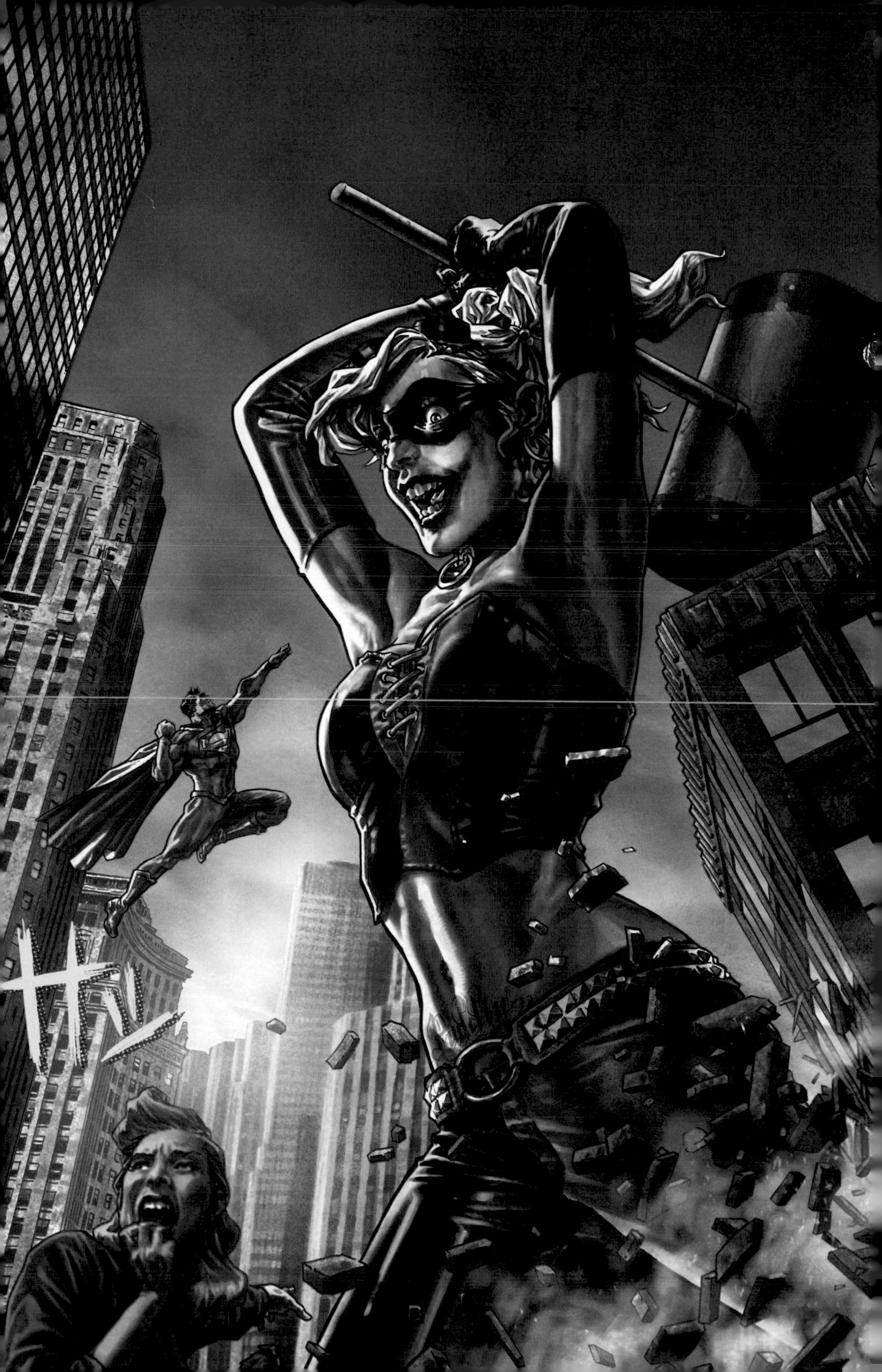
HA

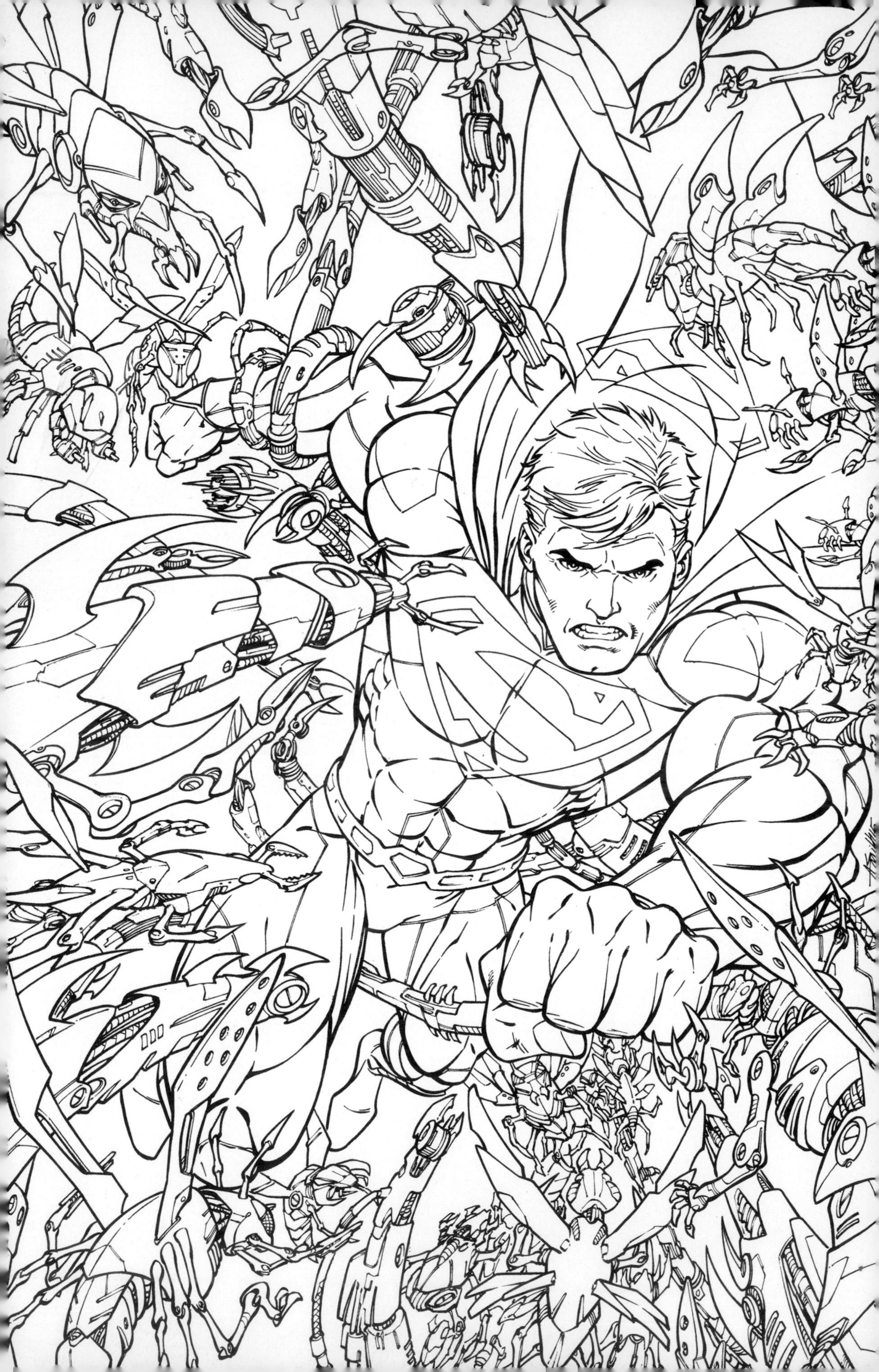

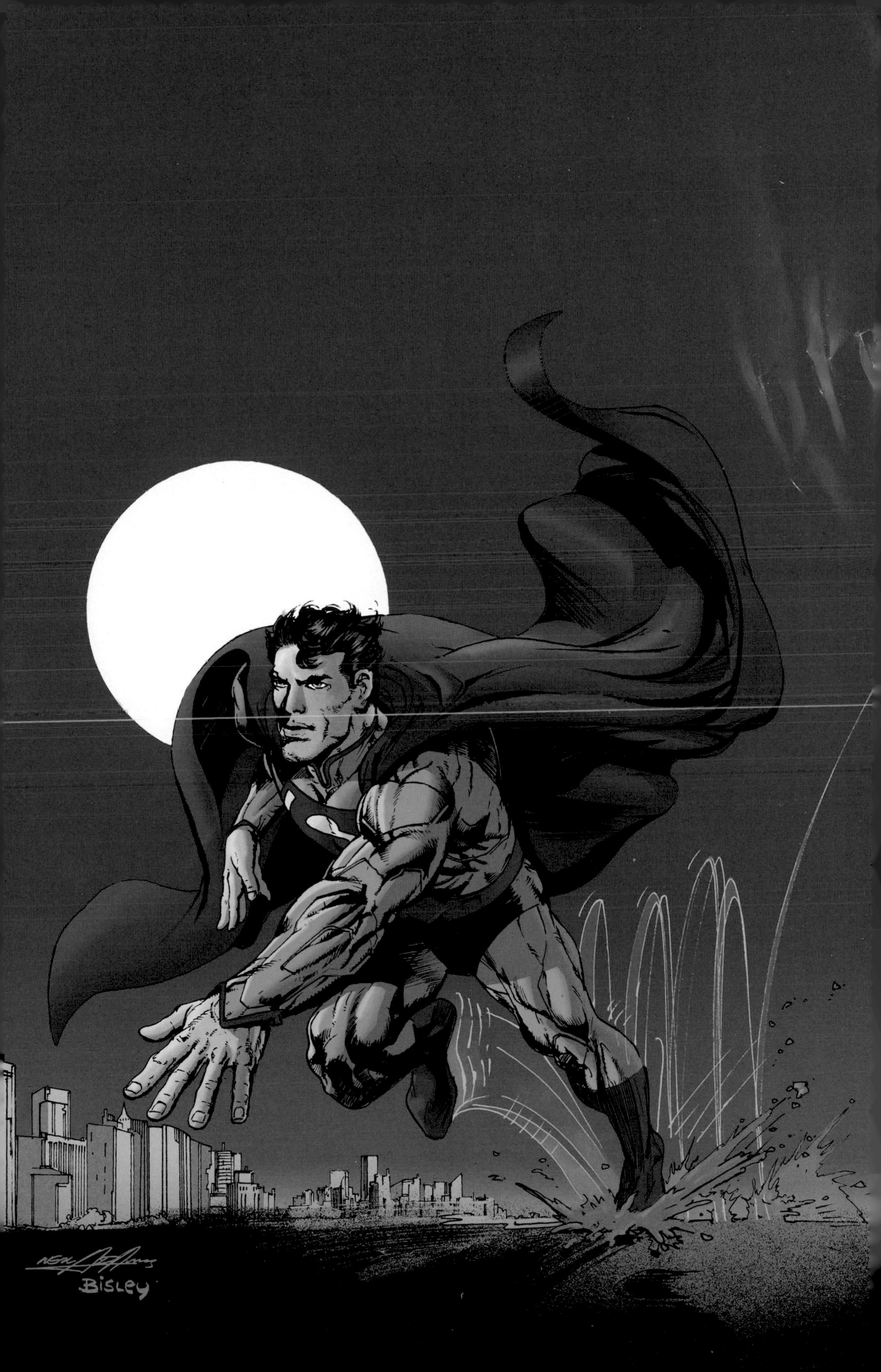
BISLEY